Classroom-based Research
and
Evidence-based Practice

SAGE has been part of the global academic community since 1965, supporting high quality research and learning that transforms society and our understanding of individuals, groups, and cultures. SAGE is the independent, innovative, natural home for authors, editors and societies who share our commitment and passion for the social sciences.

Find out more at: **www.sagepublications.com**

Connect, Debate, Engage on Methodspace

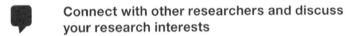 **Connect with other researchers and discuss your research interests**

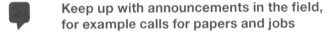 **Keep up with announcements in the field, for example calls for papers and jobs**

 **Discover and review resources**

 **Engage with featured content such as key articles, podcasts and videos**

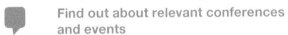 **Find out about relevant conferences and events**

Methodspace

Connecting the Research Community

www.methodspace.com

brought to you by

Classroom-based Research

and

Evidence-based Practice

Second Edition

An Introduction

Keith S. Taber

Los Angeles | London | New Delhi
Singapore | Washington DC

Los Angeles | London | New Delhi
Singapore | Washington DC

SAGE Publications Ltd
1 Oliver's Yard
55 City Road
London EC1Y 1SP

SAGE Publications Inc.
2455 Teller Road
Thousand Oaks, California 91320

SAGE Publications India Pvt Ltd
B 1/I 1 Mohan Cooperative Industrial Area
Mathura Road
New Delhi 110 044

SAGE Publications Asia-Pacific Pte Ltd
3 Church Street
#10-04 Samsung Hub
Singapore 049483

Commissioning editor: Jai Seaman
Assistant editor: Anna Horvai
Production editor: Ian Antcliff
Copyeditor: Sarah Bury
Proofreader: Jonathan Hopkins
Indexer: David Rudeforth
Marketing manager: Catherine Slinn
Cover design: Lisa Harper
Typeset by: C&M Digitals (P) Ltd, Chennai, India
Printed in Great Britain by MPG Printgroup, UK

Library of Congress Control Number: 2012950639

British Library Cataloguing in Publication data

A catalogue record for this book is available from the British
Library

ISBN 978-1-4462-0921-9
ISBN 978-1-4462-0922-6 (pbk)

Contents

About the author

Dr Keith S. Taber is Reader in Science Education at the University of Cambridge. He is a member of the Faculty of Education where he is Chair of the Science, Technology and Mathematics Education group. He has formerly been Programme Manager for the Part-time PhD in Education, and Deputy Programme Manager for the MEd and MPhil in Education programme. He teaches educational research methods across Master's and doctoral programmes. He supervises research students, especially in areas of science education, gifted education, student thinking, understanding and learning.

Keith's background is in science teaching and he is a Chartered Science Teacher. He formerly taught in comprehensive secondary schools, and further education, and undertook his own MSc and PhD degrees by undertaking part-time research whilst teaching. His MSc was based on a case study exploring an issue of concern in a large secondary school. His doctoral research explored an aspect of students' conceptual understanding and development, during college study. He was the Royal Society of Chemistry Teacher Fellow for 2000–2001, during which time he developed a range of classroom materials to support teachers in diagnosing and responding to common student learning difficulties.

Keith is the editor of the journal *Chemistry Education Research and Practice*, and part of the editorial team of the journal *Studies in Science Education*, as well as being a current or former member of the editorial board of a range of other educational journals. He has written/edited a number of books, and has published many research reports and articles for teachers.

Foreword to the first edition

This is a book about teaching and learning, and – in particular – about researching teaching and learning. In writing the book, I am setting out to support teachers (and those preparing for teaching) in developing their skills in critically evaluating research reports, and in planning and carrying out their own small-scale school- (or college-) based research. I am assuming, in particular, that many readers will be getting their first taste of classroom enquiry – usually in terms of the projects undertaken on university courses. The book will be particularly useful to:

- those undertaking initial teacher education courses
- those setting out on higher degrees (such as MEd, MA or MPhil) involving classroom research and
- classroom teachers who have identified enquiry into teaching and learning as a focus of their individual or departmental development plans.

I am particularly aware of the needs of students ('trainees') undertaking initial courses of teacher education, such as the Post-Graduate Certificate in Education (PGCE). PGCE courses require academic assignments that demonstrate critical reading of research literature, and most also include at least one project-based assignment that involves undertaking small-scale enquiry (research). The rationalisation of higher education qualifications in recent years means that any qualification labelled '*post-graduate*' is by definition at Master's level, and this has put an onus on universities to clearly demonstrate that the *Post-Graduate* Certificate in Education involves a level of academic scholarship equivalent to the start of a Master's degree course. This is leading to universities increasingly seeing their PGCE as the first part of a Master's degree, and has led to an increased scrutiny of the way the students ('trainee teachers') write about both published research and evidence collected during their own school-based placements.

> The distinctive focus of educational research must be upon the quality of learning and thereby of teaching. With few exceptions, the classroom, the transaction between teacher and learner in all its complexity, are what research should shed light upon.
>
> (Pring, 2000, p. 27)

This book is about teaching and learning, and it is about educational research: both areas where a great deal has been written. Teaching and learning are obviously core professional concerns of all teachers, and there are good reasons for many PGCE projects to be based in these topics. These are key areas that student teachers need to learn about as they are central to the new teacher's development – and in terms of a student research project, they are 'do-able'. That is not to say that there are not other very important areas of educational research, such as (for example) educational leadership and school organisation, but these are usually more difficult topics for the student teacher to tackle. Those undertaking projects in these other areas will also find a great deal of the book remains applicable, as many of the examples I use have been chosen to make general points about issues that arise when research is undertaken in educational contexts, especially when the research is carried out by teachers.

It is not the purpose of this book to tell everything there is to know about teaching and learning – a comprehensive review of such a large topic would require a much more substantial volume. Nor is this book a handbook of education research methods – that would be another heavy tome. The present volume offers an introduction to both areas – an introduction that should help equip the reader to be confident in critically reading the research literature, and in appreciating the nature, limitations and possibilities of small-scale, practitioner, classroom research. This volume invites the reader to engage with issues around teaching and learning, and with educational research. It will provide a useful overview for all readers, but I hope many will be enticed to explore both of these areas further.

Keith S. Taber
Cambridge, October 2006/August 2012

Foreword to the second edition

One constant in education is change. Those entering a career in education need to be prepared to face, and be able to cope with, a great deal of policy and organisational change. In the time since the first edition of this book was published, the educational scene in England, where the author is based, has seen, *inter alia*, changes in curriculum and assessment policy; shifts in the status of many schools; the removal of government support for the (government-initiated) professional body regulating teachers; changes in the funding of undergraduate and teacher education courses; changes in the funding of teacher professional development support (including the abandonment of the much-heralded Master of Teaching and Learning initiative); and an attempt to bring about shifts in the provision of initial teacher education.

A particular concern for many working in teacher education and development has been rhetoric emerging from the UK government suggesting that the PGCE route does not offer the strongest preparation for teaching because it would be better if new teachers were inducted into the profession in real schools rather than the ivory towers of universities. To someone working in a university where every aspect of our initial teacher education programme has been judged 'excellent' by the government's own inspectorate, and where trainees for teaching study on a genuine partnership course (working with teachers in schools for much of their time), it is clear that such (surely, deliberately) misleading public statements must be ideologically driven, as they are clearly *not* evidence-based.

The rhetorical tactic here is to imply that there are two ways of preparing to be a teacher: either working in real schools, learning how to do the job by teaching real classes, with support from experienced current classroom teachers; or by attending lecture courses from so-called academic experts who do not teach in the schools themselves. Given *that* choice, most of us would acknowledge that the option with real experience of schools is likely to be preferable. Therefore, the fallacious argument is made that more initial teacher education should take place *in the schools* ***rather than*** *in universities*. This is just one example highlighting how important it is that all those entering teaching are prepared to be appropriately critical of educational dogma, and to acquire the knowledge and skills to seek out evidence and evaluate it carefully.

As someone who has worked in education for three decades now (initially in secondary education, then further education, then in initial teacher education, now primarily working with higher-degrees students), I have come to expect a regular flow of high-profile official pronouncements on all sorts of matters. These are often well intended, but not always well informed by research evidence, and they are seldom sufficiently critiqued and tested before being used as a basis of new policies and initiatives. Sometimes these innovations have positive outcomes, sometimes negative outcomes, and most usually, mixed outcomes, but inevitably they tend to lead to unforeseen consequences. For example, in my subject area of the sciences, the introduction of the national curriculum overcame the common problem of students dropping key science subjects at age 14 (something that science teachers' representatives had been keen to address), but required teachers to work to an imposed curriculum that gave too little flexibility to teachers to meet the particular needs of different classes of students. So, for example, many of the most able students found science a shallow subject based on a great deal of memorisation – hardly an authentic reflection of science itself.

I mention this example because I recall a national chemistry teachers' conference where an official from the curriculum authority confidently proclaimed that none of this was a problem because the prescribed curriculum only required a proportion of the time allocated for teaching the subject, so teachers had plenty of scope to supplement the required topics with other material as they saw fit. The spontaneous response from the teachers present seemed quite unanimous. In their experience of actually teaching the curriculum, this claim was complete nonsense. According to the official view, the prescribed curriculum only required part of the time assigned – but that view did not seem to be informed by any empirical evidence.

Despite the appearance of constant flux, something that is a real source of much teacher stress and frustration, a number of important things do not really change very much in education. The need to be critical of ideologically motivated policies and initiatives is one example. Such innovations may improve things, but that is an empirical question to be tested through research. So the need for careful research is certainly a constant. The fundamental nature of learning and teaching does not change. But research can help us to better understand and so support learning; and changes in curriculum, new teaching approaches, new technologies to support teaching, and so forth, all bring new variations on teachers' work, which can be informed by research.

This second edition of the book is of course itself changed from the first edition. However, the structure and features of the first edition, which seem to have been appreciated by many readers, are largely unchanged. The changes I have made are largely a matter of updating and selective additions. There are many of these, and here I will just highlight the most significant. An opportunity has been taken to address some topics that received less attention than others in the first edition. The parts on educational research ethics and data analysis have been expanded – in the former case the topic has now been given its own chapter for the first time. The first edition had little to say about 'mixed methods' research. This was in part a deliberate choice, as I have found the term is sometimes used in misleading ways, and this can be unhelpful for new researchers. However, the term is increasingly adopted to describe research studies, and I find many students look to describe their own research with this label. I have therefore explored the notion in more detail in this new edition.

The book was originally conceptualised as a resource to support those new to educational research in making sense of key ideas, and in particular to support critical reading of research studies. For this reason a number of published research studies were used as exemplars of key points through the text. This feature remains, but in the new edition I have also made reference to examples of small-scale student studies as examples of the kind of projects that are viable for those taking courses such as the PGCE. I have drawn here on the recently established *Journal of Trainee Teacher Educational Research*, which publishes examples of the research undertaken by trainee teachers from my own institution whilst on school placements. This has been a useful resource in revising the book, as the studies are open access on the web, meaning that anyone with internet access can download them for free. This has allowed me to draw on features of these studies knowing that all readers can access the full reports if they wish.

I introduce some of these studies in a new chapter (Chapter 5) at the end of the first part, before drawing upon them for examples used later in the book. This new chapter focuses on a theme which will be especially relevant to many readers: the particular nature of research undertaken by teachers or students working in schools, and the approaches to research that are most likely to be viable for someone in that situation. This new addition gives more attention, in particular, to case study methodology, a strategy that often suits teacher research particularly well.

In updating this aspect of the book I have been forced to face an issue that perhaps did not get treated in sufficient depth in the first edition. That is the nature of action research (AR). I commonly find new classroom researchers, whether teachers or full-time research students, are keen to use AR for their projects because they see it as about making aspects of education better. Yet, of course, we would hope all educational research should ultimately make education better, so that is not sufficient to make a study AR. I have had some difficult conversations with well-meaning full-time research students looking to improve some educational feature, who are determined they are doing AR, despite having no classroom or students of their own, and no teacher-collaborators sharing their research aims, or working with them on designing their study.

PGCE students, and teachers taking higher degrees, often have a better claim for adopting AR, as they are in a position to seek to improve their own actual classroom practice in the here-and-now through their research. Yet, even in many of these cases, the studies they design have little more in common with AR (as it is widely understood) than they are examples of practitioner research. In the new edition I take a position that argues that classroom-based research undertaken by teachers who need to report their research in academic formats is often best *not* conceptualised as AR, and that, indeed, many of these studies are better thought of as case studies.

I know AR has, quite rightly, gained considerable prestige among the teaching community, and this stance may not be welcome to some. I do not mind if readers agree or disagree with me, as long as they are prepared to engage with the issues I raise. For, as I explain in the text, the labels we choose to give things remain secondary as long as we carefully detail our research and explain the rationale behind our decisions. I refer to the example of an excellent small-scale classroom study carried out by a trainee teacher on school placement that is described by its author as AR. The author justifies his decision to consider his work as AR in relation to published scholarship on AR. I actually consider his work to be a case study. At the end of the day, however, what actually matters is that the report is detailed, clear and well argued. This allows us to make judgements about the quality of the work, and its relevance to our own teaching contexts – regardless of how we might like to categorise it. That, I suggest, is the mark of a good research report.

So this second edition can be seen as an updated, enhanced and selectively expanded version of the original book. I have been very pleased to hear that so many students and teachers found the first edition useful, and I hope the new features enhance the book for future readers.

PART I

Learning about educational research

This book is organised into three parts. This first part, learning *about* educational research, introduces key ideas that anyone who wishes to be informed about research in education should be familiar with. Chapter 1 considers the nature of teachers *as professionals*, and why learning from published research, and even carrying out your own classroom research, is nowadays often considered an integral part of both being a professional teacher, and of post-graduate teacher education. Then, Chapter 2 offers a taste of what educational research is about, by offering examples of the kinds of claims about classroom teaching and learning found in published research. As well as providing an overview of the scope of research, this chapter introduces some studies that will be used as examples later in the book, and gives the reader an opportunity to ask themselves about the kind of processes and evidence that would enable researchers to make the knowledge claims they do.

To those coming to study education from some academic fields – those where particular ways of working are well established and applied by all those working in the field – it may seem that educational research is an immature field. Certainly, the widely different approaches taken may seem catholic and eclectic, if not anarchic. However, the initially confusing range of research strategies is not an indication that 'anything goes' in education research. Different approaches to research are based on different sets of fundamental assumptions and beliefs about what research is capable of finding out. Any particular study needs to use an approach consistent with the underpinning assumptions the researchers make – and the reader needs to recognise (but not necessarily share) those assumptions to appreciate the status of the claims being made.

Chapter 3 explores this issue and offers a simple model to help readers new to educational research. Approaches to research in education can generally be seen as falling into two clusters that reflect two distinct traditions. It is important to appreciate this distinction, as researchers in these two different traditions are usually trying to develop very different forms of knowledge, and use different ways of going about this. These research traditions offer different types of findings that need to be understood and applied in different ways.

It is suggested in the book that thinking about and undertaking research takes places at three levels: the 'executive' level where the basic assumptions underpinning research are established, the 'managerial' level where a strategy is adopted and research is designed, and the 'technical' level where data is collected and analysed. In much classroom research the same person acts as the executive, the manager and the technician (often whilst being in the class as the teacher at the same time!), but it is important to recognise the different roles. Chapter 3 considers the highest level where the most basic assumptions are set out, and introduces the two main clusters of approaches ('paradigms') for undertaking educational research.

This issue is sometimes presented as some kind of paradigm war, with different researchers having fundamentally different views about how to do research. However, the approach argued here is based on a consideration of the nature of the specific research foci being studied. Research into school attendance patterns will be different from research into teacher beliefs about pedagogy or research into students' second language skills, because attendance patterns, teacher beliefs and language skills are different kinds of 'things', and that has consequences for what kind of knowledge we are able to obtain about them, and how we need to go about acquiring that knowledge.

Chapter 4 moves to the next level, where some key strategies ('methodologies') used in educational research are introduced. Chapter 5 then considers the particular situation of the classroom teacher who is interested in undertaking enquiry into the teaching and learning in her or his own classroom. This chapter considers the strengths and weaknesses of different methodological choices, from the particular perspective of the teacher-researcher, and offers examples of the kinds of classroom studies possible for someone in this context. In particular, the chapter introduces examples of what teachers-in-training, new to classroom research, can achieve as part of their professional placements in schools. It is suggested that often case study offers a suitable approach for teachers interested in balancing a desire to explore or solve classroom issues or problems with the expectations of writing a formal research report for an academic course.

The second part of the book, learning *from* educational research, builds upon this introduction by exploring how teachers can critically read and evaluate research studies. The final part, learning *through* educational research, provides a guide for teachers or students setting out on their own classroom research projects. Here the 'technical' level of actually doing the research is discussed. That part looks at how to operationalise the basic ideas about research from Part I, through the collection and analysis of data, and how to report research (drawing upon the criteria used to evaluate accounts of research in Part II). Throughout the book I discuss examples from published studies to demonstrate key points.

Before looking at how we can effectively critique and carry out research, though, we need to get a basic understanding of the role and nature of educational research in teaching.

1

The professional teacher and educational research

This chapter:

- considers the nature of professionalism in teaching
- presents the notion that a 'strong' model of teacher professionalism is linked to the ability to both critique research claims to inform one's own teaching and to carry out small-scale research to develop practice
- explains the importance of research to studying education at post-graduate level
- explains the rationale for the structure and style of the book.

This book provides an introduction to research into classroom teaching and learning. It is *not* a textbook on teaching and learning that draws upon classroom research, and so provides teachers with lessons from research that they should consider adopting in their own teaching. Such books exist (see the list of further reading at the end of the chapter), and are useful, but this book is as much about the nature and processes of classroom research as it is about the outcomes. The reader *will* find many examples of research findings considered in the following chapters, and a careful reader will learn a good deal about teaching and learning by reflecting upon these findings.

However, the book is as much about *how* teaching and learning can be explored through research as it is about what research has found. There are a number of linked, but distinct, reasons why a book for teachers, and those starting out on a teaching career, should have such a focus. These reasons are both principled and pragmatic.

On the pragmatic side, teachers, and especially students on courses of initial teacher education ('teacher training'), are increasingly being expected to demonstrate 'evidence-based' practice, or 'research-informed' practice. Indeed, practitioner (teacher) research has become very common in recent years, so that in many schools it may be normal, or even expected, that teachers engage in research as part of their work (McLaughlin, Black-Hawkins, Brindley, McIntyre, & Taber, 2006). This tendency may well increase as senior managers seek to develop their schools through engagement with research (Wilkins, 2011). This book is designed to help teachers develop the skills for making sense of, and planning, classroom research.

On the more principled side, this move to require teachers to be research-savvy, or even research-active, may be seen as part of the development of teaching as a profession. Teaching has been *referred to* as a profession for a very long time, and has been (in general) a graduate-entry career for some years. However, professionalism is more than earning a living – the key feature of *the professions* is that they are self-regulating groups of professionals. In the English context, for example, it was as recently as 1998 that the government handed over responsibility for registration of teachers to the General Teaching Council for England, a body representing teachers, and having the power to debar them by suspending registration. Even then, registration depended upon being awarded 'Qualified Teacher Status' through the government's criteria.

Incredibly, the English government decided to abolish this (supposed) professional body of teachers in 2012, and replace it with an agency that was directly controlled by the government ministry. This clearly brings into question whether teaching in England can really be seen as a profession, if its regulatory body is in the gift of an agency external to the profession itself. This suggests that despite any rhetoric about the professional standards and responsibilities of teachers, teachers in England are not trusted by government to be professional enough to regulate themselves, i.e., to be fully professional.

Despite this, the present book is driven by a view that teaching should be a profession, and that qualified teachers should have the status of professionals. Professionals have to use their specialist knowledge and their professional experience to make judgements of a kind that cannot simply be based on following lists of rules. Of course there are rules that teachers should follow, but to be an effective teacher one has to constantly make quick decisions relying on professional judgement in the myriad situations where there are no simple straightforward rules to tell you what to do next.

We would expect any professional to be well informed about developments in their area of work, and to follow guidelines for 'best practice'. This is, of course, the case in teaching, but for many years we have seen what I would characterise as the 'weak' model of professionalism in teaching in this regard.

──── The weak model of teacher professionalism ─────

In this weak model, the teacher fulfils the requirement to follow 'best practice' without taking a major responsibility for exploring what that might mean. In this model (which, of course, is a caricature – but nonetheless represents the general pattern followed in the past by many teachers) teachers are told what research has found out during their initial 'training', and are updated from time to time – perhaps through courses or staff development days, but largely via centralised official 'guidance'. In other words, the government commissions research, interprets it, forms policy, and issues 'advice'.

In at least one instance, the case of the 'National Strategies' in England, one could be forgiven for thinking that the government issued enough guidance to allow teachers *never* to have to again think for themselves. That is, at least, if any busy teacher found enough time to study all the files, and booklets, and videos, and charts and sundry other material that were produced and distributed at great expense. (Much of this guidance was fundamentally sound, and well intentioned, but the sheer volume, and mode of dissemination, were more suited to keeping a store's retail staff updated with the latest products than informing the professional work of qualified graduate teachers.) So in this model, the teacher teaches, but others (with more time and other skills perhaps) are given the responsibility to find out *how* they should teach.

Secondary science teachers, for example, were provided with a great deal of material about teaching science to 11–14 year olds, and much of this drew upon some of the vast amount of research into teaching that subject which is available around the world. Key points from the research were summarised into succinct bullet points suitable for being presented to teachers in development sessions, and translated for teachers into advice on how to teach topics and sequence material.

Question for reflection

Given that teachers are busy with preparing, teaching and assessing, and all the other work involved in carrying out their duties, is it not a good idea for the authorities to interrogate and interpret research to guide teachers in how to do their jobs more effectively?

I am not suggesting here that such attempts by government agencies at guiding teachers in their classroom work are completely inappropriate, but there are problems with such an approach. The first is in terms of that notion of professionalism. No matter how well meaning a government, and no matter how skilled its advisors, it is not the profession. If teaching is the concern of the teaching profession, then the profession should be taking the lead, not being told what to do. The government is of course a major stakeholder in education, but its agenda is inevitably political. Governments should act politically, but professions are meant to be independent and self-regulating.

A five-part lesson is right out ⸻

There is, of course, a distinction between what governments *require* teachers to do, based on education policy, and guidance that is meant to *suggest* how they may best go about it. In theory, guidance is just that, and teachers are free to decide when it is best not to follow it. In practice, much of the guidance issued by government translates into *expectations* on teachers: for example, what school Inspectors *expect* to observe during inspections that may have serious implications for schools. (Or sometimes, just what school management teams fear Inspectors will expect to observe.) This can lead to ridiculous, unintended outcomes, so that at one time teachers in many English schools were expected to plan all their lessons with three distinct, discrete parts, because an effective lesson has three parts, and if Inspectors called they would expect to see a three-part lesson.

Clearly the advice to break a lesson up into three parts was well intentioned, but it would be a nonsense to have a general rule that all effective lessons (for 5 year olds or 16 year olds, in whatever curriculum area) will have three parts. Yet for a while in England many teachers were pressured to be seen to be following this fiat as though it had some kind of divine authority:

[In structuring your lesson] shalt thou count to three, no more, no less. Three shalt be the number thou shalt count, and the number of the counting shalt be three. Four shalt thou not count, neither count thou two, excepting that thou then proceed to three. Five is right out.

(Chapman et al., 1974)

However, as was pointed out in the *Times Educational Supplement*:

There is no stone tablet that decrees every lesson must consist of three sections. "And, yea, thou shalt teach every lesson as a perfect trinity. Thou shalt have no other lesson structure but this. He that forgeteth the starter activity, main section and plenary shalt be struck down and forsaken."

(Shaw, 2012)

If teachers are to be professional, then they need to question such expectations – not for the sake of being difficult, but to ensure they are confident that the guidance is appropriate in their professional context. A teacher must be free to *not* follow guidance that they judge as inappropriate in a particular teaching situation. To do this, without penalty, they need to be able to argue a case for their actions (to colleagues, to school managers, to parents and governors, to school inspectors, and to those most intimately involved, the learners), *based on evidence*.

Before the reader starts to suspect that they are being asked to be some kind of sub-versive element – disrupting the carefully researched and disseminated approaches recommended by government agencies – it is important to point out that the government itself explicitly recognises that this weak model of professionalism is not appropriate. There is a very good reason why government and the profession accept the need for teachers who are critical and reflective in considering advice. This is that educational research seldom offers clear unambiguous guidance about the best way to teach. This will be no surprise to teachers with backgrounds in social science or the humanities. It is not difficult to find different research studies that at first glance offer opposite con-clusions. (The reader will meet some examples later in the book.)

Such contradictory research findings may sometimes indicate shoddy work (and this book will provide skills in making judgements about the quality of research), but it is often the case that such apparent contradictions may derive from well-executed studies. This leads us to ask how it can be possible that two carefully undertaken studies can sometimes lead to apparently opposite conclusions.

Educational phenomena are complex

Schools, children, classrooms etc. are very complex entities, and it is seldom possible to make statements about *teaching history*, or *learning to play a musical instrument*, say, which are as definitive as the statements we can make about the melting point of lead, or the type of landscape produced when glaciers retreat.

General statements about teaching and learning are often *too general* to inform teacher decision-making in relation to specific classes. Whilst there are some important general principles that are always useful, it is not possible to assume that research that showed X worked in classroom Y will *necessarily* tell you anything about your class Z.

In the case of the guidance to science teachers issued as part of the National Strategies initiative, some quite complex and nuanced research was summarised in terms of a few general principles and recommendations for practice, which were abstracted from the peculiarities of particular schools, classroom and classes of students. The need to provide simplistic summaries of the research suitable for including in published guidance led to oversimplistic accounts unlikely to enable teachers to significantly change their existing ways of working (Taber, 2010b).

The method of 'delivery' of the recommended research-based pedagogy reflected a centralised approach: materials written at national level were used to prepare trainers (appointed as 'consultants') to present ideas and teaching materials to groups of teachers, who would then 'cascade' what they had learnt to colleagues in their schools. The pedagogy being recommended to teachers was a constructivist one which acknowledges the way each individual learner interprets ideas differently and has to make sense of them in terms of their own existing understanding and learning context (Taber, 2011a). The pedagogy used to teach the teachers about this involved mass-produced presentations delivered through a scripted teacher-centred classroom approach. This perhaps tells us something about either the level of confidence in the recommended approach, or the level of funding made available to support the programme of 'consultants' 'delivering' the 'training'.

Because of the complexity of the individual classroom context, most detailed ideas from educational research need to be tested out to see if they *transfer* to our own context and apply in our classes. Moreover, we can save ourselves a lot of work and anguish if we are able to read research in ways that help us filter out ideas that are unlikely to 'work here'. Again, that is something that this book sets out to help develop.

The effective application of the ideas in teaching would require careful exploration of their implications by trying out approaches with classes, and then reflecting upon the outcomes, supported by dialogue with other professional colleagues – ideally with both those experienced in the teaching approaches (having some expertise) and others still becoming familiar with them (and so more directly able to relate to the challenges faced by the relative novice). It is this combination of exploring ideas with experts and peers that many students find so useful on a PGCE or similar course.

The strong model of teacher professionalism

Although the widespread incidence of teacher-research is a relatively new phenomenon, in practice teachers have always had to find out 'what works here'. In the first edition of this book I quoted the statement from the then standards used to evaluate new teachers, i.e., that:

> Those awarded Qualified Teacher Status must [demonstrate that] they are able to improve their own teaching, by evaluating it, learning from the effective practice of others and from evidence. They are motivated and able to take increasing responsibility for their own professional development.
>
> (TTA, 2003)

I suggested that this was part of what might be characterised as a *strong* model of teacher professionalism: each classroom teacher is expected to actively evaluate his or her own work, and to seek to improve it – using evidence.

Undermining the strong model

Since that edition of the book was published, a new set of 'Teachers' Standards' has been introduced (Department for Education, 2012), which are worded somewhat differently. These include requirements that a teacher must:

> demonstrate a critical understanding of developments in the subject and curriculum areas, and promote the value of scholarship. (p. 6)

> take responsibility for improving teaching through appropriate professional development, responding to advice and feedback from colleagues. (p. 8)

These changes could be considered to reflect potentially significant shifts in emphasis: that the focus of the teacher's development efforts should be less about what is happening in their classroom and more on developments in their subject; that the key source informing the development of teaching should be the advice of other teachers, rather than the evidence collected through the teacher's own classroom enquiry. These shifts could again be seen as ideologically driven: to downplay the role of pedagogy compared to the structure of the discipline being taught; to emphasise the importance of teachers being guided by (the authority of) others, rather than seeking their own solutions to classroom issues.

Prerequisites of strong professionalism

Whether the rephrasing of the Teachers' Standards was deliberately intended to undermine aspects of teacher professionalism or not, to some extent, researching one's own professional work is now an accepted 'part of the job' for today's teacher. This certainly does not mean teachers are expected to 'reinvent the wheel'. As the 2003 professional standards suggested, the starting points for improving teaching are a reliable evaluation of current strengths and weaknesses, and having access to ideas about what 'effective practice' might be. So teachers need to know:

- what might be considered 'effective practice' in other classrooms (and be worth testing out in the present context); and
- how to collect suitable evidence to inform evaluations of (a) existing practice, and (b) the effect of any innovations introduced.

This clearly requires the teacher to have both the procedural knowledge to undertake small-scale classroom enquiry, and 'conceptual frameworks' for thinking about teaching and learning that can provide the basis for evaluating their teaching. In other words, the professional teacher needs both the ability to do her own research and knowledge of what existing research suggests (Taber, 2010c).

———So, do teachers need to be educational researchers?———

The strong model of teacher professionalism puts more responsibility and autonomy in the hands of the individual teacher. It is primarily the teacher's role to make decisions about how to teach, but – being a professional – these decisions must be justifiable. Teaching decisions can be justified in terms of theory and practice: knowledge drawing on published research and the analysis of evidence collected in the classroom.

So, *in a sense*, the teacher is an educational researcher. But there are also other individuals who have the specific job description 'educational researcher'. It is important to realise that there is in principle a substantial difference between the 'research' that teachers are being asked to undertake as a matter of course and the academic research being undertaken by professional educational researchers. The latter have an in-depth training in research methodology, substantial time (and institutional resources) for research, and an obligation to produce 'public knowledge' (Ziman, 1968). The expectations on academic researchers, in terms of the level of scholarship, the rigour of research and the generalisability of findings, do not apply to teachers (this theme is developed in Chapter 5). Teachers may often be *capable* of this type of work. Indeed, sometimes teachers are able to demonstrate that their research does indeed meet these expectations, and publish their findings in research journals (a possibility considered in Chapter 12). However, in general, it would be totally unreasonable to expect this of busy classroom teachers as a matter of course: teachers have other responsibilities and priorities.

So there is a spectrum here, then, rather than a dichotomy, with published professional academic research at one pole and small-scale practitioner enquiry undertaken to improve one's own teaching at the other pole. There is a minimum expectation for teachers to be active at one pole, and nowadays in many schools teachers are encouraged to go further and undertake enquiry that is 'published' internally through departmental meetings, school intranets, or at meetings of schools working as 'learning networks' or 'learning communities' (see the examples in McLaughlin et al., 2006). Many teachers undertake research projects for Masters' or doctoral degrees, where basic training in research methods is provided and increasing levels of academic rigour are applied. The key message here is that all teachers are now required to be able to demonstrate research-informed and evidence-based practice, and many are going much further than this.

——— Support for the teacher-as-researcher in initial teacher education ———

So there is now a minimal expectation on all teachers to be able to show that their work is informed by published research and the analysis of evidence collected in their own classrooms. As with any other aspect of the teacher's work, it is important that teachers are supported in meeting these requirements. This is especially important during initial teacher education, if only because for many teachers this may be the only stage of their career when they have:

- ready access to academic advisors;
- ready access to a research library;
- ongoing mentoring from experienced practitioners;

- a teaching programme and timetable designed to allow sufficient time for thorough planning, reflection and lesson evaluation;
- a substantial peer group at a similar stage of development, struggling with the same issues and skills;
- regular observation and feedback on their teaching;
- regular opportunities to visit other classrooms and see teaching and learning with different teachers and groups of learners.

Few 'trainee' teachers probably appreciate just what luxury they have in this regard – at least until they move into their first teaching appointment!

PGCE (Post-Graduate Certificate in Education) courses traditionally require students to submit a variety of assignments, usually incorporating evidence of both understanding of 'theory' and the application of such ideas to classroom practice. Passing the course normally means satisfying the examiners in these assignments, as well as demonstrating all the competencies outlined in the teaching standards.

In many of the universities, the PGCE includes at least one assignment that is based on a fairly substantive project, where the student is expected to demonstrate familiarity with some area of research literature, and to undertake some type of empirical study. For example, this may be based around the development of teaching resources, with a critical evaluative commentary drawing on evidence of learning outcomes. The assignments on a PGCE are an academic requirement of the course, but have in the past sometimes been designed and judged from the perspective that the students are *primarily* engaged in a professional training course, and academic demands should not be too burdensome. Such a view is changing.

———— 'Mastering' the PGCE

In effect, the Post-Graduate Certificate in Education has become an academically more rigorous qualification. There are two reasons for this. One concerns routes into teaching. Since teaching has been considered a graduate profession, the two main routes into teaching have been by studying for an education degree or, for those already holding a degree, taking a PGCE course. The curriculum for the PGCE was largely at the discretion of the awarding university.

In recent years the government has introduced centrally determined teaching standards, which are seen as the means to qualify as a teacher. PGCE courses must incorporate these, but in addition there has been the development of a range of alternative routes to qualified teacher status for graduates (including 'school-based' routes with less input from 'the Academy', as favoured by the present UK government). PGCE is no longer the only way for a graduate to become a teacher. It therefore becomes pertinent to ask why students should enrol for a year at a university when they could train whilst employed in a school. This is not the place to debate the relative merits of PGCE, but clearly one of its characteristics is that it is an *academic* university qualification.

In parallel with these developments in preparing teachers, there has been a move to rationalise the qualifications framework at all levels of the education system. Under these developments universities have agreed to a common understanding of the level of their awards, and the terminology used. As part of this understanding, the expression 'post-graduate' is taken to mean a qualification at a *higher level* than a first degree (not just something taken afterwards). In many universities, therefore, the PGCE qualification is being developed in response to the requirement that any qualification labelled *Post-Graduate* (rather, than say, a *'professional* graduate qualification') should be substantially at M (Master's level). One of the consequences is that many students applying for a PGCE will find that universities increasingly see the PGCE as (potentially at least) the first part of a Master's programme that will be taught over the training year and the first few years in post. Applications will be considered accordingly, and applicants may be expected to demonstrate Master's level aptitude if they wish to take this route. To meet the expectations of the PGCE being a post-graduate course, universities reviewed their assignments, and the assessment criteria by which they were marked, to ensure they enabled the university to judge that the students meet the expectations of post-graduate study where:

> Much of the study undertaken at Master's level will have been at, or informed by, the forefront of an academic or professional discipline. Students will have shown originality in the application of knowledge, and they will understand how the boundaries of knowledge are advanced through research. They will be able to deal with complex issues both systematically and creatively, and they will show originality in tackling and solving problems.

> (QAA, 2001)

Such an agenda fits well with the expectations outlined above for the teaching profession. Those students who use their PGCE as the first stage of a full Master's programme will go on to write a substantial thesis – some type of synthesis of research literature or, more often, an empirical enquiry informed by existing research – and so the PGCE assignments will also become the first part of a programme of preparing students for planning their Master's project and writing their thesis.

In summary:

- in the 21st-century context of *being* a teacher, there is an expectation of engaging with, and to some extent in, educational research;
- in the 21st-century context of *becoming* a teacher, there is an expectation of being prepared to engage with, and to some extent in, educational research;
- in the 21st-century context of becoming a teacher through a *post*-graduate route, there is an expectation of engaging with educational research at a high academic level.

It is in this context that the present book sets out to offer support to teachers and students by providing an introduction to educational research into teaching and learning.

━━━━━━━━ What is expected of students undertaking research? ━━

There tend to be two kinds of student undertaking educational research. There are many full-time students (sometimes, but not always having teaching backgrounds) who enrol in research degrees in education and are, in effect, learning how to be academic educational researchers. In the case of doctoral students, the expectation is that by the end of the process they will meet the expectations of other professional academic educational researchers – they will be able to publish their work in peer-reviewed academic research journals. Master's students are not *expected* to proceed as far, but on graduating should be competent to join research projects in a professional capacity if not necessarily lead on their own research. Many Master's projects do produce material suitable for submitting to research journals. Generally, then, the expectations of academic research apply to these students.

The other kind of student undertaking educational research is primarily a teacher, but undertaking research as part of initial preparation for teaching or for professional development once in post (perhaps for a certificate or diploma, or a Master's degree, or perhaps a doctorate in education, an EdD). A primary purpose of the research training provided to these students is intended to support them in becoming effective practitioners who can use research to support their professional work, rather than to make them professional researchers.

However, the university making the award may well take the view that to fully understand research processes it is important that students are taken through the logic and rigour of thinking about and reporting their work in the way academic researchers do. This is not just because the teachers on the university course are probably academic researchers themselves, so think in those terms, nor because the university staff see teacher-researcher as an inferior type of research, unlike 'proper' academic research. Rather, the logic here reflects the way teachers in training are taught to plan their lessons.

Commonly, new teachers are expected not only to go through a clear logical process to make sure they are planning appropriate lessons, and including suitable learning activities, but also to justify their decision-making through quite detailed documentation. Yet most experienced teachers seldom plan and record their plans in quite this systematic way (or indeed have time to). However, when the teacher is starting out, it is important to make the thinking processes of lesson planning explicit, so that the reasoning can be carefully scrutinised. With experience (of planning, teaching and evaluating lessons, of teaching the 'same' lesson to various classes, etc.), the teacher builds up a vast store of tacit professional knowledge to guide her or his decision-making that the new teacher simply does not have. The logic, then, is to go through a rigorous, explicit process when starting out, which will partly become more automatic and intuitive later on.

A similar logic applies in learning to undertake classroom research. University staff often consider that the best way to ensure students are using classroom research effectively is to go through processes that mimic the rigour of academic research. This both makes sure that the students' thinking is made explicit and so is open to their own reflection and critique, and by requiring a formal report allows the assessors/examiners to make judgements about the quality of the thinking underpinning students' classroom work.

This is summarised in Table 1.1, which sets out the differences in what is expected of the different types of educational researcher. However, a strong word of warning must be added here. Each university sets its own expectations for its course, and has its own types of assignment and assessment specifications. The extent to which student teachers must adopt an academic style of presentation of their work can vary from one

Table 1.1 Different expectations on different types of researcher

	Researchers and researchers-in-training	Teachers and teachers-in-training
Undertaking research as part of professional role	Expected to produce generalisable research addressing issues motivated from the research literature, in the form of knowledge claims published in academic research journals	Expected to have the skills to undertake classroom-based enquiry to inform their own practice and to be able to justify research-informed decisions (to colleagues, inspectors, parents, etc.)
Undertaking research for a university course and qualification	Expected to demonstrate developing competence in producing generalisable research addressing issues motivated from the research literature, in the form of knowledge claims of the type published in academic research journals	Expected to show developing competence in classroom-based enquiry to inform their own practice, and *may* also be expected to frame and report their enquiry in the form of an academic research report – addressing issues motivated from the research literature, and reporting findings as knowledge claims supported by the analysis of classroom data

university to another. If you are studying for a university course, either part-time or full-time, whether as a trainee teacher, a teacher, or as a research student in education, you should familiarise yourself with the requirements of any research assignment you are set, and the assessment criteria that will be used to judge it.

The specific nature of teacher research is considered further in Chapter 5, but it is important not to think that teacher research is necessarily only of local interest, in the particular school or classroom context in which it is undertaken, and so somehow inferior to professional academic research which is taken more seriously by those making decisions about education. Teachers can have influence more widely, especially when working together through organisations like teaching subject associations. So, writing in the *Curriculum Journal* about the case of history teaching in the context of the English National Curriculum, Counsell (2011, p. 208) discusses how teachers have "built activities designed to shift pupils' ideas within particular conceptual domains". She reports that "examples of history teachers doing this are extensive, often spinning from a single, starting example that teachers pick up, reshape and then throw back into the community for continued debate". Counsell suggests that the inclusion of 'historical significance' in official curriculum attainment targets was "largely in response to burgeoning teacher discussion, by then spanning over 20 articles, many web discussions and new textbook activities".

━━━ Examples of classroom research undertaken by new teachers ━━━

As part of the process of supporting teachers new to educational research, the current edition of the book draws upon examples of research undertaken by students undergoing initial teacher education through a PGCE course, as well as referring to research published in research journals by established and experienced researchers. The inclusion of examples of student teacher research is intended to both provide exemplars and to illustrate something of the nature of teacher research. For students asked to undertake classroom enquiry as part of a PGCE or similar qualification, these examples can provide an indication of the scale of what is likely to be feasible, and how such small-scale classroom studies can be related to existing literature on aspects of teaching and learning.

This is important given that there are often limited examples of teacher research accessible to teachers starting out on their own classroom-based research. This book therefore draws upon examples of studies published in the *Journal of Trainee Teacher Educational Research*, an open-access journal that, as its name suggests, publishes reports of PGCE students' research studies undertaken whilst on school placement. The text here can only draw upon selected aspects of these studies, to support particular points, but readers can access the full papers from the journal website (http://jotter. educ.cam.ac.uk/). Each paper is a (sometimes slightly 'tidied-up') assignment submitted for examination for the PGCE qualification, by a trainee reporting work they had carried out in school during their course.

Getting the most out of this book

The book has been planned to support your reading. Different readers will have different needs, and different learning styles. Not everyone will wish to work through the book from start to finish. However, in writing a book, the best assumption is that material should be presented in the book in the order that the author wants readers to meet it! Writing a book for learners is a pedagogic task, and needs to be planned in a similar way to a lesson or course of instruction. As in classroom teaching and learning, it can be helpful for the author (as a teacher) to be explicit to readers (as learners) about how material is structured. Thus a textbook has a contents list, headings, an index, etc.

In planning this book the major considerations were:

- to break down a complex topic into more manageable 'chunks'. In particular, consideration of methodology is presented separately in the book from a discussion of common data collection techniques, to emphasise the importance of thinking about these issues separately;
- to present these 'learning quanta' in a sensible sequence. In planning that 'sensible sequence' I have largely used the principles of going from the general to the more specific, and of following the sequence in which themes are usually tackled when planning a research project;
- to discuss real examples (of published research studies including student teachers' research projects) to give readers an idea of *the variety* of educational research, and *to illustrate* the abstract ideas raised in the book. There is a vast literature on teaching and learning, so I have selected a few examples of studies that offer a range of approaches, and which provide useful contexts for discussing key points made in the text. The inclusion of examples from trainee teachers' classroom research helps readers in that situation themselves get a feel for the scale and nature of an acceptable student project.

Inevitably, this approach is imperfect. Key points from different chapters are strongly linked, and so I have included cross-referencing forwards and backwards in the text. Some 'jumping around' when reading the text not only reflects the interlinked nature of the subject matter, but is also likely to be a more effective way of learning about the topic (requiring greater engagement in reading, and also giving opportunities both to review and consolidate ideas already met, and to preview those to come).

In a similar way, understanding the strengths and limitations of research studies requires a consideration of all aspects of how those studies are planned, executed and reported. I have had to bear this point in mind when making decisions about where to locate examples in the text for them to be most effective. Such decisions are inevitably compromises, and to make best use of the examples the reader will need to use the book in a somewhat iterative way – returning to re-examine examples in the light of further reading.

Question for reflection

If the purpose of the book is to inform readers, why does the author keep posing questions for readers to answer?

I have also included a good many 'reflective questions' in the text. The suggestion is that at these points the reader stops and considers their answer to the question before reading on. In classroom teaching we often attempt to make learners' current thinking explicit, to help them see how new ideas might fit into, or extend, that thinking. The same principles can help when learning from a book – although readers are of course at liberty to ignore this device and just read on. (You might, however, first want to think about how you view those learners you teach who habitually want to be told the 'right' answers before they have intellectually engaged with the question!) Many of these questions would be a suitable basis for an informal discussion with a colleague who is also learning about educational research.

Finally, the discussion of examples of studies from the research literature in this book *inevitably* distorts and simplifies the original authors' own accounts. In attempting to draw on these studies as teaching examples, I have simplified them and been selective in which points I've considered. (This is what teachers do, to work at the level of their students.) Readers should remember that the papers discussed here that are published in research journals have passed through a strict editorial process, involving peer-review by other educational researchers (see Chapter 6). Despite any flaws, these studies have all been judged to make original contributions to our knowledge of teaching and learning.

Readers of the book will identify the literature that is potentially most relevant to their own projects, and will need to read identified studies critically to appreciate both the strengths and limitations of the research. To prepare the reader for this work, studies with a range of research foci, and differing methodology, have been selected to demonstrate the variety of educational research.

I would suggest that readers might find it useful to use a simple summary sheet to outline any paper they wish to critique, with a set of headings relating to the typical structure of research reports (such as those in Figure 1.1). Then the paper should be interrogated in terms of the key questions and issues that will be introduced in the book.

Such a summary cannot provide full details of studies, but can be a useful framework for getting an overview of what a study is about. Boxes 1.1 and 1.2 provide two examples, giving overviews of two very different educational studies. Reading these brief outlines provides a concise précis of the two studies.

> study:
>
> focus:
>
> aim / purpose/ rationale / research questions:
>
> methodology:
>
> – sample (size, nature):
>
> – data collection techniques used:
>
> – ethical issues
>
> analytical processes:
>
> findings:
>
> – type of knowledge claims made:
>
> – how does this inform education?

Figure 1.1   An outline for summarising the key points in research papers

---

Box 1.1

Outline of a research study from the *Modern Language Journal*

study: Sagarra & Alba, 2006

focus: learning vocabulary of a second language

aim / purpose/ rationale / research questions: to compare three methods of learning vocabulary (rote memorisation; the key-word method; semantic mapping)

methodology: experimental – learning of 24 new Spanish words, 8 by each of three different techniques. (Order of technique was varied for participants.)

- ○ *sample (size, nature):* 916 undergraduates in a large US university, of whom 778 provided data used in the analysis
- ○ *data collection techniques used:* immediate and delayed post-tests involving matching vocabulary to diagrams
- ○ *ethical issues:* all participants were adult volunteers, who were told the purpose of the research

analytical processes: statistical – results given as means and standard deviations; comparisons made using analyses of variance

findings:

- ○ *type of knowledge claims made:* effectiveness of learning technique – the key-word method facilitated retention more than rote memorisation, which gave better retention than semantic mapping

> ○ *how does this inform education?* could inform second language teaching – 'when presenting new vocabulary, language teachers can provide learners with a keyword or suggest that they create a keyword to help them remember the new L2 [second language] word' (p. 239)

Box 1.2

Outline of a research study from *Research in Education*

study: Biddulph & Adey, 2004

focus: 12–13 year old pupils' perceptions of history and geography lessons

aim / purpose/ rationale / research questions: to find out what pupils enjoyed in history and geography lessons in terms of topics and teaching and learning strategies

methodology: semi-structured group interviews

○ *sample (size, nature):* 12 groups of year 8 pupils from 'a variety' of different types of schools; each group of 6 pupils of the same gender, but including a range of abilities and levels of interest in the subject. (3 groups for each gender in each of history and geography)
○ *data collection techniques used:* pupils were asked to complete a prompt sheet to focus their thinking, before the group interviews, which were 'recorded'
○ *ethical issues:* all pupils were volunteers; interviewing was in same gender groups

analytical processes: not reported in the paper

findings:

○ *type of knowledge claims made:* pupils reported enjoying research/authentic problem tasks, group-work, field work, etc., but found making notes and answering questions tedious. Pupils tended not to see any relevance in the subjects to their future
○ *how does this inform education?* teachers are encouraged to be explicit about the relevance of the skills used in history and geography, and the importance of developing geographic understanding to issues that pupils would recognise as significant

---

The importance of criticising (and 'forgiving') research

It is important to read research *critically*, carefully examining arguments, and the evidence put forward, to see *if the claims made are supported by the analysis of data presented*. This book exemplifies this by exploring weaknesses and limitations, as well as strengths, in published studies. For the reader who is not familiar with the educational research literature, it could seem that some of the criticisms of studies suggest that these papers have little value.

It is easy to find fault in studies, and we can find ready reasons for this:

- educational research is difficult to do well;
- many studies are severely limited by the available access to classrooms and learners;
- many studies are severely limited by the available resources;
- most research journals have severe word limits on papers, which may prevent authors offering the level of detail they might wish.

The Biddulph and Adey (2004) study, outlined in Box 1.2, does not, for example, explain how transcribed interview data was analysed to derive the findings. However, it is published in a journal that normally publishes papers of less than 4,000 words (shorter than many PGCE assignments), which is restricting to authors. This allows the journal to report more studies, but limits the information available to the reader.

Often an individual study can only contribute in a small way to the development of knowledge. However, that does not mean that it has no value. Although it is important not to accept findings and (especially) authors' suggested implications of their research without examining them critically, it is also important not to completely dismiss a study because it has limitations.

———— Research studies and research programmes ————————————————

The research literature is cumulative, with each new study adding a little more evidence. Research is always based upon a wide range of assumptions (it has to be) and so each study will involve many choices (where different underlying assumptions and values might lead to different preferred options). The resources available then constrain what may *actually* be done.

So although individual studies may be limited, and even flawed, they may still offer useful insights and relevant evidence that may be 'suggestive' and 'indicative', even when hardly conclusive. Many researchers see their work in terms of research programmes: that is, they have a long-term interest in exploring issues and questions they see as significant, but which are not capable of being 'settled' by a single enquiry. Rather, successive studies are intended to help move understanding forward. Early studies may do little more than help establish the nature of the issue, the most useful definitions, the boundaries of the matters to be studied, and test out the suitability of appropriate approaches to research. The notion of research programmes will be revisited in Chapter 4.

———— Research writing as rhetoric ————————————————————————

A second very important consideration is that research in the social sciences (such as education) does not always match the image of 'disinterested' enquiry that is sometimes offered as a stereotype of the natural sciences. Educational researchers may be inspired by issues that link to their personal values. Educational researchers may, for example, be strongly motivated by issues of social justice, equality of opportunity, or (say) the importance for society of supporting an intellectual elite. When researchers have strong commitments to such principles, then their writing may be intended to be largely rhetorical, to argue the case for the educational policies that best reflect values they feel are important. (Just as a government may have ideological reasons for seeing teaching as a craft that requires on-the-job training to produce skilled workers who are responsible to managers and government agencies, rather than as a true profession where individual professionals are expected to take responsibility for their work, being held accountable by the profession itself.) Such writing will clearly marshal a case to support their arguments.

Perhaps in an ideal world such rhetorical writing will be clearly distinct from research reports that should document empirical studies in an objective fashion, without being reported with any 'gloss' or 'spin'. Even if such an ideal were feasible (if it were possible to be 'objective' in making all the myriad decisions that lead to a particular study having the final form it does), that is not the current state of affairs. Many papers published in respectable research journals offer 'empirical studies' that are clearly biased by such concerns. The use of the term 'bias' may suggest something necessarily negative, but perhaps we should make a distinction between bias as preference and bias as prejudice. Researchers are allowed their preferences, but should not prejudge empirical questions before they have undertaken careful and thorough empirical studies. Phillips and Burbules point out that although we may not consider subjective writing as appropriate in research, it is not sensible to expect research to be value-neutral:

> Every enquirer *must* adopt a framework or perspective or point of view. It is a truism that, given this framework or perspective, he or she may see phenomena differently from the way other investigators see them.
>
> (Phillips & Burbules, 2000, p. 46)

The responsibilities of writers and readers ⎯⎯

The reader of educational research is invited to 'buy into' the account being provided by the author of a research paper. It is the author's responsibility to make the case for any conclusions offered. However, it is the reader's responsibility to check the argument proposed. An argument's worth depends upon both its logical structure and the strength of the evidence offered. Inevitably, any argument presented in an educational research study will in part depend upon data, and in part upon the interpretation of that data – an interpretation that draws upon the author's own theoretical perspectives. A reader's evaluation of the argument will similarly depend upon the theoretical perspectives that they have developed about the topic.

By the time you have completed the book you should have developed a good basic framework for interrogating studies in order to evaluate them to inform both your own teaching and your own classroom enquiry. You should also be able to apply this framework to recognise the strengths and weaknesses of your own work, and so be able to plan and report work that you yourself would consider competent and informative. At that point you can feel you are ready to be a professional teacher in terms of the 'strong' model of teacher professionalism.

————Further reading ————

The present book only offers an introduction to classroom research, and I hope many readers will wish to take their reading further. This book is also, I believe, unusual, as I have given a lot of space to critiquing specific published studies. This was a deliberate decision, and was intended to support those new to educational research in thinking about how to read research critically. I hope this feature also makes the book more interesting to those who wish to do classroom research, but are not that interested in methodology – as the book is in a sense as much about teaching and learning as it is about doing research. For those readers who find the discussion of studies into these areas of particular interest, there are a number of good books around introducing scholarship and research on teaching and learning. I have suggested several useful titles below.

I also hope that most readers of this book will decide that research methodology is actually an interesting area in its own right, and will want to delve deeper – at least into those aspects linked to their own classroom research. There are a great many texts available, both about educational and social research in general, and about particular methodologies and techniques. A number will be recommended at various points later in the book. Here I am just suggesting three very useful books. The Wilson text goes into more detail than the present volume on a number of important topics, whilst still being written with the classroom teacher in mind. Of the more advanced texts, the Cohen et al. book is a classic text and, whilst written and presented in a more formal style than many other texts, offers a fairly comprehensive overview of education research. Robson's text is very readable and is a favourite of many students.

Cohen, L., Manion, L., & Morrison, K. (2011). *Research Methods in Education* (7th edn). London: Routledge.

Joyce, B., Calhoun, E., & Hopkins, D. (2002). *Models of Learning: Tools for Teaching* (2nd edn). Buckingham: Open University Press.

Moore, A. (2000). *Teaching and Learning: Pedagogy, Curriculum and Culture*. London: RoutledgeFalmer.

Muijs, D., & Reynolds, D. (2001). *Effective Teaching: Evidence and Practice*. London: Paul Chapman Publishing.

Robson, C. (2002). *Real World Research: A Resource for Social Scientists and Practitioner Researchers* (2nd edn). Malden, Massachusetts: Blackwell.

Sotto, E. (1994). *When Teaching Becomes Learning: A Theory and Practice of Teaching*. London: Continuum.

Wilson, E. (Ed.) (2012). *School-based Research: A Guide for Education Students* (2nd edn). Thousand Oaks, California: Sage.

2

What is this thing called educational research?

Central to educational research ... is the attempt to make sense of the activities, policies and institutions which, through the organisation of learning, help to transform the capacities of people to live a fuller and more distinctly human life.

(Pring, 2000, p. 17)

This chapter:

- discusses a range of different research topics related to teaching and learning
- introduces the kinds of findings that are reported in accounts of educational research
- asks you to start thinking about the kinds of evidence that can support the claims made in educational research, and how that evidence could have been collected.

This chapter gives some examples of the outcomes of educational research – the findings and conclusions about aspects of teaching and learning that researchers claim to show in their published accounts of research. Taken together, these studies give an indication of the *range* of foci that such research projects can have. More importantly, this chapter should get you thinking about how such findings are derived.

What does educational research find?

This chapter, then, gives a taste of the kind of things that educational research investigates, and the types of suggestions and recommendations that derive from research. Often these suggestions and recommendations are potentially significant for teachers, in that they may indicate that changes of teaching behaviour would lead to more desirable classroom outcomes. As professionals, teachers want their work to be informed by research. However, changing familiar ways of doings things may be difficult, uncomfortable and, indeed, risky (as it may well take time to become as effective in applying new skills and approaches). It is therefore important that teachers do not simply take up every potentially relevant recommendation they find proposed in a research report. Rather, *teachers must be confident that change is likely to be worthwhile*.

So, changing teaching behaviour on the basis of research is only advisable when we are convinced that (a) the research has been done well (an issue considered in more detail in Chapter 6), and (b) is likely to apply in our own professional context – which may be quite different from the sites where a published study is carried out (an issue explored in Chapter 7).

In this present chapter the range of educational research into learning and teaching is illustrated in terms of reference to a small number of (mostly) recent studies. This chapter considers findings that should be of interest to all teachers, as it touches upon a range of topics that are central to classroom teaching and learning. It does, however, only describe a selection of the great number of studies about teaching and learning being published. The reader is advised to look at these 'findings' with a curious eye, and to reflect on how the authors came to their conclusions.

Questions for reflection

As you read about the claims that researchers have made, you should be asking yourself a range of questions:

- How do they know?
- How confident can I be that the claims are justified by the evidence?
- What kind of evidence would be needed to support such a claim?
- Do these findings have a limited range of application (for example, to a certain age range, or subject area, etc.)?
- How could I find out if these findings apply to my professional context?

Bibliographic details of all of the studies mentioned in this chapter are listed at the back of the book. This will enable you to locate the original accounts if you decide to read them to make *your own* judgements about the extent to which the authors have a convincing case for the claims they make. Some of the studies are also discussed in more detail later in the book, where they are used as examples to illustrate the nature, strengths and limitations of different approaches to educational research.

——— What kind of things does research tell us about student thinking? ———

One area of educational research explores student thinking about various topics – whether it is their understanding of the subject content that makes up the curriculum of school, or their views about aspects of school life and classroom learning.

What do pupils think of school subjects?

It can obviously be useful for teachers to be aware of how students perceive their subject. In a paper in the journal *Music Education Research*, Button (2006) reports on a study exploring the perceptions of Music held by 11–14 year-old students. He reported that there were a number of gender differences in student responses to a questionnaire. Girls had more positive attitudes to the subject, being more enthusiastic about, and interested in, music, where boys reported being more anxious about taking part in musical activities. Three-quarters of the girls, but only about half the boys, reported having access to a musical instrument at home.

In a study of 12–13 year-old students' perceptions of history and geography lessons, reported in the journal *Research in Education*, Biddulph and Adey (2004) suggest that "pupils were unable to distinguish between subject content and the learning process" (p. 3) when asked about their enjoyment of particular topics and teaching approaches (see Chapter 1, Box 1.2). So pupils had enjoyed learning about Mary Tudor by designing posters or learning about Antarctica by writing poems, but could not separate out the influence of the subject material from their experiences of learning through a particular type of activity. This could be seen to suggest that for many pupils particular content is not intrinsically interesting or boring, but may be made the basis for enjoyable lessons as long as teaching and learning activities are chosen to engage the students.

Writing in the journal *Thinking Skills and Creativity*, Burnard and Swann (2010) report a study exploring students' perceptions of their experiences of working with professional artists running workshops outside the usual school curriculum. They identified three themes that seemed especially important to the way students experienced these workshops as different from standard curriculum fare. These were the way the artists related to the students; engagement of the emotional side of learning; and the significance of the physical context for learning. Burnard and Swann (2010, p. 79) found that the learners valued the "non-hierarchical, 'real world' relationships with artists which they felt were different from the kinds of relationships they shared with their teachers", where "the artists participated as co-learners alongside the pupils" in a "shared compositional project [where] artist and pupil investigated and experimented together, each taking something different from the opportunity for learning". That the students responded to relationships they perceived as "real and human" may offer an important message for all those working with young learners.

Do students accept mutually inconsistent ideas?

An important programme of research that continued through the twentieth century explored children's developing cognitive abilities, and in particular the complexity of logical thought typically available to learners at different ages (Sutherland, 1992). However, in the past few decades much attention has shifted from general capabilities to considering the patterns of student thinking in particular subject areas.

Stylianides and Al-Murani (2010) reported a study in the journal *Research in Mathematics Education* to follow up survey responses suggesting that students accepted contrary ideas. These students agreed that one particular argument provided a mathematical proof of a particular assertion, but also agreed that another argument demonstrated a counter-example to the same assertion. A general statement cannot both be true (i.e., for all cases) and be shown to be false in some cases: so this seemed illogical. One interpretation was that the students held a misconception about the nature of mathematical proof, and did not appreciate that a proof and a counter-example could not both be possible. However, when Stylianides and Al-Murani interviewed students who offered the contradictory responses, they found that there were other explanations for this discrepancy. For example, a student might separately find both the argument for the proof and the argument for the counter-example convincing (not spotting a flaw in the latter argument) without noticing that they were agreeing with two contradictory statements. In interviews, students would realise this, and appreciate they needed to change their judgement of one or other of the arguments.

I have found similar apparent contradictions in my own work in science education: students may agree with apparently inconsistent statements about the same focal topic. For example, colleagues and I have asked upper secondary students in England, Greece and Turkey to agree/disagree with statements about the bonding in salts such as sodium chloride (Taber, Tsaparlis, & Nakiboğlu, 2012), and found that respondents will often agree both with 'canonical' statements (reflecting the scientific understanding) as well as with alternative statements reflecting common misconceptions inconsistent with the science taught in school. However, in chemistry topics, students are often asked to think about several apparently inconsistent models of the same concept (atomic structure, oxidation, acids, etc.), and so they may feel quite justified in agreeing with contradictory statements, considering different models "as alternative narratives that could be employed to make sense of chemistry" (Taber, 2000c, p. 411). This difference between mathematics and science suggests that research into aspects of student thinking needs to be undertaken within the context of particular teaching subjects.

How do students understand ideas they meet in lessons?

In terms of student thinking about curriculum topics, there is a vast amount of research. This is especially so in science, where research has revealed students often hold 'alternative conceptions' or 'alternative frameworks' that are inconsistent with the curriculum models that are presented as target knowledge in school (Taber, 2009b).

For example, in 1983, Watts published a study in the *European Journal of Science Education* claiming that secondary-age students understood the key physics concept of 'force' in ways that did not match scientific understanding. Furthermore, Watts (1983) claimed he had discovered eight distinct 'alternative conceptual frameworks' that described the ways that students thought about forces. Watts argued that his findings would inform teachers trying to teach this concept in school science. However, such 'findings' are not always universally accepted. In 1994, Kuiper published a study in the *International Journal of Science Education* claiming that secondary students "in general do not have a set of mutually consistent ideas about force, and that it is not therefore correct to describe such understanding as 'alternative frameworks', which implies a coherence in student ideas" (Kuiper, 1994, p. 279).

Questions for reflection

Why might two studies produce such contrary findings? What considerations might a teacher use to decide which (if either) study forms the better basis for informing their teaching?

Are pupils constructivist learners?

This area of research has been seen as significant as it is strongly linked to theories of learning and models of good teaching. So-called 'constructivist' perspectives emphasise the importance of learning as being a process of building on existing knowledge and experience (Taber, 2011a). There are many flavours of 'constructivism' but teaching approaches believed to be consistent with such beliefs about learning (sometimes identified as 'progressive', 'student-centred', 'active' learning, etc.) are often contrasted with so-called 'traditional' approaches, which are considered to be based around a model of learning as knowledge being transferred from the teacher to the students – usually largely by the giving of notes to the class, or directing students to read textbook passages.

Teaching can be said to be about making the unfamiliar familiar. In a study of 13–14 year-old English students learning about Japan in their geography lessons reported in the *British Educational Research Journal*, Taylor (2011) presents examples of how learners *make sense* of an initially unfamiliar distant land by relating it to their own existing knowledge and experiences – constructing conjectured explanations of Japanese customs and scenes in terms of what is familiar. This process is largely facilitated by dialogue – allowing learners to share their ideas, and allowing the teacher to model student understanding and judge how to scaffold new learning.

In 2004, the journal *Educational Research* published a study by Kinchin which concluded that secondary school students had an "overwhelming preference … for a constructivist learning environment", thinking this "would be more interesting, more effective at developing students' understanding and would permit them to take greater ownership of their learning" (Kinchin, 2004, p. 301). According to Kinchin, this work is significant because "not only that students would be receptive to moves by teachers towards more constructivist principles in the classroom, but also that a failure to promote such a transition may contribute to an epistemological gap between teaching and learning styles that will be an impediment to meaningful learning" (p. 301).

Question for reflection

What do you feel Kinchin would need to do to make the case for their being "an epistemological gap between teaching and learning styles"?

Asking students to provide their views about schooling and teaching (sometimes known as 'pupil voice' or 'student voice') has become more common in schools, and so has been the focus of research. In one paper in the journal *Research Papers in Education*, McIntyre, Peddar and Ruddock (2005) reported a study where 12–13 year-old students were invited to provide feedback on their English, maths and science lessons, and this feedback was shared with the teachers. Among the findings reported, McIntyre and colleagues claim that the student feedback had a constructive focus on learning and that students had common ideas about what helped their learning. Students believed that:

- interactive teaching focused on achieving understanding;
- teaching which enables collaborative learning;

- having the ideas to be learnt suitably contextualised; and
- being given more feeling of ownership of their learning.

were all helpful (McIntyre et al., 2005).

Student voice might seem to primarily be about the students, but can also be very important for teachers according to a study in the journal *Improving Schools*. Demetriou and Wilson (2010) report an interview study with 11 science teachers within their first three years of teaching, and suggest that there are "merits of listening to the student voice for new teachers", and that:

> The teachers in our research who took the time to listen and invest an emotional rapport with their students, were the teachers who ultimately saved time – through curbing disruptive behaviour, instilling discipline and reaping the rewards of effective and genuine interest in learning.
>
> (Demetriou & Wilson, 2010, p. 64)

This would seem to be an important message for all teachers.

———— What kind of things does research tell us about learning? ————

Learning is the central purpose of education, and so it is not surprising that educational researchers have explored many aspects of learning.

Do pupils have learning styles?

One notion that teachers often come across is that of 'learning style' (preferred ways of learning), although a major review conducted on behalf of the Learning and Skills Research Centre reported that the research base for many of the popular models of learning styles was inadequate, as "Research into learning styles can, in the main, be characterised as small-scale, non-cumulative, uncritical and inward-looking" (Coffield, Moseley, Hall, & Ecclestone, 2004, p. 54). However, in a paper published in the journal *Music Education Research*, Calissendorff (2006) argues that the ways that 5 year olds learn to play the violin can best be described in terms of their learning styles. Calissendorff offers a nuanced model of what this notion of learning style means in the particular context she researched.

Question for reflection

How might one collect data that allows us to conclude that 5 year olds have preferred ways of learning?

Exploring the processes of learning

In a paper in the the *Modern Language Journal*, Sagarra and Alba (2006) reported a study showing the relative effectiveness of the 'keyword' approach to learning foreign language vocabulary (see Chapter 1, Box 1.1). In this technique, the new second language word is linked to a familiar first language word that looks or sounds similar, and students learn a sentence or mental image connecting the keyword with the first language translation of the target second language word. They give the example of 'a messy table' to connect the Spanish word *mesa* with its English equivalent, table. Teachers are often encouraged to 'teach for understanding' (Newton, 2000) and to avoid rote learning, and in general this is good advice. However, such mnemonic approaches can prove very useful in situations where the material to be learned will appear largely arbitrary to the learners. So a system based on a similar method of associations to that reported by Sagarra and Alba has been developed to help medical students learn the many technical terms used in anatomy. In that system the learners are asked to actively create a quirky mental image that will help them recall the technical term where it is claimed "that the 'crazier' or 'more illogical' an association, the better it is to help recall, retain, and remember over a long period of time and in essence 'learn' the meanings of word parts comprising medical terms" (Brahler & Walker, 2008, p. 219).

Learning can be a very complex set of processes. In a paper published in 1998, Petri and Niedderer explored how a student's understanding of a key science concept, the atom, developed over time. They reported that the student's conceptualisation passed through a number of stages, but that the student actually operated with a mixture of the different versions of the concept, rather than cleanly moving on from one to the next. In their paper, "the student's learning pathway is described as a sequence of several meta-stable conceptions", and they found that the student's notion of the atom after teaching seemed to be a complex entity – "an association of three parallel conceptions" (Petri & Niedderer, 1998, p. 1075).

Question for reflection

What kind of evidence do you think researchers would need to collect to explore an individual's learning in such depth?

Can learners regulate their own learning?

Self-regulated learning (SRL) is often seen as an important goal of education, where the learner has enough metacognitive awareness and sufficiently well-developed 'study skills' to operate as an independent learner – rather than being dependent upon a teacher to offer direction whenever a decision needs to be made: have I done enough? is this good enough? what should I do next? etc. There has tended to be a view that as these are quite high-level processes they appear relatively late in our cognitive development. However, a study reported in *ZDM: The International Journal on Mathematics Education* by Whitebread and Coltman (2010) suggests that the previous failures to recognise metacognitive behaviour in young children may be due to insensitive methodology rather than the lack of metacognition itself. Their own careful observations of 3–5 year-old learners suggested that "when the children ... were given reasons for articulating their thinking which made sense to them, they appeared to be more capable in this regard than perhaps previously indicated" (Whitebread & Coltman, 2010, p. 176).

It is obviously unrealistic to expect young children to be fully independent learners, but an effective school system should encourage learners to take on increasing levels of responsibility for monitoring and directing their own learning, to equip them for further education and life-long learning. Rogers and Hallam (2006) published a study in the journal *Educational Studies* considering the study habits of high-achieving 14–16 year-old students. In their sample they found that, typically, high-achieving boys had more effective studying strategies than high-achieving girls, as they managed to achieve high standards while doing less homework.

In a 2004 study, published in the *International Journal of Science and Mathematics Education*, Corrigan and Taylor (2004) suggest that the requirements for promoting SRL may include:

- offering students choice
- setting learning goals and timeframes (within parameters)
- opportunities to reflect
- a relaxed and supportive environment
- a hands-on, activity-based, fun learning environment
- access to a wide range of resources.

Question for reflection

How might researchers go about identifying factors that help develop SRL?

One activity that can certainly encourage us to think about our learning is to teach others what we have learnt. There is an old teacher's adage that one only really understands a topic when one has to teach it to others. This might lead us to argue:

> that (a) teachers want to help pupils to understand their subject; and (b) in many teachers' own experiences, deep understanding did not derive from learning in class, but from preparing to teach a class. The logical next stage would seem to be something like: (c) teachers need to create for their pupils a similar learning context to that they themselves experienced when preparing to teach a subject.
>
> (Taber, 2009a, p. 83)

One approach is to set older or more advanced students the task of tutoring their peers. Galbraith and Winterbottom (2010) report a study in the journal *Educational Studies* where 16–17 year-old students taking biology acted as peer tutors for 14–15 year-old students. The study focused on the peer-tutors' experiences of the process (collecting data through a shared Wiki). Galbraith and Winterbottom found, as might be expected, that acting in a teaching role supported the learning processes of the tutors. They report that the process:

- helped to support tutors' learning through testing and clarifying their understanding, and reorganising and building ideas;
- gave tutors the opportunity to revisit fundamental ideas and make links between conceptual areas;

- prompted tutors to rehearse ideas, working through them repeatedly to secure an appropriate level of understanding;
- led to reflection on tutors' own learning;
- gave tutors the opportunity to focus on key points, and to present material in a format which required engagement with basic ideas and understanding of the tutee's perspective; and
- led to tutors working through and reorganising their understanding and using mental rehearsal of peer-tutoring episodes to help focus on gaps in their own subject knowledge (Galbraith & Winterbottom, 2010, p. 331).

One suspects that a very similar list might be obtained if new teachers were asked to reflect upon their own experiences of preparing to, and starting to, teach.

Exploring the significance of language skills in school learning

One area of concern in many schools is the learning of students for whom English is an additional language (EAL), i.e., not their first language. When English language is the medium of instruction in schools, it is clear that students lacking basic language skills could struggle to learn from teaching. In a paper published in the journal *Educational Studies*, Strand and Demie (2005) report a study analysing results on national tests taken at age 10–11 in a local education authority. Strand and Demie reported that EAL students at the early stages of developing fluency in English had significantly lower 'KS2 SAT' test scores in *all* the test subjects than their monolingual peers, and this seemed to be linked to the low fluency in the language. They also found that EAL pupils who were fully fluent in English achieved significantly *higher* scores in the tests than their monolingual peers (although they recognised that this finding could be associated with factors other than language fluency).

Question for reflection

Strand and Demie report that EAL students who were fully fluent in English achieved significantly *higher* scores in standard school tests than their peers who only spoke English. Can you suggest any possible explanations for such a difference? (Does Box 4.1 offer any viable suggestions?)

———————What kind of things does research tell us about teaching? ———

If learning is the central purpose of education, then teaching is the means by which that aim is achieved. Whereas learning often needs to be studied through indirect measures, some aspects of teaching are more readily investigated. Many aspects of what teachers do in the classroom, and how they plan for lessons and organise their classes, have been studied.

What kinds of classroom discourse do teachers encourage?

Many aspects of classroom practice have been subject to substantive levels of 'guidance' with official approval (see Chapter 1), and may act as the source of criteria used to evaluate teaching. Understandably, many aspects of official policy and guidance (especially where those pronouncements do not seem to be supported by a strong evidence base) are subject to close research attention. Hardman, Smith and Wall (2005) report a study in the journal *Educational Review* that investigated the nature of classroom interaction and discourse in primary schools during a daily 'literacy hour' that was required as part of a National Literacy Strategy (NLS) – with a special focus on students with special educational needs (SEN). They reported that although the NLS was encouraging teachers to involve pupils with SEN in the literacy hour, the classroom discourse was dominated by teacher explanations and sequences of questions and answers that did not provide sufficient opportunities for *all pupils* to offer and develop their own ideas.

Questioning is a major technique used by teachers, and types and purposes of teacher questions have been widely studied (e.g., Edwards & Mercer, 1987). It has been argued that teachers should use a high proportion of 'open' questions that give students scope for a potentially wide range of responses. Research also suggests this is *not* what teachers actually do. In a paper in the journal *Educational Studies*, Harrop and Swinson (2003) reported that teachers in infant, junior and secondary schools used about five times as many closed questions (where only one answer would be considered correct) as open questions (that invite more creative thinking and have several or many potentially acceptable answers).

Question for reflection

What kind of data would researchers need to collect to be able to draw such a conclusion?

Are we teaching for creativity?

One area of major interest in education in recent years has been that of creativity. Although creativity has perhaps been associated most with artistic subjects, it is an essential part of high performance in all academic areas. So in science, for example, there is much emphasis on the logic of testing ideas experimentally, but equally important is the process of having creative ideas about what to test (Taber, 2011b). Research is needed to explore how to best teach to support the development of students' creativity.

Writing in the *International Journal of Technology and Design Education*, McLellan and Nicholl (2011) question the common practice of asking students to start to think about designing an object by considering existing examples of the same type of artefact. As they point out, "if students analyse examples of the same product that they are making, this immediately limits thinking due to the way normative cognitive processes operate" (p. 81). Following an interview study involving teachers and students in six secondary schools, these researchers suggest that:

> teachers might be advised to take a different product as the starting point for design work. This would avoid the default cueing of known knowledge about the product being designed to dominate thinking, and would therefore open up possibilities, that is, the task could be more ambiguous or open-ended.
>
> (McLellan & Nicholl, 2011, p. 88)

In a paper in the *International Journal of Science Education*, Dorion (2009) reported the outcomes of his MEd project looking at the use of drama-based activities in teaching science concepts. Not all science teachers feel confident in using such arts-based teaching approaches, but – when they *are* used – they are often found very engaging and memorable by students. One secondary student, 'Morag', I interviewed about her school science lessons spontaneously stood up and starting acting out being a molecule as she had in her science lesson! (This example is described in more detail at https://camtools.cam.ac.uk/wiki/eclipse/Morag.html) Dorion's study "focused on teachers' own drama activities in five science lessons [exploring] the drama forms, teaching objectives, and characteristics by which drama was perceived to enable learning in Science". Dorion reported that "drama activities were used to convey a variety of topics that have not yet been recorded in academic literature, and revealed a greater scope for the teaching of abstract scientific concepts through mime and role play" (2009, p. 2247).

Question for reflection

Dorion reported on a study of five science lessons where teachers considered they were already using drama-based activities in teaching science. Can we learn anything useful from such a small sample of lessons that are probably not typical of most secondary science lessons?

How are teachers using ICT in their classrooms?

One feature of modern classrooms is the increasing availability of computers and other information and communications technology (ICT), and the incorporation of such resources into teaching. Hennessy, Ruthven, and Brindley (2005) reported a study in the *Journal of Curriculum Studies* of how secondary teachers of English, mathematics, and science were integrating ICT into their classroom practice. They suggest that changes in this aspect of teaching behaviour are gradual and evolutionary, that teachers reported using ICT to enhance and develop their existing classroom practice, and adopting new ICT-supported activities that modified or complemented their current practice. In a study reported in *Educational Review*, John (2005) explored how teachers across a range of curriculum subjects used ICT in teaching. John also found that adoption of ICT by classroom teachers seemed to be "evolutionary rather than transformatory" (p. 471), with changes in teaching practice being considered to allow "a blending to emerge where teachers maintained their professional control over the technology using their pragmatic professionalism" (p. 487). John also found that there were subject-based differences in the way the teacher perceived the strengths and limitations of ICT use in lessons.

Macaruso, Hook, and McCabe (2006) published a study in the *Journal of Research in Reading* that reports that when 6–7 year-old students initially considered to be 'low-performing' were given access to supplementary computer-aided instruction in phonics over a school year, they made sufficient progress in reading skills to demonstrate comparable performance with peers who had not been considered 'low performing'. Teaching and learning are closely linked, and often studies that focus on teaching are concerned (quite naturally) with its effect on learning. In a paper published in the journal *Educational Review*, Taylor, Lazarus, and Cole (2005) report a study of 14–15 year-old students using an 'electronic learning tool' to develop their writing in German as a foreign language. The writing tool, developed by teachers, enabled students to write in ways judged as more complex, accurate and imaginative.

De Winter, Winterbottom, and Wilson (2010) worked closely with science teachers in five schools who had an interest in using new technology in their teaching, and concluded that "new technologies can support social construction of learning, assessment (both of and for learning), motivation, and differentiation and personalisation of learning, and that supporting teachers in integrating such technology into their practice can support useful pedagogical outcomes" (p. 265). De Winter et al.'s study reiterates the potential of new technologies in the classroom, whilst also reminding us that teachers need support to make best use of innovations.

Can textbooks impoverish teaching?

Teaching resources are suitable foci for educational enquiry. In some subjects, and certainly in some educational systems, teaching is often closely linked to adopted textbooks. Aldridge (2006, p. 662) argues that this is the case for history teaching in the USA, where "teachers relied on these textbooks, consequently denying students an accurate picture of the complexity and richness of American history". Writing in the journal *Teachers College Record*, Aldridge suggests that American history texts oversimplify material in ways that distort the topics being studied. He argues that when teachers rely heavily on the class text as a basis for classroom teaching, the students are "deprived of a conceptual lens that would help them better comprehend the world around them" (p. 680).

Meeting the needs of different learners

One major ongoing concern of those working in education concerns how teaching is organised to meet the needs of students who are considered to be of different 'abilities'. There has been discussion over whether students in a year group should be taught in 'mixed-ability' groups, in sets (i.e., for different subjects), in ability bands (for all subjects), or even in different schools. In a study reported in the journal *Assessment in Education: Principles, Policy & Practice*, Gardner and Cowan (2005) report that the methodology used to assess ability (and so select students for grammar schools) in Northern Ireland is flawed, as the system used for ranking candidates has the potential to misclassify up to two-thirds of a cohort taking the selection tests by as many as three grades.

There are of course many variations in practice. In many secondary schools, some subjects are 'set', with setting in different subjects starting in different year groups. In a study reported in *Research Papers in Education*, Hallam and Ireson (2005) set out to compare the pedagogical practices of secondary school teachers from across the curriculum when they taught mixed and ability grouped classes. They found that the curriculum was differentiated more in mixed-ability grouped classes (than in lessons taught to 'sets') in terms of content, depth of treatment, the activities undertaken and the teaching and learning resources used.

Question for reflection

Hallam and Ireson report that teachers of set classes differentiate work for students less than teachers of mixed-ability class. What potential factors can you identify that could be investigated as potential causes of this effect?

Hallam and Ireson report that this did not seem to be due to the styles or skills of teachers, as differences in pedagogy were found when the same teachers taught both mixed-ability and set classes.

In a paper in the journal *Educational Studies*, Lyle (1999) claims that teachers with mixed-ability classes can help their pupils develop their literacy by forming mixed-ability groups (rather than similar-ability groups) within the class:

> mixed-ability teaching provides a setting in which both low- and high-achieving students value the opportunity to work together where both groups believed they benefited … the children themselves value this way of working and … the social experience of collaboration affects the course of individual development regardless of ability.
>
> (Lyle, 1999, pp. 293–294)

Question for reflection

What type of evidence would be needed to convince you that Lyle's findings are sound?

We might see discussion on teaching students of different ability as part of a wider 'inclusion' agenda. Florian and Black-Hawkins (2010) have discussed the notion of 'inclusive pedagogy' which requires:

> a shift in pedagogical thinking from an approach that works for *most* learners existing alongside something 'additional' or 'different' for those (*some*) who experience difficulties, towards one that involves providing rich learning opportunities that are sufficiently made available for *everyone*, so that all learners are able to participate in classroom life.
>
> (Florian & Black-Hawkins, 2010, p. 826)

Florian and Black-Hawkins report on a study where they spent extended periods of time in two Scottish primary schools to investigate the approaches used by teachers and support staff both (i) to identify strategies that were effective and could be reported for possible adoption elsewhere, and (ii) to explore relevant teacher knowledge and beliefs, to help the researchers understand how best to articulate their notion of 'inclusive pedagogy' in ways most useful to classroom teachers.

Teaching to the test?

Another concern for many teachers is how assessment is often considered to channel and constrain teachers' decisions about how best to teach their subjects. This is an important topic, as over a period of decades public examinations in the UK shifted from being based almost exclusively on examinations taken at the end of courses, at age 16 and age 18, to modular courses, where examinations may be taken at different stages in the course. The belief that this has made the examination process less robust and rigorous has led to the UK government seeking to reduce the modularisation process. In a paper in the journal *Educational Research*, McClune (2001) argues that students following modular courses, where some of the credit for final grades is awarded for examination papers taken early in the course, may be *disadvantaged* compared with students taking linear courses for the same award, and being examined on all aspects of the course in terminal examinations: "upper-sixth pupils performed better than an equivalent group of pupils in the lower-sixth year when tested with the same examination questions in physics" (McClune, 2001, p. 87).

Question for reflection

What are the potential difficulties of undertaking a study that tries to make a fair comparison between examination performances of students taking examinations at different points in a course?

The A level course was traditionally a two-year course, most commonly studied in the first two years of post-compulsory education (ages 16–18) with terminal examinations at the end of the second year. A level has now been divided into two somewhat distinct qualifications, with AS level seen as the usual target for the first year of the course, and often as an indicator for whether progression to the 'A2' year should be permitted. A key issue is raised here about the nature of learning: should learning a subject be seen as the accumulation of relatively discrete knowledge, or does effective learning require consolidation and integration through teaching in one topic supporting, reinforcing and providing context for learning in other topics?

What makes for effective teaching?

Kington, Sammons, Day, and Regan (2011, p. 103) report on the Effective Classroom Practice project which "aimed to identify key factors that contribute to effective teaching in primary and secondary phases of schooling in different socioeconomic contexts". This project suggested that, among other things, the more effective teachers (Day, Sammons, & Kington, 2008, pp. 13–15):

- created a positive climate for learning by challenging pupils' ideas, inspiring them, being more innovative in their practice and differentiating amongst pupils according to abilities and interests where appropriate;
- gave more time to developing individual relationships with pupils, and focused upon building self-esteem, engendering trust and maintaining respect;
- instigated new challenges for pupils that facilitated independent learning;
- used a variety of resources, such as overhead projectors, film and teacher-made materials to raise the aspirations and inspire wider participation of pupils;
- offered opportunities for pupils to reflect, self-evaluate, engage in dialogue about learning, and recognise their own improvements, giving pupils additional confidence in influencing their own learning.

Questions for reflection

A project to investigate effective teaching across primary and secondary schools is ambitious. Can you suggest what kind of database might be needed to allow researchers to draw robust general conclusions about the nature of effective school teaching? How would you go about a project to identify what 'more effective' teachers do that makes them 'more effective' than other teachers?

—— What kinds of things does research tell us about teacher thinking? ——

Research into learning and teaching is building up detailed knowledge about how students learn, and what teachers do, and how different teaching behaviours can support (or impede) student learning. However, it is only likely that such research-based knowledge will influence teacher behaviour in fundamental ways to the extent that teachers are aware of, and trust, research findings.

Earlier in this chapter, research into student thinking was discussed. Understanding student ideas about school and learning can help us understand (and perhaps change) their learning behaviours. Understanding students' existing beliefs about topics that appear in the school curriculum helps teachers to recognise misconceptions, and to plan teaching that builds upon existing knowledge and experience. In a similar way, educational researchers explore teacher thinking and beliefs. Teachers' beliefs about teaching and learning (including beliefs that may be tacit, i.e., significant even though the teacher is not consciously aware of them) influence teaching behaviour – especially the myriad decisions that a teacher makes in the classroom every day, responding in real-time to the developing milieu. Exploring teacher thinking provides insights into teaching behaviour, and informs those charged with developing those beliefs through teacher education and continuing professional development.

Do teachers understand the intended curriculum?

Sade and Coll (2003) undertook a study to explore the perceptions of technology and technological education among primary teachers and curriculum development officers in the Solomon Islands. Clearly, technology education is an important part of education, but Sade and Coll found that the teachers in their sample had a particular (and arguably distorted) view of what technology education should be about. The sample did not seem to consider *traditional* technologies as being part of the remit of technological education, rather "… the most widely held view of technology education was that it consists of learning about, and how to use, modern artefacts" (p. 102) such as (as one of their informants volunteered) "computers, televisions, telephones, emails, photocopies, and fax machines".

There is a good deal of research that explores how students understand the topics they are taught in school, and sometimes this research reveals quite common alternative ways of thinking, at odds with the target knowledge presented in the curriculum. So, for example, many students will suggests that a lot of what happens in chemistry at the level of molecules can be explained through the idea that atoms like to complete their outer electron shells (Taber, 1998). But this is a rather strange idea. How could something like an atom 'know' how many electrons it might have, and why would it 'care'? Atoms are tiny little pieces of inanimate matter incapable of acting as sentient agents in the world. This raises the question of how so many learners acquire this same misconception of atoms going around trying to fill their electron shells. It has been suggested that in cases like this, the way the topic is taught might well be to blame. It is even suggested that perhaps teachers themselves sometimes have the same misconceptions we find among students, and are actually passing on their own erroneous thinking. When my colleague Daniel Tan surveyed trainee chemistry teachers in Singapore about one topic, it was found they demonstrated similar levels of misconceptions as were shown by the high school students they were preparing to go and teach (Taber & Tan, 2011).

There has been a good deal of research exploring the knowledge and understanding of those preparing for teaching. A study reported in the *International Journal of Science Education* looked at how those preparing for primary teaching understood an important environmental topic, the greenhouse effect (Ratinen, 2011). The author, Ratinen, reported "that primary student-teachers' knowledge about the greenhouse effect and climate change is insecure" (p. 22).

Questions for reflection

What would you use as a criterion or standard in order to make a judgement about whether a teacher's knowledge of some topic was 'secure'?

Ratinen (2011) concluded that "students have insufficiently conceptualized the wave and particle models and, in particular, the transient dipole moment of greenhouse gases" (p. 22). Would you agree that a primary teacher needed a strong conceptualisation of these concepts to be considered to have secure knowledge about the greenhouse effect?

What do teachers believe about how their students learn?

One important focus of research has been what teachers believe about pedagogy – how to teach. In a paper in the journal *Teacher Development*, Avis, Bathmaker, Kendal, and Parson (2003, p. 191) report their study of "the experiences and understandings of a group of full-time further education trainee teachers...". These were teachers-in-training who, through their course, had been introduced to ways of thinking about teaching and learning that might be labelled 'constructivist', 'student-centred' or 'progressive'. Yet they found that students' own accounts of their classroom work were "very far from our construction of a dialogic practice", instead focusing on "skill acquisition" by students, and seeing the ideal teaching context in more traditional ways (p. 203).

Ravitz, Becker, and Wong (2000) report a study exploring teacher views about pedagogy, and *teacher beliefs about student views about* pedagogy. Ravitz et al. ('and others') found that teachers thought that students could learn as well from traditional approaches (being given notes to learn) as from more progressive 'constructivist' approaches ('student-centred', active learning). However, the teachers felt more comfortable using traditional approaches, and believed their students would *also* be more comfortable learning in traditionally organised classrooms.

Question for reflection

How do the findings of Ravitz and colleagues (regarding teacher beliefs about students' preferences) compare with those of Kinchin (of students' own reported preferences) that were discussed earlier in the chapter?

Strictly, the findings of Ravitz et al. are *not contradicted* by Kinchin's work, as the informants in the Ravitz et al. study were teachers and not the students themselves. The teachers may have *false* beliefs about their students' preferences, or their students (in the United States) may indeed have *different* views to the (English) students in Kinchin's sample.

In a paper published in the journal *Teachers and Teaching: Theory and Practice*, Wong (2005) reports a study comparing the beliefs of music teachers in two different cultures (Vancouver, Canada, and Hong Kong, China). She found that both sets of music teachers in her sample held similar beliefs about the conceptual aspects of music education, but they had different beliefs about the value of music education for their students' psychological or character development. Wong reported that in Canada more classroom activities were often student-centred, based around the students' enjoyment and interest, whereas lesson activities in Hong Kong, where music education is viewed as a means of nurturing the student's temperamental development, were more tightly prescribed.

Tobin and his colleagues (Tobin, Kahle, & Fraser, 1990) have explored how teacher behaviour is linked to the way teachers conceptualise the role of the teacher. He reported a study of two science teachers, claiming that their different metaphors for the job of teaching influenced their classroom behaviour. The teacher who saw the role of the teacher as being a resource for learners taught very differently from the teacher who saw his job as being an entertainer or the 'captain' of the ship (i.e., class).

What do teachers believe about how they learn?

As readers of this book will appreciate, teachers are expected to undertake professional development throughout their careers to update and develop their knowledge and skills. As with any 'learning activities', such courses will only be effective if teachers engage, and so it is important to understand their experiences of such 'training'. Garet and colleagues (Garet, Porter, Desimone, Birman, & Yoon, 2001) report an American study, published in the *American Educational Research Journal*, which explored teachers' perceptions of the type of professional development courses that were effective. They claimed that certain 'structural features' of the courses were important, including the form of the activity, the collective participation of teachers who shared professional concerns (e.g., teachers of the same subject, or grade level, or from the same school), and the duration of the activity (Garet et al., 2001, p. 916).

Of course, teacher learning, as student learning, is not just about understanding concepts. All learners need to feel secure and confident to perform at their best, and new teachers in particular are often working in a stressful situation. Warwick, Warwick, and Hopper (2012) considered, in particular, the support available for new male teachers entering primary education, where they would be outnumbered by the female students on their course, and the female staff in the schools. One strategy adopted was providing a 'male-only' support group for trainees. They found that "the introduction of the male-only group was an effective strategy to address the issue of being vulnerable and feeling 'isolated' in a female-dominated environment" (p. 67). Warwick, Warwick, and Hopper also reported that during the academic year when the group was adopted "all male trainees had successfully completed their examined placements and none had withdrawn from the course, significantly reversing trends from previous years". This cannot be assumed to be directly due to the introduction of the support group (it *might* have been the case anyway in this particular cohort for other reasons), but the finding is certainly suggestive, and the research indicates a promising approach to an identified problem in initial primary teacher education.

Finding and evaluating studies

The studies referred to above provide just a taste of the ongoing research being undertaken and put into the public domain to inform teachers, policy-makers and other researchers. There are now many journals publishing educational research, and university libraries usually have subscriptions to a range of these journals. Some journals publish studies across a wide range of educational topics, and some are more specialised.

Clearly, the research literature relating to teaching and learning is vast. Luckily there are abstracting services and electronic searching tools to help identify relevant studies in different topics (gender issues, ICT, gifted education…), and related to different age groups or curriculum subjects. Most libraries have access to these tools, and staff to help you use them. Identifying specific literature related to a research topic will be considered in the introduction to Section 2.

However, with so many studies, undertaken in many different ways, and sometimes offering contrary findings (e.g., the studies of Watts and Kuiper mentioned above), the task of deciding which research might be significant for our own classroom work is more challenging. We might be tempted to assume a study with a large sample size offering 'statistically significant' results should always be taken more seriously than an in-depth account of a case study of a single teacher working with one class. However, before we make such judgements, it is important to understand what researchers are doing in different types of studies and – just as important – why some researchers deliberately choose to avoid large samples and the apparently definitive results that statistical studies seem to offer. So the next chapter will explore how educational researchers think about the research process.

Further reading

There are now a good number of journals reporting educational research – such as those referred to in this chapter. Quick links to some education journals may be found at https://camtools.cam.ac.uk/wiki/site/~kst24/Education-journals.html

The somewhat disputed notion of 'constructivism' has featured quite strongly in this chapter. The term is used to describe philosophies, learning theories, teaching approaches, and sometimes even research stances. Constructivism is arguably one of the most important perspectives in thinking about teaching and learning, and it is unfortunate that the term can be used in quite different ways by some authors. An introduction to the core ideas of constructivism as a theory relating to teaching and learning is:

Taber, K. S. (2011). Constructivism as educational theory: Contingency in learning, and optimally guided instruction. In J. Hassaskhah (Ed.), *Educational Theory* (pp. 39–61). New York: Nova. (Available for download at: https://camtools.cam.ac.uk/wiki/eclipse/Constructivism.html)

3

How do educational researchers think about their research?

This chapter:

- offers a simple visual metaphor for you to think about the overall process of planning and undertaking a research study
- describes three distinct levels for thinking about research
- introduces the notion of research paradigms, and offers an introductory model for thinking about research at the highest 'executive' level of research philosophy
- explains why issues of ontology and epistemology are important when planning, or reading about, research
- presents examples to show how paradigmatic choices influence what researchers do, and so need to be considered to understand their findings
- explains how developing a conceptual framework for thinking about a research area needs to precede planning the design of a study.

Having considered some examples of the kind of findings offered by educational research in the previous chapter, we now turn to considering *how* research leads to such findings. To evaluate research we need to appreciate what educational researchers do in order to 'find' their findings. As the reader will discover, there is actually quite a range of different activities that are sometimes considered as appropriate in educational enquiries – so that educational research may seem quite an eclectic activity. The educational professional who wants to learn from published research, and perhaps even undertake educational enquiry, needs to appreciate a little about:

- *the range* of activities that can form part of educational research;
- *why* such a range of activities are used;
- *when* different approaches may be appropriate;
- *the distinct ways* that different types of studies can inform educational practice.

The shape of research project ——

Some years ago, one of the students taking the educational research course I was teaching approached me between classes with a question. He wanted to know what a research project looked like if sketched out as a shape. I did not have a good answer, as it had never occurred to me to think about educational research in terms of a shape. However, the question remained with me. Had I been asked the same question today, my answer would be that a research project has a shape a bit like a lemniscate, that is, the infinity symbol: ∞. I think the lemniscate offers a useful visual metaphor for an important aspect of the typical research project (see Figure 3.1).

A research project starts from a specific concern or interest, which is explored through an 'expansive' phase of reading 'around' the topic. This allows us to conceptualise the field

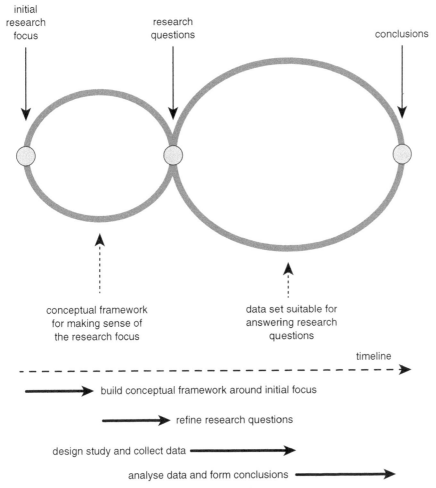

Figure 3.1 A visual metaphor for the research study

of the study (making judgements about the importance and relevance of the constructs, theories and research results reported in existing literature) to support us in refocusing on the specific research question or questions we will explore in the study. These research questions are a kind of pivot or central reference point for the whole study. So the researcher needs to be able to use both divergent and convergent modes of thinking, first to imagine a wide range of potential options in building up an understanding of 'the field', and then to refocus, having identified a way of formulating the research question(s) for the specific study to be undertaken. The need to adopt both divergent and convergent thinking in research has been considered an 'essential tension' (Kuhn, 1959/1977).

The research questions are the starting point of the second expansive phase: first, designing the study, then amassing a data set sufficient to (hopefully) enable us to answer the questions. At this stage, we move from the few lines of our focused research questions (in effect, a recognition of potential new knowledge we wish to develop), through the research design (a plan for how to answer our questions), to the establishment of an evidence base for answering the questions. Once we have collected the data we need, we then analyse this material to draw out patterns, themes, generalisations, etc. – a process of refining, summarising and generally turning a large data set into a manageable account of what we have found. Ultimately this leads to us answering our specific research questions. The challenge of analysis is to move from an often extensive data set to a few definitive statements that are able to summarise the key messages from our data – which, if all has gone well, will be the answers to our research questions. (As you might suspect, this is an ideal description, and not all research, nor even all useful research, comes to clear, simple conclusions.)

———— The research executive, the research manager, the research technician

This visual metaphor for the process of undertaking a research study suggests that a successful project will require both an overall vision of the purpose of the research to inform planning, and careful management of the different stages. 'Doing' research may be divided into activities at several levels: we might think of these levels as *executive, managerial* and *technical*. In large projects, much of the work of collecting and analysing data is carried out by research assistants, whilst the major decisions are made by a principal investigator. Of course, in many studies (and nearly always in teacher practitioner-research), the executive, the manager and the technician is the same person, but it is still very important to appreciate how these *different roles* contribute to the overall process. The extent to which the principal researcher on a project feels the need to be involved in working with the data does not only depend upon the availability of technical support (human or through computer software); it also depends upon the type of data collected, and the nature of the analysis to be undertaken.

Question for reflection

What type of data collection and analysis would make it more appropriate for a researcher to author a research report when all the work of collecting and analysing the data has been carried out by research assistants?

The 'nitty-gritty' of 'doing' is applying the techniques for collecting and analysing research data. At this level, the research plan is followed by the research technician (or the *researcher-as*-technician in a single-handed project). Common techniques for collecting and analysing data, the *tactics* of educational research, will be met later in the book (see Chapters 10 and 11). Carrying out research techniques will only comprise research when they are part of a coherent research plan, or research design, which needs to be informed by a research *strategy*. This is what is usually described as methodology: an *educational research methodology* guides the selection and sequencing of appropriate techniques in a study. The main types of methodology will be considered in the next chapter.

The present chapter considers the role of the executive, where decisions are made at the highest level. Whereas the manager sets the strategy for a particular research project, the executive may be thinking in terms of how that study fits into a coherent *programme* of research. In business (which is often considered to include schools these days), we might think of this level in terms of providing the 'vision'. However, here I will risk considering the executive level as providing the *philosophy* of the enterprise. Clearly, the philosophy needs to be established first, as this will give direction to the research to be carried out. Once this is in place, a strategy may be chosen, which will in turn guide the choice of techniques. In educational research, the 'philosophy' is usually described in terms of something called a *paradigm*. This metaphor is represented in Table 3.1.

Table 3.1 The relationships of paradigm, methodology, and techniques

Role metaphor	Level	Responsible for	See:
Executive	Philosophy	Paradigm	This chapter
Manager	Strategy	Methodology	Next chapter
Technician	Tactics	Techniques	Chapters 10 & 11

Question for reflection

Why do you think it might be important to consider questions of philosophy for someone (a) reading educational research; (b) planning enquiry into their own teaching? (It may be useful to revisit this question after reading the chapter and again after completing the book.)

Research paradigms ⸻

Often educational research is labelled as being 'qualitative *or* quantitative', and certainly many researchers favour either approaches that rely heavily on numerical analysis or those that avoid this. The qualitative/quantitative distinction is actually something of a caricature as it does not really reflect a fundamental distinction between studies (and there are many studies which draw heavily on both types of data). However, it *is* useful to identify two main types of approach to educational research that do have rather different purposes, methods, and outcomes. This distinction has been described and characterised in various ways, but is usually framed in terms of what are known as 'research paradigms'.

Some academic fields have well-accepted ways of working that are understood and followed by all those in that field. Thomas Kuhn (1996) studied the history of science and described scientists as working within 'a paradigm' or a 'disciplinary matrix' (Kuhn, 1977). The term 'paradigm' meant an example that provides a pattern, such as the examples used in language teaching to illustrate patterns in languages for learners. Kuhn believed that the researcher does not learn about her field primarily by being taught formal definitions, but more by working through examples. Kuhn was describing what he thought happens in the natural sciences, but the term 'paradigm' has become widely used in social sciences, such as education.

Questions for reflection

Do you think the natural sciences should be used as a model for research in education? What might be the arguments for and against using research in the natural sciences as a referent for *educational* research?

In experimental psychology the term 'paradigm' is often used in a slightly more restricted sense to mean a specific outline research design that can be adopted in similar studies. In education (and most social sciences), 'paradigm' has a more general meaning: studies in the same paradigm may have quite different designs, but share basic assumptions about the nature of research.

——— Paradigms in educational research ————————————————————

In education, and other social sciences, the notion of different research paradigms has been seen as important for those who want to make sense of what researchers are trying to do, and how they are setting out to do it. Perhaps unsurprisingly (in view of the complexity of social sciences), research paradigms have been characterised in many ways, with different labels used, and a number of 'candidates' for educational research paradigms may be found in the literature.

Despite this, it is commonly accepted that much educational research seems to fall into two main clusters of approach, informed by distinct perspectives on the research process. Appreciating the distinction between these two 'paradigms' offers a good deal of insight into why many studies are carried out and reported in the way they are, and what kind of lessons the reader should expect to draw from the reports. The model of these two research paradigms presented here is necessarily a simple one, but at an appropriate level for those who are new to reading educational research. I will signify these two clusters as being educational research paradigms 1 and 2, which can be denoted as ERP1 and ERP2 for brevity (see Figure 3.2).

Additional candidates for educational research paradigms have been suggested (e.g., Biddle & Anderson, 1986; Carr & Kemmis, 1986). Whilst recognising the value of some of these alternative suggestions, this model of educational research as usually being developed within either ERP1 or ERP2 seems to offer *a good starting point* for thinking about the different types of studies that may inform teaching, and will be adopted in this book. The terms in Figure 3.2 will be explored during the chapter, but we might briefly characterise these terms.

Educational research paradigm **ERP1**	Educational research paradigm **ERP2**
positivistic	interpretivist
nomothetic	idiographic
confirmatory	discovery

Figure 3.2   Distinguishing two approaches to educational research

Research is *positivistic* if it assumes it is possible to produce definitive knowledge that is objective (i.e., it can be agreed on by all informed observers); whereas *interpretivist* research assumes that the research relies upon the (inevitably somewhat subjective) interpretation of a particular human being who will necessarily bring his or her own idiosyncratic experiences and understanding to the interpretations made.

Nomothetic research looks for general patterns and rules that once discovered will be expected to be widely applicable; whereas *idiographic* research recognises value in exploring the idiosyncrasies of the unique individual case. *Confirmatory* research sets out to test a specific hypothesis to the exclusion of other considerations; whereas *discovery* research seeks to find out what might be important in understanding a research context, presenting findings as conjectural (e.g., 'suggestive', 'indicative') rather than definite.

Questions for reflection

To what extent do you expect that individual educational research studies can readily be assigned to one of the two paradigms discussed here? (And can you suggest what your response to that question suggests about your assumptions about educational research as an activity, and the type of categories that ERP1 and ERP2 are?)

   To what extent is a choice between ERP1 and ERP2 a matter of how the researcher understands (i) the nature of the world in general; (ii) what the research process is; and (iii) how it produces new knowledge? And to what extent should the choice between ERP1 and ERP2 depend upon the particular circumstances of a specific research study?

Are there qualitative and quantitative research paradigms?

Figure 3.2 does not include two of the most common terms that are used for talking about the main types of educational research, which is to refer to quantitative research and qualitative research. We could add these two terms to the EPR1 and EPR2 columns with the other descriptors, but I have deliberately not done this because there is too much ambiguity in the way that these terms tend to be used. Put simply, both of these terms are used in two very different ways. When used as technical terms:

Quantitative research collects data suitable for testing hypotheses using statistical techniques.	Qualitative research uses the researcher as an interpretive instrument whose own subjectivity (and inter-subjectivity with participants) is an integral part of the research process.

In other words, quantitative research is EPR1 research because it is positivistic and confirmatory; and qualitative research falls within ERP2 because it is intrinsically interpretive and necessarily idiographic to some extent (being based on the working relationships set up between a particular researcher and her study participants). How-ever, often the terms quantitative research and qualitative research are used much less rigorously:

Research collecting and analysing numerical data is often loosely described as quantitative research.	Research collecting and analysing data that is not numerical (usually texts of some kind) is often loosely described as qualitative research.

When the terms are used in the former sense they tell us something significant about the studies concerned, but the distinction between quantitative and qualitative *data* is much less significant in characterising a study (as examples met later in the book will illustrate). So, for example, qualitative data may be categorised, tallied to give fre-quency counts, and then used to statistically test hypotheses (which would be 'quan-titative' research) and much numerical data that is collected in research is only used to provide descriptive statistics such as averages (as part of 'qualitative' studies). My general approach in this book, then, is to avoid possible confusion by not using these terms (quantitative, qualitative) to describe paradigms or individual studies, but to limit their use to labelling types of data.

Are there really two paradigms in educational research?

Any reader asking himself or herself 'Well, are there really two educational research paradigms, or actually more?' has the author's sympathy. Educational research, like education, is socially constructed. (It is not part of the 'natural' world that would continue to exist if humans were removed from the planet.) The notion of an educational research paradigm is a way of thinking about, and making sense of, educational research approaches. What is presented here is a basic way of modelling a very complex, and ill-defined, phenomenon. This model is neither right nor wrong! It is a representation that is designed to reflect some key features of the complex phenomenon that is educational research.

However, to the extent that such a model is seen as a *prescription* of what should be done (what educational research *should* be like), it can become a 'self-fulfilling prophecy'. If research students are expected to think in terms of ERP1 or ERP2 when planning their enquiries, and write according to such a model in their theses, then such a model could increasingly come to match actual practice! Luckily this pressure may be balanced by those academics – having already had their theses safely examined – who claim original-ity in their work by seeking to extend, develop, or even overturn such models!

So the model is a simplification of a more nuanced situation, used as a pedagogic device. In teaching complex ideas from history, geography, literature, physics, etc., the educational community develops models for use in teaching. Current scholarship in an academic discipline is simplified to form curricular models that can act as target knowledge for teaching. When these models have 'the optimum level of simplification' (Taber, 2000b) they reflect the original ideas in 'intellectually honest' (Bruner, 1960) ways, whilst being simple enough to make sense to the learner. The notion of a spiral curriculum (Bruner, again) means that we look to use these models as the foundations for building more sophisticated understanding as learners progress through their schooling. This same principle should apply at *all* levels of teaching, even post-graduate level. For those just setting out to find out about educational research, then the 'two-paradigms' model offers a good starting point, as much educational research can be understood in relation to these two clusters of approaches. For those who wish to have a basic understanding of educational research to inform classroom practice, it is largely a sufficient model.

For those readers who anticipate undertaking educational research at a higher level (perhaps reading for a PhD), then it will become important to move beyond this model, to appreciate the finer distinctions within and the approaches that do not quite fit either paradigm. However, in learning (at post-graduate or any other level), it is important to build up understanding. This book will provide opportunities to apply the basic model presented here. A good curricular model provides the basis for later developing more advanced understandings. Readers are advised to make sure they are able to think with, and use, this introductory model, before looking to move beyond it. As with the students we teach, it takes time to fully consolidate new learning before it is suitable to act as a foundation for progression.

As a final point, before proceeding to the model, do not be concerned that this chapter 'only' presents a model of the nature of educational research. There is a real sense that all that research or scholarship can ever do is lead to models, even if sometimes they become so familiar and taken for granted that we act as though they are true representations of the world. Beliefs such as that the sun will rise tomorrow, or that food will continue to offer nutritional value, are in effect predictions made from models that we are *very* confident about. We more readily recognise that other beliefs (that Year 9 will continue to hand in their homework; that the AS group will get good grades; that the threat of detention is a useful deterrent) are based on models that may be incomplete and need revising as new evidence becomes available!

The philosophy underpinning the paradigms

The two aspects of 'philosophy' considered to underpin research paradigms are beliefs (or 'commitments') about the nature of the world (what kind of things exist in the world, and what is their nature?), and so the nature of the phenomena studied in research; and beliefs about the nature and status of human knowledge, and so how we might come to hold knowledge. These concerns are known technically as 'ontology' and 'epistemology' respectively. A third term you may see in your reading is 'axiology', which relates to the basic values we bring to our research. All researchers need to be concerned that their research is undertaken ethically, and this will be considered in

Chapter 9. However, some researchers working in education go beyond this, and feel that research worth their time and attention has to be driven by such imperatives as challenging social inequalities or working towards a more democratic society.

Other educational researchers may well feel that education is inherently a good thing, and that any research that can inform educational work is therefore worth doing. Finding a better way to teach about quadratic equations or ancient Egyptian society is likely to excite some researchers in this later group, but not those who feel that worthwhile educational work has to play a transformative role in changing people's lives and the society they live in. Some of *these* researchers may well feel that schools have an important role in maintaining social inequalities that are reproduced in part through the education system, so that research which simply finds more effective ways to do the traditional work of schools is a distraction. These are important issues, and it is always sensible to question the value of particular features of schooling and not take the *status quo* for granted. However, in the present chapter, the focus will be on the ontological and epistemological issues, rather than axiological concerns.

Some readers who are new to educational research may feel that they do not need to be concerned with philosophical issues such as ontology and epistemology. But if so, they are very wrong! Although it may be possible to do effective research that avoids using *the terminology*, it is certainly not possible to plan coherent research without taking these issues seriously.

———— What do we mean by a student's ability? ————

For example, several of the studies surveyed in Chapter 2 referred to 'ability'. This is an everyday word, which teachers commonly use as if it has an agreed and obvious meaning. In fact, this is far from the case. Anyone wanting to undertake research relating to student ability would need to seriously consider both ontological and epistemological questions before setting out on the research (see Figure 3.3).

Ontological concerns	Epistemological concerns
What kind of 'thing' is ability? Does it have different dimensions? Is it fixed, or does it change? Is it the type of thing that can be measured, or is it better described?	How can I find out about student ability? What type of evidence will inform me about ability? How will I know if my analysis of that evidence is reliable? How can I tell I have developed an authentic account?

Figure 3.3 How our assumptions influence our approach to research

The researcher's assumptions (either explicit or tacit) in relation to these sorts of questions will determine their research plans, as these assumptions inform all aspects of the research process. A failure to make such assumptions explicit at the start of the research process is quite likely to lead to the researcher making poorly considered decisions and failing to collect the type of evidence needed to answer his/her research questions. If this is only recognised by the researcher after it is pointed out by someone else who *does* examine the assumptions carefully (such as a tutor or examiner, for example), it may also lead to embarrassment, or worse!

Question for reflection

As you read through the descriptions of the two main educational research paradigms (below), can you identify the ontological and epistemological commitments that are associated with each?

———————— ERP1: finding the laws explaining educational reality ———

The first paradigm may be considered to be 'positivistic'. Positivism is based on an assumption that it is possible to report unambiguous truth, in terms of observable phenomena and verified facts. The term 'positivism' may be used as a label for "any approach that applies scientific method to the study of human action" (Schwandt, 2001, p. 199). A positivist approach assumes that the aims, concept, methods and model of explanation employed in the natural sciences may be applied non-problematically (Carr & Kemmis, 1986, p. 62; Walford, 1991, p. 2),

> [w]hen [positivism] is applied to educational research. ... All things are seen as predictable, regular, and capable of being fitted into the pre-determined structure.
>
> (McNiff, 1992, p. 12)

Gilbert and Watts (1983, p. 64) refer to this paradigm as a tradition "in which explanation is the goal", and associate it with such descriptors as 'scientific', 'experimental', and 'traditional'. ERP1 research is 'nomothetic' – that is, it is concerned with finding general laws – and it is commonly associated with quantitative research methodology. Biddle and Anderson (1986, p. 231) characterise research that "presumes to establish objective information about social behaviour that can be generalized" as a *confirmatory* perspective, where:

> Two methods have dominated ... the cross-sectional survey in which data are gathered, on one occasion, often from a sample of persons taken to represent some universe of human beings in whom we are interested [or an alternative approach of] manipulative experiments ... in which the investigator controls irrelevant sources of variation, manipulates an independent variable, and then observes effects in a dependent variable.
>
> (Biddle & Anderson, 1986, p. 234)

The positivist viewpoint underpinning research in this tradition is based on the belief in "a single independently existing reality that can be accessed by researchers" (Greenbank, 2003, p. 792). It is likely that many researchers in the physical sciences would see such an assumption as reasonable, and certainly, in practice, many scientists behave as though they are revealing pre-existing truths about nature. Although *concepts* such as energy, element, force or metal are human inventions, they are useful because they seem to map on to regularities in nature that are totally independent of the human observer.

However, it is important to realise that few researchers, no matter of the strength of belief in an objective reality, would consider that there are *simple* ways to find certain knowledge about that reality. The role of science can be seen as developing and refining models to give ever-improving fit to what is observed in the natural world. Perspectives that acknowledge that 'scientific research' can only provide provisional, tentative 'truths' are often labelled 'post-positivist' (Phillips & Burbules, 2000).

Question for reflection

To what extent do you think that educational research can be seen as uncovering the general laws that reveal the truth about educational reality? When might this be a suitable mind-set for exploring learning and teaching, and when might such assumptions prove problematic?

Testing hypotheses about an objective reality?

ERP1 is based upon "the view which treats the social world like the natural world – as if it were a hard, external and objective reality" leading to 'scientific investigations' which "will be directed at analysing the relationships and regularities between selected factors in that world. It will be predominantly [*sic* – not exclusively] quantitative" (Cohen, Manion, & Morrison, 2000, p. 7).

> Studies ... give stress to careful research design, to reliable measurement of variables, to statistical manipulation of data, and to the detailed examination of evidence. Hypotheses are stated to indicate knowledge claims, and these are judged to be confirmed if they are supported by inferential statistics that reach arbitrary levels of significance. Confirmed hypotheses ('findings') are presumed to generalise to populations or contexts similar to the one studied.
>
> (Biddle & Anderson, 1986, p. 231)

However, the subject matter of the social sciences, such as education, are often phenomena – institutions, processes, events, etc. – that have been set up by people with particular purposes in mind, and with various participants (teachers, students, parents, etc.) who are seen as having varying roles (swot, bully, trouble-maker, etc.) and who may have different motivations for their involvement (vocation, paid employment, desire to learn, fear of punishment, etc.). Concepts such as 'lesson', 'class', 'student', 'effective teacher', 'assessment activity', 'homework', 'detention', etc. do not relate to patterns that are found in nature outside the world of human activity and interactions. There is a very big doubt about the extent to which it is reasonable to expect human activity, such as education, to be suitable for describing through one particular 'best-fit model'.

> Researchers working within the positivist paradigm see reality as separate from themselves and expect investigators to have the same perceptions of shared phenomena and thus common understandings. Researchers working within the interpretive

paradigm see reality as a social construct and so do not necessarily expect other investigators to have the same perceptions or understandings of shared phenomena.

(Bassey, 1992, pp. 6–7)

Confirmatory research?

One of the studies referred to in Chapter 2 was Harrop and Swinson's (2003) study of the nature of questions used by teachers, published in the journal *Educational Studies*. A key referent that Harrop and Swinson cite is previous research in junior schools undertaken by Maurice Galton and colleagues (Galton, Simon, & Croll, 1980), which had reported on the proportion of teacher questions in a number of categories. This work, which is well known, is significant to Harrop and Swinson's study for a number of reasons:

- Galton's research took the form of large-scale surveys;
- Galton's studies had focused on junior schools, and had not included infant or secondary classes.

Harrop and Swinson's study used the re-examination of a relatively modest amount of classroom recording (5 hours at each of infant, junior and secondary level) – a series of snapshots from a small sample of classrooms. They explain that their research had two purposes:

> to see the extent to which the different methodology employed would produce results similar to those obtained by Galton and his colleagues;

> to examine *differences* in patterns of questioning between the three levels of schooling.
> (2003, p. 52, present author's emphasis)

Question for reflection

In terms of Harrop and Swinson's second aim ('to examine differences in patterns of questioning between the three levels of schooling'), can you formulate a hypothesis that the research could be testing?

Harrop and Swinson report that their findings in junior schools closely reflect those from a much larger survey undertaken by Galton's team revisiting their earlier study at about the same time. This suggested that their approach is able to produce valid and reliable results, and gave them confidence that their comparison across levels would be meaningful. Harrop and Swinson's (2003) study can be seen as being located in a confirmatory research paradigm (ERP1), where a specific prediction or research hypothesis is tested by collecting data suitable for statistical analysis. Their *expectation* was that the profile of teacher questions would *vary* across infant, junior and secondary levels. What Harrop and Swinson (2003, p. 49) actually found was that the profile of questions across categories "*differed very little*" in infant schools, junior schools and secondary schools.

Question for reflection

In terms of the usefulness of the research study, does it matter that Harrop and Swinson were wrong?

It would have been possible for the authors to have explored their research focus from an assumption that they would find no significant differences in the profiles of question types used in the different levels of schools (i.e., a so-called 'null hypothesis'). Had that been the case, they would have found the same results, but would have been 'right' rather than 'wrong'. The validity and reliability of a study should be judged in terms of technical competence (in building a sample, carrying out observations and analysis, etc.), without consideration of whether a hypothesis is found to be supported or not. So, in that sense, the 'negative' result found by Harrop and Swinson does not in any way undermine the study.

Question for reflection

If the 'negative' result found by Harrop and Swinson *does not in any way undermine the study*, does this imply that the choice of a hypothesis is arbitrary?

To appreciate why Harrop and Swinson predicted differences across the phases of education, we have to appreciate the *conceptual framework* that informed their study. We consider the process of conceptualising a field of research later in the chapter.

━━━ ERP2: constructing understandings of education ━━━━━━━━━━━━

Not all researchers are happy with the notion of there being 'a' truth that researchers are meant to discover:

> We do not *believe* that there is such a thing as objective (absolute and uncondi-
> tional) truth. ... We do believe that there are truths but think that the idea of truth
> need not be tied to the objectivist view. ... Truth is always *relative to* a conceptual
> system.
>
> (Lakoff & Johnson, 1980, p. 159, present author's emphasis)

The second common approach to educational research avoids the problems of trying to find universal laws or definitive accounts that tell '*the* way' things are, by dealing with the particular, and by focusing on understanding the meanings that those partici-pating in educational situations give to what they experience.

Research as developing interpretations?

Gilbert and Watts (1983) refer to ERP2 as being in the *verstehen* tradition ("in which understanding is the goal", p. 64) and they describe it in such terms as 'holistic' and 'naturalistic'. ERP2 research is *idiographic* – concerned with the individual case – and is often associated with analysing qualitative data. This paradigm may be considered as interpretivist, based upon "the belief that all knowledge claims are interpretations, and that there is nothing to appeal to in judging an interpretation but other interpretations" (Schwandt, 2001, pp. 68–69).

This interpretivist perspective may seem rather defeatist to those who assume that we can always decide between different interpretations by collecting sufficient evidence. That would be the assumption within ERP1: a hypothesis is formed, and then a study designed to collect the data needed as evidence to decide whether the hypothesis is correct. This is the basis of the experimental methods used in the natural sciences (on which ERP1 approaches are modelled). However, the interpretivist view is that such data "cannot provide any special basis or foundation for knowledge claims that is somehow free of interpretation" (Schwandt, 2001, pp. 68–69). This is not to suggest that data cannot help decide the worth of a hypothesis, but that it can only do so provided that a great deal is taken for granted. This is a theme that will be illustrated in the studies considered later in the book.

Biddle and Anderson (1986) contrast their 'confirmatory position' with what they label the '*discovery* perspective'. This term is used for approaches that

> have in common the belief that social concepts and explanations are socially constructed by both citizens and social scientists. Social knowledge and its use are both assumed to be based on values … and social facts are uninterpretable outside of a theoretical, hence historical, context.
>
> (Biddle & Anderson, 1986, p. 237)

Question for reflection

If the results of social (including educational) research only have meaning within the specific research context, then how can we know that findings have any significance elsewhere?

Research undertaken in the discovery perspective could be said to *strictly* only apply to the particular time and place (and people) where it was undertaken. Biddle and Anderson recognise the potential implication of this, that "taken to its extreme, such a critical stance decries the usefulness of all social research and claims that each event in the human world is unique and is unlikely to be replicated by any other event, ever" (1986, p. 237). However, our common experience is that what we learn in one context is *often*, if not always, valuable in other contexts. It is common for studies within ERP2 to provide 'thick description' of the specific research context, to allow the reader to make a judgement about the relevance of the study for the context of concern to the reader (see Chapter 7).

Understanding educational issues

Sade and Coll (2003) undertook a study to explore the perceptions of technology and technological education among primary teachers and curriculum development officers in 'a small island nation in the South Pacific', the Solomon Islands. In this study it was important to find out what the informants (the teachers and curriculum development officers) understood technology education to be about.

> The methodological approach selected for this research inquiry is a qualitative approach within an interpretivist paradigm. ... A qualitative approach, drawing on situated cognition and sociocultural views of learning ... was deemed to be the most appropriate approach, as the researchers wished to gain understanding of the Solomon Islands curriculum development officers' and primary teachers' perceptions. ... An added benefit ... is that such an approach allows participants to clarify ambiguity in questions. This latter issue is important in this work, since English is a third language for many Solomon Islanders.
>
> (Sade & Coll, 2003, p. 102)

In reporting their research, Sade and Coll quote examples of the comments made by some of their informants. So we are told that:

- Monica thought that technology meant things like "computers, televisions, telephones, emails, photocopies, and fax machines" (p. 98).
- Brody thought that technology was "replacing our traditional materials and old ways of doing things" (p. 98).
- Jason believed that "Technology education is learning about new things because everyday things are changing" (p. 102).

The decision to quote individuals is consistent with research within ERP2, where researchers wish to gain understanding of how individuals make sense of their worlds.

Incommensurate approaches: researchers living in different worlds?

For Kuhn, a paradigm:

- provides the theoretical basis of the field;
- is accepted by all the workers in the field;
- determines what is judged to be the subject of legitimate research in the field;
- determines the procedures, rules and standards that apply in the field.

According to Kuhn (1977), this in effect means that those researchers who share a paradigm use a commonly understood language, work with essentially the same concepts, and assume much the same meanings for technical terms. Kuhn argued that researchers working in different paradigms would, in effect, talk across each other and so they would have a limited basis for effective communication:

> the result was an incommensurability of viewpoints and a partial breakdown of communication between the proponents of different theories. ... Proponents of ... different paradigms ... speak different languages – languages expressing different cognitive commitments, suitable for different worlds. Their abilities to grasp each other's viewpoints are therefore inevitably limited by the imperfections of the processes of translation and of reference determination.
>
> (Kuhn, 1977, pp. xxii–xxiii)

Question for reflection

Given that ERP1 and ERP2 offer two very different sets of assumptions about what educational research can investigate, and how it should go about it, and what kind of outcomes can be found, do you think it will be just a matter of time before one approach becomes *the* accepted way for thinking about research in education?

Why does the reader of educational research need to be concerned with 'paradigms'?

ERP1 and ERP2 both have strengths, and can both help produce valuable knowledge that offers useful ways of thinking about educational contexts. The products of both are types of theory, or models – that is, useful thinking tools. The alert user of educational research can appreciate the strengths and limitations of each paradigm, and so can judge the likely value of the type of knowledge each offers.

Indeed, reading a study without appreciating the type of research approach being used can sometimes make it very difficult to draw out anything of value. The critical reader needs to know how to interrogate a research paper (a skill that this book is designed to help develop), but the types of questions to ask in judging the quality and relevance of research can be very different in the two paradigms.

Why do educational researchers have to be concerned with paradigmatic issues?

Even though studies from both approaches to educational research can have an important part to play in informing educational practice, it is usually considered important that any specific study can be seen to be 'located' within a particular paradigm. This is because *it is important that any research study offers the reader a coherent and consistent argument about what is being claimed.* Indeed, at doctoral level, this is the most significant criterion used to judge whether a student's thesis is satisfactory. (This theme will be revisited later in the book, when considering how to report your classroom research – see Chapter 12.)

The two different paradigms make different assumptions about the kind of knowledge that research can produce, and so lead to different sorts of knowledge claims. A study that was undertaken using an interpretivist approach (ERP2) cannot make justifiable claims in the form of generalisable laws – such as:

* mixed ability teaching *is* more effective;
* girls *are* less likely to offer answers in class;
* effective teachers *tend to* use longer wait times when asking questions in class.

Indeed, the paradigm in which a study is undertaken reflects fundamental assumptions about research that have consequences throughout a study. A choice of paradigm is based on assumptions about (some aspect of) the world being studied and the nature of knowledge that can be obtained about that (aspect of the) world. The terms ontology and epistemology were introduced earlier in the chapter: ontology concerning the nature of things that exist in the world, and epistemology being about how we can come to know about those things. For example, an (ontological) assumption that there is an observable objective world leads to different research choices than a belief that social worlds are created by participants, who each inhabit their own unique realities. It is sometimes suggested that we have to make a choice as researchers about where we stand on such issues.

Question for reflection

In recent years there has been a lot of attention given to research that is described as 'mixed methods'. This can mean different things, but is often used to describe studies that include both qualitative and quantitative analyses of data. It is sometimes suggested that mixed-methods studies form a middle path between the traditional research paradigms as they allow a mixture of approaches. Do you think it is possible for one study to be a mixture of ERP1 and ERP2 approaches?

Does a researcher have to make a binding commitment to a paradigm?

So in any particular study, we need to consider the nature of the 'reality' being investigated. However, it is possible to believe in an objective world independent of human thought (perhaps the moon would still be there, if not known as the moon, and not having the litter of human visits), and still consider some foci as best understood in more 'subjective' terms. We can objectively study *the level* of school exclusions for offences classed as bullying, but any study of what counts as bullying, why it happens, and how it feels to be bullied would need to consider the various perspectives of those who are involved as offender, victims, etc.

An (epistemological) assumption that it is possible to produce an objective account of the world that is independent of the observer leads to different research choices than a belief that the researcher inevitably becomes a significant part of the research context being studied. For example, a study that explored student learning through a survey of examination and test results could be objective (although would only be considered meaningful to those who accepted such outcomes as valid measures of learning). However, a study that explored learning through in-depth interviewing of learners is likely to channel student thinking in ways that would not have happened in the absence of the interview (e.g., Taber & Student, 2003), and so may 'scaffold' responses that reflect learning during the interview itself. (Anyone who doubts this would happen must surely also doubt the efficacy of much teacher–student dialogue carried out in classrooms to facilitate learning.)

It is important to recognise that sometimes these two different types of studies, although based on apparently inconsistent assumptions, and addressing different types of questions, may be complementary in developing our wider understanding of a research topic (National Research Council Committee on Scientific Principles for Educational Research, 2002). As an educational researcher, the key question is what assumptions we can make *about particular educational issues and contexts*, and so when it is justifiable to claim objectivity in our research, and when a more subjective interpretivist approach is indicated.

Can researchers be 'pragmatic' and use 'mixed' approaches?

Some educational researchers may carry out sequences of studies looking at a particular issue through a series of quite similar studies. But other researchers may move from one topic of interest to another, and so may feel quite different approaches are needed to investigate different educational problems and issues. Yet other researchers may follow a particular line of research (a research programme) and believe that their ongoing research informs their understanding of a topic sufficiently for them to be able to develop their understanding of the ontology of the research focus, or at least to have refined their understanding of how to best find out about it. Such changes in the researcher's thinking about the ontology and/or epistemology related to their research focus will be reflected in shifts in the methodological choices they make as their research proceeds.

The recommendation in this book is very much that the way we go about a research study needs to be informed by *our current* understanding of the nature of what we are researching and how we can learn more about it, rather than identifying ourselves as permanently working within a particular educational research paradigm.

We might consider this as taking a 'pragmatic' approach – although I would suggest it is better thought of as taking a principled approach. The term 'pragmatism' is used in a technical sense to refer to a particular stance on research (Biesta & Burbules, 2003), and one which is sometimes said to undermine the traditional objective–subjective distinction. Pragmatists see a close relationship between research and practice, and think that research processes are simply refined versions of the intelligent behaviour that allows all of us to build up an internal model of the world in which we live, and to both use that model to inform our actions, and to then modify the model itself when our expectations based upon the model are not met. This is not the place to explore pragmatist thinking in any detail, but I do not consider it is fundamentally at odds with the approach recommended in this book.

It is also very important to remember that the model of ERP1 and ERP2 (see Figure 3.2) refers to *clusters* of descriptors that are concerned with somewhat different issues:

- Whether the focus of the research is something where we should be able to expect everyone to agree about the 'facts' of the matter if we had sufficient evidence, regardless of the different perspectives that people may approach the focus from (i.e., objectivity vs. subjectivity).
- Whether the focus is the kind of thing where it is sensible to look for norms and general laws that ignore any differences between cases, or whether we can only find out what we need to know by looking at the specific details of particular cases (i.e., nomothetic vs. idiographic).
- Whether the state of current knowledge is such that we can pose reasonable hypotheses that can be 'scientifically' tested, or whether we are still at the stage of trying to find out how best to conceptualise the issues (i.e., confirmatory vs. discovery).

These three issues *can* often be related, but can also be somewhat independent, and this is why it is so important to think about the ontological nature of what we are researching, and the epistemological issues that will determine what kind of knowledge we can reasonably expect to develop about it. Later in the book we will meet (and I will question) the term 'mixed methods', which is sometimes used to describe research that is considered to either fall between, or mix together, research paradigms.

For the moment, though, I will focus on some examples illustrating how 'paradigmatic' assumptions are important in the way educational researchers think about their work.

Paradigmatic differences between researchers

When learning about unfamiliar abstract ideas, it is helpful to have examples that provide a more 'concrete' context for making sense of those ideas. This is true of the many abstract ideas we teach in the school curriculum – and equally important when learning new concepts (such as 'educational research paradigms') at more advanced levels.

Here we will briefly consider two educational research studies, which came to opposite conclusions when investigating whether secondary level students hold what are known as 'alternative conceptual frameworks' of the scientific concept of force. Considering the differences between the ways the two researchers went about their studies illustrates the notion of research paradigms, and highlights why *readers* of educational research need to pay attention to such matters when drawing conclusions from published research studies. The two studies (Watts, 1983 and Kuiper, 1994) will be available in most academic libraries. The accounts below will make sense without having read the original studies, but readers will benefit more from the following discussion if they have already had a chance to read, and judge, these papers for themselves.

Question for reflection

If you have had the chance to read the original papers of Watts and Kuiper, you should consider how *you* would explain how these two studies can come to apparently contrary conclusions.

How do we know what students learn?

One reason to study learners' ideas (see Chapter 2) is because much of the rationale of school teaching is concerned with helping learners to develop their knowledge and understanding in those areas of human activity considered important enough to be reflected in the curriculum, and in helping them develop thinking and problem-solving skills that will help them make decisions and explore and their own values and beliefs. Evaluating this aspect of what education claims to be about requires the ability to 'measure' (or describe) student knowledge and understanding, and abilities related to rational thinking, developing argument, and so forth. Such 'measurements' (or descriptions) need to be made both before and after teaching to inform judgements about the learning that may have taken place.

This is a topic where there are key ontological and epistemological issues, and these pose questions that are important for all teachers, not just researchers:

- What counts as knowledge?
- How close does a student's understanding need to be to the version presented in the curriculum for us to judge it a 'good' understanding?

- Is it possible for different students to have the 'same' knowledge or understanding of a topic?
- How can we know how much a student knows?
- Can we really ever fully appreciate another person's way of understanding a topic?
- How do we find out what a student understands when they do not have the 'right' technical terminology for talking about the topic?

Furthermore, research suggests that learning of academic subjects does not simply involve acquiring knowledge in areas where a student was previously ignorant. It has been found that often learners already have ideas about a topic before meeting it in schools. This complicates research into learning, if we see learning as *a change* in something. If what changes is the student's knowledge and/or understanding, and these are themselves difficult to characterise, then research into learning will be even more challenging. I have suggested that in research we need to think about learning as a change in *the potential* for behaviour (Taber, 2009b) – where possible behaviours might include what someone could say in response to a teacher's question, what they could write in a test, etc. That is, after learning has taken place, the learner has a different repertoire of available behaviours than before.

The use of the focus on behaviour here is not meant to reflect the behaviourist school of thought that considered that unobservables (such as what goes on inside someone else's mind) should be excluded from research (Watson, 1967). In many research studies in education, what people think, know and believe (all unobservable and only inferred indirectly) are quite central. However, it is useful to consider what kind of *phenomena* we have available to study in education. These will include teacher and student talk, and various other productions (writing), but will not include anybody's ideas or knowledge.

Phenomenon	Theoretical construct
Student talk	Student's idea
Student inscriptions (writing, etc.)	Student's understanding
Student gestures	Student's belief
Artefacts constructed by student (e.g., model of a fort or a plant cell)	Student's knowledge

This should perhaps be obvious, but psychologists believe that all normal human infants develop a 'theory of mind' that allows them to explain the social world by assuming that others (and sometimes, by extension, animals and even inanimate objects such as dolls or the wind) have minds such as their own, with similar types of motives, thoughts, justifications, etc. Because we are so used to interpreting other people's speech and other behaviour in terms of their minds, we tend to forget that our own understanding of other people's feelings, ideas, thoughts, motives, etc. are just parts of our own model of the world. That is, the process of interpreting behaviour and modelling the thinking of others becomes so automatic we tend to often think that we do actually 'know' (rather than conjecture) what others are thinking and feeling.

We read what students have written, listen to what they say, and perhaps examine models they have built, or dances they devised, or tunes they have composed, and we interpret these phenomena in terms of what is 'going on inside their heads'. However, research suggests that a person's actual knowledge and understanding tends to be highly complex and multifaceted, and that in any particular learning context the individual themselves will only access some of the mental resources they have developed. The individual will then choose to represent some (but not all) of their thinking in the 'public space', by – for example – answering a teacher's question.

That behaviour (e.g., constructing a spoken response) will rely upon the individual's skills in expressing their ideas in speech (or in model building, or in writing, or in the use of gestures, etc.). The teacher will then need to *interpret* the behaviour (e.g., the spoken response) as a data source that can provide some information about the student's knowledge and understanding. When spelt out in this way, it is clear that teachers (whether doing research or not) are involved in a challenging ongoing process of developing models of the complex mental states of others by continuously trying to interpret small snippets of data. No wonder teaching can be so tiring mentally.

We can acknowledge the value of key constructs such as a learner's 'mind', 'thought', 'idea', 'conception', 'understanding', etc., whilst acknowledging that these are not observables in educational research. Rather, as we can never see another person's knowledge, but only how they represent that knowledge through their actions in the world – what they say and do – we have to accept that a student may learn something, without ever providing us with evidence of that learning. So a young child might learn that in an emergency they should telephone 999, but never have reason to do so, or to communicate this information to anyone else. They would have learnt something, and so had the potential to apply that knowledge, but there would be no evidence of that learning outside the child's own mind.

Questions for reflection

Would you agree with the ontological claim that learning is a change in the *potential* for behaviour? What epistemological consequences would follow from accepting such a notion of learning?

However, it is also true that if a student learnt about, say, Hinduism in religious studies, and was never explicitly asked to demonstrate that knowledge, it could still be influential in their thinking, perhaps at a preconscious level (perhaps, for example, when later learning about Sikhism). Research suggests that our conscious thoughts reflect only a small part of the mental processing going on in our brains, and that much of our planning, and problem-solving, and especially creative thinking, occurs preconsciously, with just the outcomes later appearing in consciousness where we can examine and mentipulate them.

So having learnt about the way Hindus think about the relationship of the different Gods, and their manifestations as aspects of an underlying single supreme universal God, could perhaps act as an analogical anchor for thinking about a quite different topic: for example, how the children of immigrants may feel totally British yet also have a strong sense of identity based on their parents' original homeland; or how, in physics, entities such as electrons may have both particle and wave aspects. Arguably, the learning about Hinduism will be manifested in the way the learner then approaches learning about issues of citizenship or physics; but that may be something it would be extremely difficult to demonstrate, especially if the learner herself was unaware that at some level she had made this link.

This example is related to what is seen as a major question in education: that of 'transfer' of learning – how learning in a specific context can be applied more widely. That learning about Hinduism might support learning about Sikhism might be considered a kind of 'close transfer', whereas 'transfer' of understanding of aspects of Hinduism to thinking about issues of multiple identify in social science or wave–particle duality in physics would seem a more creative and 'distant' transfer. If this latter example seems far-fetched, it might be worth noting that reading about Eastern philosophies influenced Neils Bohr, one of the key physicists who developed ideas of wave–particle duality – and who chose the Tao (yin-yang) symbol as the centrepiece for his coat of arms.

Why does it matter whether students hold common 'alternative conceptual frameworks'?

The ideas children bring to lessons may match the target knowledge in the curriculum to varying extents, and may be more or less strongly held. Tenacious alternative ideas have been found to interfere with intended learning. In science, in particular, there has been a vast research programme designed to explore aspects of learners' 'informal' ideas to inform teachers of the way many students may think about topics (Taber, 2006, 2009b).

Question for reflection

It is suggested that there are two main paradigms used in educational research. Which paradigm do you think is more likely to help researchers find out about learners' thinking about topics in the school curriculum? Why do you think this?

In the early 1980s there was a burst of interest in exploring learners' thinking about science topics – and in particular finding out what ideas students brought to the class with them that might contradict or distort what they were to be taught (e.g., Driver, Squires, Rushworth, & Wood-Robinson, 1994). One classic study from this substantial literature is Watt's (1983) study of secondary students' thinking about the key concept of 'force' – which has been identified as one of the 'key ideas' in school science (e.g., Key Stage 3 National Strategy, 2002).

Identifying alternative conceptual frameworks of 'force'

Watts (1983) claimed that students across the secondary age range held 'alternative frameworks' for thinking about the key science topic of force. Indeed, Watts claimed that he had uncovered eight distinct alternative 'conceptual frameworks'. The basis of this claim was research where Watts interviewed secondary school students of different ages, and taking a range of courses. To collect data, Watts used an approach called interviews-about-instances, where simple diagrams (such as a 'stick diagram' of a person playing golf) were used as foci (Gilbert, Watts, & Osborne, 1985). In this approach, a dialogue is usually initiated with an open question (such as, 'Is there an example of a force shown here?'), with the interviewer probing to follow up initial responses. The order of presentation of foci was flexible, and Watts reported that he attempted to respond to his interviewees by reflecting back the language they used to talk about the diagrams (rather than using the formal language of the curriculum subject).

Question for reflection

Research that explores student thinking in its own terms, rather than simply judging student ideas against curriculum knowledge, has been described as 'ethnographic'. What do you understand by the term 'ethnographic', and do you think Watts' study has any features of ethnography?

Watts audiotaped his interviews, and later transcribed them to give a verbatim account of the dialogue. He then used a 'mosaic method' to piece together conceptual frameworks reflecting the ideas students presented. He reported the frameworks as pithy summaries or 'vignettes'. Watts reports eight different alternative frameworks that described the thinking of his interviewees, each of which was distinct from the notion of force being presented in school science. If Watts was correct, and students do think about forces in these various ways at odds with school science, then it is useful for science teachers to be aware of this, and to plan and teach accordingly.

According to Watts, the frameworks he reported were:

- models of student understanding;
- powerful enough to capture individual differences;
- suitable for testing with large samples.

Question for reflection

Watts described his findings as 'models' of student understanding. What might this imply about his assumptions about the type of knowledge that research into student thinking is capable of producing?

But do students really have alternative frameworks of 'force'?

Kuiper (1994) decided to check Watts' claim that students used this set of alternative frameworks to think about forces. Kuiper attempted to test Watts' model and concluded that students did *not* seem to use Watts' frameworks. Indeed, Kuiper found that "students in general do not have an 'alternative framework' for force" (1994, p. 279). We might wonder how these different researchers came to such different conclusions.

One obvious difference is that although both researchers used a sample of secondary-age learners, these were rather different samples. Indeed, where Watts undertook his original interviews in the UK, Kuiper tested Watts' theory in Zimbabwe. (Kuiper reports that additional data for his research was collected in the Netherlands, Lesotho, Botswana, Swaziland and Mozambique, although the 1994 paper is primarily concerned with the data from Zimbabwe.) However, both researchers present their results *as if* they were discussing results that related to secondary-age students *in general*. Neither paper title – 'A study of schoolchildren's alternative frameworks of the concept of force' or 'Student ideas of science concepts: Alternative frameworks?' – imply that they are discussing findings that *only* apply to one location or a particular sample.

It is not unreasonable to expect that cultural differences between such contexts as the UK and Zimbabwe could be a relevant factor (Taber, 2012b), but here there may be other explanations for the different results. Kuiper's study took a very different form to Watts' and some of the key differences are given in Table 3.2.

Table 3.2 Comparing two studies into student thinking about forces

Study	*Watts, 1983*	*Kuiper, 1994*
sample	secondary students	secondary students
sample location	London, UK	Zimbabwe
sample size	12	143
data collection	interviews	written tests
data analysis	mosaic – composite pictures pieced together	classification of responses as intuitive, intermediate, correct; factor analysis
finding	8 alternative frameworks for force	confused ideas without logical coherency

Paradigmatic commitments are shown by Watts and Kuiper

Table 3.2 shows that very different approaches were taken by the different researchers. Watts was working with a small number of individuals, but using an approach that enabled him to explore their thinking in depth, and interact with them in the research. This is typical of ERP2 and reflects the nature of Watts' study as 'exploratory' research.

Indeed Watts' study can be seen to have a strong ethnographic flavour (see Chapter 4 for a discussion of ethnographic methodology in educational research). As ethnography derives from attempts to understand 'alien' cultures, as when a Western ethnographer visits a tribal society, it may not be immediately obvious how this is appropriate in research of this type. However, research into students' informal ideas in science has revealed that learners and science teachers do have very different ways of thinking, and – for example – use many of the same words but intending different meanings. In this situation, an ethnographic approach has often been considered appropriate (Solomon, 1993). Indeed, it has been suggested that entering the academic classroom is a kind of metaphorical border-crossing for (at least some) students, as if they are entering a strange country with its own customs and culture (Jegede & Aikenhead, 1999).

Kuiper's study is more typical of ERP1, being a 'confirmatory study' looking to test a model, using statistical techniques. Kuiper uses written tests, and later uses a quantitative technique (cluster analysis) to look for common patterns. Written tests are more often associated with a normative and positivistic approach – a large sample of learners respond to a standardised task under set conditions. The researcher does not attempt to interact with the subjects during data collection. Indeed, often in such studies the researcher is not physically present, as administering the tests may be considered a 'technical' task (see Table 3.1) that can be delegated to someone with limited research skills and no specialist knowledge of the study. Often teachers administer such instruments for researchers following standard protocols.

Another major difference is in the way the two researchers go about initially sorting their data – the student responses to either interview questions or test items. Where Watts uses a 'mosaic' technique – decomposing individual responses and constructing models ('frameworks') to reflect them, Kuiper initially categorises responses into three main groups ('intuitive', 'correct' and 'intermediate'). Watts tries to describe and characterise students' ideas *in their own terms*, whereas Kuiper initially sets out to evaluate understanding *in comparison with the target understanding set out in the curriculum*. These approaches are typical of ERP2 and ERP1 respectively.

Although it would be wrong to suggest that researchers only ever find what they are looking for, it is certainly true that the way data is analysed channels the type of findings that can feasibly arise. (This is one example of the point made earlier, that paradigmatic assumptions have consequences throughout the research process.) So Watts, who set out to look at individual thinking, uncovered sets of conceptual frameworks that reflect individual differences. Kuiper classified students according to the extent that their thinking matched the 'right' answers, and found proportions of students whose thinking matched the curriculum answers to different degrees!

Only later, after using the statistical technique of cluster analysis to identify consistent patterns of responses on questions having similar [*sic*] physical contexts, does Kuiper look for alternative frameworks. At this point Kuiper accepts that the younger students commonly demonstrate a particular way of thinking that is at odds with curriculum science. However, Kuiper characterises the thinking of other students as correct, transitional (between the 'intuitive' and correct responses), or too inconsistent to be considered as any kind of coherent framework. It is significant that:

- Watts, in the role of the ethnographer, attempts to understand students' viewpoints and patterns of thinking, and does not make assumptions about which contexts learners should perceive as similar; whereas
- Kuiper, acting as a positivist, initially evaluates student responses in terms of their match to the 'right' scientific answers, and then undertakes the cluster analysis on the assumption that coherency in student thinking must be based around similar responses to questions *that would be considered* as similar contexts *from the viewpoint of curriculum science.*

Consider a student who answers two questions (that seem similar from a physics perspective) very differently, because she perceives the problem contexts as quite different and having quite different salient features. The student may be operating from a coherent understanding of the world and Watts' method allows him to probe into that understanding. However, in the type of approach used by Kuiper, that student's thinking will be considered confused because she does not give consistent responses to what are considered (from the canonical perspective) equivalent questions. For example, if the student thought that forces acted differently on smooth round objects than on box-like objects with sharp edges, then this would appear to be an inconsistent (rather than an alternative) way of thinking if we only compare the students' answers with the model 'right' answers.

Question for reflection

Watts and Kuiper were enquiring into thinking about a particular physics concept area. Can you identify any concept areas in the subject(s)/topics you teach where it might be useful to explore student thinking – and so where the same types of issues could arise in research?

An example of why we need to take ontological assumptions seriously

One major problem with Kuiper's research *as a replication study* for Watts' findings is that Kuiper's account makes it quite clear he is *not* testing for what Watts claimed to have found! Both authors talk of 'alternative frameworks' (Watts reported eight alternative frameworks based on his data on students' thinking about forces, and Kuiper claimed to be looking for alternative frameworks), but they use this term to describe different types of entity.

Watts made it clear that the eight frameworks presented in his 1983 study were *models that Watts himself constructed* to reflect aspects of his informants' thinking. He did not claim that students used these ideas consistently, nor even that any particular student's thinking would exactly match any framework.

However, it is quite clear from the published accounts that Kuiper used the term 'framework' to signify something quite different from Watts – for Kuiper, a framework actually *exists in the head of a learner*. Moreover, for Kuiper, a learner is only considered to hold a framework if it is consistently applied in those situations where (from the researcher's perspective) the framework should apply:

> The use of the term framework in the description of student understanding implies an ordered and schematic understanding of a concept. This term can be understood to mean that a particular student has a set of student ideas concerning one and the same concept which appear logically coherent and ordered.
>
> (Kuiper, 1994, p. 280)

So where Watts presented a set of *generalised thematic descriptions* that were each compiled from aspects of the thinking of several students, Kuiper expected to find these 'frameworks' fixed in the minds of particular individual students. Pope and Denicolo (1986) discussed Watts' research in some detail, and described how the kind of frameworks presented in this type of research are necessarily simplifications abstracted from the more complex patterns of thinking exhibited by the informants. They explicitly discussed how the actual thinking of individuals would often reflect 'multiple frameworks' from Watts' schemes. They warned that:

> although starting from a holistic approach, one 'end product' of his work is a much reduced description of the construing of the individuals in his study which, if taken out of context, is also devoid of consideration of the particular choices made by the researcher in his conduct of data collection and analysis.

They also suggested that:

> the busy teacher or researcher with a predilection towards reductionism may well ignore the 'health warnings' conveyed in our research report [and] indulge in a 'framework spotting' exercise using reified descriptions of frameworks and ignoring the ontology of these frameworks.
>
> (Pope & Denicolo, 1986, p. 157)

ERP1 research tends to be reductionist, and is often based on assumptions that the objects of study exist 'out there' and can be readily identified, unambiguously classified, and counted. Such assumptions may reasonably be applied to some sorts of things – as, for example, when stocktaking in a supermarket – but Pope and Denicolo suggest that Watts' conceptual frameworks are not that kind of thing. They are ontologically rather different.

In setting out to test Watts' findings by a survey approach, Kuiper is treating Watts' frameworks as being something in learners' heads, to be spotted and counted, rather than a theoretical model to organise thinking from different individuals. Kuiper's study presents a *normative* model of how the consistency of student thinking, and the match to the taught curriculum knowledge, varies across the different grade levels in the Zimbabwean sample. However, Kuiper's study does *not* have an optimal design to provide a test of Watts' model.

Question for reflection

If you accept that Kuiper's normative survey approach (ERP1) cannot negate the conclusions Watts draw from his interpretive (ERP2) study, then should you accept Watts' findings as representing students' common alternative conceptions of force?

We can accept that Kuiper's work is based on an approach that can offer useful knowledge of *the level of understanding of students within the test population,* **but** uses a methodology that is not appropriate to test Watts' model. If we take this position, then Kuiper's failure to replicate Watts' findings are not pertinent to judging that model (as he was not looking at the type of entities Watts reported). However, this is not in itself any reason to accept Watts' model either. We would still have to be convinced that Watts has 'made his case', a notion that we will return to later.

The insidious nature of our paradigmatic commitments

This example of two very different studies, which at first glance come to opposite conclusions about the 'same' issue, shows why we cannot ignore paradigmatic issues when we undertake, or read, research. Our basic assumptions about the nature of the phenomena we study, and the nature of the research process and the kind of knowledge it can lead to, continue to influence all stages of planning, executing and reporting research. Even if we do not make our assumptions explicit, they will be working insidiously as we make research decisions and write-up our accounts, and their consequences will be reflected in our work. This is represented in Figure 3.4, where we see how our fundamental beliefs influence the various stages of research.

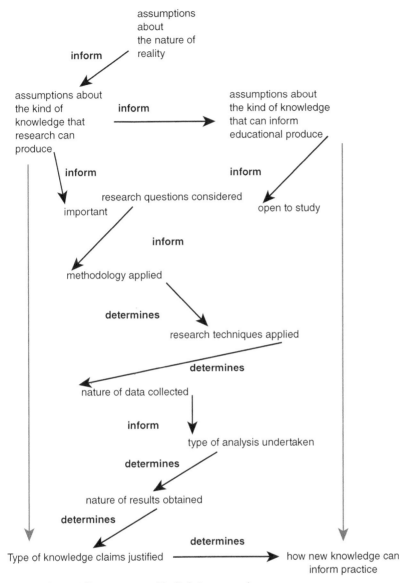

Figure 3.4 The insidious nature of beliefs in research

Question for reflection

How many of the links shown in Figure 3.4 can you identify in the examples of research studies discussed in this book?

——————————————————— **Complementary research approaches?** ———

Both research paradigms would seem to be associated with rather substantial limitations. ERP1 research uses a 'scientific' method to uncover general laws, but any findings can only be judged reliable whilst we accept the theoretical frameworks within which the research is undertaken. Critics of ERP1 approaches would argue that the complexity of social phenomena (such as learners, lessons, classrooms, schools) makes it inappropriate to look for general laws that will apply across very different contexts. Researchers who accept such an argument are more likely to undertake interpretivist enquiry, such as case study research, using approaches that explore individual cases in depth. These researchers have to accept that such ERP2 research can only strictly tell us about the particular focus chosen for research – and not about another time, another classroom, another class, another learner.

To caricature, ERP1 studies produce general decontextualised findings that are usually bound to (and so are dependent upon) the theoretical assumptions the researcher(s) used to design their study, whilst ERP2 studies produce detailed studies of very specific educational contexts that should not be assumed to apply to any other context. If developing our understanding of teaching and learning depended upon selecting one or other of these clearly limited approaches then the whole enterprise might seem somewhat futile.

These two research approaches have often been characterised as if *competing* paradigms, as "an intellectual either/or situation" (Reynolds, 1991, p. 194), which can lead to "clashes among researchers with different purposes who tend to see the others as engaged in the same enterprise as themselves, but simply doing it badly" (Hammersley, 1993, p. xix). However, the assumption that "scientific explanation and interpretative understanding are mutually exclusive categories" has been challenged (Carr & Kemmis, 1986, p. 105). Biddle and Anderson (1986, p. 239) have argued for an "integrative approach", which makes it "possible to assemble the visions of both confirmationism and the discovery perspective into a single, expanded view of the social sciences".

The perspective suggested here is that although neither ERP1 nor ERP2 can offer us totally satisfactory ways of finding out about educational phenomena, both can still offer helpful insights, and provide valuable models of educational phenomena: models which are useful because they have explanatory and predictive power. Models often have limitations, such as restricted ranges of application; and sometimes (in social science, as in natural science) the best current understanding of a phenomenon involves several different partial models, each useful in some circumstances.

It is suggested here, then, that educational research from both traditions can be *useful*, and the types of knowledge produced in these different research traditions offer *complementary* insights to inform educational practice. Indeed, the Research Council of the US National Academy of Sciences offers a vision of 'scientific' research in education that encompasses a wide range of approaches. Research in areas where little is known indicates the need for "descriptive studies [that] might be undertaken to help bring education problems or trends into sharper relief or to generate plausible theories" (National Research Council Committee on Scientific Principles for Educational Research, 2002, p. 99). From this perspective, many ERP2 studies may be considered 'scientific'.

Illustrating the complementary nature of research paradigms

Earlier in this chapter, two studies were discussed which came to very different conclusions about whether secondary-age students hold 'alternative conceptual frameworks' for the physics concept of force. We also saw that Watts and Kuiper were working in different paradigms where they approached what would seem to be the same research focus from very different perspectives. At first sight this would seem to be an illustration of what Kuhn referred to as the 'incommensurability' of different paradigms. However, it has also been suggested that research into learners' thinking about curriculum topics needs to be considered from both the interpretivist *and* the normative standpoints, especially if research is going to be useful to teachers.

> The documentation of students' ... conceptions and the way these progress is a field of work that has its roots in the ethnographic tradition with its recognition of the centrality of personal meaning and of individual and cultural differences. Yet despite this orientation, there appear to be strong messages about apparent commonalities in students' conceptions that may have implications for future directions of work in this field.
>
> (Driver, 1989, p. 488)

Other studies have claimed to be able to move from in-depth studies of individual learners to normative models of common ways of thinking (e.g., Taber, 2000a). This approach requires finding common features in the accounts of individuals, and then finding ways to test the frequency with which students more generally select items reflecting these commonalities in surveys. Part of this process involves ensuring that survey items are valid as ways of identifying the conceptions or frameworks proposed in the accounts of interpretivist studies. So, for example, David Treagust (1995) describes a process for developing diagnostic tests for teachers to identify student misconceptions. These tests consist of objective items – two-tier multiple-choice questions, where students are asked to select which of several statements is correct (the first tier) and then which of several possible explanations explains why this answer is correct (the second tier):

> ... a teacher needs a starting place for addressing known students' conceptions and/or misconceptions, and a multiple choice diagnostic instrument, informed by research in students' learning problems in a particular content area, would appear to provide a relatively straightforward approach to student assessment.
>
> (Treagust, 1995, pp. 329–330)

Sometimes a third layer is added: to ask respondents how much confidence they have in their responses.

However, the process of developing the classroom tests involves three major stages. The first stage involves determining the curriculum understanding of the topic, in consultation with subject matter and educational experts. The second stage involves identifying aspects of students' thinking about the topic, both from existing research and through open 'non-structured' interviews with learners (i.e., an ERP2 approach). Only then are the objective questions designed, piloted, and modified. This latter process also needs to involve interviewing students about their understanding of the questions, and their thinking in selecting answers to ensure that the closed response categories eventually represented in the final instrument are authentic reflections of common student ideas. A detailed description of the development of such an instrument, including accounts of the stages of testing and modifying test items, may be found in Tan, Goh, Chia, and Taber (2005) – available from https://camtools.cam.ac.uk/wiki/eclipse/diagnostic_instrument.html

———The research process ———

We can appreciate the significance of a researcher's fundamental assumptions if we consider carrying out educational research as a process. The basic steps are normally:

- selecting a focus – deciding what we want to study;
- developing a conceptual framework – forming an understanding of what is already known that is relevant to our focus;
- producing research questions – setting out the specific aims of our research;
- selecting the most appropriate methodology;
- designing the research (planning sample, schedule, forms of data collection and analysis);
- data collection;
- data analysis;
- reporting.

This is, of course, a model of a complex process. In some forms of research, these are certainly not totally separate stages that have an invariant order. However, this type of sequence is a useful basis for thinking about many research studies.

Question for reflection

If paradigmatic concerns are so important in research, why is there not a step where a choice of paradigm is made?

To appreciate the 'logic' of this sequence, the reader is referred back to Figure 3.4, which reminds us how decisions made at one point during research have consequences for what becomes possible and sensible at later stages.

The research focus

The starting point is the choice of research focus – the area that the researcher wishes to explore and find out about. Academic researchers (i.e., university teachers employed to teach and undertake related research) usually follow their own 'interests' and often have ongoing lines of research into particular issues, through which they may see individual studies as being part of a 'research programme' (an idea introduced in Chapter 1, and considered in more detail in Chapter 4). Other professional researchers ('contract researchers') work on projects financed by funding bodies or research organisations, and are directed to particular studies according to the interests of their funding agency.

Practitioners are usually motivated to undertake research to investigate and improve some aspect of their own professional practice that has been identified as a concern (this is discussed in more depth in Chapter 5). This is a simplified picture, of course: academic researchers may be directed to study areas due to available funding or a recognition that the topic is currently seen as important; contract researchers can choose which contracts to seek; teacher-researchers may be influenced by wider institutional concerns or may have their interest in a topic initiated by colleagues in universities with particular research interests.

Selecting a focus for a course assignment

Students undertaking research as part of the requirements of an academic course are in something of an artificial situation, as a primary motivation for the research is usually a report that satisfies examiners. Two important features of the project are therefore that it will enable the writing of a report that meets specific assignment assessment criteria, and that it is feasible in the timescale allowed. It is also important for the student to have a genuine interest in the topic, as a good deal of time will need to be invested to produce an acceptable report. This becomes more important as the level of the project increases: from an undergraduate or PGCE assignment undertaken over a few months, to a doctoral study that will be the main focus of work (and probably life) for 3–4 years.

A major consideration for students is their research context. For a full-time Master's or doctoral student, the choice of research sites can be made later in the research process. However, for a PGCE student, and often for a teacher undertaking research part-time, the research site may be fixed and so the research has to be situated in the placement or employing school. Academic supervisors will often be keen to suggest ideas for a research focus (as they will have to spend time discussing the students' work and reading drafts of the report). However, for a student teacher on placement the school mentor is the central person with whom to negotiate a research focus, as this will be the key person to advise what is feasible within the professional context, and to help facilitate the enquiry.

The selection of a focus for an enquiry involves the identification of the purposes of the study, such as:

- to find out if the establishment of schools with specialist status enables pupils to be better matched to their school;
- to identify problems associated with colour-blindness in practical work in science;
- to find out if girls have greater listening skills than boys;
- to investigate students' metacognitive skills and study habits;
- to study increasing the use of formative assessment techniques in maths classes;
- to find a better way of teaching about elements, compounds and mixtures in the lower school;
- to explore students' perceptions of humanities subjects in Year 9;
- to elicit teachers' attitudes to teaching citizenship within different curriculum subjects;
- to assess the value of a simple visual-auditory-kinaesthetic model of learning styles as a way of thinking about the way pupils in a Year 10 class learn.

Question for reflection

Which of the above foci might be suitable for (a) a student teacher in a placement school; (b) a teacher undertaking part-time MEd study; (c) a full-time doctoral student in a university?

Although the range of foci suitable for classroom research undertaken by teachers and student teachers is somewhat more restricted than the full range of topics explored across educational research studies, it is still vast. This issue is considered further in Chapter 5, which includes a list of examples of classroom research topics undertaken by trainee teachers on professional placements in schools during PGCE programmes (and for which full research reports are freely available in an open-access journal, *JoTTER*).

Some of the suggested foci above are presented as topic areas, some seem more like practical aims, and some are framed as questions. It is common to set out the aims of a research study in the form of one or more research questions, which need to be carefully formulated. (Selecting a focus and developing research questions in teacher-research are considered in Chapter 8.) In a doctoral study, many months may be spent honing the question(s). Before this is possible, it is necessary to review what is already known and understood about the research focus.

———— Developing a conceptual framework for research ——————————

This stage of the research process is called 'conceptualisation': where the researcher writes an account of their way of thinking about the research focus. This conceptualisation will be informed by reading of relevant literature, and will clarify key terms (what is understood by 'specialist schools', 'humanities subjects', 'learning styles', etc.). Most accounts of research include a 'literature review'. When done well, this is not just a summary of the contents of relevant papers, but a synthesis of findings that sets out how the researcher understands the current state of the field.

At this point the researcher's ontological assumptions will play a part, as the conceptualisation will discuss the nature of the things that are considered to be important to the research focus. In other words, the types of things to be investigated, and the kind of knowledge sought about them, will normally determine the research paradigm that is appropriate – which in turn will inform a choice of suitable methodology, and so the selection of specific methods, a suitable sample, etc. (cf. Figure 3.4). The conceptualisation process is therefore an essential step in the logic of any research study, and being a step it needs to be correctly sequenced. It may be tempting for a student who is undertaking classroom research as an academic exercise (and requirement), and has limited interest in its outcomes, to leave the literature review until the writing-up stage. This is a very good way of inviting additional stress, and making the task of producing a coherent research report much more difficult than it needs to be!

Selecting a hypothesis

Earlier in this chapter, we considered research by Harrop and Swinson (2003) that found that the profile of question types used by teachers at infant, junior and secondary levels were not significantly different. This finding refuted their prediction that a different pattern would be found. It was suggested above that this 'negative' finding did not undermine the value of the study. Of course, this does *not* mean that the failure to confirm the hypothesis is not an important finding.

In research undertaken from a confirmatory perspective (i.e., ERP1) there is normally an expectation of what will be found based on the existing understanding of the research field. A hypothesis is formed, which derives from a conceptualisation of the existing research, and how this might apply in the context being explored. Harrop and Swinson introduce their paper by setting out their conceptual framework for the research: the importance of the topic of teacher questions, both in view of the role they take in teaching, and in terms of previous research showing that teacher questioning is a significant activity in terms of the sheer quantity of questions teachers use when teaching.

In setting out on their research, Harrop and Swinson were effectively testing a hypothesis about *differences* between teacher questions at different stages of education: "to examine differences [*sic*] in patterns of questioning between the three levels of schooling" (2003, p. 52). It would be possible to have set out a 'null' hypothesis, i.e., that the pattern of question types would *not* be significantly different at different levels. However, Harrop and Swinson had *theoretical* reasons for expecting more open questions to be used with the older children.

> We had thought that ['Open Solution' category] questions would require more reflection on the part of the pupils than other questions so that teachers would be more liable to use them with older pupils, both because the older pupils would be more capable of handling such questions than the younger pupils and because such questions would be considered as helping the pupils to develop further their thinking processes. It seems we were wrong.
>
> (Harrop & Swinson, 2003, p. 55)

As the authors' prediction was based on their initial conceptualisation of the field, if they believe their findings are trustworthy, they need to re-examine their conceptualisation of the topic to offer a new understanding consistent with their findings. This is not a failure. The whole point of research is to develop our knowledge. In confirmatory research we are often checking our understanding (from existing research) in new contexts, or in more complex situations. Research findings often raise questions for further research – something that may make this seem a frustrating enterprise to some outsiders, but is part of the fascination for most researchers.

Conceptualising ability

Lyle concluded, from his study of how mixed-ability grouping facilitated literacy learning (see Chapter 2), that:

> ...mixed-ability teaching provides a setting in which both low- and high-achieving students value the opportunity to work together where both groups believed they benefit.
>
> (Lyle, 1999, p. 283)

Question for reflection

Considering some of the learners you work with, how confidently would you be prepared to judge their intellectual ability?

Lyle reports that the study is about *mixed-ability* teaching, yet in order to identify pupils of different 'ability' (what they are *able* to do), judgements are made in terms of pupil *attainment* (what they have *demonstrated* they can do). This is an 'ontological' issue. Choosing to use 'ability' as a way of conceptualising the difference between learners shows that Lyle assumes that it is meaningful to label students in terms of ability, i.e., that a student will have a (singular) level of ability, and that this is a relatively stable (perhaps even fixed) characteristic. Ability cannot be directly measured, so can only be inferred. By using an attainment measure to stand for 'ability' Lyle seems to assume (at least implicitly) that attainment is a reflection of ability – i.e., that all the pupils were working to their potential to a similar degree.

These assumptions may seem 'common-sense', as in everyday conversation people are labelled as 'clever' or 'dull' as though intellectual ability lies on a single scale, and as if we can readily estimate where someone lies on that scale. However, these are assumptions that would be questioned by many working in education. Sometimes it is necessary to make simplifications and assumptions of this kind for pragmatic reasons – in order to produce a research design that is viable. However, pragmatics must be balanced against the extent to which such assumptions could undermine any findings that derive from our enquiry.

Conceptualising constructivist teaching

In 2004, Ian Kinchin published a study in the journal *Educational Research*, which claimed that students would prefer to learn in a 'constructivist' learning environment. The abstract of Kinchin's paper claims (2004, p. 301):

- "an overwhelming preference among students for a constructivist learning environment"
- "Students anticipated constructivist learning environments would be more interesting, more effective at developing students' understanding and would permit them to take greater owner-ship of their learning"

Constructivism (see Chapter 2) is a commonly used notion in education, especially in terms of approaches to educational research, and in terms of teaching strategies (Taber, 2011a). However, even within a particular field such as science education, the term constructivism is used in a number of ways (Taber, 2009b).

So, a reader of Kinchin's paper needs a clearer understanding of what *this particular* author means by the term. Kinchin helps the reader here by offering an overview of how he is conceptualising this term early in the paper, both by providing a simple definition of a 'constructivist classroom', and by contrasting this with an alternative ('objectivist') perspective. In doing this, Kinchin sets up a dichotomous classification (an 'either/or' situation), depending upon "whether a teacher expects students to act as passive receivers of information (= the objectivist classroom) or as active builders of understanding (= the constructivist classroom)" (2004, p. 301). In an accompanying figure these two classroom types are related to rote learning (i.e., learning 'by heart') and meaningful learning (i.e., learning for understanding).

Question for reflection

To what extent do you feel this description of teaching styles as constructivist *or* objectivist is a valid reflection of the beliefs that inform teaching behaviours?

Kinchin describes his conceptual framework early in his paper to provide the background to his study. Pupils and teachers can have different, and changing, notions of learning. If teacher beliefs and student beliefs are mismatched (i.e., one objectivist, the other constructivist), then the classroom can become a very frustrating place. Experienced teachers will recognise the importance of this issue. Most of us have come across complaints from learners at both ends of the spectrum: about the teacher who just gives notes and expects students to somehow learn from copying them; and from pupils who feel that they are being cheated by teachers who are 'not doing their job properly' because they set up interesting learning activities, but are reluctant to dictate definitive notes and provide 'the right answers'.

Defining terms

In a 1998 study published in the *International Journal of Science Education*, Petri and Niedderer reported their research into one 18 year-old high school student's learning about the atom. Petri and Niedderer describe the focus of their study as a 'learning pathway'. This is because they are assuming that learning is not an 'all or nothing' phenomenon, where the student non-problematically moves from ignorance to knowing as a result of instruction. The authors believe that learning is more nuanced than that, with students bringing existing ideas and beliefs to class (see the discussion of Watts' study above), and that, in some subjects, progression involves learning about a succession of curriculum models of increasing sophistication.

When exploring complex phenomena, it is often necessary for a researcher to provide an operational definition that characterises and delimits the phenomenon (and allows the reader to appreciate if the researcher is actually discussing what *they* understand by the term). For the purposes of their paper, Petri and Niedderer (1998, p. 1075) define learning as "a change in a cognitive system's stable elements". They are also careful to explain that the 'cognitive system' "is the model of a student's mind constructed by the researcher" (ibid.). This is an important acknowledgement, as researchers have sometimes been considered to confuse knowledge represented in learners' minds with their own necessarily limited and partial models (Phillips, 1987).

> ## Questions for reflection
>
> Earlier in the book it was suggested that learning could be understood as a change in the potential for behaviour, i.e., a change in behaviour repertoire that may or may not be realised. (a) Is this consistent with Petri and Niedderer's "change in a cognitive system's stable elements"? (b) Would two studies defining learning in these two ways be investigating the same research focus, i.e., 'learning'?

Petri and Niedderer develop their model for the reader. They consider the cognitive system to comprise 'stable deep structure' and 'current constructions', i.e., they make a distinction between 'stable cognitive elements' which are fairly permanent features of mind, and what the learner happens to be thinking right now. Petri and Niedderer explore the stable cognitive elements in the cognitive system they construct, to describe the learning processes of one German secondary school student that they call Carl. As researchers, we have to spend time clarifying our understanding of a field before we can set about planning our enquiries. We also have to remember to set out our conceptualisation for others when we later come to report and explain our work.

▬ Further reading ▬▬

Two useful texts for anyone interested in the nature of research and philosophies informing research are books by Brown et al. and Phillips, listed below. The question of whether educational research can (or should) be considered 'scientific' is explored in the book from the US National Research Council, and in the chapter from my book, listed below. (The latter will be accessible for download to students in many universities through their library subscriptions, and a pdf of the former can be freely downloaded to anyone who registers at the National Academies Press website.) The two chapters from the collection edited by Elaine Wilson set out two key approaches (paradigms, if you like) for thinking about educational research, whilst the paper by Pring reminds us that in reality such distinctions are never absolute.

Brown, S., Fauvel, J., & Finnegan, R. (Eds.) (1981). *Conceptions of Inquiry*. London: Routledge.

Counsell, C. (2009). Interpretivism: Meeting our selves in research. In E. Wilson (Ed.), *School-based Research: A Guide for Education Students* (pp. 251–276). London: Sage.

National Research Council Committee on Scientific Principles for Educational Research (2002). *Scientific Research in Education*. Washington, DC: National Academies Press. (Available from: www.nap.edu/)

Phillips, D. C. (1987). *Philosophy, Science and Social Enquiry: Contemporary Methodological Controversies in Social Science and Related Applied Fields of Research*. Oxford: Pergamon Press.

Pring, R. (2000). The 'false dualism' of educational research. *Journal of Philosophy of Education, 34*(2), 247–260. doi: 10.1111/1467-9752.00171

Taber, K. S. (2009). 'Scientific' research in education. In K. S. Taber (Ed.), *Progressing Science Education: Constructing the Scientific Research Programme into the Contingent Nature of Learning Science* (pp. 51–78). Dordrecht: Springer.

Taber, K. S. (2009). Beyond positivism: 'Scientific' research into education. In E. Wilson (Ed.), *School-based Research: A Guide for Education Students* (pp. 233–250). London: Sage.

Taber, K. S. (2011). Constructivism as educational theory: Contingency in learning, and optimally guided instruction. In J. Hassaskhah (Ed.), *Educational Theory* (pp. 39–61). New York: Nova. (Available for free download at: https://camtools.cam. ac.uk/wiki/eclipse/Constructivism.html)

4

What strategies do educational researchers use?

This chapter:

- asks you to consider the middle, strategic, level of how we think about research in education
- introduces the notion of sampling, and considers different ways a sample can be selected
- introduces you to the main methodologies employed in educational research: experiments, surveys, case study, ethnography, grounded theory and action research
- explores what is meant by the term 'mixed-methods' research in education, and when that might be a useful way to describe a research project
- discusses a range of published studies to illustrate key points raised in the text.

The previous chapter looked at the type of 'executive level' thinking that provides a 'vision' (or philosophy) for research. This chapter considers some of the most common strategies/methodologies, adopted at the 'managerial level' of research planning (see Figure 3.1). Selecting a methodology is very important, as it guides the research plan, which in turn determines what data is actually collected and how it is analysed.

── **What is methodology?** ──

Methodology: A way of thinking about and studying social reality

Methods: A set of procedures and techniques for gathering and analyzing data
(Strauss & Corbin, 1998, p. 3)

Methodology is more than the research *techniques* – 'methods' – someone uses, and is more concrete than their paradigmatic – fundamental, philosophical – commitments. Methodology is the *strategy* used for answering research questions. It has been described as "a theory of how inquiry should proceed" (Schwandt, 2001, p. 110). A simple way of thinking about methodology and techniques (sometimes confusingly called 'methods') is in terms of strategy and tactics. Effective research has an overall coherent strategy, which outlines the general way that the research aims will be achieved. This will translate into a set of specific tactics that will address sub-goals that collectively build towards the overall aim. This is reflected in Figure 4.1, which shows the major methodologies discussed later in the chapter in the first column, followed by two further columns setting out common techniques for collecting and analysing data.

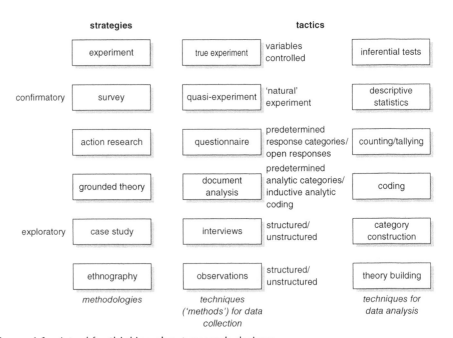

Figure 4.1   A tool for thinking about research designs

The pattern shown in Figure 4.1 seems quite symmetrical, but it is not intended to suggest that there is a simple correlation between a choice of general methodology and the more specific techniques used in a study. Rather, there is a looser relationship, in that the categories near the top of each list tend to be used in confirmatory studies (ERP1, see Chapter 3), and those near the bottom of the list are more likely in research carried out in more of a 'discovery' mode (ERP2). So various patterns may be found in the methodologies and subsumed techniques applied in particular studies, but there are some combinations that would *not* be sensible – for example, an experiment that used unstructured observations.

Can research designs be changed once research is underway?

Some methodologies are said to be *emergent*, meaning that it is not possible to plan the research in detail at the start, as the researcher has to be responsive to what is being learnt as the research proceeds. Indeed, in a 'grounded theory' approach (discussed below) it is totally inappropriate to set out a definite account of a research schedule and the data to be collected at the outset, and the flexibility within the design is seen as a strength as well as an essential part of the methodological approach. In such research, the techniques used (tactics) may be modified during the research. This is acceptable, but only within the overall coherent methodology (strategy).

However, anyone planning to use an 'experimental' design to test a hypothesis must plan the research in detail at the start, and so the techniques of data collection *and* analysis need to be firmly established before any data is collected. Research claiming to use this type of methodology, which involves substantive changes (in such matters as how 'subjects' are assigned to groups, or which statistical tests are to be applied) once the research is underway, is open to being challenged as failing to follow accepted procedures and so is potentially invalid.

As with the identification of paradigms, the recognition of suitable methodologies in educational research (and how to label and characterise them) is a 'fuzzy' area. Different authors have different ways of defining, describing and labelling both paradigms and methodologies, and this can be an unhelpful source of confusion for those new (and sometimes those not-so-new) to the field. An introductory way of thinking about research paradigms was introduced in the previous chapter, which is at the level of detail useful for those setting out on classroom research. In a similar way, the discussion of methodologies below is set at an introductory level, and readers are referred to more in-depth accounts if they wish to explore these issues in more detail. To reinforce the significant difference between methodology (research strategy) and techniques (tactics for collecting and analysing data), these topics have been deliberately separated in the book. Although techniques are mentioned here, a more detailed consideration is reserved for Chapters 10 and 11.

Common research methodologies include:

- experiments and quasi-experiments
- surveys
- case study
- ethnography
- grounded theory
- action research

There are many books that describe research methodology, which can support the development of a detailed appreciation of the distinct features of these different methodologies. The account below is intended to give an outline of the nature of these approaches.

Sampling in educational research ———

One thing that virtually all educational research studies have in common is the discussion of findings from a relatively small proportion of the potential informants! Many studies explicitly *discuss* potentially vast 'populations' of learners, but then present research that has been undertaken with only a tiny proportion of that population (Figure 4.2).

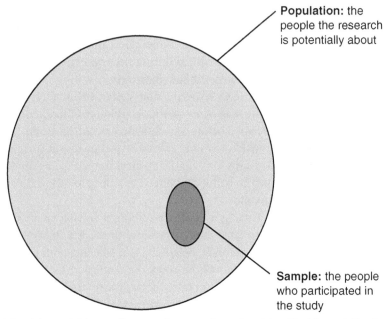

Figure 4.2 A 'sample' is usually a small proportion of an identified 'population'

Consider some titles of published research papers:

- An exploratory study of the effect a self-regulated learning environment has on pre-service primary teachers' perceptions of teaching science and technology
- Secondary school teachers' pedagogic practices when teaching mixed- and structured-ability classes
- Student ideas of science concepts: alternative frameworks?
- An investigation of pupil perceptions of mixed-ability grouping to enhance literacy in children aged 9–10
- A learning pathway in high-school level quantum atomic physics
- Constructivist-compatible beliefs and practices among US teachers
- A study of schoolchildren's alternative frameworks of the concept of force
- A cross-cultural comparison of teachers' expressed beliefs about music education and their observed practices in classroom music teaching.

The titles of most of these papers suggest that the paper is about a group of people: 'pre-service primary teachers', 'secondary school teachers', 'children aged 9–10', 'US teachers' or even 'students', 'pupils', 'schoolchildren' or 'teachers'. These are very large groups, and – of course – none of these papers present data from such large groups.

Question for reflection

One of the titles listed does not seem to derive from a group of people. What does the title 'A learning pathway in high-school level quantum atomic physics' suggest about the nature of that particular study?

Yet, we would not suggest that these titles are deliberately misleading, because no one is going to read a paper expecting it to report results obtained from *all* children aged 9–10 or *all* US teachers! We clearly expect the authors to have collected data in *some* classrooms, from *some* students, or *some* teachers. However, the more general references in the paper titles (and often in the way conclusions are phrased) suggest that it is assumed that the findings from the individuals studied tell us something about the wider group they are seen as being part of. There is no simple basis on which we can make such an assumption. This can be illustrated by some statements about 'school pupils' that could be made based on hypothetical empirical investigations that collect data from 'some' school children:

- School children are under 2.5 metres in height
- School children eat food
- School children drink milk
- School children play football
- School children support Manchester United Football Club
- School children enjoy homework
- School children are called Amanda
- School children are better at maths than English
- School children want to be educational researchers when they are older.

These statements might potentially reflect findings obtained from enquiry with *some* children, but some of them would be rather unsafe as *generalisations* about school children as a whole. The question of how we can confidently make generalisations from specific research is not a trivial one, for in fact there is no logical basis that will ever allow us to generalise *with certainty* beyond the group of people we actually collect data from! In looking at how researchers respond to this rather fundamental problem, we can again draw upon the distinction between ERP1 and ERP2 research (see Chapter 3).

Approaches to sampling in educational research

In ERP1 there are basically two approaches:

1 A sample may be constructed which is considered large enough, and *representative* enough, of a wider population to allow general findings from the research to be likely (in a statistical sense – using inferential statistics, tests designed to allow inferences to be drawn) to reflect the wider population. This approach is used in surveys (see below).
2 In experimental approaches there may be less control over the make-up of the sample of 'subjects'. However, by identifying the potential factors that may vary in a population and be relevant (think of the assumptions that need to be made here), it is possible to try to allow for these factors.

In ERP2 there is an assumption that people are individuals who vary in so many, and such complex, ways that good research reports detailed case accounts (see below) with enough context to allow the reader to make a judgement of the extent to which findings might apply elsewhere (this process will be examined in more detail in Chapter 7).

In the extreme, a study will offer an account of one case (e.g., 'a learning pathway...'). Other studies offer accounts of a range of contrasting cases to show what similarities and differences may be found across cases. Neither paradigm solves 'the problem of induction' (how to draw general conclusions from specific examples), reminding us of the value of complementary approaches (see Chapter 3), or 'grounded theory' approaches (discussed below), which offer ways of building general models, starting from specific cases.

Purposive sampling

Samples are not always selected to be representative of wider populations. Indeed, sometimes the sample for a study is deliberately chosen not to be representative and 'typical'. So in their study of teaching using new technologies, de Winter, Winterbottom, and Wilson (2010, p. 262) reported that the participants were all mentors in schools working in an initial teacher education partnership, who "take responsibility for supporting the [learning] of trainee teachers on professional placement in their school", *and* that they selected participants who "had an existing interest or expertise in using a particular 'new' technology in the classroom".

> ## Questions for reflection
>
> How might you describe the 'population' that de Winter et al.'s study was reporting on? Do you consider that de Winter et al.'s approach to sampling to be biased, and – if you do – might that undermine the validity of their conclusions?

We can only judge the applicability of a sample in terms of the purpose of the particular study. So often in ERP1 research, the aim is often to find out what is usual, normal or typical in a population (e.g., how much the average student might learn in given circumstances), and a biased sample will bias the results. In general, when a study claims to look at *what is typical in a population*, then *the sample needs to be representative of the population* the study claims to be about.

However, de Winter, Winterbottom, and Wilson were looking to produce guidance to support teachers in adopting new technologies in their teaching, and so deliberately selected their participants in order to work with those in good positions to help them identify effective approaches. In such a study, it is quite appropriate to purposefully select participants who are *not* typical of a wider population. We could argue here that the population actually being sampled was not teachers in general, but only those who had interest and competence in using new classroom technologies. Alternatively, we could suggest that in this type of study, the very notion of sampling a population is simply not relevant. The important point is that the selection of participants in the study was sensible, and so could be justified, in terms of the purposes of *that* study.

In reading about the examples of research discussed in this book, the reader should be alert to the size, mode of selection, and composition of samples of informants providing the data upon which findings are based (perhaps keeping a note when reading studies, using a form such as that in Figure 1.1). Where studies attempt to offer general findings, the reader should ask themselves whether the sample could be either diverse enough to be representative of classrooms generally, or large enough to buffer against the distorting effect of large variations between individual teachers, classes and lessons.

————————————————— Experiments and quasi-experiments ———

Experiments are set up to test specific hypotheses. In a 'true' experiment the researcher controls variables, so that only the factor which is hypothesised to have an effect differs between the experimental and control treatments. In reality, such control is rarely (if ever) possible in enquiries into teaching and learning – even if the range of potentially significant variables can be identified.

However, it is sometimes possible to make comparisons between situations that *approximate to* the conditions needed for an experiment. For example, an experimental procedure might require students to be assigned to one of two classes randomly, but the researcher may have to work with existing classes. However, if it can be shown that the two groups are sufficiently similar (on whatever measures are considered relevant), it may be possible to continue as if there was an experimental set-up. In such a

Box 4.1

Just some of the factors that may feasibly impact on educational outcomes

Student characteristic	Teacher characteristic	Classroom/school context
hair colour	age	size of screen/board
height	gender	arrangement of furniture
gender	teaching experience	type of floor covering
birth-date	level of qualification	number of windows
handedness	main teaching subject	size of windows
religious faith	other subjects regularly	direction windows face
first language	taught	closeness of classroom to road
IQ	degree background	setting of school (e.g., urban,
learning style(s)	hair colour	rural, etc.)
personality style	eye colour	proportion of students receiving
eye colour	height	free school meals
use of eye glasses	religious affiliation	management structure of school
use of hearing aid	political affiliation	status of school (academy, free
parental income	regional accent	school, church school, local
parental education (highest	handedness	authority school, etc.)
qualifications/years of	IQ	number of pupils on role
college)	seniority in school	level of staffing
parental employment status	years working in the	class size
number of older siblings	present school	teaching assistants supporting
number of younger siblings	professional development	teacher
a twin?	opportunities taken	turnover of staff
parental criminal record	marital status	admissions policy
gang member	professional disciplinary	exclusions policy
...	history	...
	weekly alcohol intake	
	...	

situation, although it is not possible to randomly assign individual learners to the two classes, there should be a random assignment (e.g., a coin toss) to determine which class will experience the 'experimental' treatment, and which will act as the control.

In making a judgement about which factors may be relevant, we will exclude from consideration many potential factors that we have, in effect, decided in advance are not important in the study. The range of potential factors we could potentially take an interest in when comparing classes is immense (see Box 4.1 for some examples).

Questions for reflection

Consider the list in Box 4.1 of some of the variables we could decide to take into account when comparing educational outcomes in different classes of students. Are all of these variables relevant to educational outcomes or can some of them be ignored? Are there some variables listed that would be relevant in some studies and not others? If so, how would you decide when these factors could be important for any particular study?

Experiments use statistical tests to check for 'statistically significant' results (i.e., those which have a low probability of occurring by chance) as well as for 'effect' sizes (as large samples may lead to *statistically* significant differences which may be of little practical importance). When quasi-experimental approaches are employed, statistical tests may also be used to check for significant difference between groups that may already exist prior to any 'treatment' being applied, and which could invalidate any differences 'after' the experimental treatment has been carried out.

So in a paper in the *Journal of Science Education and Technology*, Çokadar and Yılmaz (2010) reported a study designed to explore "the effect of creative drama-based instruction on seventh graders' science achievements in the ecology and matter cycles unit …" (p. 80). The authors report statistics relating to the achievement test scores in two classes, an experimental group (taught through drama-based instruction) and a control group (taught through lectures and class discussion), at pre-test (before teaching) and in a post-test (afterwards). The mean scores in the two groups are shown below (Table 4.1).

Table 4.1   Results from the Çokadar and Yılmaz (2010) study

Group	At pre-test	At post-test	
Control	7.63	16.86	significant difference
Experimental	7.91	19.60	significant difference
	non-significant	significant difference	

We can see from Table 4.1 that the experimental group achieved more (on average) in the post-test than the control group, but that they also achieved more in the pre-test and so might be considered to be starting from a stronger knowledge base. Çokadar and Yılmaz present the outcomes of statistical tests to tell us that in both groups achievement was significantly better after teaching (confirming what most teachers would infer from simple inspection of the change in mean scores). Readers are also told that the difference between the two groups *after* teaching was statistically significant whereas the difference before teaching did *not* reach statistical significance. In this example, most teachers would find this reasonably convincing – after all, the difference in mean scores at post-test is noticeably greater than the small difference at pre-test.

However, statistics only tell us what is likely by chance. The small difference in pre-test scores *could* conceivably mean that more students in the experimental group had some key understanding that was important for learning more about the topic. That seems unlikely, but we cannot completely rule out such a possibility. Of course, average test score are just that: it would be quite possible that students in a class with a lower average score on a test were in a better position to progress if the profile across different test items was very different in the two classes – not all knowledge is equally central for further learning. As always, teaching and learning are complex matters. A better grasp of central concepts is more important than knowing many discrete facts. Although we might find Çokadar and Yılmaz's results (in Table 4.1) convincing, we might not always be so readily convinced that a non-significant difference in pre-test scores should be ignored in explaining a significant difference in post-test scores (see Figure 4.3).

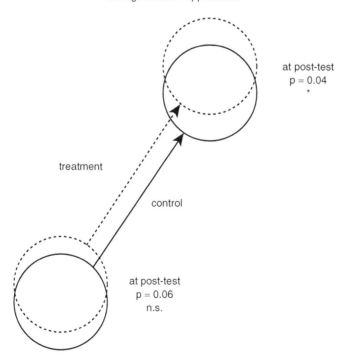

A hypothetical quasi-experiment:
comparing post-test to pre-test scores in two classes taught
through different approaches

at post-test
p = 0.04
*

treatment

control

at post-test
p = 0.06
n.s.

Differences in pre-test scores for the treatment and control
groups are found to be non-significant (p>0.05).
Differences in post-test scores for the treatment and control
groups are found to reach significance (p<0.05).
Conclusion: the intervention (treatment condition) leads to
better learning gains than 'normal' teaching (control condition).

Figure 4.3 Visual representation of learning gains in two groups of learners in a
hypothetical quasi-experiment

Question for reflection

Consider the hypothetical results of a quasi-experiment represented in Figure 4.3. Statistical tests tell us that before the intervention, the pre-test scores in the 'treatment' and 'control' group were not significantly different. However, after the intervention, the post-test scores of the treatment group were significantly higher than those in the control group. Would you be convinced this demonstrates the effectiveness of the intervention?

Statisticians have developed various techniques to address the complications of undertaking this kind of experimental study, and some very powerful statistical approaches are now available. These do, however, require specialist knowledge to apply correctly, and most teachers do not use such techniques in their own studies.

As well as the technical difficulties of experimental design, this type of work raises particular potential ethical issues, especially if there are good reasons to believe that some learners will be deliberately disadvantaged compared with others in order to investigate the effect of some intervention. Ethical issues are very important in research, and are discussed in Chapter 9.

Exploring whether modular examinations disadvantage students

One of the studies referred to in Chapter 2 was a paper in the journal *Educational Research*, where McClune (2001) argues that students following modular courses (where some of the credit for final grade is awarded for examination papers taken early in the course) may be disadvantaged compared with students taking linear courses for the same award, and being examined on all aspects of the course in terminal examinations.

Question for reflection

McClune's study compared the performance of students in the first and second year of an A level course. What factors might need to be 'controlled' to make this a fair comparison?

McClune's study can be seen as an example of working in a positivistic research paradigm (ERP1, see Chapter 3). McClune reviews the 'advantages and disadvantages' of modular assessment, and highlights concerns that students may not be 'ready' for examinations part way through a course, and may need substantial time to consolidate learning before being examined. This framing of the topic (the author's conceptual framework, see Chapter 3) may be seen as offering an implicit hypothesis – that students examined earlier in their course may be disadvantaged compared to those examined at the end of the course.

Such a hypothesis is suitable for 'experimental' testing, i.e., manipulating conditions to compare between the two situations. Such experiments are difficult to set up in educational contexts, but it is possible to use a quasi-experimental design, where instead of a manipulation, advantage is taken of the 'natural' experiment (i.e., that some students were being entered for all their examinations at the end of the course, and others taking module examinations part-way through). However, simply comparing examination grades between these two groups of students does not ensure that any differences in outcomes are due to whether students take modular or purely terminal examinations (for example, schools that tend to have less successful examination grade profiles may decide to follow modular courses to see if that helps their students, or students with strong records of examination success may be more likely to opt for courses with terminal examinations).

Designing the quasi-experiment

McClune describes how he set up a sample that was large enough to use statistical testing, and which gave him groups suitable for making a comparison based on whether or not modular examinations were followed. McClune selected candidates entered for examinations at the same time, in the same subject (physics), and having followed the same subject content specifications. As there were some common questions in the modular and terminal examination papers, McClune was able to look at students' performance on the common questions, assessed by the same criteria (i.e., mark scheme). The sample was selected randomly from all the examination centres (i.e., schools, etc.), and so as to include papers marked by all the examiners marking those questions.

Question for reflection

How would you go about selecting a sample 'randomly'?

In a truly experimental study, the researcher would randomly assign participants to one of the two conditions (in that case modular or terminal examinations). This would offer some safeguard that there is no systematic difference between the two subgroups in some factor that might have an influence (and as we have seen there are potentially many one could consider!). In a quasi-experimental study the researcher cannot assign participants to the two conditions. So although McClune built his sample based on a random choice from those students taking the examination, each student selected was inherently already in the modular (first year) or terminal (second year) condition. There was a random choice of students from within the two conditions, but no safeguard against some systematic factor(s) determining which students were in the two conditions being compared.

Clearly, any difference in the marks attained on the common questions among the two groups could be due to (a) chance – owing to the particular individuals in the samples; (b) a difference between the groups in terms of the nature of the learning achieved on courses examined by modular or non-modular examinations; (c) a difference between the two groups coincidental to their following different patterns of courses. Only an effect due to option (b) would be relevant to the focus of McClune's study. To exclude the possibility that any difference between groups was due to factors other than those of interest, one has to be able to identify and control for those factors. In education, we can never be sure of all the possible influences that may be at work (see Box 4.1), and so it is never possible to be absolutely sure we have excluded all such influences.

Using inferential statistics

To avoid the influence of chance, a large enough sample is needed to be able to use inferential statistics. McClune's sample comprised 406 students examined on the terminal route at the end of their course, and 346 taking the modular examinations halfway through their two-year course. Even when a full randomisation process is possible, inferential statistics can never completely rule out a difference between two groups being due to which individuals were randomly chosen for each treatment (rather than reflecting a true difference in the two larger populations), but they can indicate how likely or unlikely a result is to occur by chance. Generally, a result that is only likely to happen by chance less that once in every twenty opportunities ('$p<0.05$', where p is probability) is taken as being 'statistically significant'.

This means that we have to accept that a proportion of all the many thousands of *statistically significant* findings in the literature are due to random variations. We could reduce the number of such 'false positive' statistical tests produced by using a more restrictive measure of statistical significance, e.g., $p<0.01$, but this will reduce the number of significant differences we identify, and many more potentially important results will be classed as statistically 'non-significant' (see Chapter 11). Commonly, in reporting the results of statistical tests, the author will provide the probability of the result being a chance event (e.g., $p = 0.012$), and an indication of whether this is judged as statistically significant according to the commonly used (if somewhat arbitrary) cut-off values (see Table 4.2).

Table 4.2 How probability is interpreted in terms of statistical significance

Probability	Implication	Indicated
$p \geq 0.05$ (e.g., $p=0.14$)	If this was just a chance effect and the study was repeated a great many times, this result would occur in more than one in twenty of the runs (so we might think it is reasonable to assume it could be a chance result and so is non-significant, n.s.).	n.s.
$p<0.05$ (e.g., $p=0.036$)	If the study was repeated a great many times, this result would occur in less than one in twenty of the runs if this was just a chance effect (so we might think it is reasonable to assume this is *probably* not just a chance result and consider it significant).	*
$p<0.01$ (e.g., $p=0.0083$)	If the study was repeated a great many times, this result would occur in less than one in a hundred of the runs if this was just a chance effect (so we might think it is reasonable to assume this is *probably* not just a chance result and consider it highly significant).	**
$p<0.001$ (e.g., $p=0.00067$)	If the study was repeated a great many times, this result would occur in less than one in a thousand of the runs if this was just a chance effect (so we might think it is reasonable to assume this is *probably* not just a chance result and consider it extremely significant).	***

In order to carry out his analysis, McClune had to use a scoring scheme (see Chapter 11) to convert grades on previous GCSE examinations into a numerical score. This allowed him to control for the previous academic attainment of the students in the two groups by checking for any significant difference between his two sub-samples. However, inferential statistics can only give the likelihood of something being so.

That an 'analysis of variance' test did not reveal significant differences between the two groups in terms of their scores for previous qualifications is certainly not the same as saying that the two groups had *identical* GCSE results.

According to McClune's analysis:

> Pupils completing the second year of the course had a higher level of attainment than those taking the examination during the first year of study. Similar differences between upper-sixth and lower-sixth pupils were observed in both boys and girls...
>
> (McClune, 2001, p. 79)

On most questions the differences in scores between first- and second-year students were quite small. Often researchers report an 'effect size', a value which indicates the likely *importance* of a difference (it is possible for a very small, and practically irrelevant, difference to reach statistical *significance*). In this case, McClune does not need to interpret his findings this way: teachers appreciate that the difference between 64% and 69% could be very important in an examination.

Question for reflection

Why would it be difficult for a teacher to undertake the type of study described in McClune's paper?

McClune's study is an example of research that would have been of practical importance to many teachers (who had to choose between modular and terminal examinations for their students), as well as to policy-makers (who decide what type of examination system should be in place). However, the classroom teacher is unlikely to be able to carry out such research. McClune worked in a university environment, and his research was only possible with the cooperation of the examination board that allowed him to develop his sample and access scores for the students from across all the examination centres entering candidates. It is unlikely that classroom teachers would be granted this level of cooperation and access.

Surveys ——

Surveys usually look for data from large numbers of people. Some surveys collect information from whole populations of people. For example, a school could survey all its pupils, or all their parents, to find out their views on some issue relating to school policy. In such situations a high return rate, or at least making sure that everyone eligible to respond has the opportunity, may be sufficient for the findings to be of import. A more complex situation occurs when the population of interest is too large for all members to be asked to respond. In these situations, a sample of the population is surveyed. The sample has to be defined to ensure that it is representative of the wider population. One approach is to ask a random proportion of the population. If this is possible, then statistical techniques can be used to estimate how accurately the sample response is likely to represent the wider population.

Question for reflection

Imagine you are charged with finding out what 13 year-old school children think about the amount and type of homework they should be asked to complete each week. You are required to sample 0.2% of the age range nationally. How might you go about identifying the youngsters in the target population, and then contacting a *random* sample to carry out your survey?

In practice, it is often impossible to use a random sample. Where the population consists of a broad category such as 'A level students' or 'parents of pupils on the special needs register' it is unlikely that a researcher could ever access the information needed to identify all those in the population. Without this information there is no way to select a random sample.

Sampling populations in surveys

Often research in education (and other social sciences) has to settle for other sampling techniques. The strength of a truly random sample is that it avoids the researcher having to know (or guess) how different people in the population might be influenced by various factors: a large enough random sample is likely to be representative (enough) of the relevant influences. The representativeness of a non-random sample is actually often more important than its size. That is, a modest-sized sample that is representative of some population tells us more about the population than a larger non-representative sample. If you wanted to survey the 1000 students in an 11–16 school, to find out about their attitudes to truancy, it would be much better to have a sample of 50 students selected at random from all the students, than to have responses from all 200 pupils in the first year of the school.

When we do have a random sample of a population, not only will a larger sample give a better picture of the population as a whole, but it is also possible to estimate the likely 'measurement error' introduced by sampling. This is why the 'small print' on opinion poll reports often tell us that the outcomes should be considered to be accurate within, say, ±1.5%. However, when a sample is not random, and we cannot be sure it is representative of its population, it is not possible to estimate the likely error as it could be subject to systematic error. For example, we might think that a sample of 20000 people would be quite large, and could give us a good indication of Londoners' favourite football team. But if we undertook the poll at Chelsea's Stamford Bridge stadium on a match day, the results are likely to be very biased by the choice of a sample that would not be representative of Londoners as a whole. This would be like asking one class of primary students who their favourite teacher was, and assuming the results applied to the population of pupils in the school as a whole.

When we cannot access a random sample, there is a danger of our sample not being fully representative of the population we are interested in. We can try to *construct* a representative sample, but this may not be easy. We may look to build a 'stratified' sample which includes people from identifiable subgroups of the population of interest, with these subgroups represented in the same proportions in the sample as they are in the population. For example, consider a survey to find out which factors have the most influence on whether students apply to study at university. A sample that was composed of a disproportionate number of students from wealthy backgrounds, or of those with graduate parents and siblings at university, is likely to give distorted results. The problem for the researcher is that to avoid this distortion she must be able to both know *which* factors might be relevant (is gender? is ethnic background? are there regional factors? is there a difference between urban and rural areas? etc., cf. Box 4.1), and be able to build a stratified sample which has representative proportions of respondents matching those in the wider population. This can be a very challenging task.

Question for reflection

The problem of deciding which factors need to be considered when constructing a representative sample for a survey is about *including* all sections of a population. The problem of deciding which factors need to be controlled in a fair experiment is about *excluding* effects due to potentially confounding variables. Is there a sense in which these are similar problems, linked to how ERP1 studies (see Chapter 3) seek objective knowledge?

Some types of survey do not use representative samples. The weakest type of sample is based on convenience sampling. So, for example, a survey of 'primary age children' may be based on surveying the children in the nearest primary school where access is offered. This clearly leads to severe limits on the extent to which results may be generalised to 'primary school pupils' in the wider population.

There are, however, forms of sampling that fall between stratified and convenience sampling. Purposeful sampling can build a sample that includes some representation from certain groups without attempting to build a fully representative sample. So for a survey of staff perceptions of pupil behaviour in a school, the researcher may seek out newly qualified teachers (NQTs), recent appointments and supply teachers to be included in the sample on theoretical grounds (i.e., that these staff are most likely to experience misbehaviour), as well as including some established staff and senior post holders. There will be no attempt to make the sample represent the population in proportional (numerical) terms, but some members of identified key groups will deliberately be included. It may even be that a decision will be taken to include *all* the NQTs, even though this gives a distorted sample, if their perceptions are seen to be particularly valuable. As always in educational research, what is important is that such decisions are clearly reported and explained in any formal account of the study.

In a study published in the *British Educational Research Journal*, Brooks and Everett (2009) reported on graduates' perceptions of the value of having obtained a degree. Clearly, the potential population of graduates is immense, and in selecting their 90 participants, Brooks and Everett recruited graduates from six institutions that they considered to occupy different 'market positions' within higher education:

- an Oxbridge college
- a college of the University of London
- a redbrick university
- a 1960s campus university
- a post-92 university
- and a college of higher education.

The implication here is that because there is a perceived market in higher education, with institutions being seen at different levels of prestige, then degrees could be seen as more valuable (e.g., by potential employers) when awarded by some institutions rather than others. Given this premise, it was sensible to ensure that the study sample included graduates from institutions with different prestige in the 'market'.

Question for reflection

Many people working in education find the application of market thinking inappropriate, and the categorisation scheme used by Brooks and Everett might be seen as elitist. Some might even feel that using such a scheme is inconsistent with democratic values that should seek to improve education for all, rather than imply some institutions are in some sense inferior to others. Do you think that adopting such a classification should be avoided on ideological grounds?

Some of us might be uneasy about explicitly adopting such a sampling frame. However, if Brooks and Everett recognised this difference in prestige, and considered it important, it would have been inappropriate to have ignored it, as this could have undermined their research. Had they been ideologically opposed to such a situation, they could have positioned their research from an axiological stance (i.e., reflecting their values) to explore this issue, and see if their results would support arguments for change.

Brooks and Everett, instead, draw the reader's attention to another severe limitation of their study with potential to bring their results into question:

> It is important to remember that our sample was self-selecting: respondents offered to be interviewed after receiving a letter about the project from their alumni office, or seeing an advert on the 'Friends Reunited' website. It is, therefore, likely that the sample over-represents those who have had more successful learning careers and/or transitions from higher education into work – as it is probably much easier to talk about perceived successes than perceived failures.
>
> (Brooks & Everett, 2009, p. 347)

Question for reflection

Should Brooks and Everett have realised in advance that interviewing a self-selected sample was likely to have biased their sample, and so designed their study to avoid this limitation?

The self-selecting nature of the sample *is* a major methodological flaw in the study, and so the quote above offers a major caveat to the study findings. Yet the paper is published in a prestigious journal, after being subject to peer review. Often research involves compromises. Sometimes methodological decisions are heavily influenced by ethical considerations that make it inappropriate to do what would be most informative (see Chapter 9). Research is also always subject to major limitations of resources – an issue discussed in some detail in the following chapter (Chapter 5) – including the available access to study participants. Sometimes, as researchers (just like as teachers) we have to accept that we have to settle for doing what is possible, when we clearly are not in a position to do what we would ideally like to do. It is worth noting that limitations are not necessarily a bar to publishing work. All research results are subject to some limitations, and a good research report acknowledges these and discusses how they may have influenced the results obtained. Reviewers who advise editors on whether submitted manuscripts are suitable for publication (see Chapter 6) are required to make an evaluation on whether the research is worth reporting despite such limitations and compromises.

Surveying teacher beliefs about pedagogy

Ravitz, Becker, and Wong (2000) report a study exploring teacher views about pedagogy and teacher beliefs of student views about pedagogy. Their specific research focus was on the relationship between teacher pedagogy and the use of computers in teaching.

They distinguish "two overarching approaches to teaching that represent different and somewhat incompatible models of good pedagogy" (Ravitz et al., 2000, p. 3 – cf. 'Conceptualising constructivist teaching' in Chapter 3). These are:

- Traditional transmission instruction – "based on a theory of learning that suggests that students will learn facts, concepts, and understandings by absorbing the content of their teacher's explanations or by reading explanations from a text and answering related questions"
- Constructivist-compatible instruction – "based on a theory of learning that suggests that understanding arises only through prolonged engagement of the learner in relating new ideas and explanations to the learner's own prior beliefs".

Questions for reflection

The two categories used in Ravitz et al.'s study seem to offer both a rather simplistic dichotomy of approaches to teaching and a somewhat caricatured picture of these two approaches to pedagogy. How would such a conceptualisation fit a study undertaken from a 'confirmatory' or a 'discovery' research paradigm (see Chapter 3)?

Ravitz, Becker, and Wong undertook a survey to collect their data. Their published report gives details of how, where, and when they went about this. Their study was based on a national survey undertaken through a questionnaire issued in the USA during Spring, 1988.

Designing a hybrid-sample

Ravitz and colleagues explain how they built a sample of schools with three components. As well as schools included on the basis of 'probability' (selected by chance), they also deliberately included schools that were known to have a high level of provision of computers, and schools considered to be substantially involved in educational reform (i.e., where it might be expected that teachers will be using more 'constructivist-compatible' instruction). In each school the questionnaire was to be answered by the school principal, the technology coordinator, and a probability sample of teachers. Ravitz et al. reported that over 4000 teachers responded to the questionnaire, and that over half the sample was from the schools selected at random.

Ravitz and colleagues reported (2000, p. 11) that, overall, the teachers gave similar ratings to both approaches in terms of the student knowledge gains that could be achieved (44% for the traditional approach compared to 42% for the constructivist approach), although more thought students would gain most useful skills by the constructivist approach (29% for the traditional approach compared to 57% for the constructivist approach). They also found that most of the teachers surveyed felt more comfortable with a traditional approach (64% traditional compared to 28% constructivist), and most also thought that their students would prefer the traditional approach (53% compared to 37% constructivist).

Question for reflection

In another study discussed earlier, Kinchin reported that secondary-level students overwhelmingly preferred a constructivist approach, but Ravitz et al. found that most teachers believe that students would be more comfortable when taught with a traditional approach. Does this simply mean that the teachers surveyed by Ravitz et al. had incorrect beliefs about their students' views on teaching?

Strengths and weaknesses of a survey approach

The Ravitz et al. study offers some examples of the limitations and the advantages of a survey as a research methodology. A severe disadvantage of a survey is that responses are limited to the options or categories offered. So this study is undertaken within a confirmatory paradigm (ERP1), where the relevant categories are decided at the outset. The researchers had to characterise the main pedagogic approaches as clearly distinct categories (in this case, a dichotomy), and decide upon questions about views and behaviours that would link to these pedagogies – informed by their reading of previous research. Such an approach produces 'objective' data that is readily analysed and is suitable for statistical interrogation. The survey approach also allows a sample to be built up that is both large enough to make statistical comparisons, and includes categories of respondent of particular interest to the researchers. In this case, the carefully built sample provides the possibility of identifying nine groups of respondents:

	Principals	ICT coordinators	Teachers
Representative of schools nationally	—	—	—
Schools with strong ICT provision	—	—	—
Schools known to be involved in educational reform	—	—	—

By making comparisons between responses across different questionnaire items it is possible to uncover statistically significant correlations. So Ravitz et al. found that teachers conceptualising teaching in certain ways, favouring

- an inquiry approach
- being a facilitator and
- organising class time around multiple, simultaneous small-group activities

were more likely to report doing certain class activities:

- week-long projects;
- student journals;
- designing assignments where students had to "represent the same idea in more than one way";
- hands-on activities;
- reflective student essays.

The authors were also able to report that respondents selecting responses linked to a constructivist approach were more likely to report frequently, using activities considered (by the authors themselves) to be constructivist:

> Overall, those who selected the constructivist belief alternative on each survey question were about one-half a standard deviation higher on an index measuring the sum of the number of constructivist activities engaged in (monthly) than teachers who chose the traditional transmission belief statement (or who selected the middle response).
>
> (Ravitz et al., 2000, p. 50)

Surveys, especially large-scale surveys such as this, clearly offer considerable scope for reporting on general patterns and trends, subject to the proviso that respondents only provide information on the particular points (and often using predetermined response options) that are built into the survey. They are strong on providing a 'big picture' where researchers feel they already know what it is important to ask, and where the research is not concerned with the particular features (views, behaviours, understanding, etc.) of individual respondents.

——— Case study ———

Case studies are very common in education, and involve the in-depth exploration of a particular case. Case studies are useful in complex situations where the number of significant variables may exceed the number of cases, making control of variables impossible. We can see how teaching and learning phenomena might well fit into this pattern. Defining the case is an important step here, as there is much flexibility. Examples of the 'unit' being studied in a case study include a teacher, a class, a group of students who work together, a lesson episode, a module in the scheme of work, a year group, a school, a local education authority (LEA), etc. Cases are often quite limited units of study, such as in Duit and colleagues' study based on the "analysis of one specific classroom discussion episode" (Duit, Roth, Komorek, & Wilbers, 1998, p. 1060), although this is not always the case. So Freebody (2003, p. 80) noted how "the [US] National Institute on Student Achievement, Curriculum, and Assessment ... conducted a Case Study of the entire Japanese school system with particular reference to the teaching and learning of Mathematics and Science."

According to Yin (2003), a case study has a number of characteristics. A case study is an empirical enquiry that explores a phenomenon within its context, rather than attempting to isolate it. Consider a school where the classes are set in half year groups and where the two top maths sets are taught by different teachers (at different times – as one half of the year group has English when the other has maths) in different rooms. The head of department notices that the profile of test scores is consistently much lower in one of the two top sets although they are meant to be parallel. This could clearly be something to do with the teacher, or the pupils, or the interaction between the two. The timing of the lesson or the learning environment could be factors. It may be that one class has PE immediately before two of its maths lesson each week, and arrives excited and tired. Or it may be that one of the teachers has a non-teaching period directly before some of her sessions with her class and is mentally 'fresher'. There are many possible factors at work, and isolating variables (e.g., move the classes to different teaching rooms; now try moving the lessons to a different time of day) is not likely to be a feasible strategy for understanding what is going on. It is not even clear if the timetable and classroom are merely background context or significant features. In this situation, building up a case study that explores in some depth what is happening in the class suspected of under-performing may be a suitable approach to developing useful new insights.

'Triangulation' within case studies

Yin suggests that case studies cope with these situations by using multiple sources of data (allowing 'triangulation', discussed in more detail later in the book, especially in Chapter 8), looking for *convergence*. This is similar to a grounded theory approach (see below) although, unlike grounded theory, Yin notes that in case-study research "prior development of theoretical propositions to guide data collection and analysis" are appropriate (Yin, 2003, pp. 13–14.) Yin suggests that "case studies are the preferred strategy when 'how' or 'why' questions are being posed, when the investigator has little control over events, and when the focus is on a contemporary phenomenon within some real-life context" (p. 1).

A case study of student learning?

In a 1998 study published in the *International Journal of Science Education*, Petri and Niedderer reported their research into one 18 year-old high school student's learning about the atom. Petri and Niedderer (1998, p. 1075) claim to 'describe' "one student's learning process in a course on quantum atomic physics in grade 13 of a German gymnasium (secondary school)". They refer to this student as Carl. This description is in terms of what they call a 'learning pathway':

> The student's learning pathway is described as a sequence of several meta-stable conceptions of the atom, starting from a planetary model. His final cognitive element 'atom' following teaching is displayed as an association of three parallel conceptions including his initial planetary model, a state-electron model and an electron cloud model.
>
> (Petri and Niedderer, 1998, p. 1075)

Questions for reflection

As research studies offer participants assurances of anonymity, we can be confident that Carl's real name was not actually Carl. Do you consider the decision to refer to the student as Carl (rather than 'student X' or similar) to be appropriate, given this was not actually his name? In view of the discussion in Chapter 3 (pp. 58–60), would you consider Carl's learning pathway to be an educational phenomenon, or something else?

This is a very interesting study, but we might ask why we would be particularly interested in one particular learner (who is no longer a school student).

Why do we care about Carl?

In reporting the conceptual framework (see Chapter 3) supporting their work, Petri and Niedderer make a distinction between 'stable cognitive elements', which are fairly permanent features of mind, and what the learner happens to be thinking right now. This distinction is important, but problematic for researchers. Although we may be more interested in the 'stable cognitive elements', we only ever have access to what students (tell us they) are thinking now. The 'stable elements' are theoretical constructs (parts of models we construct to make sense of phenomena such as student comments) and must be inferred from data based on the public representations of the 'current constructions'. (In other words, what a student says and does now is assumed to reflect what they are currently thinking, which draws upon the cognitive resources – concepts, facts, etc. – they are currently accessing, which are likely to be only a fraction of those potentially available.)

This is just one complication of exploring student understanding. Learning is a complex and subtle phenomenon, and even when researchers correctly interpret what students say, do and write, each particular datum offers only limited access to current understanding. It is known that students may sometimes hold manifold conceptions of the same topic (Taber, 2000c) so that learning may often be better understood as a shift in the profile of use of 'versions' of concepts in various contexts, rather than as switching between holding different conceptions (Mortimer, 1995). In-depth study of individuals, carried out over extended periods of time, are needed to explore the shifting sands of the learners' 'conceptual ecology' (Taber, 2001). For researchers who hold such a perspective, the subtleties of learning are best explored through case studies of individual learners, such as Carl.

Petri and Niedderer provide contextual information on the course being taught, and when particular ideas were covered in lessons. The authors were involved in developing teaching about the topic of quantum physics at high school level, so it is important that they offer the reader information about the nature of the instruction. They also give an account of the data they collected and how it was analysed.

Use of multiple data sources in case-study work

A range of data was collected during the study (Petri & Niedderer, 1998, p. 1078):

- observations and a pre-questionnaire
- video tapes of the entire unit and the group work of four students

- short, spontaneous interviews
- three semi-structured interviews in small groups
- one semi-structured final interview with all students
- one semi-structured interview with some students three months after
- written material from each student.

The collection of different types of data provides the basis for an in-depth qualitative analysis. However, it is important to recognise that in some studies such a multitude of data sources provides less redundancy (allowing comparison and cross-checking between different types of data) than may at first seem the case. We need to be aware of the 'degrees of freedom' inherent in the focus being studied.

If researchers wanted to know if a student knew a simple fact, e.g., whether the letter B is a vowel, it may be sufficient to ask one question. However, we know from research that student understanding of many concept areas is much more complex than this, with students holding manifold conceptions that can be elicited in different contexts. To explore student thinking in these areas, it is necessary to ask a range of questions (or set a range of tasks) varying contextual and verbal cues in the questions. The more 'degrees of freedom' in what is being explored in research, the more 'slices of data' are needed to build an authentic representation.

Studies of learning are attempting to see how something that is already a complex target for research (e.g., an individual's knowledge and understanding) is changing over time – and this requires that a suitable range of probes are used at several points during the learning process. The 'degrees of freedom' are greater, and so more slices of data are needed to construct a useful model of the system studied. (If this seems a little abstract, refer to the examples discussed in Chapter 8.)

Generalising from the case?

No matter how careful and proficient the researchers may have been in producing their model of Carl's learning about quantum physics, it remains a case study of a single learner. Petri and Niedderer's study tells us little about the learning of Carl's classmates, or of students studying the topic elsewhere. We might *assume* that students of various ages, studying various other school topics (the causes of political revolutions, the effects of previous ice ages on landscape, the significance of natural evil to understanding conceptions of God, etc.), might demonstrate learning with somewhat similar characteristics. We might *expect* that all humans have brains that work in similar ways and that the learning of 'academic concepts' (Vygotsky, 1934/1994) depends on similar processes across learners and topics, but Petri and Niedderer's case study of a single learner's learning pathway for one concept cannot offer any direct evidence to support such (ontological, see Chapter 3) assumptions. Not only that, but the rationale for selecting case study – the complexity of learning processes and the individuality of learners – suggests that we should be careful about drawing general conclusions from one case. This is a general problem of case studies that some researchers believe grounded theory, discussed below, can overcome.

The terms nomothetic and idiographic, introduced in the previous chapter, were coined by Wilhelm Windelband (1848–1915), who was interested in distinguishing the natural sciences from 'historical science'. Windelband (1894/1980) suggested that:

- The nomothetic "sciences are concerned with what is invariably the case";
- The idiographic "sciences … are concerned with what was once the case".

Carl completed his study of high school physics some years ago now. Petri and Niedderer are only *directly* telling us about what was once the case.

Instrumental and intrinsic case studies

An important distinction is between instrumental and intrinsic case studies. An instrumental case study looks at an example, perhaps what is seen as a typical example (e.g., of a lesson, of a school, etc.), in detail, in the hope that it will provide insights that will be considered as worth testing out in other similar cases. So if a case study of truanting in one school revealed that parent attitudes were a major factor in whether children truant, then staff in other similar (*sic!*) schools concerned with truancy rates might consider it *likely* that the same thing could be true in their school context as well.

An intrinsic case is studied because there is something of special interest about that particular instance. So, for example, if one teacher consistently achieves much greater progression rates (of students selecting to take the subject further) than her colleagues teaching similar classes the same subject in the same institutional context, then a case study to build a detailed account of her work with her classes might offer indications of what was happening to bring about such desirable outcomes. Similarly, if a school finds that a disproportionate number of students are excluded from classrooms for behaviour misdemeanours that occur during mathematics lessons, it might suggest that a case study looking at student misbehaviour, and what triggers it, in that particular department could be informative. It might not represent what is happening in other departments, but that is less important as the issue of concern seems to be located in that particular curriculum area.

Multiple case studies

In recent years there has been the development of the approach of using multiple case studies. This is an approach to increase the generalisability of results from case studies. A series of case studies are undertaken (sometimes selected because of contrasting features), each with the type of detail suggested above, and then another layer of analysis across the cases is employed. As each case requires considerable attention, and as often the cases are undertaken in a range of research sites, such an approach is seldom suitable for a PGCE project, and may not be suitable for the classroom teacher. However, such an approach might well be suitable as the basis of a project for a higher degree student.

For example, Dorion developed a programme of research to explore the potential to use drama-based techniques in teaching secondary science (e.g., role play and physical simulations of systems, such as when students are asked to 'be' molecules in a gas, or charges flowing through a conductor). As an MEd project, Dorion undertook a multiple case study where each case was focused on a lesson taught by a teacher who used drama techniques in science lessons. He analysed each lesson in detail as a discrete case, before then offering a synoptic analysis that led to a model for how such approaches could be used in teaching. He later reported this stage of his work in the *International Journal of Science Education* (Dorion, 2009). For his PhD research, Dorion then undertook another multiple case study, this time himself teaching lessons in different schools drawing upon the model he had developed, but again seeing each lesson, and student learning in it, as a discrete case, before then looking for common themes that arose across the cases.

━━━ Ethnography ━━

Ethnography is an approach that is used in anthropology to explore unfamiliar cultures. The problem facing anthropologists studying a new culture is to try to find out about 'alien' rituals and customs in terms of the meanings they have for the people in that culture. So, the type of methodology developed, 'ethnomethodology',

> is concerned with how people make sense of their everyday world. More especially, it is directed at the mechanisms by which participants achieve and sustain inter-action in a social encounter – the assumptions they make, the conventions they utilize, and the practices they adopt.
>
> (Cohen et al., 2000, p. 24)

At first sight, ethnographic methodology may seem inappropriate when the researcher is exploring aspects of teaching and learning in their own society. After all, ethnomethodology is designed to find out about *other cultures*. However, there may well be situations when those researched can be considered as members of a different culture, so that an ethnographic approach is appropriate. This might certainly be the case when the researcher would be considered a member of a different social class for example. A well-educated intellectual in a professional role such as a teacher or an academic researcher should not *assume* that disaffected youths from disadvantaged backgrounds will share the same cultural values and assumptions.

Ethnographic approaches have been adopted by researchers when attempting to explore learners' understandings of curriculum topics. In science, such studies have shown that learners commonly hold alternative conceptions or 'misconceptions' of many topics (see https://camtools.cam.ac.uk/wiki/eclipse/eclipse.html). Research suggests that 'children's science' may often be coherent, theory-like and highly tenacious (Taber, 2009b). The researcher trying to understand how a student understands a topic area has to try to put aside their own way of thinking and try to 'see' the topic 'through the eyes of the learners', to try to 'get inside' the mind of the learner. This is considered to be analogous to the anthropologist trying to learn to think like a newly discovered tribe, to understand the way people in that culture 'see' their world. This was the approach taken by Watts, although not by Kuiper, in the research into student thinking about forces discussed in Chapter 3.

In Chapter 2, reference was made to Florian and Black-Hawkins' (2010) study on 'inclusive pedagogy', where the researchers not only wished to observe teaching behaviour and the teacher thinking that informed it, but also asked: "how can examples of inclusive pedagogy in action be articulated in ways that are useful to other teachers and supportive of their practice?" (p. 815). In anthropological terms, this might be considered an attempt to provide an 'emic' account, one that is intended to be meaningful in the terms of the culture investigated. That is, Florian and Black-Hawkins do not just want to be able to report their findings in a form of interest to other researchers and theoreticians, but also wanted their findings to make sense to teachers so that they might consider adopting strategies reported as being useful and effective.

Describing the careers of primary pupils

Pollard and Filer (1999) report a study of pupils' primary school 'careers'. Their book is based around four detailed case studies of individual primary pupils, based on ethnography. They describe the primary aim of their work as "to create an accurate description of the perspective, social practices and behaviour" (1999, p. 2) of the people they are studying. Ethnographic approaches rely on detailed observations recorded as field notes. Pollard and Filer describe the main methods of their approach as "discussion, interview, collection of documents and a great deal of 'participant observation', with copious fieldnotes describing events, and a 'research notebook' to record analytic ideas and fieldwork experiences" (p. 2).

An important feature of this type of research is that it may take a good deal of time to 'immerse' oneself in the culture before beginning to see the patterns of meaning that the informants use to understand their lives. Research notes need to be as 'unfiltered' by existing theories as possible, to avoid imposing some inappropriate pre-existing theory or schemes onto the data:

> Ethnographic studies are carried out to satisfy three simultaneous requirements associated with the study of human activities: the need for an empirical approach; the need to remain open to elements that cannot be codified at the time of the study; a concern for grounding the phenomena observed in the field.
> (Baszanger & Dodier, 2004, p. 10)

It has been noted that ethnography is much better at producing theoretical accounts than offering ways to validate such accounts:

> Ethnographic methods offer means for generating theory. By the same token, these techniques are poor ones for testing theory, since the data obtained by the researcher were not gathered systematically and do not represent any population of events to which the researcher may wish to generalize.
> (Biddle & Anderson, 1986, p. 238)

To some extent, this limitation is overcome in grounded theory research.

━━━Grounded theory ━━

> Grounded theory methodology … is a specific, highly developed, rigorous set of procedures for producing formal, substantive theory of social phenomena. This approach to the analysis of qualitative data simultaneously employs techniques of induction, deduction, and verification to develop theory. Experience with data generates insights, hypotheses, and generative questions that are pursued through further data generation. As tentative answers to questions are developed and concepts are constructed, these constructions are verified through further data collection.
>
> (Schwandt, 2001, p. 110)

Grounded theory (GT) is a difficult methodology for a novice researcher to adopt, especially where an enquiry has a tight timescales. So when Schraw, Wadkins, and Olafson (2007) undertook a GT study of academic procrastination (reported in the *Journal of Educational Psychology*), they collected data over eight academic semesters – this timescale was due to the demands of the GT methodology, and not a result of any procrastination on the part of the researchers! Despite not being especially suitable for a novice, it is important for all educational researchers to *know about* this methodology, because:

- it provides a model for interpretivist research which may overcome many of the limitations of much 'qualitative' enquiry;
- it is commonly used as a referent in interpretivist research.

In other words, many studies make references to using approaches 'informed' or inspired by GT. One of the originators of GT has described "the fervent adoption of GT terminology and selective application of discrete aspects of GT methodology" in qualitative data analysis as a "multi-method cherry picking approach" (Glaser & Holton, 2004). The reader of such accounts needs to appreciate what is meant by GT research, and to be able to judge whether studies that 'name-check' GT are following the methodology closely enough to be able to claim the recognised benefits of this approach.

Key features of grounded theory studies

Theoretical sensitivity: "to enter the research setting with as few predetermined ideas as possible … to remain sensitive to the data by being able to record events and detect happenings without first having them filtered through and squared with pre-existing hypotheses and biases" (Glaser, 1978, pp. 2–3). This is similar to the approach taken when using ethnomethodology.

Theoretical sampling: GT studies have an *emergent* design, in that the collection of data leads to hunches and hypotheses that inform what data should be collected next, i.e., "sampling on the basis of emerging concepts, with the aim being able to explore the dimensional range or varied conditions along which the properties of concepts vary" (Strauss & Corbin, 1998, p. 73). This is clearly antithetical to experimental research where the procedures for data collection and analysis need to be established at the outset. For example, Schraw and colleagues reported that in their study, "participants during Phase 1 were selected randomly; participants in Phases 2–4 were selected using theoretical sampling" (2007, p. 14).

Coding: In GT studies there are well-established procedures for coding data – "the analytic process through which data are fractured, conceptualized, and integrated to form theory" (Strauss & Corbin, 1998, p. 3). A key feature is the 'constant comparison' method, whereby new data is compared to existing codes to check fit and as necessary modify the codes; and where modified sets of codes are then tested back against data collected previously. This iterative process is intended to ensure that the codes used *emerge from* the data, and are *not imposed on* the data. 'Substantive' coding (based directly on describing the data, on a line-by-line basis) shifts to a theoretical level as categories are developed to organise the codes, and a core category of central significance is identified.

Theoretical saturation: GT is only considered as ready for publication once theoretical saturation is reached. That is when new data collection (indicated by theoretical sampling) does not lead to any further changes to the theory, as the scheme of categories and their properties and relationships fit new data without further modification, i.e., "The point in category development at which no new properties, dimensions, or relationships emerge during analysis" (Strauss & Corbin, 1998, p. 143). In their report of their GT study, Schraw and colleagues inform the reader that during the first phase of their study they found that "the focus group and individual interviews saturated the codes that were necessary to understand the phenomenon of academic procrastination" (2007, p. 15). At the end of their study they invited participants to review their draft findings (a process called 'member-checking'), which "helped to assure that the final paradigm model was fully saturated, dependable, and credible" (p. 17).

Is the model saturated?

We can apply this notion of saturation to Watts' model of learners' conceptual frameworks for understanding force (see Chapter 3). Watts did not claim to be using GT, and acknowledged that his study produced a model *suitable for further testing*. He claimed his results had similarities with the findings of other studies, but this in itself cannot be seen as strong evidence for the value of his findings. A reader of the research is likely to look for evidence that the model produced is both an authentic reflection of the data collected (i.e., the analysis is careful and comprehensive) and that the findings are likely to be of wider relevance. In this regard, Watts' paper shows that he based his model on a sample of 12 students of a range of ages in several schools in London, England (see Table 4.3).

Table 4.3 The Watts (1983) sample by age and gender

Age	11	12	13	14	15	16	17	*
Females	1			1	3	1	1	7
Males		1		1	2		1	5
Total	1	1	0	2	5	1	2	12

The question that a reader might ask is that:

- *if* the analysis of data from twelve informants, over a wide age range, from one geographical location, provided evidence of eight alternative frameworks,
- *then* how can Watts (or the reader) be confident that increasing the sample, by interviewing additional students, would not have led to a larger set of frameworks being developed?

This is, of course, the generalisation issue raised earlier in this chapter: to what extent are Watts' results (from a limited sample) capable of being applied to 'school children learning physics' in general? Watts' study is convincing in suggesting that secondary students do come to class with alternative conceptions of the force concept. However, in reading Watts' research, the reader must question the generalisability of the findings because:

- the sample cannot be considered to be large or representative;
- the analytical procedures do not assure a saturated model;
- the description of the informants and research sites are insufficient for readers to make judgements about degrees of similarity with their own teaching contexts (cf. Chapter 7).

These are issues shared by much research based on the analysis of qualitative data. Although GT offers a way of overcoming these limitations, it requires a commitment of resources (and especially researcher time) that is seldom possible (see the next chapter for a consideration of the resources needed for studies based upon different methodologies). This is why there are many more studies claiming to *draw upon* GT methodology than genuine grounded theories in the literature. Juliet Corbin, who has written a lot about GT approaches, has been quoted as suggesting that "a lot of people claim to be doing Grounded Theory studies. But ... a lot of work being done all over the world ... that claims to be theory ... bears no resemblance to theory, Grounded Theory or otherwise" (Cisneros-Puebla, 2004).

Ready for testing?

As Watts recognised, his study was 'exploratory'. This did not prevent the study being published or recognised as significant. Although teachers may not have confidence in the generality of the model of alternative conceptual frameworks presented, the broader finding that the students usually come to class with their own alternative understandings of forces has important implications for teaching this topic.

A full GT study will produce a theoretical account of a situation that is grounded in the data, is saturated, and is suitable for widescale *testing*. So GT can "explain what happened, predict what will happen and interpret what is happening in an area of substantive or formal enquiry" (Glaser, 1978, p. 4). The notion of testing would seem to link GT to 'ERP1' research, so although the methodology of GT is certainly interpretivist, the full procedure can lead to a 'bridge' between the two main approaches to educational research (Taber, 2000a):

> Of course a theory can be tested. Although validated during the actual research process, a theory is not tested in the quantitative sense. This is for another study.
>
> (Strauss & Corbin, 1998, p. 213)

Substantive and general theories

In one of the studies mentioned in Chapter 2, Calissendorff (2006) reports a study into 5 year olds learning to play the violin, where she used a GT approach to data analysis. However, Calissendorff acknowledges that although she has reported what she considers to be a 'substantive theory' of student learning *in her particular focal context*, further theoretical sampling would be needed before it could be developed into a more general GT:

> A substantive theory, based on the study of a small group, does not have the same explanatory scope as a larger, more general theory. For a substantive theory to become formal, it needs to be expanded and compared with other theories.
>
> (Calissendorff, 2006, p. 94)

So, for example, it would be possible to undertake a GT study of a phenomenon such as giftedness within a single school – looking to find out how giftedness was understood, identified, experienced and responded to, etc. by management, teachers, support staff, pupils (considered gifted or not), parents, etc. To make this a GT study, it would be necessary to use ongoing theoretical sampling until any new data was redundant because the data analysis had saturated (where collecting more data did not add anything more to the model being built). The 'substantive' GT would offer an in-depth and nuanced theory for understanding how giftedness was understood *in that school context*. However, it could only be the starting point for a formal theory of giftedness in schools or society more generally.

A grounded study of teacher mind-sets?

Few studies in education claim to follow the full GT procedures, but many do claim to adopt methods from this approach. The extent to which adopting *some tactics* outside the context of a coherent GT *strategy* is advisable has to be judged on a case-by-case basis. Tobin (1990) reported a study of the beliefs and teaching behaviours of two science teachers, and concluded that the teachers held *metaphors* for their roles as teachers that influenced the way they taught:

> Peter's teaching behaviour was influenced by metaphors that he used to conceptualize teaching. Peter described teaching in terms of two metaphors: the teacher as *Entertainer* ... and the teacher as *Captain of the Ship* ... Sandra's teaching was influenced by the metaphor of *Teacher as Resource* ...
>
> (Tobin, 1990, pp. 51, 53)

This fascinating study is reported in great detail in book form (Tobin, Kahle, & Fraser, 1990), and it is only possible to discuss some key points here. Tobin's study was based on his own belief that teachers have significant metaphors for their classroom work:

> An assumption underlying this study was that many of the teachers' beliefs and knowledge about teaching and learning are metaphorical ... metaphors underlie the understandings ascribed to important concepts about teaching and learning.
>
> (Tobin, 1990, p. 35)

> ## Question for reflection
>
> Why might we consider Tobin's assumption that he should look for the metaphors that teachers relied on to guide their role in the classroom as an 'ontological commitment' underpinning his study?

Triangulation: the data collection processes used in Tobin's study

Tobin's study offers an example of research where a range of different data-collection techniques were used (i.e., triangulation) to build up an authentic picture of an educational focus. There was a ten-week period of data collection:

> Participant observer data collecting strategies were employed. These involved observing classrooms, interviewing teachers and students on a daily basis, working with students during class time, obtaining written responses to specific questions, examining student notebooks and test papers and analyzing teacher assessments of student performance.
>
> (Tobin et al., 1990, p. 16)

The research team reported that they took care "to ensure that data were obtained from a variety of sources and that multiple perspectives were represented in the data obtained" (Tobin et al., 1990, p. 17). A precise schedule for collecting data was deliberately not established at the start of the project. Rather, flexibility was retained to allow the researchers to follow up interesting leads:

> As the study progressed, the research team made decisions about the aspects of teaching and learning on which they would focus, the data to be collected and procedures to be adopted in collecting and validating data.
>
> (Tobin et al., 1990, p. 17)

> ## Question for reflection
>
> Tobin does not claim his study developed grounded theory, although there are certainly aspects of the methodology that reflect GT methodology. Can you identify features of the study that (a) do, and (b) do not match such a GT approach?

Can we consider Tobin's study to be GT?

Although GT is a well known and much discussed methodology in the social sciences, it is rare to find published studies about teaching and learning that claim to be GT. In part, this is surely because the approach is very demanding – being unpredictable and open-ended, and requiring a commitment to a time-consuming and rigorous approach to data analysis. Tobin and colleagues' study certainly has several features that reflect a GT approach. The collection of a number of different 'slices of data' is one feature of GT research (although this is not uncommon in interpretive studies, such as case studies). The use of an emergent design – where decisions about data collection are made throughout the study in the light of consideration of the data already collected (i.e., 'theoretical sampling') – is another feature of this approach to research.

However, at least two features of Tobin's study would compromise its consideration as GT. One factor is the limited duration. Although ten weeks of fieldwork is a considerable commitment for a research team, it still seems to represent a predetermined window. In principle, in genuine GT studies there is no predetermined time limit on data collection – this should continue until there is 'theoretical saturation' (see above), that is, until new data is not offering any more refinements of the model being developed. Secondly, GT research is meant to have an open agenda, where the researchers do not enter the field with preformed notions of what they might find. The extent to which this is actually a practical possibility is much discussed, but it is clear in this study that Tobin was *looking for* the metaphors that teachers held of their teaching roles, and *expecting* to find that these influenced teaching behaviour.

Is Tobin's study ethnography?

Tobin and colleagues' study also shares some of the features of ethnographic work. Their period of fieldwork included a good deal of observation, compiling field notes, and collecting the kind of in-depth data that allows insight into another culture. Tobin and his colleagues were keen to try to understand the meanings that Sandra and Peter gave to their work, and to the interactions they entered into in the classroom. Although Tobin's study would probably not be considered as 'an ethnography', the case studies of Sandra and Peter (like many examples of case-study work in education) are certainly built using an approach informed by ethnographic methods.

Action research

Action research (AR) is characterised in terms of purpose: it is "the study of a social situation with a view to improving the quality of action within it" (Elliott, 1991, p. 69). Whereas much research is carried out to satisfy intellectual curiosity – to explore an interesting phenomenon, or answer an intriguing question – *action* research is designed to bring about change in a personally experienced situation. This makes AR a common approach to *practitioner research* in professions such as teaching. There are many professional problems that teachers may attempt to address through AR; for example:

- poor student behaviour
- limited student understanding of a topic
- intimidation and bullying behaviour within a group
- lack of interest in a topic
- poor quality of homework
- not enough student involvement in discussion
- stereotyped gender roles during practical activities.

AR is not characterised by the particular data collection techniques used, but by the attitude to the knowledge developed. AR may well produce reportable new understandings, and these may be applicable elsewhere, but the aim of the research is to solve a problem or improve a situation. Where a solution is found, it will be implemented even if this compromises the collection and analysis of data – if a suspected solution is not helping, it will be abandoned to try something else, even though it may not yet have been rigorously evaluated:

> The fundamental aim of action research is to improve practice rather than to produce knowledge. The production and utilization of knowledge is subordinate to, and conditioned by, this fundamental aim.
>
> (Elliott, 1991, p. 49)

AR involves cycles of trying out ideas, and testing them out in practice. McNiff (1992, p. 38) describes a formulation of the action research cycle:

- I experience a problem when some of my educational values are denied in practice
- I imagine a solution of the problem
- I implement the imagined solution
- I evaluate the outcomes of my actions
- I re-formulate my problem in the light of my evaluation.

Question for reflection

Earlier in the book it was suggested that many research studies need to be understood as contributing to particular research programmes, with each study building upon and seeking to extend those that have already been completed. Is there a case for suggesting that 'an AR study' following the action research cycle might be better seen as a chain of studies within a programme rather than as a single discrete study?

AR is successful if it improves practice, and the researcher needs sufficient evidence on which to base such a judgement. However, action research is highly contextualised, and reports (where reports are produced) may well offer little readily generalised knowledge to inform other practitioners. Indeed, although AR is a common form of research, very few studies in most educational research journals seem to be *presented as being* AR. (Perhaps this is one reason why there are now journals specifically concerned with AR and studies carried out by AR.)

Question for reflection

Can you suggest why few genuine AR studies are published in research journals?

In teaching, we need to make decisions in the classroom based on our current best understanding of what the available evidence suggests, rather than delaying action until there is a watertight case that supports each of the myriad decisions. Imagine if every decision you made in the classroom as a teacher (e.g., to ask a particular question at this moment in time; not to reprimand that student at this point; to make this simplification in explaining this concept to that student...) had to be justified through a formal logical argument, supported by well-documented evidence!

Later in the book it will be suggested that in 'academic' research the researcher needs to demonstrate that findings are rigorously supported by the analysis of systematically collected data, to make a strong case that the conclusions are valid. Although AR seeks an evidence base for effective decision-making, it is used to directly support the actual work of teaching (here, and now) rather than developing formal theoretical frameworks shown to have general application. AR is therefore often concerned with producing good-enough evidence for making quick decisions about the teaching that is ongoing now, rather than seeking to produce abstract knowledge that incrementally develops educational theory. Such AR is not held up to the evidential standards of academic research, but relies on evidence that is 'fit for purpose' – where the purpose is to inform our immediate work in the classroom.

Question for reflection

As AR prioritises informing action rather than developing the evidence base expected in academic research, is it suitable as a basis for a teacher's project that has to be formally reported for a university assignment?

An intervention study on pupil literacy

In a paper in the journal *Educational Studies*, Lyle (1999) makes a claim that working in mixed-ability groups helps pupils develop their literacy. Lyle's paper tells us that the research context was a single primary school that requested the help of education students to support reading in Year 5. Twelve undergraduate students were involved, and each worked with a mixed-ability, mixed-gender group of pupils for one afternoon per week for ten weeks. The pupils were drawn from three school classes, and Lyle outlines the work undertaken (1999, p. 285).

The study was based in a single school. This raises the question of the extent to which this school may be 'typical', and whether the 48 pupils involved in the study can be seen to be representative of children of this age group (9–10 year olds, as referred to in the title of the paper). The context of the study was an intervention. Pupils were taken from the normal class context and worked in specially formed groups with second-year undergraduates on a specially devised scheme. This type of activity is not so unusual in primary schools, but the reader will wonder whether the study findings would translate to groups working with the normal class teacher (in the busy classroom managing many groups at once). Again, this does not negate the value of the study, but it raises questions about the extent to which the research context can be considered similar to other contexts where readers may wish to apply the findings of the research.

Could Lyle's study be considered as collaborative action research?

AR is a very common form of activity in education, as well as in other professional areas (such as health care). In its purest form, AR involves practitioners enquiring into aspects of *their own* professional context that they consider problematic, or capable of being improved. The key impetus of AR is to improve the professional situation, that is, to produce 'knowledge-in-action' to inform the practitioner's own practice. AR often involves interventions, introducing changes, which are then evaluated before being adopted, dropped or, often, modified for further cycles of AR.

Lyle is not acting as an action-researcher in the usual sense. He is not exploring a problem in his own professional practice, and indeed he clearly has a strong academic interest in the topic. However, the study does discuss an intervention that was introduced to address an issue identified in the school. In this sense, we may see this project as a *collaborative* AR study where teachers work with academics to explore an issue of concern to the teachers. When seen in these terms we would expect concern for improving the problematic situation to take precedence over the collection of evidence to make a case for new knowledge in academic terms. If seen in AR terms, then Lyle describes an intervention that does seem to have been very valuable for the literacy development of the *particular* 9–10 year olds.

Promoting self-regulated learning

In a 2004 study, Corrigan and Taylor suggested that the requirements for promoting self-regulated learning (SRL) may include:

- offering students choice regarding learning goals and timeframes
- opportunities to reflect
- a relaxed and supportive environment
- a hands-on, activity-based, fun learning environment
- access to a wide range of resources.

Corrigan and Taylor (2004, p. 49) suggest that SRL is promoted by learning conditions, "where external regulation is minimal" (p. 49), that is, where the conditions of learning are flexible, offer choice, are student-centred, promote active learning, and where learning is project-/problem-based.

> ## Question for reflection
>
> Corrigan and Taylor describe the methodology they chose to use as "a qualitative approach within an interpretivist paradigm" (2004, p. 51). What factors might lead to the researchers making such a methodological choice?

Corrigan and Taylor describe their study as an "exploratory research inquiry" (2004, p. 51), and such exploratory work would tend to be considered to fit within the interpretivist research paradigm (ERP2, see Chapter 3). Corrigan and Taylor suggest that such an approach would be most appropriate because (a) a quantitative approach would be "of limited use" in view of their small sample size, and (b) they "wished to gain an in-depth understanding of the effectiveness of SRL as a pedagogy…" (2004, p. 51).

An in-depth approach is suitable for an exploratory study where it is considered that the existing knowledge about the field is sketchy, or of limited relevance to the context being explored (see Chapter 7). Collecting data in-depth often means working closely with a small number of informants instead of obtaining data from a larger sample. Quantitative methods are indeed of little value in these situations where there is no specific hypothesis to test, and a modest sample size. Presenting the decision-making in this way fits the 'ideal' way of undertaking research, with methodological decisions determined by the type of study being undertaken, which is in turn determined by the way the research conceptualises the field and formulates questions (see Chapter 3).

However, Corrigan and Taylor's wording can also be read to imply that their choice of a qualitative approach was determined by the practical constraint of working with a small sample. Research decisions are often constrained by pragmatic considerations such as this. This is especially the case when *practitioner*-researchers enquire into aspects of their practice, as the research site and potential foci for enquiry are often fixed by the practitioner's institutional and teaching context (see Chapter 5).

Whether this is problematic depends upon the aims of the research. If a teacher wishes to contribute to our general knowledge about an issue, then being restricted to a fixed research context could be a major limitation. However, if a teacher is seeking to address a specific problem in current practice through AR, or to develop a detailed understanding of some features of her own professional context (Why is there such a high level of non-attendance *in our* Year 8 cohort? Why *do my* Year 10 class have such problems in understanding the current topic?) through a case study, then being restricted to a single research site is not a problem, as that location is the only one where the most relevant data can be collected.

Question for reflection

Corrigan and Taylor are working in the context of higher education: to what extent can their study be seen as action research?

Corrigan and Taylor describe their sample as 'purposeful': "6 volunteer participants (5 female and 1 male) … intended to reflect the views of a range of students with different performance levels within the SRL project" (p. 52). In their paper, the authors are quite clear that their focus is "the effectiveness of SRL as a pedagogy for use with pre-service primary teachers" (Corrigan and Taylor, 2004, p. 51), and their data derived from one sample drawn from one cohort of trainee teachers in one institution.

Are the findings from AR context-bound?

Taylor and Corrigan refer to their informants as being *pre-service primary teachers*. It would have been possible to design a multi-site study with a much more robust sample that could allow knowledge claims to be made which derive from a much more diverse group of *pre-service primary teachers*. However, Corrigan and Taylor's decision-making in their research makes more sense if it is considered as an example of action research (AR). Corrigan and Taylor are *practitioners* (in higher education) looking to make improvements in *their* professional work. They had introduced changes to *their* teaching to attempt to encourage stronger SRL in their students, and so the main focus of their research was evaluating that intervention. AR takes place within the problematised context, and seeks understanding for the practitioners involved in that context. AR:

- *empowers* practitioners to develop as teachers, but
- *constrains* research design as data collection is limited to the specific context of the intervention, and must be planned around the opportunities that the intervention allows.

This is something that teacher-researchers need to be aware of when planning their own research studies (see Chapter 8). It is also a theme that will be developed in the next chapter. The problems of reporting action research are considered in Chapter 12. It is also important not to identify teacher research with AR, as although much teacher research is AR, a great deal is not. We might say that it is *a necessary, but not sufficient,* condition of AR that it is carried out by practitioners looking to improve their own professional work. That is, all AR should be practitioner research (or at least research where practitioners are intimately involved in both motivating and planning the research) – but that does not mean that all practitioner research is necessarily AR.

What about research that seems to adopt some other methodology?

As I have suggested throughout the book so far, there is no single, simple way of describing types of educational research that all educational researchers would totally agree with, although the six categories of research strategy described above are widely recognised as key methodologies. However, if you read widely you will find reference to other categories of methodology that some writers use. For example, there are particular approaches called lesson-study and design experiments, which may not seem to sit clearly in any of the categories above. Some authors make a major distinction between what are sometimes called pure and applied studies, and some consider evaluation studies as a category by itself.

The thrust of the argument in this book is that such labels are less important than the principles that inform a research design. So, for example, many evaluation studies look to see how effective some particular educational programme initiative is, and so *could* often be considered to be case studies of that programme or initiative. It is less important that we label a particular enquiry as case study, evaluation study, or some-other-kind-of study than it is we are clear about whether the particular research design adopted makes sense in terms of the purposes of the research, and the (ontological and epistemological) assumptions built into the study.

What about 'mixed-methods' studies?

However, one particular research label that has been increasingly adopted to describe educational research studies in recent years is that of mixed methods (Creswell, 2009; Creswell & Plano Clark, 2007). You are very likely to read studies that are described by their authors as mixed methods, and so it is worth considering what this might mean. Unfortunately, there are least three senses in which the term mixed methods tends to be used:

- A study is described as mixed methods because it uses several different techniques to collect and analyse data – I will label this meaning as MM-T (for techniques).
- A study is described as mixed methods because it collects and analyses both quantitative and qualitative data – I will label this meaning as MM-D (for data).
- A study is described as mixed methods because it includes elements of both main research paradigms (ERP1 and ERP2, see Chapter 3) – I will label this meaning as MM-P (for paradigms).

MM-T: studies that draw upon a range of data collection and analysis techniques

Although studies are sometimes referred to as 'mixed methods' because they use a range of different techniques, this is not an especially helpful label. A survey might be based on the use of one instrument, e.g., a questionnaire, but some methodologies commonly lead to research designs involving the use of multiple methods. So case studies, for example, may commonly include elements of observation, interviewing, document analysis, and perhaps questionnaires. These different techniques are not 'mixed' together, but rather coordinated to (a) respond to different specific research questions or (b) provide triangulation to increase the confidence with which interpretations may be made. Ethnographies, AR and GT all tend to used multiple techniques. Little is to be gained by using the term 'mixed methods' when it is often more informative to describe a study as a case study (for example) than being 'mixed methods'.

MM-D: studies that collect and analyse both qualitative and quantitative data

The distinction between quantitative data and qualitative data is one that is commonly noted when talking about research. Data that derives from measuring or counting items is different in nature from data that describes the nature of phenomena. Quantitative data *seem* more objective (as, surely, any competent observer following the protocol carefully should produce the same measurement or count) whereas qualitative data have to be interpreted through a particular researcher's own conceptual frameworks. There is a clear sense of the two different research paradigms at work here.

However, the careful reader will suspect things are often not really as clear-cut as that. If the quantitative data consists of an observer's tally of the number of times a teacher uses a dialogic technique of referring back to a perspective previously offered by a student in class discussion, then the definitive-looking numbers depend upon both the observer's interpretation of what 'counts' as an instance of using this teaching technique, and their skill at noticing and recording every example in a busy classroom (and their knowledge of the various contributions pupils have previously made in the class). The apparent precision of such data may sometimes be misleading.

Moreover, as was pointed out earlier in the book, the way data *is processed* during analysis is as important as its original form. Many studies that collect qualitative data proceed to fragmenting the data and classifying the deconstructed fragments, and then to counting up the frequency of different types of event (this is discussed further in Chapter 11). Sometimes statistical techniques may then be applied to this secondary quantitative data to test hypotheses. On the other hand, data that is initially collected as frequency counts is sometimes used in largely descriptive ways – to report frequencies, averages, ranges, etc., rather than to test hypotheses. The distinction between qualitative and quantitative data is therefore important, but there is nothing inherently special about studies which collect *both* qualitative and quantitative data. In principle, qualitative, quantitative and mixed-data sets can each be analysed in descriptive, statistical or mixed ways.

MM-P: studies that draw upon elements of contrasting research paradigms

The term 'mixed methods' can have somewhat more significance if it is used to refer to studies that seem to mix up elements of apparently contrasting research paradigms. However, even here we should be careful about what such 'mixing' might mean. The idea that mixed-methods studies draw upon different research traditions might seem to fit with a model in which studies lie on a continuum between those that are very positivistic at one pole, and those that depend very much upon subjective interpretation at the other pole (perhaps as represented in the scheme shown in Figure 4.4).

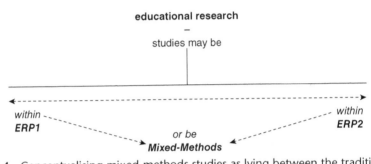

Figure 4.4   Conceptualising mixed-methods studies as lying between the traditional research paradigms

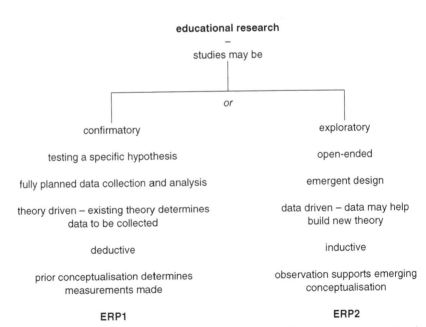

Figure 4.5   Some of the contrasting features of studies in the two main educational research paradigms

This is a seductive idea, but we might wonder what it could mean for a study to be somewhere 'between' positivist and interpretivist (or between nomothetic and idiographic, or between confirmatory and discovery). Figure 4.5 sets out some of the key differences between studies drawing on the two main research traditions.

Figure 4.5 reminds us that the logic of research in the two paradigms is quite different. However, it is useful to bear in mind that a study might address a number of related research questions (RQs) in relation to some topic or issue. It may be that different research questions might draw on different features of current knowledge about a topic: some perhaps linking to aspects where existing knowledge is much more robust than others. These different RQs might well be addressed by different approaches. This need not be incoherent as long as the different parts of the research are underpinned by consistent programmatic assumptions.

Consider a study which had the research questions:

- How often does bullying occur in this class?
- What do students in this class understand bullying to be?

The first (positivist) question assumes there is a clear definition of bullying which would allow bullying incidents to be identified and counted; the second (interpretivist) question assumes that 'bullying' is a socially constructed category given meaning by individuals. If a researcher attempted to simultaneously answer both questions, they would need to recognise that they could not assume that 'bullying' in the two questions was referring to the same thing. (That is, there is a potential confusion in terms of 'ontology', see Chapter 3).

It might make more sense if the research was undertaken in two phases: first, to develop an understanding of what the students understood bullying to be, and then to investigate how common bullying (as students understood it) was. Of course, it is quite likely that different students would construe bullying differently, and the second phase of the research might show that the frequency of bullying incidents in the class would be perceived quite differently by students with different notions of what counts as bullying. Whether we would consider this hypothetical research as a study with two distinct phases, or rather as two related studies, is somewhat arbitrary. (Cynically, we might suspect that if an academic researcher carried out this research, they might be happy to see this as two distinct studies if they felt there was sufficient data for the work to be reported in two publishable research papers.)

Research studies and research programmes

The idea of a research programme was introduced in Chapter 1. A research programme involves an ongoing series of studies building upon one another (see Figure 4.6, which adapts the visual metaphor for a research study met in Chapter 3). The research programme is defined through a 'hard core' of commitments that researchers in that particular tradition share, and an agreed plan for developing understanding in the topic through particular lines of research. The philosopher Imre Lakatos (1970) suggested that theory developed in the programme acted as a 'protective belt', as it was always understood in ways that were consistent with the hard-core assumptions, and could be sacrificed (replaced, modified) to protect those assumptions if the interpretation of new evidence required it. However, the programme was only worth supporting as long as such changes in the theory in the protective belt were seen as progressive (for example, offering better explanatory and predictive power – rather than just constantly patching up the theory in an '*ad hoc*' fashion to fit data already collected).

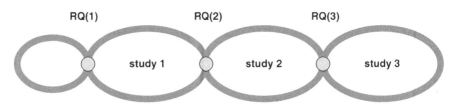

Figure 4.6 Studies may build upon each other in a research programme

The commitments in the hard core of a programme may be ontological commitments to the way some aspect of the world is understood. The developmental psychologist Jean Piaget undertook a large number of studies over many years in a programme he referred to as 'genetic epistemology' (Piaget, 1970/1972). The programme of work assumed some basic general principles about the nature of intellectual development

Piaget's programme assumed that children developed intellectually by passing through a number of stages of development that were domain general and invariant. That is, Piaget thought that any child was at some general level of development that determined the sophistication of their thinking across any subject area or topic. Piaget also believed that every person passed through these general stages in the same (i.e., invariant) order. This latter belief was tied to a model of how development proceeded, which saw each developmental level as enabling the child to interact with its environment, and to makes sense of that interaction in particular ways that provided the resources needed to begin shifting to the next stage of development. So a fully developed adult is capable of 'formal operations' that allow us to mentipulate ideas and symbols in the mind, so supporting abstract thought. However, according to Piaget, that is only possible because the individual has constructed the structures for thinking in that way through earlier experiences of simpler 'operations'. Piaget's model is said to be constructivist, and has been influential in informing constructivist ideas about learning that were met in Chapter 2.

Piaget developed his methodology and his theory over many years. His original methodology was based on naturalistic observation – following young children around the school to eavesdrop on their conversations (Piaget, 1959/2002). However, that proved to be an inefficient way to collect the kind of data that was needed, and Piaget developed an alternative approach, called the clinical interview, where children would be asked a sequence of prepared questions about particular topics. Piaget developed his theory to refine his model of stages (introducing and characterising sub-stages). He also introduced various auxiliary ideas.

One of these, called 'horizontal décalage', was needed to explain why it was that often children seem able to operate with more advanced thinking in some topics than others (something that seemed to threaten the hard-core assumption). Horizontal décalage protects the assumption of students having specific intellectual levels by considering that the level refers to a potential sophistication of thinking, which can only be applied (and so observed) in a particular domain or problem situation once the child is familiar enough with the content of that domain or problem. Piaget's ideas became very influential, so many other researchers around the world adopted his ideas, accepted his basic hard core premises, and undertook research within the Piagetian programme (Modgil, 1974). There is still much work continuing today in this tradition.

We might consider that action research (AR) is like a programme of research directed at a particular issue or problem. Each cycle of AR is like a single research study in a programme of research. Sometimes we can think of 'mixed-methods' studies that address related questions by different approaches in the same way: what is presented in a research report as a single study may include questions that are actually tackled sequentially, so what was found in an early phase of the study (using one methodology) was then followed up in later phases (using a different methodology). Ultimately, it does not matter if we consider this one study or several, nor whether we accept or reject the label 'mixed methods', as long as the research report explains the different parts of the research clearly, and justifies the design of the different aspects of the research.

Evaluating a classroom simulation using 'mixed methods'

Many readers will have come across simulators that allow people to learn to drive cars, or to fly aircraft, without the potentially serious risks of making mistakes in the real situation. Perhaps readers might think it would be a great idea for someone to devise a simulated class, where we can develop our teaching prowess without worrying too much about getting things wrong. Well, in a paper reported in the journal *Educational Media International*, Mahon, Bryant, Brown, and Kim (2010) reported a study of an attempt to use just such a simulation. They explain that their paper "discusses an educational simulation ... to assist pre-service teachers (PSTs) in gaining more experience managing student behaviour" (p. 121). This study was informed by the research questions: "Can a computer-simulated classroom provide an authentic environment for the learning of strategic decision-making in regard to classroom management for teacher candidates?" (p. 128).

The following extract from their result section gives a flavour of their findings:

> The majority found it to be a creative and intriguing approach to studying classroom management. For example, one PST responded, "I thought it was interesting and a great way to practice teaching strategies in a controlled setting." Other PSTs saw it as a way to introduce classroom management, calling it "eye-opening".

Another stated, "It gave me an idea of how to control a classroom and how an entire class can be affected by not knowing what strategies to use."

There were generally two themes relating to negative comments and recommendations for improvements. Either PSTs had problems with the structure of the simulation experience, or they took issue with the technology. For example, they commented that there needed to be more structure to the running of the simulation itself and more practice with the system prior to playing. Others disliked the fact that only the teacher could use the voice chat, while one commented, "The system seems too clunky to be able to react the way I would in real life."

Although some PSTs found the simulation too chaotic to enhance their learning, the majority of students did report that they learned something about classroom management techniques from the experience. These comments generally fell under the themes of observations of inappropriate management techniques and ideas for improving techniques.

(Mahon et al., 2010, p.129)

Question for reflection

Given the study's research question, and the nature of the findings, what type(s) of methodology do you feel might have been used in Mahon et al.'s study?

The authors report that their study participants were 20 undergraduate pre-service teachers and that they used "a mixed method". The authors also refer to their study as an experiment: "the experiment was designed to simulate a testing situation. The PSTs participating in the experiment were seated together in a small computer lab" (Mahon et al., 2010, p. 127). Readers are informed that "data sources included instructor/facilitator notes and observations" and "a questionnaire designed to capture student assessment of the simulation [that] included both open-ended items [and] Likert rating scales" (p. 128). So, for example, students were asked to rate the simulation as a tool for helping them think about classroom management issues on a 5-point scale (where 1 indicated 'poor' and 5 indicated 'excellent').

When reporting the methodology used in a study it is important to be clear about how data is analysed, as well as how it is collected. In this study, the authors report that "the majority of data was analyzed using constant comparative thematic coding appropriate to the qualitative method" (p. 129), that is the kind of analysis used in GT studies (as discussed earlier in the chapter). The data from the Likert scales were in the form of ratings on a numerical scale, and for these particular questionnaire items "mean responses were calculated" (p. 129), that is, an average value was found on each of these items from the ratings of the 16 students who returned the questionnaires. (Averaging Likert scale points in this way is only strictly valid if those responding considered the numerical points to be equally spaced out on a scale.)

In their published report, Mahon and colleagues do not state the actual mean values they obtain on particular items, but rather offer a narrative results section (part of which is quoted above). This seems to be constructed from three types of element. There are statements which tell us what proportions of the respondents reported: "The majority found it to be a creative and intriguing approach to studying classroom management ... the majority of students did report that they learned something about classroom management techniques from the experience" (p. 129). These types of statement seem likely to derive from the Likert items where most of the students rated the simulation at points 4 or 5 against particular criteria.

A second type of statement talks about themes in the data: "There were generally two themes relating to negative comments and recommendations for improvements. ... These comments generally fell under the themes of observations of inappropriate management techniques and ideas for improving techniques..." (p. 129). These findings likely derive from the thematic analysis, where student comments to items were grouped together into statements that were interpreted by the researchers as making similar points. Finally, these general statements about typical evaluations and common themes are supported by quoting specific examples from the data-set to illustrate categories of response.

In effect, this study is an evaluation of an education innovation used in initial teacher education. The authors themselves call it an experiment, but it is hard to see how this label is appropriate, given that there was no explicit hypothesis being tested, and the simulation was not being judged against any kind of comparison. Indeed, there was no attempt to measure how well the PST managed behaviour in the simulation, nor whether their actual classroom management skills were either improved after using the simulation compared to before the simulation, or in some way better than those of a comparison group of PSTs who had not used the simulation. Such loose use of terms such as 'experiment' is not helpful to those who read research reports, and reminds us that it is important to make our own judgements about the nature of the studies we read about.

The paper appears to report one group of students using one simulation on one occasion in one particular teacher training context. There is no attempt to persuade us that these students are typical of those in initial teacher education programmes generally, nor that the conditions in which they used the simulation are likely to be typical of how such innovations might be applied in other institutions. It is not described by the authors as being a case study, but it would seem to be one: we find out about what happened in one particular case of the use of a simulation to help new teachers think about behaviour management issues. Case studies often draw on a range of data sources, although the results section of the paper seems to draw largely on the questionnaire.

The student questionnaire in this study collected both qualitative data (in the form of freely composed text) and quantitative data (in the form of numerical ratings). However, the numerical data is not subjected to any kind of statistical tests, as would be the case in a so-called 'quantitative' study. For example, if a matched group of students had completed a parallel questionnaire after having experienced a more traditional form of behaviour management input (perhaps a lecture with some illustrative video material, followed by workshops including student role-play), then it might have been possible to process the ratings on the two sets of Likert items to test specific hypotheses. For example, a hypothesis might have been: *Students in the simulation group will rate the usefulness of the input in helping them think about classroom management issues more highly than those in the lecture/workshop group.*

If statistical analysis had shown significantly higher ratings in the simulation group, then the hypothesis would be supported (and the study could sensibly have been considered an experiment). However, Mahon et al. only report having undertaken descriptive analysis on the numerical data and so their study seems to be fairly typical of many ERP2 studies that explore a particular instance of something and offer a detailed descriptive account of what was found out. In summary, then, Mahon and colleagues describe their study as an experiment (which it is not) and as using mixed methods (which is not very informative), but it might better be characterised as a case study to evaluate one instance of teaching and learning through a simulation.

Using mixed methods to get a picture of the working lives of school principals

A rather different study name checking 'mixed methods' was reported in the *Journal of Curriculum Studies* by Spillane and Hunt (2010). These authors state their aim as "to describe the work of US school principals, identifying both dominant patterns and differences across principals in one mid-sized urban district" (p. 295), and describe their study as "a mixed methods descriptive analysis". This is rather a complex study, and the brief account here necessarily ignores a great deal of interesting detail.

The study was located in "a mid-sized urban school district in the south-eastern US" and "data collection involved 52 principals and 2400 school personnel. Of the 52 schools there were 30 elementary schools, eleven middle schools, seven high schools, and four alternative/special education schools" (p. 296). The study used a range of data sources:

- 'experience sampling logs' (where principals would be prompted to complete a survey about their current activities at 'random' times they were not forewarned of)
- a questionnaire completed by school principals
- a questionnaire completed by school staff managed by the principals
- observations of some principals
- interviews with some principals.

The logs and questionnaires contained closed items that provided data suitable for statistical analysis. The researchers used an approach called cluster analysis that takes advantage of the processing power of modern computers to look for similarities across the patterns of responses relating to different principals. In this study, the cluster analysis identified three 'clusters' of school principals. So an advanced quantitative analytical technique was used to suggest that the different principals could, as a simplification, be considered to be members of three distinct groups. The different clusters were given suitable descriptive labels:

- 'administration-oriented'
- 'solo practitioners'
- 'people-centred practitioners.

However, in the next stage of the study, a rather different approach to analysing data was used. First, three principals were selected for more detailed attention, one from each of the clusters identified in the previous analysis. Then:

> A grounded-theory approach was employed: we read and re-read observation notes and interviews identifying themes and patterns. Once we settled on particular themes, we re-read our interviews and observations and used survey and log data to triangulate and search for disconfirming evidence.
>
> (Spillane & Hunt, 2010, p. 300)

So once statistical methods had been used to identify clusters of principals, the focus shifted to three individuals who were used to construct what were in effect case studies, drawing upon multiple data sources, and using analytical techniques typical of interpretive ('qualitative') studies. So, in this paper, quantitative survey data is analysed statistically, and then a principled selection of the qualitative data (relating to three individual principals) is analysed thematically.

The results reported in the paper are of two distinct types. So we are told, drawing on quantitative data, that "the 20 principals in the 'administration-oriented' group spend the bulk of their time (nearly 70%) managing personnel, budgets, resources, students, the campus, and schedules. These principals spend much less time (20%) on curriculum and instruction and the bulk of this time (16%) was devoted to reviewing student classroom work, data, and standardized testing" (p. 304). But we are also presented with detailed narrative accounts of the work of the principals exemplifying the different clusters. So in the case of the principal from the administration-oriented cluster, Mr Smith, who held "an administrative certificate and a Master's degree" and had "eight years of teaching experience" (p. 305), we are told that:

> Mr Smith's classroom visits tend to be brief and involve minimal interaction with teachers. ... Mr Smith's classroom visits involve brief exchanges, especially with students. Indeed, students and their work appear to be at the heart of Mr Smith's approach to leading and managing instruction. ... Mr Smith's focus on student achievement is not confined to his classroom visits. A key focus of his efforts as principal involves identifying students who are not performing well and intervening to ensure they succeed.
>
> (Spillane & Hunt, 2010, pp. 306–307)

We might choose to conceptualise this research as two linked studies: the first identifying 'types' of school principal, and quantifying aspects of their use of their time etc., followed by a second study which built case studies as exemplars of each type (and which was only possible once the cluster analysis had identified the basic groupings). However, we can also appreciate the logic of combining the different types of analysis in the same research report where the survey and case studies offer complementary data offering a fuller overall picture of the work of school principals in this particular educational context.

My own 'bias', as may be clear from my comments earlier in the chapter, is to be suspicious of the description of mixed methods, as it often seems to stand in place of a thorough consideration of methodological issues informing research. However, whereas our biases may often be quite reasonable in the light of our past experiences, we should avoid prejudice: for example, we should not prejudge research before we have carefully considered it. I might not have chosen to describe Spillane and Hunt's work as 'mixed methods', but they do, and they report research that encompasses the use of quantitative and qualitative methods, informed by different paradigmatic commitments, and show effectively that careful combining of methodologies can be both principled and informative.

——— Further reading ———

Some useful follow-up readings on the main strategies used in educational research are listed below. Both Stake and Yin have written authoritatively on case-study approaches. Robson's book is quite old now, but still very useful for anyone new to thinking about using statistics in their research. The Glaser and Strauss book is the classic text on grounded theory, and although much has been written since, is a fascinating account of the processes 'discovered' by the originators of the methodology. (My chapter in the Wilson book is a much simpler overview of GT methodology and a useful place to start reading about GT, but I would recommend Glaser and Strauss to get a real feel for what is involved.) There are many books about action research, and they often seem to offer quite different views of what AR is/should be, but McNiff and Whitehead bring the authority of having been involved in working with practitioners undertaking AR over many years. The article from *Teacher Development* is a review article, which is critical of the notion of mixed methods as championed by Creswell in his influential book on research design. I suggest that if you read the review article, you should also take a look at the book to make up your own mind (and perhaps if you decide to read the book, you should also read the review article).

Creswell, J. W. (2009). *Research Design: Qualitative, Quantitative, and Mixed Methods Approaches* (3rd edn). Thousand Oaks, California: Sage.

Glaser, B. G., & Strauss, A. L. (1967). *The Discovery of Grounded Theory: Strategies for Qualitative Research*. New York: Aldine de Gruyter.

Hammersley, M., & Atkinson, P. (2007). *Ethnography: Principles in Practice* (3rd edn). London: Routledge.

McNiff, J., & Whitehead, J. (2009). *Doing and Writing Action Research*. Los Angeles: Sage.

Robson, C. (1994). *Experiment, Design and Statistics in Psychology* (3rd Revised edn). London: Penguin Books.

Stake, R. E. (1995). *The Art of Case Study Research*. Thousand Oaks, California: Sage.

Taber, K. S. (2009). Building theory from data: Grounded theory. In E. Wilson (Ed.), *School-based Research: A Guide for Education Students* (pp. 216–229). London Sage.

Taber, K. S. (2012). Prioritising paradigms, mixing methods, and characterising the 'qualitative' in educational research. *Teacher Development, 16*(1), 125–138. doi: 10.1080/13664530.2012.674294

Yin, R. K. (Ed.) (2004). *The Case Study Anthology*. Thousand Oaks, California: Sage.

5

How can teachers research their own classrooms?

This chapter:

- explores the specific nature of teacher research, and in particular of research that is directed at addressing issues and problems within a specific professional context
- considers the kinds of foci most suitable for classroom research projects
- considers the kinds of constraints that need to be considered when selecting a research strategy, and discusses the extent to which common methodologies are suitable for small-scale teacher research
- considers some examples of case studies carried out by new teacher-researchers as part of their initial teacher training course
- explores some limitations of action research as a potential methodology for classroom research, and considers how these could be addressed.

In this chapter the focus is on research carried out by teachers in their own classrooms, relating to their own teaching, and the learning of their students. However, the chapter begins with a brief consideration of what I label two modes of research.

Two research modes

It is helpful to think about two modes of educational research that have somewhat different priorities and purposes. Both modes involve the collection of research data in particular contexts, to answer questions and develop new understandings. The distinction is based upon *the relationship between the research context and the aims of the research*.

Theory-directed research

Much research carried out by professional researchers, such as university academics, is primarily driven by a desire to develop new *generalisable* knowledge about some aspect of the world. We might call this research 'theory-directed', as the primary purpose is to construct, test or develop theoretical knowledge that deals with abstract concepts and categories. To be useful educational research, this work must clearly be seen as applicable to real teaching and learning contexts; but it is framed in terms of general ideas that can be related to a wide range of contexts (even when the research is reporting from one specific case). Most of the examples of research studies already referred to in this book can be considered to fall into this category.

Question for reflection

Consider the various studies referred to in Chapter 2, illustrating the range of education research. (a) To what extent would you assume the findings are likely to be relevant well beyond the specific contexts where data was collected? (b) What features of the way a report is presented are likely to help persuade you that its findings are likely to apply beyond the specific learners, classrooms, teacher, and/or schools sampled?

Researchers undertaking theory-directed research will usually collect data from particular contexts and informants that they hope can to some extent 'stand for' general categories of activities, episodes, people or institutions. So the research may be about French lessons, or primary children's handwriting skills, or attitudes of physics teachers towards students who appear maths-phobic … or whatever. In order to carry out the research the researchers will need to identify and negotiate access to specific research sites (e.g., particular schools and classrooms) and observe and talk to particular people (such as teachers, learners, school managers, parents, etc.) identified in the hope that this will allow them to construct general knowledge about 'French lessons', or 'primary learners', or 'physics teachers' (or whatever) *in general*.

In this type of research, the collection and analysis of data inevitably provides knowledge of the specific contexts and participants, but this is not the prime purpose of the research, which is to abstract generalised knowledge that applies *to the categories of* event, person or institution. Clearly, in this mode of research the typicality or representativeness of the contexts and informants sampled is of major importance (see the discussion of sampling in Chapter 4), and questions of the generalisability of the findings from the specific data collected are paramount. Even a case study that explores a particular instance considered to be special in some way, and so of particular interest in its own terms (i.e., an idiographic study, see Chapter 3), may be undertaken in a theory-directed mode (e.g., finding out what is so effective about some teachers may produce results of application in helping *other* teachers improve their practice). Theory-directed research is represented in Figure 5.1.

The key feature of theory-directed research, as represented in Figure 5.1, is that the starting and end points of the research are located in the domain of abstract ideas: the problem is framed in general terms, and the results are interpreted in terms of those general ideas, even though the empirical work of collecting data necessarily involves particular participants (learners, teachers, school managers, parents, etc.). Such theory-directed research is often undertaken by full-time students carrying out an empirical research study as part of their course, or by academics who have a particular interest in a research topic. Such research may also be sponsored by funders (e.g., governments, charities, commercial organisations) to inform policy development and practice in education.

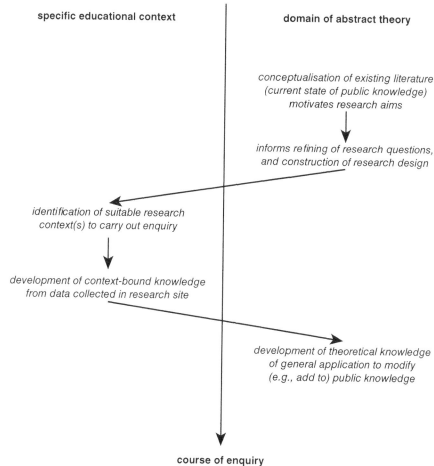

specific educational context

domain of abstract theory

*conceptualisation of existing literature
(current state of public knowledge)
motivates research aims*

*informs refining of research questions,
and construction of research design*

*identification of suitable research
context(s) to carry out enquiry*

*development of context-bound knowledge
from data collected in research site*

*development of theoretical knowledge
of general application to modify
(e.g., add to) public knowledge*

course of enquiry

Figure 5.1   The nature of theory-directed research

However, there is no reason why teachers cannot be motivated to undertake classroom research because *they* are interested in a theoretical issue, or believe there are gaps in the research literature. In practice, teachers are usually restricted to exploring those issues suited to the context(s) where they already have access (an issue considered below). So it would make little sense for an early-years teacher to decide to undertake theory-directed research into the reasons why some students drop out of courses in higher education, or for a teacher in a highly selective school to decide to explore the role of teaching style in successful mixed-ability teaching.

For trainee teachers on placement in schools, in the process of meeting and considering a wide range of new educational ideas, it may be very sensible to base a classroom research project around some theoretical idea or question from their university classes or reading that particularly intrigues them. One such trainee teacher explained the motivation behind her classroom enquiry:

> The concept of personal epistemology, or what individuals know about knowing, is an increasingly significant field within educational psychology. There is, however, little research focused on the epistemological beliefs of primary school

children. I intend to focus on the area of personal epistemology in order to answer my research questions:

1   How do children define knowledge?

2   What do children perceive to be reliable sources of knowledge?

3   How do children believe the knowledge they need for their future development can be acquired?

                                                                    (Dawe, 2012, p. 32)

So Dawe's research questions are not about the specific children she was working with on professional placement in school, even though they were her study participants, but are clearly framed as about 'children' more generally. Although, as will be discussed later in this chapter, the constraints on small-scale projects such as Dawe's inevitably limit what can be achieved, Dawe published her research report, thus allowing her to make a modest contribution to scholarship in what she considered an under-researched area.

Context-directed research

As we have seen, there is nothing, in principle, to stop teachers undertaking theory-directed research, although in practice few full-time teachers are in a position to identify and spend time in suitable research sites outside their own immediate professional context, so are often restricted to exploring questions that can be addressed in their own institutions. Understandably, it is more common for teacher-researchers to be *motivated by* a particular issue, or perhaps a perceived problem, relating to their own practice or professional setting. The teacher may be less interested in the mechanisms of learning than in helping (her or his) students to learn, or less concerned with the causes of behavioural problems than with ensuring orderly lessons, for example. This does not mean that the teacher is not interested in developing understanding, but usually the primary concern is doing a good job, and any new understandings developed are most valued when they can inform practice: to bring about higher levels of learning or to overcome rowdy behaviour or meet some other professional goal. Indeed, given a choice between finding a better way of achieving a teaching goal or overcoming a problem in professional practice, or instead developing a better understanding of the underlying issues, the teacher-researcher will often be more concerned with the practical outcomes than the underlying theory.

Now, the research carried out in a particular context because we are interested in effecting changes in *that* context is not necessarily different in its form from research that is theory-directed. Sometimes the only difference might be that the research site has not been selected on the basis of its representativeness of other comparable contexts. So it is quite possible that careful context-directed research could, in principle, offer insights to develop general theoretical knowledge, but this is not its prime purpose, and so it is not primarily judged in those terms. Context-directed research is represented in Figure 5.2, where a dashed line is used to show

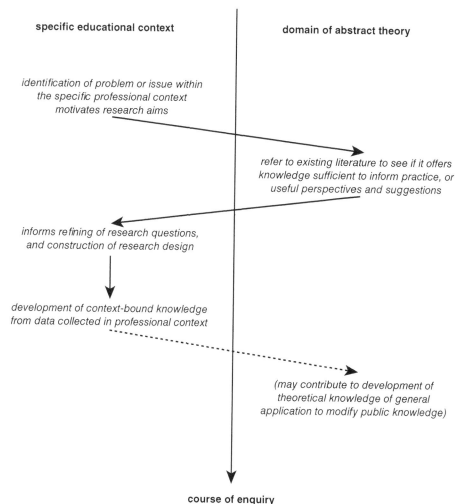

specific educational context   **domain of abstract theory**

identification of problem or issue within the specific professional context motivates research aims

refer to existing literature to see if it offers knowledge sufficient to inform practice, or useful perspectives and suggestions

informs refining of research questions, and construction of research design

development of context-bound knowledge from data collected in professional context

(may contribute to development of theoretical knowledge of general application to modify public knowledge)

course of enquiry

Figure 5.2   The nature of context-directed research

that although such research may contribute to the development of general theory, this is not always the case.

The key feature of context-directed research, as represented in Figure 5.2, is that the motivation for the research derives from something specific in the professional context, and the research is successful if context-bound knowledge is developed which can better inform future action in that context (regardless of whether or not findings are seen to be generalisable to other contexts elsewhere).

It is just a model

In Chapter 2, I suggested that it is useful to think of there being two education research paradigms, reflecting two general ways of thinking about educational enquiry. I also pointed out that this was a gross simplification, but might have some pedagogic value as a model to help think about the many different ways research is described. I am doing something similar here. There is not an absolute distinction between theory-directed and context-directed research, and it is quite possible to find studies which seem to be hybrids, or something in between these two types of research. However, just as the two-paradigms model can be useful, so can this model of two research modes. So Table 5.1 sets out a simple comparison between these two modes of research, summarising some of the key differences between them.

Table 5.1 Comparing two modes of research

Mode of research	Theory-directed	Context-directed
Motivation for research	Limitations of current theoretical knowledge	Scope for improving aspects of the professional context
Priority	Generating abstract generalisations to inform theory	Generating local knowledge to improve work within the professional context
Incidental	Understanding the specific research sites selected for data collection	Possibly generating insights that may be worth testing for wider relevance
Judged by	New contributions to theoretical knowledge	Potential to improve professional context/practice

Questions for reflection

Do you think this model of theory-directed vs. context-directed research applies to students undertaking educational research as part of a university course? Which research mode – theory-directed or context-directed – is likely to be the basis for classroom research undertaken by full-time university students in initial teacher education whilst they are on professional placements in school? What about the teacher registered for a part-time research degree, undertaking classroom research for their thesis?

Is research designed to solve problems and improve practice always context-directed?

Making a distinction between context-directed and theory-directed research might suggest that theory-directed research is only about ideas, and is not motivated by practical problems. This is not so. Educational research is about teaching and learning, and the institutions and contexts in which teaching and learning occur, and is very much concerned with the problems faced by teachers and learners in real classroom and other educational settings. The feature that characterises theory-directed research is its concern to develop general ways of discussing and thinking about aspects of teaching and learning, so that what is learned in one context can best inform what is going on elsewhere. It is in the nature of academic research, in whatever field, that it seeks to transcend the specific. Even if the research is about a specific case, it is approached and reported in ways such that it can potentially be valuable in understanding other cases.

Question for reflection

Consider a busy teacher who wishes to address some issue or problem that has been identified in their practice. They feel they have limited time for reading research literature, and cannot prioritise time for writing up any formal account of their research. In these circumstances, any research undertaken to address the teacher's concerns is likely to be context-directed. Whilst this is understandable, do you think there might be any arguments that the teacher should consider working in a theory-directed mode instead?

Is context-directed research theory-free?

Figure 5.2 suggests that even in context-directed research the teacher-researcher will engage with theories discussed in the educational literature. After all, issues and problems arising in the local context are likely to have strong similarities to those found elsewhere, even if the precise nexus of circumstances surrounding the specific concern is unique. It clearly could be of value for this teacher to do some reading into what has been tried elsewhere, and what seems to have been successful in similar situations.

Moreover, even if what is sought is personal knowledge about how to improve practice here and now, it is clearly sensible to learn enough from addressing the present problem to be in a better position to solve similar problems if they arise with other classes, or after moving to work in a different school. This is going to require some *personal* theorising about the current situation to be able to abstract from it any general principles that might be applied in the future. Such personal theorising does not need to reflect how ideas are commonly described and understood in scholarly literature. However, if colleagues are facing much the same problem in their classes, as will often be the case, it will be valuable to have a common way of talking about the issues, and the existing literature may provide this.

In effect, then, context-directed research can be very similar to theory-directed research, with two major exceptions:

- In context-directed research the identified issue or problem in the local practice is the starting point for and target of the research
- In context-based research there is no expectation to formally report outcomes and relate them to existing research literature.

I have focused on this distinction at some length because, whilst much teacher research is context-directed and fits these characteristics, the research that is undertaken by student teachers, or teachers registered for higher degrees, *is often subject to formal requirements to report outcomes and relate them to existing research literature*, even when the enquiry is motivated by issues or problems in practice.

━━━ Suitable foci for classroom research ━━━

Teachers often take up research as a response to an issue or problem they have identified in practice. They wish to solve the problem, or address the issue, and so set out (a) to find out more about the issue, and/or (b) to make modifications to practice that may improve matters. In this situation, the research foci suggest themselves, as they are the starting point for undertaking the research. However, teachers may also decide to undertake classroom research for professional development reasons, to develop their insight and skill in classroom work and perhaps to demonstrate capabilities whilst working towards recognised qualifications. In the context where the fully professional classroom teacher is expected to be research-informed, and capable of undertaking systematic enquiry into practice (see Chapter 1), acquiring research skills is important. Undertaking a small-scale classroom research project is often the focus of a higher degree in education, and initial teacher education courses often include assignments based upon some small-scale classroom enquiry. In these contexts, the teacher needs to identify a suitable focus for classroom enquiry.

The *Journal of Trainee Teacher Educational Research (JoTTER)* was set up as a web-based journal to offer examples of the kinds of classroom studies that can be carried out by trainee teachers on professional placements in schools – for example, as part of the one-year Post-Graduate Certificate in Education (PGCE). The journal offers examples from the initial teacher education partnership based at the University of Cambridge in England (Taber, 2010c), which illustrates something of the range of topics tackled by graduate trainee teachers working in schools. Table 5.2 reports the foci of empirical studies reported in *JoTTER* (all of these research reports are available freely to anyone with internet access from http://jotter.educ.cam.ac.uk/). It is clear from Table 5.2 that even beginning teachers are able to enquire into a wide range of research foci, in different curriculum areas, and with pupils of different ages.

Table 5.2 A range of contexts for classroom research undertaken by trainee teachers taking a Post-Graduate Certificate in Education course

Learner context	Curriculum context	Focus of study
5–6 year olds & 10–11 year olds	Primary school	Pupils' teacher gender preference (Lang, 2012)
6–7 year olds	Behaviour management	Use of sign language with hearing children (Mottley, 2012)
6–7 year olds & 10–11 year olds	Modern foreign languages	Pupil perspectives on learning a new language (Whitwood, 2012)
7–8 year olds	Handwriting	Left-handedness (Hayes, 2011)
7–8 year olds	Study skills	Pupil perceptions of knowledge and learning (Dawe, 2012)
9–11 year olds	Study skills	Pupil perceptions of intelligence (R. Smith, 2012)
10–11 year olds	Collective worship	Pupil perceptions of purpose and value of collective worship (Rutherford, 2012)
11–12 year olds	French	Pupil use of target language (Morgan, 2010)
11–12 year olds	Science	Group work and peer assessment (Armsby, 2011)
12–13 year olds	Spanish	Impact of an exchange trip (Forbes, 2010)
12–13 year olds	Religious studies	Gender grouping and discussion work (Dowley, 2012)
13–14 year olds	English	Students' creative story-telling (Greaves, 2010)
13–14 year olds	French	A videoconferencing project (Michell, 2011)
13–14 year olds	German	Self/peer assessment (Turner, 2010)

Learner context	Curriculum context	Focus of study
13–14 year olds	Literature	Learning about a novel (Healy, 2010)
13–14 year olds	Music	Differentiation for students who are extra-curricular musicians (Walsh, 2012)
14–15 year olds	Mathematics	Conceptions of mathematical proof (Payne, 2012)
15–16 year olds	Latin	Foci of teacher assessment (A. Smith, 2010)
15–16 year olds	Science	Teaching about 'how science works' (Dry, 2010)
16–17 year olds	Geography	The role of fieldwork in learning about rivers (Mutton, 2010)
16–17 year olds	Geography	Teaching through 'active learning' techniques (Hicks, 2010)
16–17 year olds	Religious studies	Use of 'evidence sheets' (Yevsiyevich, 2011)

Teachers-in-training undertaking initial teacher education courses in university are in an unusual position. Technically, they are still students rather than teachers, and will be expected by their university tutors to be engaging with theoretical issues met during their university courses. However, when placed in schools they become members of school staff (and in secondary school, teaching departments), being expected to take on the professional role of a beginning teacher – with due concern for the learning and welfare of the particular classes and students assigned to them. It was suggested above that university researchers are often motivated to undertake theory-directed research and then select research sites where this can be carried out, whereas the teacher-researcher is most often motivated to undertake research by some aspect of the professional context, and draws on theoretical ideas as metaphorical lenses to investigate that context.

The trainee teacher expected to carry out a classroom enquiry as part of their teacher education course would seem to have 'a foot in both camps', as both an academic scholar expected to engage with the theoretical background to educational work, and as a classroom teacher expected to focus on the teaching and learning in their own classes. This suggests that their classroom research could be either theory-directed or context-directed, and could include elements of both as the trainee teacher seeks to demonstrate how research informed by some of the various theoretical ideas met at the university can support their classroom work. We can find examples of these features in the studies reported in *JoTTER*. So, for example, Hicks (2010) reported research into how "active learning can be incorporated into A-level geography teaching" (p. 153). This work was motivated by an issue he identified in relation to a class of 16–17 year olds he was assigned to teach:

> As part of my placement I took over an AS-level class of nineteen students. ... In the last examined topic in the January grades ranged from [the top grade available] to unclassified. Several members of the group failed to attain their predicted grade. Issues had existed over the behaviour of some members of the class during lesson time.
>
> (Hicks, 2010, p. 155)

Here, Hicks' starting point is an issue in practice, and that motivates an exploration of existing literature for ideas about he might respond to this issue in his teaching.

Yet, another trainee teacher working with the same age group and subject presents his work rather differently, starting from an interest in an aspect of subject teaching: "fieldwork is seen as synonymous with geography and is connected with the subject more strongly that it is with others, like history or science" (Mutton, 2010, p. 84). Where Hicks starts from an issue arising in the context of his teaching, Mutton sets out the aim of his study as about a general issue of importance in subject teaching – which will be explored in a particular context where he has access to a suitable group of potential study participants: "in this assignment I am going to investigate the effectiveness of fieldwork as a teaching and learning method, looking specifically at rivers in the context of a group of Year 12 students who participated in a four-day residential fieldtrip to Derbyshire" (Mutton, 2010, pp. 84–85).

In a sense, Mutton has, by framing his work as theory-directed, set himself a different type of success criterion than Hicks with his more context-directed aims. Where Hicks needs to show that his study can inform his teaching of the target group, Mutton is seeking knowledge that can be abstracted from his research context to make claims about a general issue of teaching and learning in his subject. Of course, as Hicks and Mutton were novice educational researchers undertaking their research as teachers-in-training, we might feel their projects should be judged successful if:

1 They learnt something from their enquiries to inform their work with other classes they would meet later in their teaching careers.
2 They acquired confidence and skills that would encourage them to adopt a research-based approach to future problems and issues they might meet in their classroom work.

However, by reporting their work systematically, and making it publicly available in *JoTTER*, it also has the potential to inform the work of other teachers, trainees and students.

———— Considerations informing a choice of research strategy ————

The previous chapter introduced the range of research strategies (methodologies) that are commonly adopted by educational researchers in their work. This raises a key issue for classroom teachers who may wish to undertake research into their own teaching contexts: which strategies are most suitable for use by the classroom teacher?

The answer suggested in this chapter is two-fold. First, it is important to note that the choice of a research strategy should be informed by the same range of considerations regardless of whether the researcher is a classroom teacher who sees enquiry as part of being a fully professional teacher or an academic researcher employed primarily to undertake research. In both cases, there is a logic that must be followed to ensure that the research we carry out has a reasonable chance of providing useful information that can inform educational practice (whether directly or through contributing to the wider literature). That logic was represented in Chapter 3 (see Figure 3.4) and will be discussed in more detail in the final section of the book (see Chapter 8 on 'Teachers planning research'). However, it is also the case that all research projects are constrained by limited resources that restrict what it might be possible to achieve. Key resources might include:

- Timescale – when we need the research done;
- Personnel – the people-hours available to do the work;
- Access – permission to work with and be informed by those who can provide the information we need;
- Equipment and materials – to support the collection and analysis of data;
- Skills – the necessary research skills to effectively apply particular data collection and analysis techniques;
- Dissemination opportunities.

Anyone undertaking research needs to think very carefully about both of these sets of considerations – research coherence and resource constraints. A poor choice of research strategy that does not match the research questions can invalidate research, whilst an overly ambitious research plan that cannot be properly resourced is unlikely to get much beyond the planning stage.

Question for reflection

If you are planning your own classroom-based study, consider which of these resources (listed above) might be sufficiently limited to put serious constraints on what it may be possible for you to achieve.

For a classroom teacher, resources for carrying out research are likely to put severe restrictions upon opportunities for undertaking some types of enquiry. However, there is much that can be achieved by teacher-researchers who are realistic about the resources available to support their classroom enquiries.

Timescale

The timescale for a research study is the overall duration from inception to presenting results. Professional academic researchers commonly take on projects where the timescale is measured in years, or at least quite a few months. In many cases the timescale is relatively fixed, often established by the sponsors of the research. For teachers working in schools, the timescales for research projects may be quite variable. Often, the nature of school-based work is such that results are needed quite urgently to address particular issues and perceived problems. So a school's senior management team may ask a teaching department to make changes to improve some aspect of practice that can be introduced for the next school year (if not sooner), giving little time to research problems or test suggested solutions.

When the teacher initiates the research it may have an even shorter timescale. So a teacher may be unsatisfied with some aspect of classroom practice, such as student behaviour in a particular class, or failure to address students' learning difficulties in a particular topic. These are problems which are immediate, and the teacher will hope to address them whilst working with the current class, rather than seeing them as issues for a long-term project.

Teachers may also undertake research studies as part of professional development associated with academic qualifications or some externally funded initiative. In the case of classroom research undertaken as part of higher degree study, courses may be of one- or two-year duration (for Master's degrees) or longer (for doctorates). In these cases, there will be the advantages of a somewhat longer timescale, and support and structuring by the higher education institution offering the course, but often the actual period available to collect and analyse data is considerably shorter than the total length of the course. For teachers in this situation, it is very important to be realistic in considering what will be possible in the time available.

So, for example, teachers will often be attracted to action research (AR) as an approach to classroom research, and in many ways this is absolutely appropriate for the classroom practitioner. However, AR is a cyclical process, where the researcher undertakes iterative stages of both research and reflection upon that research to inform further stages. Whilst this makes it especially suitable for classroom work (see the comments about access below), many teachers find it challenging to meaningfully undertake more than one cycle of research within the timescale for completing a Master's degree thesis (the suitability of AR for studies that need to be formally reported is considered in more detail later in the chapter).

Similarly, many teachers who learn about grounded theory (GT) are attracted to this approach because it offers the sense of rigour that implies trustworthy, reliable research outcomes, without necessarily involving large representative samples or complex statistical methods. Yet to undertake GT studies properly implies an open-ended commitment to continuing further 'theoretical sampling' and the consequent rigorous analysis and re-analysis of data sets, until one can claim to have 'saturated' the model being developed. So whilst research designs that draw upon aspects of GT are often appropriate for teachers, a full GT study is a risky option for anyone working within a limited timescale.

One of the most intense contexts for teachers undertaking research is when teachers-in-training who are placed in schools temporarily, and who only have a limited period to get to know their classes, are expected to carry out a small-scale research project. This will be just one feature of an intensive placement where the new teacher is required to demonstrate development in a range of basic teaching competencies. Because of the extreme nature of the constraints on undertaking research in such contexts, the beginning teacher in such a context has to be especially careful to plan something that is both viable in the time available, and yet worthwhile as an activity. The studies published in *JoTTER*, referred to above (see Table 5.2), provide some examples of the kinds of studies that have proved viable under these circumstances.

Personnel

Academic researchers, such as university staff, are often expected to undertake research as a core part of their work. Indeed, funded projects based in universities and research centres are usually able to employ designated staff to spend most or all of their time working on a project. Teachers and other educational practitioners, such as teaching assistants, however, are employed primarily to facilitate learning, rather than to enquire into it. In recent years, teaching has increasingly come to be seen as a research-based profession (see Chapter 1), where teachers are not only expected to be aware of current research, but – increasingly – to be skilled in collecting and analysing data to evaluate teaching and to inform improved practice. Yet teachers are seldom offered significant protected time for this type of activity; rather, it has increasingly been seen as just another thing that teachers do as part of their job.

Often the focus of a teacher's research is their own classroom, and the teaching and learning occurring there. A teacher-as-researcher has an immense advantage in researching their own classroom in terms of both motivation (the issues are immediate and affect our work directly) and deep knowledge of the research context. However, it may be harder to be objective in evaluating one's own work than when commenting on other classrooms. There is often a tendency to justify our own actions (which after all, were what seemed justified when we acted!), when we might be more critical of others. Conversely, some teachers are prone to be a little too self-critical, and not so forgiving of themselves as they might be of others.

From a practical point of view, there is a more significant problem in enquiring into one's own practice, which is the difficulty of simultaneously being the practitioner and the researcher: both roles that require attention and concentration. This can lead to role-conflict, when 'the researcher' needs to take time out from being the teacher to note down a comment or observation, or a potentially valuable insight, or just needs time to step back from the classroom activity to reflect, but 'the teacher' has a responsibility to maintain the flow of the lesson. There may sometimes be the possibility of teachers working together as 'critical friends' or co-researchers to support each other by observing each other's classrooms, but often in teaching this depends upon making special arrangements as colleagues are usually teaching their own classes when we might want their help. Teachers-in-training may have a particular advantage here, especially when trainees are paired with a peer on professional placement.

This is a key constraint on the way classroom research can be planned. So, for example, an academic researcher might observe a class with an observation schedule to tally frequencies of particular events, or might eavesdrop on an extended conversation that is taking place among one group of students as they work together on a problem, or even temporarily remove a learner from the classroom context for a short interview (with the permission of the classroom teacher, and consent of the learner, of course – see Chapter 9). These options are generally not available to the teacher researching their own classroom. Again, an exception here is the teacher-in-training who, whilst assigned a class, is always under the supervision of the qualified teacher legally responsible for that class. Whilst this does (and indeed sensibly should) not mean that the qualified teacher will always be present in the classroom, they should be available and may well be keen to support the beginning teacher's research by focusing classroom observation upon particular areas. Other teachers generally have to find alternative approaches, such as relying upon a combination of very short contemporaneous notes, writing up impressions as soon as possible after lessons, and recording the classroom (with voice recorders and/or video cameras, for example).

Access

Educational researchers need to gain access to suitable contexts in which to undertake their research. External researchers need to negotiate access with schools, where 'gatekeepers' (those responsible for looking after the interests of the children and the school – see Chapter 9) will need to be persuaded that the intended research is potentially worthwhile and will not disrupt the school or be detrimental in any way to the learners. In this regard, the teacher-researcher normally has a major advantage. The teacher who wishes to undertake research into his or her own classroom has automatic access, although this is accompanied by the major responsibility to ensure that their research follows appropriate ethical guidelines (again, see Chapter 9).

Where teaching is seen as a research-informed profession, then we should *expect* teachers to be collecting data in their classroom that will inform their practice. We might see the setting and marking of tests, and indeed any work which the teacher scrutinises, as a form of data collection to inform the teacher's work, and these activities not only are well-established, but also have become expected parts of the teacher's classroom work. In increasing numbers of schools, research of various kinds is becoming seen as a key part of school development (Wilkins, 2011), and the phenomenon of teachers enquiring into teaching and learning in their classes is therefore coming to be seen as the norm. In these schools, teachers can normally use their 'insider' status to readily organise wider access to other groups of students within the school where this is appropriate.

The teacher-in-training on placement in a school is for many purposes seen as a member of staff and so has this privileged insider position. Schools that work in partnership with higher education institutions to provide placements for initial teacher education should be aware of, and signed up to, the expectations placed on the teacher-in-training in regards to course assignments which require the collection and analysis of research data. Generally, schools see this as a very healthy and useful activity. However, as in other aspects of school placement, it is important for the trainee to carefully discuss her or his research plans with the nominated mentor and/or the usual teacher of the class(es) that will be the context(s) for the research activity.

What is more difficult for the classroom teacher is to undertake research that requires data collections beyond the school. So it is unusual for teachers to undertake surveys that collect data across large numbers of schools, or to undertake systematic observations in schools other than their own (except where this is seen as meeting a particular school development need). That type of activity tends to require particular resources (for example, to cover the absence of a teacher observing in another school), and negotiation of access (e.g., persuading other schools to cooperate in collecting survey data) that are often more problematic for the classroom teacher. For example, the study discussed in Chapter 4, where McClune (2001) analysed examination scripts from a large number of examination centres required access to data that would be unlikely to be granted to a teacher in a school.

What may well be possible is for teachers to work together on a project, within or even across institutions. Michell (2011) reports in *JoTTER* how he set up videoconferencing between his class of Year 9 (13–14 year old) students studying French in an English school and their quatrième counterparts in an English class in a French

Collège (secondary school), taking advantage of an existing link between the two institutions.

> Collège B had already been involved in a letter exchange with pupils in School A and, although this had largely fallen by the wayside, the prospect of a closer link between the two schools appealed to the staff in both language departments. They were more than willing to participate in this project and I owe a debt of gratitude to the Collège's English teacher...
>
> (Michell, 2011, p. 60)

Equipment and materials

Funded research projects provide for necessary resources in their budgets to cover various costs. This might include the printing and posting of questionnaires, travel costs for researchers, specialised computer software, and recording equipment such as video-recorders and voice-recorders. The classroom teacher is unlikely to have comparable sources of funding. Some reprographics costs may be available from departmental budgets or other school funds, especially when the research activities are an inherent part of the teaching and learning processes in classrooms. However, such funds are unlikely to stretch to extensive or glossy new teaching materials to evaluate (as can be the case in funded projects).

Schools will have basic computer equipment, and a range of other communications technology as part of general stock used to support teaching. Indeed, these days, many students come to school with devices capable of recording audio or video of a quality that matches the best research kit of a few decades ago! Specialised software (for example, to support data analysis) may be more difficult to access as it is often expensive, and there may be a limited case for such expenditure if the applications are not likely to be used elsewhere in the school. Increasingly, though, the combination of inexpensive communications devices and freeware downloadable applications provides an accessible source of equipment suitable for recording and analysing classroom research data.

Skills

A more significant issue is that of research skills. Many research techniques are based upon activities we all undertake regularly. Interviewing is a means to use conversations to find out information, and observation is based on watching what is going on: we all posses *some* skills in these areas. However, most novices at research interviews or observation find that there is much scope to develop more sensitivity (at hearing what people are trying to tell us; at seeing what is significant in a scene), and better decision-making (about what to ask, what to focus observation on). Such skills can be developed through use, interspersed with self-critical reflection on performance, and, where possible, advice from a colleague who has more experience. In terms of carrying out classroom research to inform teaching, it is certainly usually better to proceed from a limited skill-base than not to proceed at all.

Similar points may be made about using recording equipment such as video cameras and audio recorders. Modern equipment tends to be very user-friendly, but use in a busy classroom can be problematic. Setting up a video camera within one's own classroom (when you are teaching and so unable to operate the camera) usually means a choice between settling for a long-shot which will capture an overview of the classroom, but little detail, or a predetermined selection of a particular target area (the board, where you often stand to talk with the class, or perhaps one particular group of students) where only some of the action of interest is likely to take place. Modern digital voice recorders are very good at picking up sound – but in a busy classroom may well record a cacophony of overlapping talk and background noise. Again, by trying things out, the novice researcher soon finds out what will collect useful data in a particular classroom context. The teacher relying on effective data collection to support a sponsored project, or a study required for a teaching qualification or higher degree, is well advised to practise techniques and pilot interview questions or observation schedules until they are satisfied they have reasonable competence, before using these techniques in an important project.

As well as requiring skills in data collection, research requires analytical skills. It is not unusual for the novice researcher to plan the collection of data, but to expect the analysis of data to be quite straightforward. This is seldom the case. Whilst compiling descriptive statistics is well within the capability of most teachers and other classroom researchers, the use of quantitative methods (i.e., statistical testing) demands considerable knowledge and understanding of the logical basis of the tests used, the kind of data they can be applied to, and how to interpret the statistics produced. The actual 'number-crunching' requires careful attention to detail, or the use of computer packages which do the processing very quickly, but require familiarity with how to correctly set up and enter data to make sure that the results are meaningful. Qualitative analysis may seem less daunting, but there is a range of distinct approaches that can be used (see Chapter 11), and – as with data collection – sensitivity and skill will develop with practice.

Dissemination

Whilst it may seem strange to suggest that dissemination opportunities might constrain choices made in undertaking a research project, this is an area where the experience of the academic researcher and the classroom practitioner are quite different. Professional educational researchers may be contracted to produce reports in a particular form, and are often funded to travel to talk about their research at conferences. They are usually expected to submit their work for publication in research journals, and outcomes are sometimes only published some years after the research was conducted.

Classroom practitioners seldom have funding support to report their work at research conferences, but may well be invited to report back to a departmental or school staff audience. Practitioners are able to send reports of their work to academic journals (and to practitioner journals), but the preparation of papers can be time-consuming, and few are published without a process of authors being asked to make one or more rounds of revisions to the submission in response to peer review (see Chapter 6). This process can be drawn out (typically several months delay between submission and hearing whether a journal may be interested in publication), and it may be difficult to justify prioritising the time required when one has other professional priorities.

None of this should be taken as suggesting teachers should not seek to report their work, as potentially many studies carried out by classroom teachers offer valuable potential insights for other teachers and researchers. The Galbraith and Winterbottom (2010) study into peer-tutoring discussed in Chapter 2, and published in the academic research journal *Educational Studies,* is an example of a report of research carried out by a teacher with students in his own school. This study was the basis of an MEd thesis, where there was already an expectation that the teacher's research would be informed by a thorough literature review, follow a rigorous design, and be reported through formal academic writing. However, much classroom research that is context-directed – i.e., primarily intended to tackle perceived problems and issues in professional work, and so improve practice – will adopt an approach (i.e., action research, see Chapter 4) that is not ideally suited to formal academic reporting.

Suitability of common research methodologies for teachers' classroom research

The previous chapter outlined some of the most common strategies used in educational research studies. All of these approaches are represented in the research literature, but – of course – they are not all equally suitable for any particular study. The choice of a research strategy needs to reflect the fundamental ontological and epistemological assumptions informing the research questions (see Chapter 3), as well as what is feasible in the research context.

Experiments

Experiments test the effect of some intervention by comparing outcomes in the presence or absence of that intervention. In principle, experiments may be deliberately organised to provide a 'fair test' by comparing the effects of two different conditions (e.g., learning about *Hamlet* through textual analysis versus learning about *Hamlet* through putting on a production of the play). Alternatively, we might take advantage of a 'natural' experiment if the two different conditions are already in place (Ms Jones teaches chemistry by conceptual themes such as acidity, oxidation, etc., illustrated by the different groups of elements; Mr Smith teaches the same course organised by groups of element, in each case exploring different concepts where relevant to the group). In either case, the major difficulty is normally in knowing that we are comparing 'like with like', that is, that any differences in outcome we detect are likely to be due to the difference in treatment we think we are testing, and not some other difference(s) between the two conditions. Experiments are notoriously difficult to set up in educational contexts. In simple terms, there are two approaches one might take (see Chapter 4). The most direct approach requires the researcher to control for all factors (e.g., student prior knowledge) that might influence outcomes (e.g., student learning) so that the experimental and control conditions are identical, apart from the one factor being investigated. Otherwise we need to use large samples, random assignment to conditions, and statistical methods to analyse the data.

Questions for reflection

Consider an intervention you might introduce in your teaching in the hope of increasing student learning, motivation or positive behaviour. What factors would have to be held constant to test, in a 'controlled' way, whether the intervention really did have any effect?

Imagine you wished to study the potential benefits to a group of learners of going on a school trip. How easy would it be to find a suitable group who did not go on the trip to undertake a 'fair' comparison with those who did?

Often in educational contexts we are not even sure we can identify all the factors that could be relevant to particular educational outcomes. The differences between classes and teachers will often be significant, and yet we usually cannot run both the control and experimental conditions with the same teacher and class: once students have experienced an educational programme, we cannot erase the effects of that experience so that we try a different approach (and of course it would not be ethically acceptable, even if it were possible). We can see this if we consider some of the examples in Table 5.2. A number of these studies were intended to find out the effects of particular educational experiences.

So, for example, Mutton (2010) wanted to find out about the value of taking students on a geography field trip. In principle, one could explore learning or attitudinal changes of students who went on a field trip with a control group who did not. However, if a school uses field trips, it is very unlikely to have another group of similar learners (same age and ability range, same interest in the subject, studying the same topics for the same examination course, etc.) who are taught the same content without the field trip. It *might* be possible (but much more difficult to organise) a comparison with students (same age and ability range, same interest in the subject, studying the same topics for the same examination course, etc.) at a 'similar' (*sic*) school who do not use field trips, but could we assume that the teaching in the school sending their students on field trips was in *all other ways* comparable with the teaching in the comparison school? It should be clear that organising a 'fair' test is often highly problematic.

Statistical methods can sometimes help here. Although schools vary considerably, and it is difficult to find good matches between schools, it may be possible to build up a sample by randomly assigning enough schools to the experimental or control condition to use statistical tests to compare results. As long as schools are randomly assigned (so they have an equal chance of being in the experimental or control condition), then it becomes *unlikely* that large average differences in outcomes between the two samples will be due to random differences between the schools (rather than the presence or absence of the intervention). This approach has been used in the epiSTEMe project (www.educ.cam.ac.uk/research/projects/episteme/), a funded initiative that explored an approach to designing teaching sequences in lower secondary science and mathematics teaching. However, even in a project staffed with academic researchers, recruiting enough schools to provide a sufficiently large sample proved challenging. This is the kind of approach that becomes feasible on a large scale, but is usually beyond what a single teacher can organise.

This approach also requires that the researcher can assign schools to conditions, and usually teachers and schools will not change their way of doing things just for our research. More commonly, we have to work with 'natural' experiments by building a sample to compare schools or classes that are already doing things in different ways. If we found that (a) some schools send students on overseas exchanges visits to support language teaching and some do not, and (b) that generally students got better grades in modern languages when they attended schools that sent them on overseas trips, we might conclude that the trips supported learning enough to make a difference. However, if it transpired that schools usually decided not to send pupils on such trips when (i) the students generally came from homes where families could not afford to fund additional educational opportunities, and/or (ii) student behaviour was such that trips were seen as inappropriate on safety grounds, and/or (iii) the languages departments were understaffed and could not cope with organising trips, then it seems quite possible that the lower grades in these schools can be adequately explained *without* considering the opportunity for trips abroad. We might suspect the trips would be valuable for language learning, but we could not consider the grades as good evidence because we do not have a fair comparison of 'like-with-like'.

Experimental methods become viable *in principle* for the teacher-researcher when the teacher-researcher can randomly assign children to an experimental and control group. For example, imagine that Mutton had formed two equal size groups of students by a drawing of lots and one group had gone on a field trip, whilst the other group did not (but otherwise received the same teaching). Here it might be possible, in principle, to make statistical comparisons between the two groups if there were enough students in the study. However, if Mutton suspected that field trips were beneficial to the students, he might not feel it ethically and professionally appropriate to have half the students excluded from this opportunity in order to test an experimental hypothesis. (Such ethical issues are considered in more detail in Chapter 9.)

Even if Mutton had thought this was justified, any statistically significant differences found between the two groups might still be due to systematic factors other than the value of the field trip itself. For example, students excluded from the trip, seeing their peers being allowed to take the trip, might have become demotivated and even bitter. This might have led to more negative learning and attitudinal outcomes for this group than would have been the case *if no one* at all had gone on the trip. So although randomisation is meant to avoid systematic bias in samples, it cannot avoid systematic effects that are indirect consequences of the research process itself.

The issue here is that people can react to being involved in a research study. Teachers who are enthusiastic (or dubious) about some educational innovation often inadvertently communicate this, and their expectations (of success or failure) to the learners. Students who are provided with something novel in their lessons may react to the novelty itself (often finding the change from routine itself quite interesting, or in some cases threatening) regardless of what the innovation is. Unfortunately, many innovations that are successful when first tested cease to be effective once they are adopted by less enthusiastic teachers, or become familiar to the learners. All these considerations act as 'threats' to the validity of an educational experiment. Experiments have their place in educational research, but tend to be unsuitable for most teacher-led classroom research projects.

Surveys

The nature of a survey (see Chapter 4) is to explore the opinions of a population about some issue, either by asking all members of the population, or by sampling the population in a way that allows us to infer the opinions of the broader population. Surveys certainly have their place in schools. For example, if a school's governing body was considering changing school dress (uniform) policy, it might decide to survey the views of the staff, the students, and their parents. Surveys can be useful within a class context. A teacher may wish to find out about the reading habits (amount of time spent reading, what kind of books, etc.) of students in a class to inform the choice of books to be studied in class. A real example is given by Whitwood (2012), who reports in the *JoTTER* on a study she carried out while on professional placement at a primary school. She was interested in how pupils at two different grade levels (Year 2 and Year 6) responded to being introduced to learning a new foreign language. As part of her study she included "a very simple questionnaire that would give me clear results and would be completed efficiently by all pupils" (p. 334). Simple questionnaires designed to survey perceptions or attitudes with teaching groups are a common feature of many small-scale classroom enquiry projects.

Usually, teachers' classroom research involves more than just investigating students' views. Whitwood's study involved an intervention, whose reception by the children was evaluated by a combination of the questionnaire and group interviews. So although the techniques used in surveys (such as questionnaires) may be used in teacher research, this is usually only one part of a research design, such as a case study, and then we would not consider the research to be a survey as such. The distinction being made here relates to the levels of educational research discussed in Chapter 3. A questionnaire may be the main technique (tactic) employed in survey methodology (strategy), but can also be one of the techniques used as part of other strategies, such as a case study, for example.

Ethnography

It is not uncommon for research carried out in classrooms to be reported as having an ethnographic flavour or drawing upon ethnography. Teachers are certainly well placed to appreciate the culture of the classroom. However, ethnography is a rather particular tradition, and is perhaps best seen as a somewhat specialised approach requiring a particular academic background and enquiry skills. Teacher-research can certainly be informed by reading relevant ethnographic studies, and often has an 'ethnographic flavour', but for most teachers choosing to 'do' an ethnography in their classroom would be ambitious, unless they have a suitable background from having studied a discipline such as anthropology.

Grounded theory

Grounded theory (GT) has a number of features (see Chapter 4) that make it problematic for anyone looking for a methodology to undertake a research project as part of a teacher education course or higher degree. In particular, GT is suitable for enquiries that can be open-ended in terms of both research design (something that will often make university supervisors uncomfortable in student projects) and, in particular, timescale. Despite these complications, GT is an excellent approach for someone interested in exploring a complex, and currently not well understood, phenomenon, as long as they are comfortable in taking an iterative approach (where ongoing data analysis informs the next steps of data collection), and they are prepared to commit as much time to the enquiry as may be needed to reach 'saturation' (i.e., a fully developed theory).

GT is therefore an ideal approach for a teacher who recognises a major and long-term issue in their professional context, and is happy to set out on an open-ended enquiry to better understand what is going on. Depending upon the particular issue and professional context, the ongoing study might involve shifts in focus (between teaching groups, for example) and indeed may well involve iterations over different terms and years, using analysis of the data collected (perhaps from interviewing students or analysing student work, for example) to refine data collection instruments (such as interview questions or tasks set as student activities) for use with the next topic, or next class. This type of iteration ('theoretical sampling') is a core part of GT and can be a very effective approach to research that can gradually provide a clearer and more nuanced understanding of an issue. However, if a project has an inherent time limit, GT is not appropriate. So a student teacher on professional placement may have to complete their project in less than a term, and even a higher degree student may often only have one or two terms for data collection: in these situations, GT is not usually a viable choice of methodology.

Action research

Action research (AR) is a very common approach to practitioner enquiry in areas such as education. Indeed, the nature of AR (see Chapter 4) is such that it is ideally suited to addressing problems in a teacher's professional work, as it is focused on problem-solving rather than the generation of abstract knowledge – that is, it is context-directed (as represented in Figure 5.2), rather than theory-directed (as represented in Figure 5.1). However, as with GT, the very strengths of AR can sometimes act as a limitation for those who are undertaking classroom research as part of a formal educational qualification.

Many research projects have a structure whereby precise research questions (RQs) are formulated, informed by a literature review, and then the research is designed to answer the RQs. Data is then collected, and then analysed, and this allows (in an ideal world!) answers to be found to the RQs. There is often then a formal report (for example, submitted to a university as an assignment or thesis) that sets out specific knowledge claims based upon the research, and supported by the logic of the research process (e.g., see Figure 3.4). Even when the research is based in a single specific context, there is an expectation that the findings will be related to general issues discussed in the literature, and will identify implications for practice and/or further research well beyond the original research context.

However, in an AR study, there are usually a series of successive activities – each informed by the previous activity, and informing the next – where activities may be stopped or modified in full flow before there is 'full data set' to support making a formal case that any specific RQs have been answered. The 'shape' of an AR study does not fit the visual metaphor of the lemniscate, as suggested in Chapter 3, but rather is a sequence of ideas about what to do next, actions planned and executed accordingly, and evaluations of the effects of the actions to inform the next cycle (see Figure 5.3).

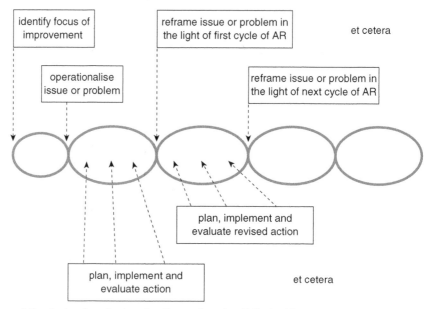

Figure 5.3 A visual metaphor for the cycles of activity in AR

As the purpose of AR is to help us do a better job, the teacher undertaking AR is likely to cut short any intervention that does not seem to be having the desired effect, rather than continue just to keep collecting data. This can make AR sound a 'sloppy' activity, rather than rigorous research – but this is because AR is designed to find solutions to problems in practice, and it prioritises doing that rather than developing formal research findings. So AR is certainly a very appropriate way for classroom teachers to undertake classroom enquiry. However, if a teacher is undertaking classroom research as part of working towards an academic qualification, and the university requires a formal research report structured as a case for research findings (see Chapter 12), then it *may* be difficult to clearly meet the requirements based on an AR project. (This is something the teacher concerned should certainly check with the course documentation and supervisor.)

It seems then that:

- AR is often an effective approach for teachers to adopt in carrying out classroom-based research to address problems identified in their professional work;
- learning how to undertake AR as part of initial teacher education or continuing professional development is very worthwhile;

but

- features of AR may *sometimes* make it a problematic basis for classroom enquiry that has to be reported as a formal research study.

This may create a dilemma for some teachers looking to start out on classroom research, and unsure if AR is a suitable approach. I return to this issue later in the chapter.

Case study

The final major type of methodology discussed in the previous chapter was case study. A key feature of a case (see Chapter 4) is that it is one instance of many, which can be studied in detail to help us understand the case itself better. Case study is suitable when we wish to explore a complex phenomenon, which would be disrupted were we to take it out of its 'natural' context (even if that were possible). Case studies often deal with phenomena where it would be difficult or unhelpful to try to tease out the different variables that might be relevant (usually because they are likely to interact in ways we cannot predict), and where there are just too many factors involved to consider an approach such as an experiment – which, as we have seen, would require a control of variables that is seldom possible in education.

Case study is often a very suitable methodology for classroom research because teaching and learning present the kind of complex phenomena that are most suitable for case studies. The choice of a research methodology should always be made once the research issue or questions have been clarified, to make sure that the approach chosen has potential to meet the aims of the research. Case study is often used when we want to develop a clearer, more detailed picture of something, or to understand what is going on in some complex situation. Educational issues are often of this type, so case study is often a sensible choice for teachers seeking to find out more about a problem or issue in their professional practice.

As well as often being a suitable strategy for answering research questions raised by classroom teachers, case study is often a sensible choice on pragmatic grounds. As was suggested earlier in the chapter, research designs have to be feasible given the resources available to researchers. So, for example, experiments are seldom viable in small-scale research in naturalistic settings (such as classrooms); large-scale surveys require access to representative samples of populations; ethnography requires particular research skills; and grounded theory requires an open-ended timescale. For many purposes, case study and AR seem the most viable options – and some questions have already been raised about the suitability of AR when the teacher-research is subject to formal academic expectations.

Identifying foci for classroom research ———

Consider three examples of classroom studies undertaken by teachers-in-training as part of their initial teacher education programme (and reported in the *JoTTER*):

- R. Smith (2012) explored students' perceptions of intelligence, and how this might be linked to the way they approached challenging work.
- Walsh (2012) explored the issue of how to differentiate music teaching to meet the particular needs of those students that undertook regular extra-curricular study of music.
- Turner (2010) investigated the use of targets set by students themselves in an attempt to raise achievement in speaking German in a mixed-ability class.

These authors identified these topics as being suitable for small-scale research projects, which could be reported in university assignments, to demonstrate that they could apply theoretical learning, library work and classroom research skills in order to develop their own personal understanding of aspects of teaching and learning and so inform their professional work as teachers. These studies illustrate different approaches to identifying foci for classroom research projects.

Smith (2012, p. 288) set out to investigate "how children in year 5/6 think about intelligence, either as something fixed or as something changeable, and if this bears any relationship to whether they rise to a challenge or give up". Her choice of focus was informed by reading about research that suggested that children's notions about the nature of intelligence would influence their attitudes to dealing with challenges in learning. Someone who thinks that intelligence is something firmly fixed at birth might readily respond to a difficult problem by thinking they were too 'stupid' to ever solve the problem, and so soon decide not to waste more time and effort on it. However, someone who believed that intelligence is something we can develop is more likely to feel it is worthwhile persevering with a difficult problem. This clearly has relevance to how children respond in classrooms, especially when faced with the kinds of challenging task best suited to extending their understanding of a topic.

Walsh (2012, p. 161) explained *her* study was motivated by what she framed as a 'problem', that is:

> The problem for music teachers is finding the means by which to differentiate within mainstream classroom music lessons for, and enhance the learning of, students who are taking part in extracurricular activities. Where these students have developed musical skill outside the classroom, they are insufficiently challenged by pedagogic strategies that challenge those who have not and so their learning is hindered.
>
> (Walsh, 2012, p. 161)

Turner (2010) reports a study that started from what she perceived as a problem that she had met in practice: "throughout my training, it struck me that regardless of actual overall linguistic ability, there is often a discrepancy between a pupil's ability to speak the language as compared to their comprehension and writing skills" (p. 2). She explained that she "sought to affect not only my teaching practice but also to help students increase their subject based attainment" (p. 4). Here, Turner's starting point is an issue in practice that motivates an exploration of existing literature for ideas about how she might respond to the issue in her teaching.

Question for reflection

Can you relate these projects to the distinction between two modes of research (theory-directed and context-directed) suggested earlier in the chapter?

Earlier in the chapter, I introduced a model that might be useful for thinking about the difference between most research carried out by academic researchers (which I suggested was theory-directed) and much research carried out by teachers about their own classrooms and schools or colleges (which I labelled as context-directed). This was strongly linked to the motivations that drive research. These tend to be different among professional researchers and teacher-researchers. So academic researchers usually seek the kind of generalised knowledge that is abstract enough to be relevant well beyond any particular sites where the research was carried out. Teacher-researchers, however, tend to focus primarily on understanding and improving the particular teaching and learning contexts in which they work, rather than developing theoretical knowledge. These different categories of researcher tend to have these different concerns because of their professional roles: teachers are primarily paid to focus on the teaching and learning in their own classrooms, whereas academic researchers are expected to contribute research of wide relevance to the published research literature.

The special situation of the teacher who is a student (or vice versa)

This raises the question of how we can best understand the research carried out by a student teacher, or a teacher-in-service who is also a student. Such research can respond to a number of different motivations:

- Problem-solving: to solve problems and improve practice
- Professional development: to develop professional skills and competences
- Qualification: to meet the criteria for an academic reward
- Theory-generation: to contribute to public knowledge by developing new theory.

Often the teacher-as-research-student is motivated by several of these possibilities, but there are likely to be tensions in a research project where too many of these motivations are prioritised.

In the example of the student teacher projects considered above, there were various emphases. Smith's work seems to be motivated primarily by her academic scholarship, and reading about prior research. She identified a finding that she was interested in exploring in the particular context where she was teaching. Her work seems to be theory-driven in the sense that she was using her placement school as a suitable context to test out the relevance of an idea presented in research, rather than trying to solve a particular problem that had arisen in her own practice.

By contrast, Turner's study seems to be motivated by something she had observed during her time working in classrooms, and that she saw as a problem for her as a subject teacher. We might suggest that this study is context-driven, although it is quite likely the problem is one that is found in many language classrooms.

Walsh frames her study in terms of a problem that faces music teachers generally. In most compulsory music lessons in most schools there are likely to be both pupils who only study music in that context, and others who may spend considerable time receiving tuition in learning an instrument – or perhaps regularly singing in a choir. These extra-curricular musicians deserve music lessons that challenge and stretch them, but may be considerably advanced in their learning compared with many classmates. A programme of research developing theoretical knowledge supporting classroom pedagogy to deal with this general issue could be very valuable to music teachers. But Walsh was one, a novice classroom teacher, working with a small number of classes in one school context. So although her project was motivated by a general problem, her own research was necessarily contextualised very locally. Walsh focused on two of her Year 9 students, 14 year-old tuba-player 'Geoff', and 13 year-old violinist and choral singer 'Kitty'. In developing and testing an approach to differentiation that might work for Geoff and Kitty, Walsh would obviously develop her own professional knowledge in ways she would expect to inform her later work with other musicians and classes.

It is also quite possible that by reporting her work with these two students in *JoTTER*, Walsh's study could offer useful ideas for approaches that other music teachers might wish to try out and adopt in their own contexts. However, she was clearly not in a position where she was likely to be able to make a major contribution to developing new theoretical knowledge that could be abstracted from particular contexts and so claimed to be of general application. This would likely require undertaking work with extra-curricular musicians in classes across a wide range of teaching contexts.

In all three cases, whatever the initial motivation of the research, it led to new knowledge of a particular 'local' teaching context:

- exploring a general issue of interest within a particular context to develop personal/professional knowledge that could inform one's own teaching in the future (R. Smith, 2012);
- applying a general principle to a specific context to address a particular issue faced now in professional work (Hicks, 2010);
- addressing a general problem in subject teaching within a specific teaching context to better meet the needs of current students and develop understanding of the issue for future teaching practice (Walsh, 2012).

In each of these cases the relationship between the general (theoretical) and the specific was primarily in one direction: ideas from existing academic and professional literature were explored in the particular local context. This is quite appropriate given the position of the researchers concerned, as new teachers. However, in each case, reporting their work in the literature makes available an account of how these ideas played out in one particular educational context, and so can potentially provide valuable insights for other researchers and teachers. This leads us back to an issue raised earlier in the chapter: that action research (AR) may be a problematic choice of methodology for the teacher who is also a student expected to produce a formal academic report of their classroom research.

———— Action research does not always fit well with academic course requirements ————————————————————————————————

Earlier in the chapter the main strategies (methodologies) applied in educational research were considered as possible approaches to be adopted by teacher-researchers. It was suggested that action research (AR) was often an effective approach for teachers to adopt in carrying out classroom-based research to address problems identified in their professional work, *but* that features of AR may sometimes make it a problematic basis for classroom enquiry that has to be reported as a formal research study.

In other words, teacher-researchers who are not studying for a formal qualification, and who are not undertaking research supported by a sponsor expecting a formal report, may well find that action research offers a very sensible approach to being an effective practitioner striving to be a better teacher (both in terms of external targets and personal satisfaction): one who innovates and who collects evidence to inform decision-making that solves problems and improves practice. So for any reader of this book who does not have the constraints of writing a formal report in a specified format for external scrutiny, then the concerns expressed here about AR will not apply.

In some academic institutions, AR is encouraged as a basis for teacher development through higher degrees; and forms of writing which focus on the reflective aspects of AR, and the personal development achieved, are acceptable as the basis for academic theses (McNiff & Whitehead, 2009). However, many universities expect a research report to have a particular form and structure, and in particular to make a case for what has been learnt in a particular way (such as in the model presented in Chapter 12). At doctoral level, in particular, examiners usually expect work that could be reported in peer-reviewed research journals (and much Master's degree work can also meet these standards), where a key criterion is that the work makes an original contribution to developing *public* knowledge.

However, the core concern of AR is to improve practice in the professional context, and so although new knowledge is generated, this tends to be personal knowledge closely linked to the local context rather than abstracted theoretical knowledge that can claim to be generally applicable. The problem is not that the work is based in a single teaching and learning context, but rather that AR is not set up to produce the kind of knowledge suitable for dissemination in peer-reviewed research journals or academic theses (see Chapter 6). Work that may be very valuable and effective as AR can still fail to support the writing of a project report or research thesis that meets the expectations of examiners in many institutions, if the normal priorities of AR are emphasised to the exclusion of the expectations of formal academic research. A particular, additional, problem with AR is that it is especially suited for cycles of activity and evaluation, and so often an AR 'project' will require timescales that extend beyond what is available for teachers on formal university courses.

Should the teacher-as-research-student avoid AR?

This raises a potential dilemma for the teacher-as-research-student (the trainee teacher completing a teaching qualification or the in-service teacher undertaking a part-time degree course) as AR is often highly suitable for practitioner studies, but may not be ideal for producing a report or thesis that meets university expectations. This dilemma is spelt out in Table 5.3.

Table 5.3 To AR or not to AR, that is the question...

To undertake AR...	...or not to undertake AR
I am a teacher/student teacher, who wishes to learn to use research to make me a better classroom teacher and improve my practice...	...and I am undertaking a formal qualification where I am expected to undertake and report classroom research.
A powerful way to become a good teacher-researcher would be to develop skills of AR, which will be flexible and responsive to support my changing professional experiences...	...but to meet the expectations of my current qualification, I am expected to produce a report which demonstrates an academic approach to research.
My professional development will be supported by selecting an issue of concern in my professional context, and then following through on as many cycles of AR as are needed for me to be satisfied with the improvement in my practice...	...but the timescale I have for my project is strictly limited, and I will have to begin working on the report of my work by a specific date.
I expect to inform my AR by appropriate reading to provide me with some useful ways of thinking about the issue, and some suggestions for ways to proceed, but my focus is on what is happening here...	...but in my formal report I am expected to: motivate research questions from the existing literature (even when my initial focus derives from a problem in practice); show how I have answered those questions; and relate my conclusions back to the conceptual framework identified from my literature review.
I am interested in becoming a better teacher, and in improving the professional context here in my classroom, in my school, with my classes...	...yet I will be expected to write up as if what I have found out is of wider applicability, although I know that each teacher and each classroom and class is unique.

When to avoid AR

The dilemma referred to above only applies when AR would not fit the expectations of a university or other sponsoring or evaluating organisation. So the teacher who is also a student tempted to adopt AR as their methodology should first familiarise themselves with the expectations and assessment criteria that will be used to judge their work. In some cases, there may be no conflict between the AR and the kind of research expected.

Questions for reflection

Is your research related to a formal academic qualification? If so: (a) Do you know the formal requirements for undertaking and reporting your research, and the criteria by which your work will be evaluated? (b) To what extent would an AR project allow you to meet the expectations of your supervisor(s) and examiner(s)?

Where the kind of research required does not match the AR approach, then another choice of methodology needs to be made. Often this will be a case study approach (see below) as case study can support practitioner research that is context-directed whilst still meeting the expectations of academic research. There is an argument that it might be possible to design a study to allow you to both do AR and be adopting another research methodology such as a case study. You could perhaps initiate an AR study, and then decide to document the AR process in sufficient detail to construct a formal case study from it; but that does seem to move away from the spirit and priorities of true AR, where the focus is on improving an educational situation rather than contextualising it through formal theory and documenting it at the level needed to write an academic report. A better option in this situation might be to undertake a case study, which will allow the testing out of an innovation or problem solution of the type that would be introduced in AR, albeit within the constraints of a single cycle of research.

━━━ Practitioner research need not be action research ━━━

Students often report that they wish to undertake AR because they are keen that they use their research project to address some aspect of practice they would like to improve (i.e., context-directed research, see Figure 5.2). However, if they are looking to meet the requirements of a formal course assignment or thesis, they then often acknowledge that in the study they will only be able to complete one cycle of AR because of time and other constraints – which compromises an AR approach (see Figure 5.3). They then proceed to undertake a careful literature review (as required for their course assignment, but not normally expected in AR), formulate formal research questions, set out a research design to attempt to answer those questions (in a single cycle of

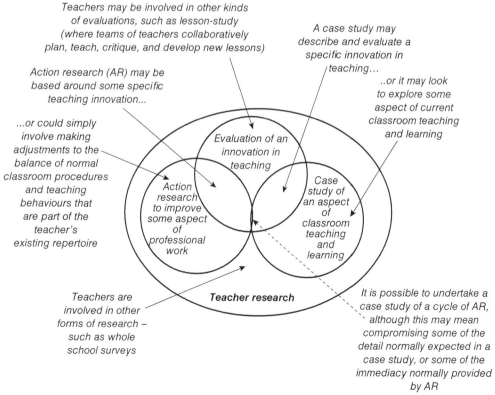

Figure 5.4 Some common types of teacher research

research, rather than employing the iterative approach of AR), and proceed to collect a full set of data sufficient to offer an argued case for the extent to which they were able to answer the question (usually meaning substantially more data than is necessary to make a professional decision about the next action we should take as a practitioner). This seems some way from the way AR is meant to be integrated with usual teaching practice and organised around such practical questions as 'How do I improve things here so that my values as a teacher are better met in my teaching?' (see Figure 5.4).

One of the attractions of AR is that is allows us to initiate changes we hope will improve practice, and evaluate those changes. Yet there is an asymmetry in the relationship between AR and problem-solving in teacher research. Research undertaken to improve practice is a necessary, but not a sufficient, condition for AR.

AR must be carried out by practitioners looking to improve some aspect of their professional practice...

...but...

...teachers carrying out research to improve some aspect of their professional practice need not be undertaking AR!

So, for example, Dry (2010) described his study of a sequence of lessons where he taught the science topic 'space' through lessons designed to emphasise the nature of science (undertaken as part of his PGCE course and later published in *JoTTER*) as 'an action research project'. Dry wanted to respond to recent changes in curriculum expectations by foregrounding teaching about the nature of science, rather than the science 'content' of the topic, and considered his study an 'intervention' (p. 228). Drawing on a range of authors, Dry identified a number of characteristics claimed for action research, and considered the extent to which his study met these expectations. Dry's detailed considerations are summarised in Table 5.4.

Table 5.4 The reflections of one student teacher on whether his study was action research (after Dry, 2010, pp. 220–221)

Reported characteristics of AR	*Dry's characterisation of his own (2010) study*
"a strategy for social research in which practitioners research the effects of changing an aspect of their practice"	the study concerns an intervention
deals with practical issues or problems	"clearly true of this intervention", since it addresses an issue faced by all science teachers working under the English National Curriculum
"the effecting of change, not only the study of current practice, is inherent in action research"	true of the innovation
"an action research project involves the active participation of practitioners"	Dry was both the researcher and the practitioner responsible for teaching the class involved in the intervention

Reported characteristics of AR	Dry's characterisation of his own (2010) study
action research is cyclical	not true here in any substantial sense
AR works towards collaboration	"collaboration with colleagues was not explicitly built into this study"
"Technical action research aims to improve practice. Practical action research aims to also develop the professional understanding of the practitioner(s) involved. Emancipating action research seeks to change the parameters imposed by a system or organisation…"	"The distinction between technical and practical action research is almost non-existent in the present case where the researcher is also the practitioner, since change in practice will only come about as a result of an understanding on the part of the researcher-practitioner. So this project may be described as practical action research"

Dry noted that his "study uses an action research methodology since it is concerned with investigating the effect of changing the way [class] 10YSep are usually taught, rather than studying in detail a pre-existing situation, which would comprise a case study" (p. 229). Case study is said to be 'naturalistic', suggesting that it is a methodology suitable for investigating things as they are, rather than a basis for change. However, teachers innovating in their teaching is a 'natural' part of education. Hamilton (1980, p. 78) explains that case study "claims to be naturalistic and builds upon the analysis of real-life situations … rejects the technology of manipulation (i.e. randomisation, matching and replication) that is the defining attribute of experimental social research".

What this means is that an external researcher who wanted to constrain and change the conditions of learning in a classroom to investigate some effect cannot be considered to be undertaking 'naturalistic' research, *but* if the teacher herself decides to try something new for pedagogic reasons, then that innovation is a natural part of the educational process, and might make a suitable focus for a case study. So if the teacher implements some change that she thinks might be beneficial for teaching and learning, then that innovation could be the focus of a case study to explore what happened in the innovative situation. Dry studied in some depth an identified sequence of lessons to teach one topic to one specified class using the collection and analysis of a wide range of data sources (Dry, 2010). In the published report of his work, he set out both the boundaries and context of his study:

> The intervention to be described in this report took place during six consecutive sixty-minute physics lessons of a year 10 group at a coeducational 11–16 comprehensive school in England. The lessons fell in February and March 2009. All 17 students in the group had chosen to take three science GCSEs instead of the school's default option of two GCSEs. The class, known as 10YSep, was mixed ability, with a fairly wide range of students present. … The class were following the OCR Gateway GCSE syllabus. … At the start of this intervention, the class's usual teacher, who had taught them since the previous September, was replaced by the present author, an education student placed at the school for the purposes of Initial Teacher Training specialising in physics.
>
> (Dry, 2010, p. 228)

Dry made a good argument that his study met most of the key characteristics of AR (see Table 5.4), which are in any case described differently by different authors,

although he conceded there was not a perfect fit. However, if we accept that innovations may be the subject of case studies as long as those innovations are part of the normal development of teaching (and not an artificial context set up to meet the needs of an external researcher), then in many ways Dry describes a case study of the teaching of a particular topic to a specific class through a sequence of lessons. The published study offers a standard report format, similar to a 'scientific' paper (see Chapter 12), including a literature review, and an account of the collection and analysis of a range of data.

Question for reflection

How important is it that we know whether to best identify Dry's 2010 study as action research or case study?

This leads us to the question of whether Dry's study really was AR, as he argued, or a case study, or some kind of hybrid, or perhaps even both of these at the same time. The reader, perhaps more concerned with learning to use research to better understand and develop their teaching than the technical labels applied to studies, may think this is a moot point, and not of any great consequence. Indeed, for practical purposes it does not really matter because Dry has:

- presented a claim for how to understand his work (i.e., as an intervention investigated by AR);
- attempted to justify his claim by describing how he understands AR, supported by reference to recognised experts on research methodology;
- acknowledged where his claim is weak and his study does not fit with common descriptions of AR;

and, most importantly,

- presented a very clear, detailed explanation of his research design, so we can see what he did, and why he did what he did, and how his conclusions follow logically from the analysis of carefully planned data collection.

This allows the reader to understand the logic of his study, and the reasoning behind its design and execution, and so allows us to reach a judgement on the validity and significance of his findings, regardless of whether we think the study is AR or not. The examiners who assessed his report recognised that Dry had undertaken a valuable and well-explained study; had undertaken suitable scholarship in terms of both research methods and subject teaching; and had demonstrated his knowledge, understanding and competence relating to classroom research. There is an important lesson here, in that it is less important how we label our work, than that we set out a detailed explanation of what we have done and why. Dry saw his work as an AR study that did not match all of the usual features of AR. I would characterise his study as a case study of an innovation to improve an aspect of the teacher's practice, reported in sufficient detail to be informative to other teachers and researchers. Either way, his examiners thought the work was of high quality, and awarded him a prize for the study.

Exploring an educational idea or issue through a ━━━ case-study approach

Case studies look at a particular instance of some educational phenomena: assessment policies in one school; teaching and learning of thermodynamics in one class; classroom interaction in one lesson; beliefs and attitudes of one teacher, etc. One of the case studies reported in the *JoTTER* explains that "the 'phenomenon' in question ... is the single one-week Spanish exchange trip and the case study will focus on just four pupils within this" (Forbes, 2010, p. 116). Case studies may be used in both theory-directed (see Figure 5.1) and context-directed (see Figure 5.2) modes of research. This links to the difference between what are known as 'instrumental' and 'intrinsic' case studies.

Instrumental and intrinsic case studies

In an instrumental case study, a case is considered a suitable example of a more general class of such instances to be useful in exploring a general issue where the nature of the research issue/questions suggests more will be learnt by studying a particular case in detail than by surveying many cases in less depth. So the research may be motivated by a desire to develop understanding of particular kinds of events or processes (i.e., theory-directed), and the case is an instrument for addressing the research questions.

An intrinsic case study, however, looks at a particular case because that case is of special interest for some reason. It may be a case that is far from typical, but allows us to learn about some special features of that particular case – perhaps a school or teacher achieving especially impressive outcomes (low truancy, high examination scores, low teacher turnover, excellent retention in a school subject, etc.), to find out what particular combination of factors could be at work in that case.

Often the teacher-researcher is interested in addressing issues and problems in practice, and may be interested in questions such as:

- How can I get my final year class to get more engaged in revision?
- How do I encourage my students to undertake group work more productively?
- Why do my students have such difficulty with understanding force and motion?
- Could peer assessment support my students in developing better metacognition without using excessive class time?
- How do I challenge the small group of gifted students in this class?
- What can I do to integrate the new student into my tutor group?

This suggests that where a teacher-researcher undertakes a case study, it is often going to be an intrinsic case study, where the case is of particular importance because it is *my* school, *my* class, the topic *my* students are struggling with: the case is of intrinsic interest because it relates to the researcher's own professional practice.

In general, where a case study is undertaken by a teacher in context-directed mode (to address issues and problems identified in practice, see Figure 5.2), it is likely to be an intrinsic case study. Where, instead, a teacher is interested in learning more about how some general theoretical issue (dialogic teaching, student misconceptions, formative assessment, student understanding of multiple representations, etc.) links with their professional practice, they may select a particular case (e.g., teaching a particular topic with a specific class, or a suitable lesson for group discussion work, etc.) because they think it is a suitable context for exploring the issue. So where a teacher-researcher selects one class, one lesson, one topic, one group of students, as a suitable context for undertaking theory-directed research (see Figure 5.1), rather than because the issue derives from concerns about *that* class, topic, etc., then we would consider this an instrumental case study.

Is a context-directed, intrinsic case study suitable as a basis for academic research?

Given the discussion above about the possible problem with AR as a basis for research that has to meet academic requirements, the reader might wonder if the same problems apply to an intrinsic context-directed case study. Certainly, some of the examples of research questions suggested above (such as 'How can I get my final year class to get more engaged in revision?') seem to be rather parochial in nature. However, an intrinsic case study of this type can be perfectly suitable as the basis for an academic project as long as the researcher's understanding of the original practice-based issue is developed through a review of relevant research literature, leading to the specification of research questions that will allow the building of a suitable design for the case study (i.e., collecting and analysing relevant data to seek to answer the research questions) within a suitable time schedule.

The case study will be planned, carried out and reported as a single cycle of research (although it will likely lead to recommendations for how the research can be refined or taken further), unlike the AR process of successive cycles of activity and evaluation. Most importantly, if the case study needs to be reported in a formal academic style, the work must be planned and reported so that the findings of the case study can be explicitly linked back to the wider research literature. So the 'optional' feature shown Figure 5.2, illustrating the context-based mode of research, is an essential part of a case study that must be reported as academic research – as shown in Figure 5.5. So, for example, Yevsiyevich (2011, p. 14) saw her implementation of a new learning tool (evidence sheets) in a Year 12 (i.e., for 16–17 year old) religious studies class as "a piece of action research", but she intended her study not only to bring about change in the professional context of her teaching placement, but also to "present pedagogical inquiries to the RS community".

If you are carrying out your research as part of an academic assignment, it is important to familiarise yourself with the criteria by which your report will be judged before you start planning your study. For an undergraduate, or an initial teaching education assignment, it is likely to be sufficient that you relate your findings back to the literature to show how what you found links with previous research. In the previous section I discussed Dry's research study undertaken during his PGCE. As pointed out above, Dry submitted to the university a formal report of his research, which was later published in *JoTTER* (Dry, 2010). He described his study as AR, but provided a detailed

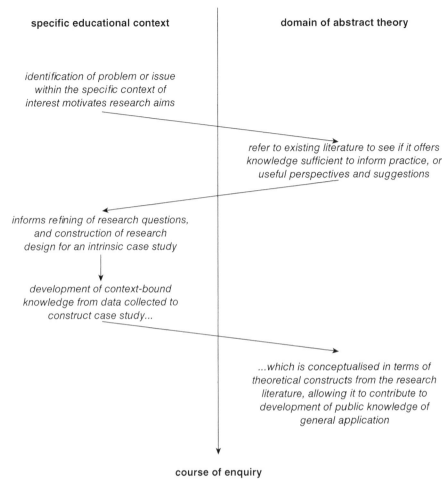

specific educational context

domain of abstract theory

identification of problem or issue within the specific context of interest motivates research aims

refer to existing literature to see if it offers knowledge sufficient to inform practice, or useful perspectives and suggestions

informs refining of research questions, and construction of research design for an intrinsic case study

development of context-bound knowledge from data collected to construct case study...

...which is conceptualised in terms of theoretical constructs from the research literature, allowing it to contribute to development of public knowledge of general application

course of enquiry

Figure 5.5 An intrinsic case study may be undertaken in context-directed mode, but can still be formally reported to add to public knowledge

and clear exposition of the purpose of his study; the findings of a review of relevant reviewed literature; specific relevant research questions; an explained research design; an account of the analysis of data and the conclusions reached; a discussion of the results, and how they related back to the original motivation for the study and the reviewed literature; and a consideration of the limits of the study and possible directions for further research (in effect, he followed the model suggested in Chapter 12).

For a PhD study, there will be an expectation that you have added to our understanding of a topic in a modest, yet substantive (non-trivial) way. Often in a Master's dissertation, well-established theory or previously proposed innovations may be tested out within a specific context to see if it helps make sense of, or improve, practice in that context. Both for trainee teachers and teachers in service, it is important that any findings are also clearly linked to professional learning that can inform future practice. This is demonstrated in this comment from the report of Forbes' PGCE research project published in *JoTTER*:

> I am aware that one case study cannot offer enough evidence to support general-isations about all learners in a similar situation, and that is by no means the intention of this study. I wish instead to look closely at *how* the Spanish exchange trip impacts upon the attitudes and productive language skills of these four particular Year 8 pupils, with a view to discovering how I, as an MFL teacher, can maximise the benefits of exchange trips for pupils in the future.
>
> (Forbes, 2010, p. 116)

Forbes is right that we cannot assume that our local findings apply in other contexts – in different schools, with other students taught by other teachers. A key issue for making results useful to others is to provide enough detail of the context of your own research to allow other readers to make judgements (what is called 'reader generalisation') about whether you are working in a comparable situation to their own professional context where your findings are likely to be pertinent (see Chapter 7).

——— Case studies and teacher research

Providing such detail, known as 'thick description' (Geertz, 1973), is one of the features of a well-written case study. Table 5.5 shows how this and other features of the case study methodology can be applied in classroom-based enquiry.

Table 5.5 The nature of classroom-based case studies

Characterisation of case study	Application in classroom-based research
Case study explores one instance from among many possible instances	The case could be: some aspect of teaching and learning in one of our classes; one lesson; the teaching of one topic; one student in one of our classes; an identified category of students (e.g., those labelled gifted) in a class; an identified group of students working together in a class; an examination paper; one teaching activity; etc.
Case study is naturalistic	We enquire into an aspect of teaching and learning as it occurs in the usual classroom context. For example, the case study is often of a real teacher working in his/her own school with his/her own class, as part of the normal timetable or other school activity. The case study may be of an innovation, where that innovation is introduced by the teacher as part of the normal process of trying out new approaches in teaching.
The case cannot readily be separated from its context	For example, we may look at one episode that is part of a lesson; one group of students working in the context of a class; one topic that is part of a teaching scheme…
	We can *identify* the specific instance that is our case, but we cannot dissect it from its natural context without severing connections that are inherent to the nature of the case: and the case cannot be fully appreciated without some knowledge of its context.

Characterisation of case study	Application in classroom-based research
Case study accounts provide 'thick description'	The researcher has an extensive and intimate engagement with the case and so can collect detailed and nuanced information, often from a range of complementary sources. Reporting a 'thick description' allows readers to compare the context of the case with other contexts they may be familiar with, and so make judgements about the likely relevance of the findings to their own work.
Case study commonly involves collecting a range of types of data	Case study is often selected when a phenomenon is seen as complex, and involves a range of interacting factors. This is often the case when we explore aspects of teaching and learning where many 'variables' are at work. Case studies often involve the collection of data from several of documentation, observation, interview, focus groups, questionnaires, etc. Often it is possible to 'triangulate' the different data sources to see if they offer a consistent picture of the case.

Avoiding the muddle of 'mixed methods'

As suggested in Table 5.5, it is common for case studies to draw upon a range of data sources. Eisenhardt (1989, pp. 534–535) wrote that "case studies typically combine data collection methods such as archives, interviews, questionnaires, and observations. The evidence may be qualitative (e.g., words), quantitative (e.g., numbers), or both." Consider, as an example, a teacher who decided to implement dialogic teaching approaches into a sequence of lessons with one class because she thought this would help students engage better with the ideas being presented. To explore the effect of this innovation, she might decide to undertake a case study of the teaching and learning in the sequence of lessons. This might derive from the teacher having read about dialogic teaching (Staarman & Mercer, 2010) and so deciding that she would implement some of the ideas because she wanted to better understand the nature of the approach; or it may be something that had been suggested by a colleague who knew she was unhappy about the teaching and learning in this particular class.

Questions for reflection

Can you relate these two hypothetical scenarios to the distinction between theory-directed and context-directed models of research? Can you relate the labels 'intrinsic' and 'instrumental' to the case study in these scenarios?

As part of the hypothetical case study our hypothetical teacher might:

- use a voice recorder or video camera to keep a record of classroom interaction;
- analyse students' written work carefully to look for evidence of their understanding of the material discussed in class;
- use a questionnaire to survey the students' views about the use of the new approaches;
- interview some students about particular aspects of the classroom interactions identified from the classroom recordings, to ask them about the thinking behind their contributions.

Such a case study would collect a range of data, of various kinds, directed at both teasing out different features of the case and testing out the inferences drawn in analysis – by comparing the messages from different 'slices' of the data. The questionnaire might include items with closed response options, when analysis might lead to tallying and reporting the numbers of responses in each category.

As suggested in Chapter 4, some people might describe this as a 'mixed-methods' study, as it used a range of data collection techniques and provided different kinds of data suitable for analysing in particular ways. However, it was also pointed out in Chapter 4 that the term 'mixed methods' is used in a range of ways, and might best be reserved (if used at all) for research that combines fundamentally different research approaches. Yet case study offers a single coherent methodology, within which we can design studies that sensibly collect and analyse a range of data. I would suggest that calling this type of study 'mixed methods' is both potentially confusing and also entirely unnecessary. So in her research (reported in *JoTTER*) on how seating arrangements influence discussion in a Year 8 class, Dowley reports that:

> The three methods of research used here – non-participant observations, questionnaires and informal interviews – allowed me to break my research into three distinct parts, in order to give me small pictures that will build up to show the findings of my case study.
>
> (Dowley, 2012, p. 231)

This seems a logical approach within the strategy (methodology) of a case study. Describing it *as* a case study offers a clear label for the research without inviting the 'muddle' of what different people understand by mixed methods.

Further reading

The studies carried out by trainee teachers whilst on professional placement, and reported in the *Journal of Trainee Teacher Educational Research*, may be accessed at: http://jotter.educ.cam.ac.uk/

A consideration of the nature (and problematic aspects) of action research is given in: Tripp, D. (2005). Action research: A methodological introduction. *Educação e Pesquisa / Education and Research, 31*(3), 443–466. (The journal is online at www.scielo.br/revistas/ep/iaboutj.htm)

PART II

Learning from educational research

This part considers some key ideas that can be used to *evaluate* educational research. There are at least two different ways in which we might wish to judge a report of educational enquiry:

- Are the claims justified?
- Are the claims relevant?

In other words, as readers and potential users of educational research, we wish to know whether a study has been competently executed, so that we can have confidence in its findings, and also whether what was found in the research is likely to have implications for our own professional context or area of concern. These are different issues as there may be very good reasons why an extremely competent piece of research should not be assumed to apply 'here' – just as the findings of a study that initially appears highly relevant may need to be treated cautiously if its methodology seems fundamentally flawed.

It is very important to appreciate this distinction, as publication of research in an international peer-reviewed research journal *should* suggest that the study has been competently carried out and carefully reported, but does not give any assurances that the findings are transferable to our own professional context. Chapter 6 considers how we can evaluate the quality of research studies, and Chapter 7 explores how we might judge the relevance of research to our own professional context. Both of these chapters will draw upon some of the key points about educational research discussed in Part I.

Finding literature

Before evaluating research reports, we need to be able to identify potentially relevant studies. There is now a vast research literature in education, and it may seem difficult to know how to start finding suitable reading. In searching for relevant literature, it is useful to identify suitable key terms. We should be aware that sometimes there are alternative terms used for much the same thing by different authors, but this will normally become evident when we start reading. So if I searched for learners' 'misconceptions' in the topic of 'chemical reactions', I would find papers which led me to realise that 'misconceptions' are sometimes called 'alternative conceptions', and that 'chemical reactions' are sometimes discussed under the heading 'chemical change'. I can then extend my search with these new terms.

We still need to know where to start searching, and there is a range of possibilities here. A student studying a course will normally have been assigned recommended readings and these will normally cite other literature. Often we can identify likely further studies of interest from these citations. Once we start on this 'paper chase', it can become self-perpetuating. It is important to be able to make judgements about relevance from reading abstracts and quick scans of material. It is important to know what justifies committing serious time for close study, as not everything that sounds like it will be useful is actually that central to our interests. If there are no obvious starting points in course reading lists, then supervisors, course tutors or school mentors *may* be able to make suggestions, but remember that it is your job as the researcher to locate the literature relevant to your study. Tutors may help, but it is not their role to do this for you.

Library staff, however, often do see it as part of their job to help students in literature searches, and will be able to introduce the main abstract services and databases that list a great deal of the available material. This will often allow a fairly systematic review of all material that is tagged with keywords of interest to your search. Nowadays, many of these search facilities can be used off-site by password-controlled access from your home computer.

Although less systematic, a search engine such as Google Scholar can also be useful in finding relevant literature that may be helpful in developing a conceptual framework (i.e., an informed way of thinking about the topic, see Chapter 3) for your study. It is also useful to peruse the copies of recent journals in the library, although this can easily lead to a lot of time spent finding a great many interesting articles, few of which are directly relevant to the task in hand. This is great for expanding your thinking, but may not be helpful in meeting deadlines. Time can pass very quickly in a well-stocked library.

Most journals are now accessible online, and indeed some are now only published that way. Articles published electronically are assigned a unique identifying code, a DOI (the 'digital object identifier'), which is unchanged even if the journal web address changes for some reason. So if you wanted to read my paper 'Vive la différence? Comparing "like with like" in studies of learners' ideas in diverse educational contexts' (Taber, 2012b), published in the open-access journal *Educational Research International*, you could access it by typing the DOI (10.1155/2012/168741) into an internet search engine.

A list of journals relevant to educational research can be found at https://camtools. cam.ac.uk/wiki/site/%7Ekst24/education-journals.html, with links to the journal home pages. Most journal sites allow you to search the archive of issues by keying in your search terms. Often, once you have identified a paper of interest, the journal sites often also offer links to other papers by the same authors, and sometimes to other more recent papers that cite that paper (these features may extend beyond the specific journal, but are often limited to that particular publisher's own portfolio of journals).

If the journal is archived in JSTOR (www.jstor.org), a digital platform that includes over a thousand journals, then when you have identified an interesting article, you will be able to search for related items across the whole of the JSTOR platform. Usually the most recent volumes of a journal are not included in JSTOR, but its archive includes a great many classic studies, and its education section lists well over 100 different periodicals.

Usually, when accessing papers online, you will also be able to download the citation in the format needed for bibliographic applications that help you manage and correctly cite the literature you refer to. These applications take a little time to learn to use, but can save a lot of effort and angst in the long run. Whether you decide to use such an application, or simply keep your own list of bibliographic details, one very important piece of advice is to *always* make a note of the full bibliographic details at the time you identify and access any material you may later wish to cite in your work. Many hours can be wasted trying to rediscover what 'Smith, 2008' (or, worse, 'Smith') referred to, months later when you are writing up.

Most journals require a subscription to access papers (but some are open-access, and so free to all). Universities subscribe to many of these journals and can allow students access from any computer (including off site) using a password-based security system. Therefore, not being able to physically get to the library after a busy day in school is no longer a good reason not to have explored a wide range of research literature. Teacher-researchers who are not registered for university qualifications may find there are arrangements for local teachers to use university library facilities, although this would not usually extend to subscription access when working away from the library.

6

Teachers evaluating research quality

This chapter:

- introduces ways of thinking about research writing
- discusses the different types of publication outlet for research writing
- considers the importance of peer review in ensuring quality standards
- discusses quality criteria that allow readers to evaluate research reports
- introduces notions of validity and reliability, authenticity and trustworthiness of research
- raises the issue of whether concerns about the ethical conduct of a study should undermine confidence in its conclusions.

―――――――――― **Three metaphors for thinking about research writing** ―――

For the reader new to research writing, and perhaps apprehensive about the task, it may be useful to adopt three metaphors that can provide guidance: the author *as story-teller, as advocate,* and *as teacher* (see Box 6.1).

Box 6.1

The research author as story-teller, advocate and teacher

Effective educational research writing can be seen in terms of:

- The *literary* analogy: A good research report has a narrative that leads the reader through 'the story' of the research.
- The *legal* analogy: The author needs to make the case by a careful, logical argument, drawing upon convincing evidence.
- The *pedagogic* analogy: The author is a communicator, charged with informing readers about the research.

———— **Different types of research require different types of evaluation** ————

A key point to be taken into account when judging research reports is that different types of studies set out to do different types of things, and it is not appropriate to judge them all in exactly the same way. This is closely tied to the idea that educational research is usually undertaken within a 'paradigm' that informs all aspects of the research process, and determines the nature and significance of the claims being made (see Chapter 3). It is strongly suggested, therefore, that the present chapter should be read after the previous chapters (which introduce and explain the main distinction between different types of educational research). So, in research undertaken within ERP1, the researcher is attempting to find out about, and record, some aspect of an objective reality. The researcher attempts to uncover that reality whilst having as little influence on the researched situation as possible. The informants in such research are often considered as 'research subjects' in the very real sense that in many studies the individual subjects are assumed to represent members of a wider population, and to be interchangeable with other members of the population.

However, research undertaken within ERP2 is likely to see informants as participants, perhaps even co-learners, in the research (Taber & Student, 2003), and jointly involved in the process of constructing the research account. There is no assumption that the researcher merely reports what was already there, as the researcher has entered the research context and is interacting with the other participants. There is often a deliberate attempt to collect data from individuals in such depth that the accounts developed reflect the personal history and unique character of the informants. Such research does not assume that participants can be non-problematically swapped for other members of some wider population without changing the findings of the research. The issue of generalisability – whether findings might apply elsewhere – is often a key concern when reading this type of research.

———— **Judging whether educational research claims are justified** ————

There are several issues that will influence whether we consider research reports to offer justifiable findings. When reading a research report, especially one that claims to demonstrate that major changes in professional practice are needed, we need to ask ourselves a number of questions:

- Is the account detailed enough for the reader to make judgements?
- Is the account honest?
- Is the focus appropriately conceptualised in the research?
- Is the methodology appropriate?
- Are the techniques applied in a technically competent manner?
- Do the conclusions logically follow from the findings?

A failure in any one of these stages may invalidate the conclusions and make any recommendations dubious. (This should be borne in mind when planning and carrying out classroom research – see Chapter 8.) A further question we should consider is:

- Has the research been conducted in an ethical manner?

Question for reflection

Should it matter *to the reader* if research findings have been obtained by unethical means as long as all the criteria for offering justified knowledge claims have been met?

—————————————————————————————————————— **The peer-review process** ——

An initial question that can be usefully asked about any study we read is, 'Where is it published?' Research reports can be published in research journals (primarily intended for academics), professional periodicals (primarily intended for practitioners), in conference proceedings and on personal websites, for example. In general, if a study is published in a recognised international research journal, it can usually be assumed to have some worth.

Publishing in academic research journals

Such a journal will normally be published by a commercial academic publisher, or a recognised research institution or learned body; will have an editorial board and/ or advisory board drawing upon international experts in the field; and will require all submitted studies to undergo 'peer review' by several 'referees'. This means that the editor sends papers for comment to recognised experts in their field, and bases decisions about what to publish on their recommendations:

> The referee has to both critique the arguments made (are the claims justified in terms of the evidence presented?) and judge whether the study offers new knowledge claims that are both robust and substantive enough to justify publication. Few, if any, studies can be considered definitive, so a judgement must be made about whether a study offers the basis to inform future work...
>
> (Taber, 2012a, p. 6)

The most prestigious journals have rigorous quality standards and reject most of the material they receive. Moreover, most papers that are published have to be revised by the authors to meet the criticisms and suggestions of referees – so peer review is a process that improves as well as selects what is published. The following comments are extracted from an editorial suggesting what authors should expect referees to look for in a journal submission (Taber, 2012a):

> A key feature of any publishable contribution is that it should be clearly argued, so that any knowledge claims made can readily be seen to follow from the presentation of empirical data and/or analysis of literature offered.
>
> ...a referee needs to make a judgement about the degree of novelty of a submission. ... A review may show novelty by offering an analysis or synthesis of existing literature that goes beyond simply cataloguing existing publications on a topic, to reveal a previously unnoticed pattern or trend across published studies. ... In empirical work, novelty might be quite nuanced ... a paper will not set out to simply replicate prior research, but to move beyond it by following up ideas and questions deriving from previous studies.

...readers will normally expect the literature review to set out a conceptualisation of the issue or problem being studied. This usually motivates the specific research question(s) that are being addressed in the study.

...the authors of each submission need to persuade referees that their research design offers a coherent and suitable approach to tackling the research question(s)...

All studies in which human subjects are participants, regardless of the approach taken, need to adhere to ethical guidelines. This is something that it is especially important to bear in mind when research is carried out with one's own faculty colleagues or students, when issues of informed consent and confidentiality may become more problematic.

Question for reflection

The examples of quality criteria for peer review listed above are taken from an editorial in a specialist journal concerned with chemistry education. Which of these points are likely to apply in other areas of educational research?

Journal websites will provide information on editorial boards and procedures. Submitted papers are usually read and evaluated by at least two experts in the field before being accepted for publication. The reviewers are usually anonymous (to avoid them being subject to pressure from authors) and often the authors are asked to submit a 'blind' version of their manuscript that disguises their own identity so that the work must be judged on its own merits. The system is not perfect – it is often possible for a referee to realise who the author of a paper must have been (so some journals use a 'single blind' approach, where referees are told who the authors are, but not vice versa) and editors have to rely on referees making judgements objectively rather than allowing personal friendships or antagonisms to influence their recommendations. However, the system provides a safeguard which the community can trust, that most papers published have sufficient merit.

Publishing in practitioner journals

Some practitioner periodicals, aimed at and largely written by teachers themselves, also use peer-review procedures. However, the criteria used to evaluate papers may be less stringent. For example, accounts that are considered to provide useful illustrations of good practice may be accepted for publication in such periodicals, without needing to demonstrate any substantial contribution to new knowledge. Such periodicals often also publish 'opinion'-based pieces meant to stimulate discussion that need not be based on wide readings of existing literature, nor new empirical evidence. It is often quite acceptable for such articles to be based on selective literature and anecdotal evidence. These contributions may indeed stimulate useful discussion among readers, but when carrying out a review of literature they should not be confused with reports of research. Such material may certainly be referred to and cited, but personal opinion (even if published) and research findings should be given appropriate weight in building up an understanding of a topic. Where researchers do publish articles about their empirical work in practitioner journals, they are often required to simplify their theoretical background and limit the number of academic references made in order to meet the style of the publication (and the assumed preferences of the professional readership). High-quality work may be published in such journals, but it is sensible to assume that empirical studies reported in practitioner journals *may* not have been as carefully vetted as those in academic research journals.

Online journals

Most international research journals allow papers to be accessed via websites (through electronic subscriptions or payment per article downloaded), and the research reports are no different from those in paper copies of the journals (and so have the same status). Often these journals publish the paper 'online first', sometimes many months before the paper copy. There are increasing numbers of journals that only publish online, which may be most reputable. For example, the author edits an electronic-only journal called *Chemistry Education: Research & Practice* (*CERP*). *CERP* has an editorial board, and advisory board drawn from recognised experts internationally, uses the accepted peer-review process and is published by a learned society (the Royal Society of Chemistry).

However, it is important to bear in mind that *anyone* could start and publish a journal online, and – if unsure – a reader should look to see who the editors and board members are, to confirm they are likely to ensure quality standards: are they well known in the field? Do they work at prestigious universities or research institutions? Are they drawn from a range of countries? Most genuinely international journals related to education will have boards including academics from North America, Europe, Australasia, etc.

The 'grey' literature: conference papers

Material presented at conferences is often also published in one form or another. The status of conference papers is variable. Some prestigious conferences review papers according to the same type of peer-review process used in journals. However, as one of the advantages of conferences is allowing reports of recent and ongoing work, it is more usual that only a proposal/abstract written months before the conference will have been reviewed. Conferences have different rules about what needs to be included in such a proposal. In particular, some conferences require the abstract to include reference to research results and conclusions (which allows referees to review the proposal more rigorously) and others do not (allowing more up-to-date work to be presented, as the results did not need to be available when the proposal was made, many months before the conference). Paper copies of papers distributed at a conference, or made available by the author later, *may* have been through a minimal peer-review process.

When formal books of proceedings are published, there may be further peer review and revision of papers *after* presentations – although this may not always reach the standards of top journals. Sometimes conference papers, and other such literature – discussion papers and position papers that may be distributed without being through formal peer-review processes – are referred to as 'grey literature'. This reminds us that the quality and status of such papers is very variable. Such papers are not necessarily of low quality, but the readers should take extra care in reading them critically. Some 'grey literature' (especially papers given at the annual British Educational Research Association conference) is archived at 'Education-line' as part of the British Education Index service (www.leeds.ac.uk/bei/index.html).

The 'grey' literature: publishing on the web

Publishing papers electronically on a website has become very common. Individual researchers sometimes publish papers online on personal websites. However, as researchers are judged by their publications in research journals, some caution is needed in considering these papers. Usually such papers are reprints (i.e., making available writing previously published) or pre-prints (making available papers due for publication in journals or books) or conference papers. If papers appear to have no information about where they have been published, submitted or presented, then one may suspect that they either fall short of publication standards or report work-in-progress not yet ready for formal reporting. Various organisations may also publish research through the web. This can include reports commissioned from reputable researchers by charities and other organisations, and research digests commissioned by organisations such as education authorities. The status of the hosting organisation, the independence and reputation of the authors, and the extent to which reference to other relevant literature is included can all help the reader make a judgement about the quality of the 'research' reported.

Teacher research on the web

In recent years, there has been encouragement for teachers and other professionals to carry out small-scale research, with limited funding support from sponsoring organisations. The UK government offered 'Best Practice Research Scholarships' (BPRSs) for some years, requiring those receiving the support to produce a report for publication on a website. A good deal of classroom research of this type is now available. The BPRS scheme required the practitioner-researchers to have a research mentor to advise on the project, but the level of research training available within such schemes is usually limited, and the detail required in reports is often minimal. This is quite reasonable, as award holders may well have been deterred by the thought of having to produce a lengthy report at the end of the project, and the research was often of an action research nature where the main aim was to improve practice rather than create new public knowledge. There must be a question over the extent to which such limited reports of 'best practice' can inform teaching and learning more widely, but this source of literature can certainly provide ideas and examples for other teachers to consider.

——— Is the account detailed enough to make further judgements? ———

The reader of research papers needs to be able to make judgements about the nature, quality and significance of the research reported. Making such judgements requires the report to include sufficient detail of how the focus was conceptualised, what data was collected, and how it was analysed, to be able to decide whether the researcher's findings seem justified.

Data analysis always involves some level of data *reduction* (see Chapter 11). In studies using quantitative analysis we have to assume that counting, coding and calculating have all been carried out carefully. There are equivalent technical procedures involved in analysing qualitative data. The reader has to trust that coding has been carried out carefully and sensibly, and that fragments of data used to illustrate categories and themes are representative of the wider data set. It is never possible to know for sure how well this work has been done, and so we usually have to assume that researchers are technically competent in these matters if they appear to have followed appropriate procedures (and they have published in an international peer-reviewed journal).

The reader should, however, be given enough detail in an account to decide whether the types of procedure applied are appropriate. Some examples of the types of questions that the reader should be able to answer from the information given in a paper are given in Boxes 6.2 and 6.3.

Box 6.2

When reading an ERP1 study, we need to have enough information to answer several questions

Questions we may ask about ERP1 studies might include:

- Is the sample size large enough?
- Is the sample representative of the population?
- Does the data collected address the research question/hypothesis?
- Is the statistical test used appropriate for this type of data?
- Have the outcomes of statistical tests been clearly presented?
- Is it clear how statistical findings are interpreted?

Box 6.3

When reading an ERP2 study, we need to have enough information to answer several questions

Questions we may ask about ERP2 studies might include:

- Were interviews long enough for in-depth discussion?
- What types of questions were used in interviews?
- Did the researchers record informants' comments verbatim?
- How much of the data collected was transcribed?
- How was the data sorted and coded?
- How did the researcher(s) decide when they had sufficient data?
- How did the researcher(s) decide when they had undertaken sufficient analysis?

Any paper that does *not* allow these types of questions to be answered restricts our ability to judge its quality, and so limits the weight we should give to its findings. Journals are often under pressure to keep papers short (to publish more studies in the available pages), and so editors often look to see if they can persuade authors to make papers concise – and there are often stringent guidelines on paper length (4–6000 words for many journals). This makes it difficult for an author to give a full report of a major research project in the space available. Whilst recognising these constraints, a research report should give sufficient detail to allow readers to know:

what was done

and why

and how.

If this is not clear, the paper is of limited value as a contribution to knowledge. One of the characteristics of the shift towards electronic, online publishing is that journals often allow authors to include 'supplementary information' linked to the online version of their paper. For web-only journals, judgements about paper length can be made on academic grounds (is the paper detailed enough, without including trivial information or material on irrelevant side issues?) without worrying about the need to keep an issue within a limited number of pages (as major costs of hard-copy journals include the production costs of printing the material, and the distribution costs of posting journals out to subscribers around the world, both increased if more pages are printed).

—— Is the account honest?

The reader of educational research has no real way of safeguarding against fraudulent accounts of research, which are occasionally identified. A famous example concerns very influential research on the 'nature versus nurture' debate, where studies into twins who had been separated soon after birth were used to attempt to determine the extent to which such characteristics as 'IQ' were determined by genetic inheritance, and how much by upbringing. Years after these studies became widely reported in textbooks, doubts over the research surfaced. There were questions over how so many pairs of separated twins had been identified for use in the research, why the statistics did not shift in the ways expected as the sample size was increased, and why there was no trace of reliable records of the research assistants who had supposedly collected much of the data!

This type of fraud is probably very rare, as professional researchers who are caught out are likely to lose their jobs, reputations and careers. (Though in this case, the researcher was knighted, and doubts only arose after he died and it was found that all his records had been burnt.) Studies that are undertaken by researchers from established universities or institutes of similar standing, that are published in recognised research journals with international editorial/advisory boards, and that use peer-review procedures are very unlikely to be deliberately dishonest. It would not be impossible to prepare a paper with fabricated data that might seem genuine to reviewers, but this would go against the values and 'epistemological hunger' (or desire to understand and know) that brings most researchers into academic work.

Bias in educational research

A more insidious type of dishonesty concerns the extent to which researchers allow their biases and expectations to flavour their findings. We all have biases, but the good researcher will not allow them to prejudice their work as they are more interested in having a better understanding than proving their hunches correct. Of course, that is 'easier said than done'. In ERP1, carefully followed procedures should minimise the effects of researcher bias. Although the choice and definition of concepts and categories will limit what could be found in a study, these choices should be clearly stated. This is a much more difficult issue in interpretivist research. One suggestion is that researchers do not assume they can be totally objective, but make their assumptions and expectations explicit, so the reader is aware of the direction that any bias would shift findings. A grounded theory methodology (see the previous chapter) should provide the same types of safeguard against bias as the procedures used in ERP1 research, but *only* if the full GT process is carefully carried through.

It should also be recognised that many interpretivist researchers would argue that, when dealing with the world of ideas, feelings, beliefs etc., there is no objective truth, only the understandings constructed in human minds and through their interactions. This is a fair point, but where such research claims to explore the ideas, beliefs or understandings of teachers or learners, the reader has a right to expect the research account to be an interpretation that owes more to the informants than the beliefs and opinions of the researcher.

Is the research paper a fraud? ———

The Nobel-Prize-winning immunologist Sir Peter Medawar (1963/1990) posed the question of whether the scientific paper is a fraud. Medawar was raising the issue of how research in the natural sciences is often reported as if it is a straightforward, linear process. Hypotheses are proposed, tested, supported or refuted – and a neat account is published. The messy reality of crazy conjectures soon ditched, false starts, mistakes, laboratory mix-ups, data lost to contamination, power-failure, computer crashes, or researchers being delayed returning from lunch, and so forth, seldom appears in the account. (Although most of us have heard the story of how penicillin was discovered by accident because some dirty glassware used in experiments had been left unwashed when the scientist took his annual leave. Modern health and safety standards would likely have seriously delayed a discovery that has saved many millions of lives.) The result is that the final paper presents a very convincing argument for the smooth path to the findings – how can it have been otherwise?

The contexts of discovery and justification of findings

Interestingly, Medawar did not feel that any of this actually mattered in terms of *the findings*. Rather, he was concerned that research papers may offer a very poor image of what the *process* of research is actually like. Medawar was drawing upon a recognised distinction between *the context of discovery* and *the context of justification*. In other words, it can be argued that it does not matter how ideas came to be formed, or what false moves were made in exploring them, as long as there is a sound argument for why we should be confident they are right once we have tested them.

So, it does not matter (to take an almost mythical example) if the chemist August Kekulé came up with the idea for the molecular structure of the compound benzene when he dozed off and had a dream about snakes. This has no significance for whether the structure should be accepted. What does matter is the eventual evidence that led to chemists accepting the structure that Kekulé (quite literally) dreamed up. Scientists must report *this evidence* accurately and honestly, and in enough detail for it to be checked by other scientists replicating the work. As long as this is done, stories of how they may have started off with a different hypothesis, or perhaps dropped a flask part way through an experiment and had to start again, are not considered relevant and are not reported.

Question for reflection

Medawar was a scientist (trying to understand the immune system). Can his analysis be applied to research in classrooms?

Subjectivity in research accounts

To a natural scientist (or the teacher with a background in the natural sciences), some research reports in education and other social sciences must seem rather personal compared to the dry, third-person accounts they are used to reading. Many research papers in the social sciences are written in the first person, and have an almost biographical nature. These accounts may include features of personal history that 'explain' research interests, or include anecdotal material to indicate how hunches arose. False starts, rather than being omitted, may even seem to be celebrated in some reports. This type of writing is not ubiquitous in educational research, but is common in studies from ERP2, where it is recognised that research has a subjective element. If a researcher sees herself as an integral part of the context being studied, interacting with the informants in a process of co-constructing data (see Chapter 3), then it makes sense to write an account where the researcher's role is recognised rather than obscured.

It is sometimes suggested that when a practitioner writes up their research in third-person style ('the teacher-researcher interviewed the student', rather than 'I interviewed the student'), this is dishonest as it attempts to present an objective account that underplays the researcher's intimate involvement in the research context, and so give the impression that the (teacher-)researcher was able to stand back and observe as an outsider. Some new teacher-researchers do adopt this third-person style, and usually there is no intended dishonesty, but rather an attempt to emulate what they believe research writing is meant to be like. The author once read an assignment from a trainee teacher offering an account of both an observation of a teacher's lesson and of how – at the end of the lesson – the observer approached the teacher and offered a rather critical evaluation of the teaching observed. I was concerned about this assignment at two different levels. For one thing, the trainee was meant to have critiqued his own teaching and not that of one of the teachers working in his placement school. Secondly, whilst most teachers involved in mentoring trainees are open to discussing apparent limitations in their own teaching rather than wishing to be seen as paragons of classroom practice, it was hardly the place of the not-yet-qualified novice, still developing insight into both the job of teaching and the context of the placement school, to undertake an aggressive criticism of the fully qualified, experienced teacher.

When I broached these issues with the trainee, it transpired that he *was* actually presenting a critique of his own teaching. 'The teacher' he referred to in his assignment was himself, described in the third person. The classroom observer who was so critical of the teacher was also the trainee. In order to offer a 'scientific account' (and therefore in his mind a more rigorous one) the trainee referred to himself separately as both 'the teacher' and 'the observer', and reported his internal reflections on his lesson in the form of a dialogue between these two characters. In his attempt to be scientific and rigorous he managed to provide a distorted and misleading account. If you are reporting your own actions as a teacher-researcher in educational research writing, then describing yourself in the first person, as 'I', is not only acceptable, but often sensible.

Potential conflicts of interest

Question for reflection

Would you believe a study that claimed a computer program was effective in supporting student learning if that study was sponsored by the company selling the software?

One related issue is when researchers may be seen to have a 'conflict of interest'. For example, one of the studies mentioned in Chapter 2 (Macaruso et al., 2006) found that computer-based supplementary phonics software enabled students considered to be 'low performing' to catch up with their classmates. The second author of the paper, Hook, was a consultant involved in the design of the software. The third author, McCabe, was actually the Director of Research and Product Management at the company that developed the software. This is something the reader may wish to bear in mind when reading the study. However, these affiliations are reported at the end of the study, so that the potential 'conflict of interest' is acknowledged. Whilst ideally we might prefer an evaluation of the software that can be seen as independent, the developing company is both prepared to support research into their products (which may not happen otherwise), and presumably highly motivated to use the findings from research to improve and develop their software.

——— Is the focus appropriately conceptualised in the research? ———

There are many different ways that a project can be conceptualised. Any research paper will have a specific focus (and/or research questions), and the first part of any research account is usually setting the scene for the research by offering a way of thinking about the research context. This introductory section of a paper will explain key ideas that are being used to think about the research, and will discuss existing literature the author thinks especially relevant (see Chapter 3).

The reader may also have a view about how the topic is best understood, and which existing literature provides useful insights into the topic. It can be very thought-provoking to read the work of researchers who see things very differently from yourself, but you may decide not to be influenced by the findings of research which derives from a very different way of understanding the research focus.

Validity

The notion of *validity* is often used to judge research, especially in ERP1. There are different flavours of validity, but basically this is about measuring what you believe you are measuring. For example, a study of boys' and girls' involvement in lessons might measure how often pupils answer the teachers' questions. If it is found that girls answer fewer questions, this can be used to suggest that they are less involved in lessons – if we believe that we have used a valid indicator of involvement. A survey of pupils' attitudes to school science might include a question phrased, 'Do you think science is interesting?' Pupils responding might think that the question was about the science they hear about in the news and not have school lessons in mind when answering. School science is at best an imperfect reflection of science (Kind & Taber, 2005), so this would invalidate the question as a means of finding out about attitudes to *school* science.

The role of the conceptual framework in *making the case*

Part of the reason that the conceptualisation stage (see Chapter 3) is so important in research is because of the imperative in writing up studies to 'make the case' – providing readers with a coherent argument that convinces them that the conclusions drawn from a research study (and so the implications for practice that may be recommended) are based on sound logic. It is in the nature of a logical argument that any one single flawed link undermines the whole argument. Yet most research studies are in themselves only able to explore and report a single aspect of an issue.

For example, Kinchin's (2004) study of students' preferred type of learning environment offered respondents a choice of two caricatured classroom styles. Kinchin argues that "a mismatch between teachers' and students' epistemological views is likely to perpetuate problems in the classroom" (p. 310). This is a reasonable opinion, but is not supported purely by the data presented *in this study*. As is necessarily the case with so many studies, the evidence actually presented offers support for part of an argument, the rest of which relies on findings from other work (and which are built into the conceptual framework for the research presented at the start of the study).

One key way that educational researchers think about their own enquiries is from within a much more extensive conceptual framework (based upon previous research and scholarship) that provides the wider context for their research. It was the physicist Isaac Newton, now seen as a kind of archetypical scientist who (in a seemingly atypical modest comment) suggested that if he had seen further than others it was because he had stood on the shoulders of giants. Appropriately, as he was Warden of the Royal Mint, Newton's comment is represented around the edge of the British two-pound coin. In this sense, at least, natural science can provide a useful model for research in education – even if within the educational community there may be somewhat less agreement on who those giants actually are. (Many people's lists would likely include Piaget, Vygotsky, Bruner, Ausubel, Dewey; but what about Montessori, Froebel, Gardner, Papert, Sternberg, Bernstein, Rousseau, et al.?)

Sadly, some commentators now feel that Newton's famous comment was actually a way of putting down one of his scientific competitors – Robert Hooke. Newton and Hooke were involved in a priority dispute and Hooke was known as a rather short man. It is suggested that Newton was less concerned with recognising the work of people like Galileo or Copernicus, than hinting that he had nothing to learn from the diminutive Hooke. Whatever Newton's motivation, the phrase has become associated with the iterative and accumulative nature of research and scholarship.

Is the methodology appropriate?

Decisions about methodology derive from fundamental (paradigmatic) assumptions about the nature of what is being researched, and how knowledge may be generated through research (see Chapter 3). These assumptions will normally be apparent (either explicitly or implicitly) in the way a topic is conceptualised in the introduction to a research paper. However, if the reader feels that that methodology chosen is inconsistent with the way the topic has been set out in the introduction to a paper, this will limit the degree to which any findings are likely to be considered as addressing the initial research questions/focus.

Are the techniques applied in a technically competent manner?

As suggested above, one has to assume that much of the data handling in a research project has been carried out carefully and proficiently. However, there are technical issues that will be addressed in research reports that should be carefully considered. Statistical tests are usually only applicable to certain types of data, and may require minimum sample sizes. A test that is only valid where a population has a normal ('bell-shaped') distribution may not be informative if applied to a bimodal ('two-humped') distribution.

In a similar way, an in-depth analysis of interview data would normally assume that the informants' words were recorded verbatim, and another approach (e.g., the researcher making notes of the interview after the event) may not be considered rigorous enough. As always, though, we may have to accept methodological complications. Classic sociological research from the so-called Chicago school used covert participant observation to undertake ethnographic studies of groups such as street gangs – a methodological approach that interspersed participating in the observed group's activities with finding private opportunities for discrete note-making.

Reliability

In ERP1 research, it is usually assumed that the researcher measures some aspect of a pre-existing reality. In principle, the researcher can be substituted by another without influencing the findings. One way to test this assumption is to check inter-researcher consistency. For example, two researchers could independently use the same observation schedule in the same class, or code the same data into the same categories. This can lead to reliability coefficients, which are closer to 1 the greater the level of agreement between the two observers. It would normally be expected that, although there is inevitably some variation, there should be substantial agreement between researchers.

In some research, the checks of inter-researcher reliability are also used as a way of improving reliability. For example, in coding data, the researchers may all code the same sample independently. They then meet to discuss any disagreements, and decide which coding category/criteria they should use, until they feel they have developed a common understanding of the coding scheme. This is similar to the moderation process used by examination boards to ensure similar standards across examiners.

This type of checking is not possible in a study with a single researcher. It is also less significant in studies where the researcher considers they are co-constructing data with informants (ERP2 approaches), as here the data would be expected to be influenced by the researcher, and inter-researcher reliability is not a relevant consideration (Piantanida & Garman, 2009). This type of research account is not *fiction*, but it is a personal construction of the researcher reflecting their values, understandings, perceptions, and the formative experiences that brought them to the research – and so as long as we appreciate that, then the personal element does not invalidate the account.

You should not believe everything you read in research reports

The distinction between 'fact' and fiction may get stretched in interpretive research. In Chapter 3 we found Watts (1983) reporting students' alternative conceptual frameworks relating to a curriculum topic, but acknowledging that these were the outcome of a process of analysing individual student comments, and then constructing coherent synthetic models of different ways of thinking revealed. Watts' conceptual frameworks were not fictions, but they were constructions of the researcher following an analytical process, and not 'factual' accounts of specific students' thinking.

Later in the book (in Chapter 11), I report on the experiences and attitudes of Gill and Barry, two pupils in a school where I was teaching and where I undertook a case study. Gill and Barry *are* fictions. The narrative account of Gill's (and Barry's) experiences in the school is a device to present a readable summary of the conclusions of a detailed case study that drew on an extensive evidence base. This vignette presents research-based findings through the narrative device of fictional students who stand for the many pupils who contributed to the research. Importantly, it is made very clear that Gill and Barry are just literary devices, and the vignette acts as an overview of research reported in full detail elsewhere in the thesis.

Some educational researchers would go further than this. Behar (2001) published a paper in the *International Journal of Qualitative Studies in Education* that was "an extract from Nightgowns from Cuba, a novel-in-progress [which] is a mix of autobiography, ethnography, and fiction ... [that] focuses on the delicate relationship that developed between Regla, the maid, and her employer Naomi, a Jewish immigrant and socialist from Poland, as the two women encountered each other in a small rural town in Cuba in the late 1930s" (p. 107).

Good literature reflects truths about the human condition, and many novels are informed by detailed research. However, not everyone would consider the novel as a suitable form of educational research. Education tends to straddle the social sciences and the humanities, and those with strong social science backgrounds are likely to consider that fictional writing of this kind has no place in a research journal. Certainly readers are given few clues as to which aspect of the fiction are based on evidence or personal experience (if such a distinction is even meaningful in this form of 'research'), and which are just creative outputs of the researcher-novelist's imagination. Any reader tempted to report their own research in this way in a university assignment should certainly check first whether this would be considered acceptable.

Alternatives to validity and reliability

It is sometimes suggested that traditional notions of validity and reliability are not appropriate in interpretivist research, where accounts instead need to be trustworthy and authentic (Guba & Lincoln, 2005). Although these approaches use different techniques, there are still issues of technical competence in the way that data is collected and analysed (see Chapters 10 and 11), which can allow us to judge the trustworthiness of studies. We also expect studies from ERP2 approaches to offer rich ('thick') descriptions of research contexts that we can recognise as authentic accounts.

One important technique often used in ERP2 is 'triangulation' (see Chapter 4). As with validity, this is a term that has many variants of meaning. However, the key point is that different data sources, and often different forms of data, are collected and compared. The researcher would often expect these different sources to offer a coherent picture, and when this is not the case, then the researcher should comment and try to explain the discrepancy. There may be good reasons, for example, why a teacher and learners have different understandings of what happened in the same lesson – or, indeed, why a 'bully' construes an episode rather differently from the 'victim'. Although consistent interpretations of several 'slices of data' (to use a GT term) do not *ensure* the researcher has made a good job of making sense of the data, the effective use of triangulation gives the reader *more confidence* that the researcher has produced a *trustworthy* and *authentic* account.

Where research is intended to explore the understandings, beliefs, views or experiences of others – such as teachers and learners – it may be possible to show these informants draft accounts of the researcher's reports to get them to comment (so-called 'member checking'). This is not always feasible, and there is clearly no assurance that informants will always be able to give objective feedback on the extent to which an account does reflect their original contributions. However, it is a useful technique in some studies.

——Do the conclusions logically follow from the findings?——————

A report of research needs to offer a logical argument. The findings of the research need to follow logically from the results – from the analysis of data. Any recommendations (for further research, for good practice) should then follow from the findings in a logical manner. It might seem a fairly trivial matter to check this, but much educational research has a strong rhetorical flavour (see Chapter 1). It is not unusual for the discussions and conclusion to research papers to mix a consideration of the results of the paper with a range of other considerations (beliefs, opinions, viewpoints). It may well be that recommendations at the end of the paper do logically follow from accepting the presented findings AND all the assumptions leading up to them (about the way the field is conceptualised AND the choice of methodology AND the decisions made when collecting and analysing data) AND other assumptions or beliefs introduced and argued in discussing the findings. The use of capitals here implies that the conclusions are only sound if *each* of the components of the argument are accepted. A reader who is not convinced by these additional considerations could logically accept *the findings* of the study, but still not accept the implications drawn and recommendations made.

The rhetorical function of research: the value of mixed-ability teaching

In a 1999 paper introduced in Chapter 2, Lyle reports research that argues for the value of mixed-ability grouping in teaching. In the abstract of Lyle's paper (1999, p. 283), two claims are made:

1 In analysing the children's comments, it is argued that mixed-ability teaching provides a setting in which both low- and high-achieving students value the opportunity to work together where both groups believed they benefited.
2 The study suggests that interactions among peers can facilitate literacy development in individual children.

Interrogating knowledge claims

There are several points worth noting about these claims. Claim 1 is about the pupils' perceptions. Lyle reports that children of this age value working in mixed groups and believe they benefit. However, the wording of the claim is noteworthy – it *could be interpreted as meaning that an analysis has been designed to illustrate an existing thesis. This would be a much weaker claim (i.e., if evidence was selected and arranged for such a purpose).*

Claim 2 is about learning, and is somewhat firmer, although phrased with the careful term 'suggests'. However, this is not a claim about the value of mixed-ability groupings. Knowing that peer interactions can help individual children develop their literacy *in itself* tells us nothing about whether we should set up such interactions by organising pupils into mixed-ability groups within the class.

As reported in Chapter 4, Lyle's study was an intervention that might be seen as action research (AR). There are inherent difficulties in writing up AR, as the 'action' to improve the educational practice takes precedence over a rigorous research design (see Chapter 12). Lyle provides a good deal of evidence in the form of quotes from two focus group interviews – with those students in the class identified as low-attaining pupils, and those identified as 'high-fliers' (p. 288). The comments made by the pupils quoted in the paper are summarised in Table 6.1.

Table 6.1 Pupil observations in Lyle's 1999 study

Group	Reported
Both groups	• having someone to break down words, explain word meanings, and suggest words was useful • making new friends
Group 1 (below average attainment)	• group reading was helpful • sharing ideas in group work was useful • the specific activities in the intervention were helpful • that writing activities helped reading and spelling • they had learnt content in the intervention (i.e., geography content related to the materials used) • discussion was a useful way of deciding upon the best idea • group work involved skills such as listening and taking turns
Group 2 ('high-fliers')	• the student teachers helped them • helping others can consolidate new learning • helping others may lead to developing strategies that will be useful in one's own learning • helping others may initiate new learning if you need to find new things out to help them • the intervention activities were enjoyable • having an audience in mind is useful when writing • their writing improved during the intervention • they had learnt new curriculum knowledge • learning new concepts/concept words • skills such as listening were needed for effective group work • group work helped them achieve more than they could alone • pupils whom they had considered stupid were actually nice once you got to know them • group discussion can help identify good ideas

Question for reflection

Which of the reported pupil beliefs provide strong evidence for the effectiveness of mixed-ability groups in developing literacy?

This listing of Lyle's findings necessarily paraphrases and simplifies a long section of Lyle's paper offering detailed material from his data, but essentially covers the points made. The evidence presented seems to strongly *suggest* that the pupils quoted generally found the intervention valuable, and that these pupils did indeed benefit from the mixed-gender, mixed-ability group work with the undergraduate students.

Does Lyle's study demonstrate the benefits of mixed-ability grouping?

There were at least four significant aspects to the intervention:

- the pupils worked in small groups
- special activities were devised
- the groups had the full-time support of an informed adult helper
- the groups were mixed-ability.

Many of the positive outcomes could relate to the special activities devised for the group, or the full-time presence of a 'teacher' assigned to the group, or the value of group work itself. The mixing of 'abilities' probably *was* valuable as it becomes more likely that weaker readers will have someone who can help them, and the more able can reinforce and consolidate learning by taking on the 'teacher' role. Yet, the study was not set up in a way that enables the reader to know how much additional benefit the grouping strategy provided:

- Perhaps similar-ability groups might have had similar or better outcomes?
- Perhaps the use of mixed-gender groups facilitated the smooth running of groups more than the mixing of attainment levels?

The report of the study does not enable the reader to do any more than speculate on these issues.

Questions for reflection

Would it be appropriate for a researcher who has strong grounds for believing that students learn more effectively when organised in mixed-ability groups, to use similar-ability groups (to compare with mixed-ability groups) in his research? To what extent must ethical considerations compromise methodological decisions?

In a study such as this, a believer in the educational value of mixed-ability grouping has to balance the ethical imperative (to 'do no harm') against the methodological imperative (a rigorous research design). This issue is discussed further in Chapter 9.

Research writing as rhetoric

In absolute terms Lyle's paper tells us that a particular intervention organised in a particular way, with some pupils in one particular school, was thought by the pupils to be helpful in their learning. The intervention used groups that were judged to be mixed ability, and that may be a factor in some of the findings. The critical reader may well wonder how Lyle expects to convince the article's audience, given the limitations of the study, that the evidence presented leads to the conclusions offered. Certainly, in terms of the empirical evidence, the logical chain supporting the author's conclusions is delicate.

However, Lyle has not set out to present an account of a rigorous test of the value of mixed-ability grouping, and his study should not be judged in this way. Although the paper reports a research study, it makes little pretence at being an objective – in the sense of disinterested – investigation. Lyle begins the paper by suggesting that government guidance encouraging setting is not supported by research, and then reviews literature that demonstrates the limitations and problems of grouping pupils in this way.

Lyle's study is conceptualised (see Chapter 3) from a socio-cultural perspective, where learning is seen in terms of facilitating conditions where teachers and students can co-construct meaning (1999, p. 294). Lyle argues that collaboration with peers changes the contributions of the individual children in the class, and recommends that when planning their lessons teachers should consider how they will group children as well as which activities they will provide (p. 294). The gist of Lyle's argument is that teachers should "adopt practices that allow children to use talk as a meaning-making tool in collaborative settings" (p. 295).

The study is then set within a *rhetorical* context that is designed to make an argument that government preference for setting may be ill-informed, and that schools and teachers should not accept this view uncritically. The author sees his task as one of persuading readers of the potential value of mixed-ability grouping despite official guidance suggesting grouping by ability improves achievement (p. 294). So Lyle does not present disembodied findings, but rather interprets his data in terms of theoretical ideas from the underpinning conceptual framework supporting the research. In other words, Lyle makes claims that cannot be directly shown to follow from the data presented:

> As the children either read, or listened, to each other reading, each was involved in actively construing and interpreting the text. Subsequent discussion mediated the higher function of reading for meaning, as the children reflected on their thinking together.
>
> (Lyle, 1999, p. 293)

Lyle did not collect data to demonstrate these points *directly* (the pupils' comments were certainly not framed in terms of 'construing', 'higher cognitive functions' and 'reflection'), but rather he presents this as a reasonable interpretation from within the conceptual framework used in the research.

Caveat emptor ———

The reader of educational research is invited to 'buy into' the story being told by the author of the account. It is the author's responsibility to make the case for any conclusions offered. However, it is the reader's responsibility to check the argument proposed. Inevitably, any argument presented in an educational research study will in part depend upon data, and in part upon the interpretation of that data – an interpretation that draws upon the author's conceptual framework.

In some examples of ERP1 (see Chapter 3) research, where hypotheses are tested, research writing is expected to be largely objective, following the model idealised (if not always achieved) in the natural sciences. In natural science, research is influenced by values relating to objectivity, accuracy, transparency in reporting, etc. However, much writing in education is not disinterested but is informed by other values, for example relating to social justice. It is quite legitimate for a researcher to take such a stance (if education is not based in our values, then it may be considered to have little value), and to use research in support of championing their beliefs. As a reader of educational research, it is important that we are aware when this is happening, and can learn to identify the chain of argument for any research claim. Lyle's study would seem substantially flawed from the standards of experimental research. However, Lyle is quite open about his own beliefs, and allows the reader to clearly see the extent to which his interpretations derive from the data or from his own conceptual framework. This is common in ERP2 studies, where it is considered difficult for a researcher to be an objective observer of phenomena (see Chapter 3). The important criterion here is that the researcher should present the work honestly, making the subjective elements as explicit as possible, so that the reader can make up their own minds about the soundness of the underpinning values supporting the work. Where this is done, such as in Lyle's paper, it is perfectly legitimate to write rhetorical papers. Then journal referees and editors will make judgements on their suitability for publication in particular journals.

What makes for effective teacher development?

Garet and colleagues (2001) report an American study, published in the *American Educational Research Journal*, which explored teachers' perceptions of the type of professional development courses that were effective (see Chapter 2). They claimed in their paper that certain 'structural features' of the courses were important, including the form of the activity, the collective participation of teachers who shared professional concerns (e.g., teachers of the same subject, or grade level, or from the same school), and the duration of the activity (Garet et al., 2001, p. 916).

Garet et al. claimed that the core features of "professional development activities that have significant, positive effects on teachers' *self-reported* increases in knowledge and skills and changes in classroom practice" (p. 916) were:

- a focus on content knowledge ("our results confirm the importance of professional development that focuses on [subject] content");
- opportunities for active learning;
- coherence with other learning activities (p. 936).

(It is interesting to note that we might well make the last two points about *children's* learning in schools!)

Garet et al. (2001, p. 919) report that their study was based on a 'Teacher Activity Survey', where they "surveyed a nationally representative sample of teachers" who had attended professional development (PD) activities sponsored by a major sponsor. They reported "receiving responses from 1,027 teachers ... an overall teacher response rate of 72%". The findings were based on "self-reports of teacher experiences and behaviour". Their report of their study explains:

- how they selected their sample (p. 919)
- how they designed the questionnaire to elicit information about 'structural' and 'core' features of PD activities (p. 919)

- how they identified effective PD activities ("we asked each teacher in our national sample to indicate the degree to which his or her knowledge and skills were enhanced ... to what extent they made changes in their teaching practices...", p. 929).

Question for reflection

How would you position Garet et al.'s study in terms of the two educational research 'paradigms' introduced in Chapter 3?

Garet et al.'s knowledge claims are based on a statistical analysis of teacher responses to different items in the questionnaire used for the survey (2001, pp. 915–916). By comparing responses to items related to various aspects of the types of PD received, and the perceived effectiveness of the PD activities, the researchers were able to conclude that certain types of feature made the professional development activities more effective. In considering Garet and colleagues' claims, we need to consider both strengths and limitations of the study. The sample size and the response rate are both encouraging features. The published report offers a good deal of detail about how the sample was constructed, and how the questionnaire was designed and how the analysis was undertaken. All of this gives the reader confidence that this was a competently undertaken study, i.e., one that should be considered to offer valuable knowledge.

Input constrains output

However, there are two *inherent* limitations in this study. The first concerns the overall epistemological stance of the authors. Their research is clearly situated in the educational research paradigm described in Chapter 3 as 'confirmatory' (i.e., ERP1). Garet and colleagues built into their questionnaire items that asked teachers about specific, specified features of the PD activities they had attended. These features had been identified by a reading of the literature, and so were limited to features that had already been identified as potentially being important. Such an approach is not able to identify any other features teachers considered significant but which they were not asked about in the questionnaire.

Links in a chain

The second limitation is that the survey did not include any independent measure of the effectiveness of the PD (e.g., such as an Inspector or school principal judging any change in teaching). The perceptions of potential key features of PD were related to the teachers' own perceptions of any changes in their teaching. So the survey was able to relate features of PD to teacher *perceptions* of PD effectiveness – but therefore the survey only informs the reader about the effectiveness of PD activities to the extent that teachers' reported perceptions are valid indicators of changes in their own thinking and teaching. This is not to suggest that teachers are not offering accurate judgements – but (as we often find) a particular research study is only able to offer evidence for part of the chain of logic needed for a convincing argument. In this study the reader has to make assumptions about links that are not directly addressed (the availability in existing literature of the most relevant factors to include in the survey; the extent to which teacher reports accurately reflect actual changes in teacher skills and classroom behaviours) to be convinced that the findings do tell us about the most significant features of effective PD activities (and perhaps then only in the US context where the survey was undertaken!).

Interpreting statistical findings

McClune's (2001) paper, introduced in Chapter 2, indicating that modular examinations may put students at a relative disadvantage (see Chapter 4) offers a detailed account of how he went about his research, and designed his sample, and accessed and analysed data. McClune demonstrated differences between the attainment of first- and second-year A-level students in his sample that, overall at least, were unlikely to be due to chance. He took reasonable measures to ensure that the two groups were not wildly different in terms of previous academic success.

Although McClune's study took care in sampling students, the findings relate to the common questions in one year's examinations for one examination board, in one A level subject. (Even in this limited context the study represented a considerable undertaking.) Despite the careful way the study has been conducted and reported, it cannot be considered to have *proved* that *in general* students following modular courses are disadvantaged compared with students taking linear courses. It is still possible that:

- significant results are due to the random sampling (unlikely but therefore, by definition, *possible*);
- the academic abilities of the two groups were different in some way not uncovered;
- there may be other relevant differences between the two year groups that have not been considered;
- the findings were an artefact of the particular common questions in that year's examination;
- the findings may relate to some aspect of the way this particular examination board sets and marks papers;
- the findings may not be generalisable to other subjects.

This is not a criticism of the research, which is presented here as an example of a well-executed and documented 'experimental' study, but an observation on the inherent limitations of any single research enquiry.

———— Has the research been conducted ethically? ————

Educational research should follow ethical guidelines (such as those provided by the British Educational Research Association – BERA, 2011). It is important that educational research does not harm or distress students, teachers or others who may be asked to help with our research. Ethical issues are especially sensitive for teachers who are conducting research in their own classrooms, as the dual role of teacher-researcher complicates the relationship with participants (Taber, 2002b). Key aspects of undertaking ethical research are discussed in Chapter 9.

In terms of reading research, readers must take a view about any paper they find which they consider includes data obtained unethically. Disregard for ethical standards tarnishes research, and some would argue that anyone using knowledge obtained in this way is implicitly condoning the unethical approach, signalling that such ways of working are acceptable. Others would argue that disregarding knowledge obtained through such research is to confuse means and ends, and that the inconvenience or discomfort of informants is compounded if the research outcomes obtained are then discounted. It is not clear what the 'right' approach is here and a reader's stance might depend on the extent of disregard of ethics, the context of the work (thinking about ethical issues has developed over the years – see Chapter 9), and the potential importance of the findings.

Further reading ——

The Evans chapter listed below goes into more detail on key issues of research quality. The Medawar chapter, originally a radio talk, discusses the nature of formal research reports: what they highlight, and which aspects of the research process they often sideline. The Taber editorial (from which extracts were presented above) offers advice to authors and reviewers on the criteria to be used when judging if a submission is suitable for journal publication. The editorial is from a specialist education journal, but discusses general principles (and is available open-access to anyone who registers with the journal website).

Evans, M. (2009). Reliability and validity in qualitative research by teacher researchers. In E. Wilson (Ed.), *School-based Research: A Guide for Education Students* (pp. 112–124). London: Sage.

Medawar, P. B. (1963/1990). Is the scientific paper a fraud? In P. B. Medawar (Ed.), *The Threat and the Glory* (pp. 228–233). New York: Harper Collins, 1990.

Taber, K. S. (2012). Recognising quality in reports of chemistry education research and practice. *Chemistry Education Research and Practice, 13*(1), 4–7. (Available from: http://pubs.rsc.org/en/journals/journalissues/rp#)

7

Teachers evaluating research relevance

This chapter:

- considers how teachers can learn from reading research, especially in terms of informing their own classroom practice
- introduces the notions of statistical and reader generalisation
- considers how a detailed account can help readers make judgements about the likely relevance of findings elsewhere
- explains the importance of theoretical considerations in making judgements of research relevance

In Chapter 6 it was suggested that when evaluating studies, we need to ask ourselves a number of questions:

- Is the account detailed enough to make further judgements?
- Is the account honest?
- Is the focus appropriately conceptualised in the research?
- Is the methodology appropriate?
- Are the techniques applied in a technically competent manner?
- Do the conclusions logically follow from the findings?

If the answers to these questions are 'yes', then the teacher who is interested in *applying: research findings will *also* want to know

- 'Does it apply here?'

Readers have to be able to judge the extent to which the findings from studies may be transferred from the context of the study to the context in which the reader is working.

Transfer of knowledge – does it apply here?

A key issue in reading an account of a research study is deciding whether it is relevant to our own context. In Chapter 6 some key questions were suggested which will help judge the quality of research accounts. However, even a high-quality study may have little to offer to inform a very different educational context. The term 'generalise' is often used to describe how research applies beyond the specific original context. There are different ways of interpreting generalisability, and two common concepts will be discussed.

Question for reflection

How do approaches to building samples (or selecting cases) influence the generalisability of research findings?

The reader may find it useful to review the ideas about sampling in Chapter 4, and intrinsic and instrumental case studies in Chapter 5, before proceeding.

Statistical generalisability

Research studies that sample larger populations look for statistical generalisability. This means that the sampling techniques used are designed to ensure that the results obtained when analysing data collected from the sample allow inferences to be made about the wider population.

So, for example, a survey *of teenage girls'* attitudes to participating in PE lessons in school would collect data from *a sample of* teenage girls. If the sample was large enough, and representative enough of the wider population, then it is possible to make statistical generalisations. If it was found that 12% of the teenage girls wanted to avoid PE lessons because they found them embarrassing, then (given a representative sample, etc.) it would be possible to assess how precisely that sample figure would be reflected in the larger population. Similar techniques are very common in public opinion polls, for example near elections, when the actual percentages of the sample giving different responses are quoted with a likely sample error (e.g., ±2%). The larger the sample size used, the more precisely the sample results should respond to the results that could have been obtained had it been possible to ask the whole population of interest. However, this always assumes there are no biases in the composition of the sample. If our sample of teenage girls was made up of those we found reading in the school library because they had brought notes to class to excuse them from PE lessons, whilst their peers were all out on the school field engaged in hockey practice, it could not be considered representative of teenage girls in general.

Reader generalisability

Any individual teacher or student, or any particular class or school, is likely to be *in some ways* quite like a good many other teachers or students, or classes or schools. Yet, each teacher or learner or class or lesson is also in many ways unique. Statistical techniques are used to help draw general conclusions about typical, average or common aspects of specific populations (maintained 11–16 city schools; gifted pupils in French classes; special-needs coordinators in secondary schools, etc.). Whereas these nomothetic (ERP1, see Chapter 3) studies attempt to balance out individual differences to offer a general picture, interpretivist studies (ERP2) may deliberately emphasise and even celebrate individuality.

Most interpretive studies do not work with large sample sizes, and indeed may select participants to study for theoretical reasons (because they provide interesting cases) that value the uniqueness of the individual case rather than see them as primarily a representative of a larger population. A case study of a lesson, for example, will present a detailed account of that lesson, hoping to provide the reader with as much of the context as possible to provide an *authentic* account that helps the reader understand that lesson. Conclusions drawn from the lesson may help us understand other lessons that may be similar. The difficulty is in knowing *how similar* that lesson may be to our own lessons.

The researcher needs to provide enough context ('thick description') – of the students, of the physical environment, of the teacher–class rapport, of the subject matter, etc. – for a reader to make a judgement about how likely it is that insights drawn from that particular case may be useful in understanding the lessons that we are interested in (as teachers, as researchers, as appraisers of teachers, etc.). This is called *reader generalisability*, because the reader has to make the judgement. The author cannot tell us, as they do not know about our context. Both the researcher and the reader have responsibilities in this process. Judgements of relevance rely upon the person making the judgement having a good understanding of both contexts. The researcher cannot be expected to know about the reader's context of interest, and so it is only the reader who can make the judgement. However, the researcher has a responsibility to provide a detailed, balanced and carefully composed account of the research context that can provide the reader with the basis for making a judgement.

Setting the scene

When a study is carried out in a particular context, it is normal to report something of the context of the research. Surveys, as suggested above, may well investigate broad populations rather than particular contexts, and true experiments are supposed to be conducted in clinical conditions where the influence of extraneous variables are controlled or excluded (although, as we have seen, that ideal is difficult to achieve in educational research). In research in ERP2 traditions (see Chapter 3), such extraneous variables are not eliminated, as they are accepted as an integral part of the complex phenomena of classroom teaching and learning, and so they cannot be removed without destroying the 'natural' situation being investigated. Rather, researchers seek to describe what they considered as the most relevant features of the context. So Smith, reporting in *JoTTER* (see Chapter 5) on work undertaken on a professional placement, sets the scene as follows:

> The study took place in a non-selective mixed comprehensive upper school (ages 13–19) in rural Hertfordshire. The school is a specialist Humanities College. ... Latin is started from scratch by the highest ability pupils in Year 9. These highest ability pupils are selected on the basis of pupils' achievement in modern languages in ... teacher assessments. These sets get two hours per week for Latin in Year 9 and five hours every two weeks if they elect to do Latin in Years 10 and 11. Numbers for

GCSE are varied with currently 16 in Year 10 and 23 in Year 11. I have focused on the Year 11 group whose attainment grades in class tests vary from A*–C with no students with special educational needs. I started teaching them from January and was able to share lessons with their current teacher to take them through the verse prescription for GCSE of 'Nisus and Euryalus' …

(A. Smith, 2010, p. 44)

Questions for reflection

Reflect on your personal response to reading this brief introduction to the research setting:

i   To what extent does it start to provide you with a mental image of the setting of the research that could support you in reading the rest of the account of the study?
ii To what extent does this outline description suggest that Smith was working in a professional context that might be similar to your own teaching context?

Transfer between contexts: SRL

In a 2004 study (introduced in Chapter 2 and discussed in Chapter 4), Corrigan and Taylor suggested requirements for promoting self-regulated learning (SRL). They described their sample as 'purposeful': "6 volunteer participants (5 female and 1 male) … intended to reflect the views of a range of students with different performance levels within the SRL project" (2004, p. 52). Developing self-regulated learning is an important goal for schools (see Chapter 2), and this is closely linked with the currently popular 'assessment for learning' and 'pupil voice' movements. Schoolteachers will want to learn from research about how to best encourage their students to develop greater independence as learners. Studies on this topic are therefore to be welcomed.

Corrigan and Taylor offer some suggestions for the conditions that are likely to encourage self-regulated learning. However, the reader looking for research to support evidence-based practice has to decide whether this study offers any relevant findings. Even though we may believe (a) that Corrigan and Taylor are highly competent and skilled researchers, and (b) that their findings do represent a valid interpretation of the data they collected, the critical reader will still wish to ask about the extent to which these findings could apply elsewhere – i.e., can they be generalised?

Degrees of separation?

In their paper, the authors are quite clear that *their* focus is "the effectiveness of SRL as a pedagogy for use with pre-service primary teachers" (Corrigan and Taylor, 2004, p. 51); and that their data is derived from one sample drawn from one cohort of trainee teachers in one institution. Although the study cannot possibly be considered to demonstrate beyond doubt that these conditions would work with other trainee primary teachers (in other cohorts, in other institutions), nonetheless it would seem reasonable for other teacher-trainers to consider the findings that *may well* also apply in their own professional contexts. This judgement might lead to teacher-trainers considering whether the findings might inform their own professional practice.

The further a context is removed from that of the original study, however, the less confidence we might have in the findings being relevant. Trainee teachers are mature individuals, highly motivated in their studies, who have previously learnt to be successful students in school (Taber, 2009a), who clearly value learning, and are in the process of learning a lot more about learning itself. This does not apply to students in primary or secondary schools, or even to many students in further education. Teachers working with students at other levels might well consider Corrigan and Taylor's study to offer useful ideas *for testing out* in their own classrooms, but would be ill-advised to *assume* that the types of strategies recommended in this study can non-problematically be transferred to very different settings.

Nested context

So we have seen that the researchers reporting interpretive studies (such as case studies) need to offer readers a 'thick description' to help them understand the context of a study. That context may well be a manifold one – having several possible levels that need to be unpacked and described. Duit, Roth, Komorek and Wilbers (1998) published a study of student group work, where they reported on how one student group in one classroom worked on one assigned task in one lesson.

> ## Questions for reflection
>
> What aspects of 'context' would you feel are needed in a thick description of this case study of a single classroom episode to allow readers to feel they have a full picture of the case? If you read that this study concerns a group of students talking about a magnetic pendulum (of the kind sold sometimes as novelty desk 'furniture'), does this help you decide whether the study may offer insights to inform your own classroom work?

Duit and colleagues tell their readers that their "case study focuses on the events in a group of five female students" during one particular group activity in part of a lesson (p. 1065). The authors provide a good deal of information about the context of the group work to help the reader situate the episodes within the lesson and beyond (and, of course, they have to do this *in addition to* setting up the research question in terms of their conceptual framework for the research, and explaining their research methodology). The reader is also offered context in terms of both the students and the teaching.

We are told that the class was "an academically streamed grade 10 class of a German grammar school [of] 25 students (16 female and nine male students)" (p. 1062) taught by one of the paper's authors. The reader is told about the immediate context of the studied episode in terms of how the teacher set up the group discussion task through a whole class discussion and a summary of what the students had been studying in previous lessons. Duit and colleagues also explained the nature of the context at the level of the teaching sequence focusing on the magnetic pendulum (which swings chaotically) "taught in four 90-minute lessons spread over a two-week period" (p. 1062). They had *also* explained the rationale for a teaching unit on the magnetic pendulum within a wider project to explore the potential of teaching about 'non-linear systems' (i.e., systems which do not have simple predictable behaviour). This is traditionally thought a difficult topic, but it is a very important one – for example, weather systems are non-linear, or 'chaotic'.

> The general aim of the project [was] to examine the educational significance of theories on non-linear systems, that is, to analyse whether or not the core ideas of these theories are worth teaching and learning, and to investigate whether they are accessible to students.

> (Duit et al., 1998, p. 1062)

The scheme of work is summarised, so that the reader is able to make sense of the dialogue reported in the group work in terms of what the students have done and seen in the previous episodes in the sequence (as well as knowing how students are expected to progress from the reported discussion in subsequent learning activities). A fair part of Duit and colleagues' paper is spent offering readers the conceptual, methodological ('theoretical') and contextual background to make sense of the episode that is the focus of the study. However, without this detail, it would be difficult for a reader to evaluate the significance of the data discussed even within its original teaching context, and it would be very difficult for a teacher working elsewhere to evaluate whether this episode, involving a particular group of students working on a particular task, has any relevance at all to their own classroom work.

Finding resonances across the degrees of separation

Duit and colleagues are interested in the social processes by which the students negotiate meanings and whether they can individually take away new understanding from the discussion task. This is a theme of interest to any teacher who sets up group discussion work in class, although only a minority of teachers are likely to ask their students to think up explanations for the chaotic behaviour of a magnetic pendulum. Indeed, although the specific nature of the task (explaining the behaviour of the magnetic pendulum) may seem rather esoteric, by offering enough context for other teachers to make sense of the logic of the teaching scheme, and appreciate the learning objectives of the group discussion, Duit and colleagues offer an account that can be read by *any* teacher using group discussion work to help them understand more about what goes on in that type of group discussion activity.

This may seem counter-intuitive, but given the unique nature of every class and every lesson, offering thick descriptions need not close down the range of contexts to which findings may be seen as relevant (e.g., only in German schools, in streamed grade 10 classes studying chaotic systems). Actually, it can have the reverse effect by allowing readers to see when something reported in a particular unique 'other' context is likely to resonate with our understanding of what goes on in our own rather different teaching context.

This does not undermine the point made above, that the more different two contexts are, the less likely we are to be confident we can transfer findings from one context to the other. We might question how relevant Duit et al.'s study would be to group work in, say, the earliest school years, or to group work in initial teacher education, or among doctoral students collaborating on a research project. However, the detailed context may allow teachers of other secondary students to make a judgement that key features of the context are similar enough for the findings to be relevant in somewhat different contexts. For example, reading the account of the study, there seems no reason to assume that the location of the research in the German system would prevent it from applying in other national systems where similar pedagogies are used (and the detailing of context enables us to appreciate the pedagogical approach within which the episode was embedded). Moreover, by explaining the teaching context of the episode in some detail, Duit and colleagues make it possible for teachers of history or religious studies, for example, to abstract from a report of students talking about some seemingly esoteric physics, features likely to be just as relevant to discussion work in their own classrooms.

Findings, generalisations and mechanisms

As a reader of educational research, it is important to be able to distinguish between three types of information that researchers will present through their papers. Many research papers present:

- findings: what we found out in this context from these informants;
- generalisations: what we think this might tell us about a wider set of contexts or the wider population we think our sample represents;
- conjectured mechanisms: what we think is going on here.

These are all perfectly legitimate features of a research report: they all contribute to the author telling the story of the research, making the case, and teaching about their understanding/models of the phenomena studied. However, sometimes authors (inadvertently or deliberately) do not cleanly separate these features, and the reader must be alert to the transitions from what had been found, to what this might suggest, to why we think this could be going on. (It may be useful at this point to review the discussion of Lyle's study in Chapter 6.)

Why are modular exams a bad idea?

One of the studies referred to in Chapter 2 was a paper in the journal *Educational Research*, where McClune (2001) argues that students following modular courses (where some of the credit for final grade is awarded for examination papers taken early in the course) may be disadvantaged compared with students taking linear courses for the same award, and being examined on all aspects of the course in terminal examinations. McClune's research design is considered in Chapter 4. Here it was reported that he found a difference in the average examination scores on a set of questions between 406 students taking their terminal examination and 346 students answering the same questions during a modular examination halfway through their course.

McClune had built his sample so that the two groups were considered to be comparable (see Chapter 4), and inferential statistics suggest that the differences in average performance found can be assumed to represent differences that would probably apply to the wider populations (statistical generalisation). This means that we would expect that – all other things being equal – a student would be likely to get a better score on these questions if taken as part of a terminal rather than a modular examination.

Theoretical generalisation...?

However, there is a second, different type of generalisation being made. Statistical techniques can tell us that different samples from the wider populations were likely to give similar results, but statistics cannot tell us whether similar findings would have been found:

- on different questions;
- in an examination set by a different board using different styles of questions;
- or in a different examination subject.

Yet McClune writes about his research findings as though they tell us something about terminal and modular examination *in general*. We can consider this to be a kind of 'theoretical' generalisation, as it is based upon the conceptual framework supporting the research design. This type of transition is very common in research reports and is quite appropriate: it is important that researchers offer the bigger picture that shows readers why their findings might be important for our practice. But the reader needs to be able to recognise this shift, and make his or her own judgements about whether it is reasonable to generalise in this way.

Sampling is not just about selecting particular people to participate in research – it can involve selecting schools, subjects, age ranges, particular examples of student work, particular questions in an examination paper, the particular lessons observed in a classroom, the particular years to compare to find trends in educational statistics, and so on. In each case, we need to ask whether it is reasonable to assume the sample can offer generalisable results.

...is supported by a feasible mechanism

This transition is linked to something else McClune offers in discussing his results: an interpretation of what might be going on. McClune suggests the differences found (between the examination performance of the two groups of students in the analysis) could be due to the increased maturity and examination skills of the older students and/or the increased opportunities to consolidate learning about the examined material during the two-year course.

This is not something that could possibly be revealed *by the findings themselves*; the data collection and analysis does not concern these matters. Rather, the author is offering feasible mechanisms as a conceptual framework within which the results make sense. Indeed, these considerations may be considered as part of the initial conceptualisation of the research: concerns that led to the hypothesis being tested. All of this is perfectly valid and proper. The author has a responsibility to give enough detail, and a clear enough account, to enable the reader to distinguish what was found in the specific research context, what the author thinks this might mean more widely, and how the author makes (*sic*) sense of the findings.

We should also be aware of the rhetorical value of the suggested mechanisms in generalising the significance of the research. If we accept that McClune's suggestions may well explain *why* there was a difference between the two experimental groups, then we are more likely to accept (on theoretical rather than deductive 'logical' grounds) that we can generalise his findings to other contexts where increased maturity, increased examination skills and greater opportunities for consolidating learning may apply. In other words, by presenting his results deriving from a sample of examination questions from one examination board in one subject, in terms of plausible explanations that would seem to apply across examination subjects, McClune makes a case that his specific findings may have *general* relevance when comparing modular and terminal examinations.

Question for reflection

Do you consider there to be any parallels between the theoretical generalisation offered by McClune in his study and the reader generalisation that may be undertaken by a hypothetical history teacher reading Duit and colleagues' account of the group discussing the magnetic pendulum?

Educational research looks at complex foci, such as classroom teaching and learning, where there are always a vast number of potential factors that we consider relevant to a particular educational episode (e.g., see Box 4.1). To make sense of this complexity we have to be able to make decisions about what is significant in any particular situation. People learn to spontaneously make such judgements all the time (to make sense of living in a complex environment), although sometimes they tend to assign significance too readily (leading to all those superstitions about Friday the 13th and crossing the paths of cats, etc.). As educational professionals we try to assign significance in more careful, principled ways. But ultimately we have to rely on existing knowledge, often in the form of feasible theories (explanatory schemes linking different concepts, informed by an evidence base) that seem well-enough supported to make these judgements. So when McClune uses theoretical generalisation to suggest his study findings may be significant beyond the particular examination papers considered, he is applying theoretical knowledge about what *seems likely* to be important in making a difference, and what can *probably* be discounted. This is the same type of judgement as the reader of Duit and colleagues' study of group work will make in deciding whether the findings from that study are likely to be relevant to the use of group work in their own subject teaching.

———— Further reading ——————————————————————————

The Dawson case study recommended here is reported in a chapter in an academic book, *but* is also part of the publishers' electronic 'Humanities, social sciences and law' collection. This means it is available electronically as a downloadable chapter and will be included in many university libraries' subscriptions. The chapter provides an inter-esting, and easy-to-read, account of a case study of some teaching and learning. The author provides a good deal of context about the study and offers samples of classroom dialogue to illustrate the points being made. Dawson also explains carefully the meth-odological and ethical issues arising in the research, making this a good model for any aspiring case-study researcher to read.

The article suggested is published in an open-access journal and considers the nature of 'replication' (i.e., repeating published studies in new contexts) in education, and when repeating someone else's study in a new setting might count as original research.

Dawson, V. M. (2011). A case study of the impact of introducing socio-scientific issues into a reproduction unit in a Catholic girls' school. In T. D. Sadler (Ed.), *Socio-scientific Issues in the Classroom: Teaching, Learning and Research* (pp. 313–345). Dordrecht: Springer.

Taber, K. S. (2012). Vive la différence? Comparing 'like with like' in studies of learners' ideas in diverse educational contexts. *Educational Research International, 2012*(Article 168741), 1–12. doi:1 0.1155/2012/168741

PART III

Learning through educational research

As pointed out in Chapter 1, there is an increasing expectation that teachers should be able to undertake small-scale empirical classroom studies to inform their own practice. Research students on MEd, MA, MPhil, EdD and PhD courses are expected to show they can competently carry out all stages of such research, but increasingly trainee teachers on PGCE courses are also expected to undertake small research projects. This part offers advice on the process of undertaking small-scale classroom research, building on the familiarity with educational research provided by Part I, and an awareness of how we judge the quality of studies, drawing upon the principles discussed in Part II.

This part has five chapters concerned with planning the research (Chapter 8) and ensuring it meets ethical standards (Chapter 9), collecting the data (Chapter 10), analysing the data (Chapter 11), and reporting research (Chapter 12). As earlier in the book, key points are illustrated by drawing upon examples from published studies, including examples of student work carried out on school placement. For practising teachers, looking to make the first tentative steps towards practitioner-research, the following chapters should offer sufficient guidance for the moment. However, if you 'get the bug' and come to view being a fully professional teacher as to imply being a teacher-as-researcher (with classroom enquiry as an intrinsic part of teaching), then you will find there are many more detailed books available to help you develop into a more sophisticated classroom practitioner-researcher.

8

Teachers planning research

This chapter:

- takes the reader through the process of planning their research study
- considers the role and importance of carefully worded research questions
- discusses what needs to be included in designs for different kinds of research
- illustrates the general principles through a more detail consideration of designing a case study
- explores when multiple data sources can provide opportunities for triangulation.

Approaching practitioner research

This chapter offers advice to the teacher looking to undertake their own classroom enquiry, whether purely for informing their own practice or as part of course requirements at higher degree level (PGCE, MEd, etc.). In Part I, we saw how research should always start from a consideration of basic assumptions about the nature of what we are studying, and what we can know about it, as these assumptions inform decisions about the type of research strategy (methodology) to choose. It will have been clear from the examples of published studies discussed in the book that our basic assumptions influence all that follows in the research process (see Figure 3.4). This chapter, then, takes the reader through the stages of planning his or her classroom research, and highlights the various decisions that need to be made during the planning process.

The focus

The first stage of any research project is to identify the focus (see Chapters 3 and 5). This will be an issue that is considered to warrant close attention. For professional educational researchers, the research focus often derives either from suggestions in the existing published literature or from their own previous research. Such researchers are often working in a 'research programme', where individual studies both derive from and lead to further research (see Chapter 1). Each study is one part of an ongoing incremental programme gradually exploring and developing understanding of a theme. This is one reason why many small-scale educational research studies that are published in the literature can seem to be highly flawed when considered individually. Often an individual study depends heavily for its rationale on other related studies. Findings from any individual study may seen tentative and highly contextualised *unless* seen as a single piece in a large 'jigsaw'. The feminist thinker Barbara Thayer-Bacon talks of knowledge construction in terms of producing a quilt where: "we may all begin on the quilt together, or we may decide to go off on our own, or in smaller groups, and begin by making our own smaller pieces first, which will then be added to the others to form the quilt" (Thayer-Bacon, 2000, p. 7).

For the teacher-researcher, the focus often seems to suggest itself. Often such research is context-directed (see Chapter 5) and undertaken to explore some aspect of the professional context. So for a classroom teacher undertaking research, there is often a very strong professional motivation as the research is about better understanding an aspect of teaching and learning in our classroom, solving a perceived problem, or improving some aspect of professional work which is considered to be sub-optimal. Even if a study is being undertaken as part of course requirements (e.g., for a PGCE or Master's course), it makes sense to identify an area where there are clear grounds for believing that research can potentially inform improvements for the teacher(s) and learners involved. Some people would see this as one kind of validity criterion that should apply to research (i.e., so-called catalytic validity, where research *should* always look to improve things for the participants), although others would argue that it is also important to develop new knowledge for its potential for application in the future.

So in her report in *JoTTER* of research undertaken on school placement during her PGCE course, Healy (2010, p. 312), a secondary English and Drama specialist, explains how she had become "increasingly interested in the role of Speaking and Listening in the classroom", given what to her mind was a "lack of emphasis on oral communication in British classrooms". Being assigned a Year 9 class that "had had relatively little experience of Speaking and Listening and almost no Drama experience", and aware that the scheme of work required this class to next work on writing "an empathetic response to a novel", Healy considered setting a text she thought would be "appropriate for Speaking and Listening activities and Drama work" (p. 313). Healy decided that, to inform her planning of what might seem to the students an innovative approach to their learning, she "wanted to gather information from students about their thoughts and experiences of Speaking and Listening, and Drama".

There are many possible foci for practitioner research, but here are few examples of the kinds of issues that might motivate research:

- test results indicate that understanding of a particular topic is disappointing
- learners indicate that they find the materials used to teach a particular topic to be uninspiring (they are more likely to use the term 'boring')
- the teacher feels that boys in the class volunteer answers to questions much more than the girls
- learners in a class are very competitive about marks/scores received, but make little effort to act on specific feedback given

- the teacher is concerned that lessons are insufficiently differentiated to both support and challenge the wide range of abilities present
- published research indicates that learners are likely to misunderstand key concepts in a topic as many come to class with existing intuitive beliefs that are inconsistent with curriculum knowledge
- very few students wish to continue studying the subject once it ceases to be compulsory

The list of student projects in Chapter 5 (Table 5.2) suggests something of the range of foci suitable for small-scale classroom research.

What do we already know about this?

Whatever the focus selected, it is unlikely that there does not already exist a body of research that would seem to be relevant. Clearly, it is usually helpful to find out what is already known about a topic before starting out on research. Even if we believe that the focus is contextualised in such a way that findings from elsewhere may not be applicable, it is useful to look at what others have done, and what they have found, to inform our own work. Ideally, we would search out, read and evaluate all relevant prior research. This is certainly expected (in principle) at doctoral level, although will normally be considered unrealistic in smaller-scale research. For the busy practitioner, there may be problems of access to libraries and time for reading. Nonetheless, time spent identifying, reading and considering the most relevant studies can be invaluable in informing practitioner-research (see Part II).

Keeping records of material read and summary notes of key points (e.g., developing an annotated bibliography of sources) is useful, but if a report is needed with a literature review, then time will need to be spent developing an overview or synthesis of the research (see the section on research conceptualisation in Chapter 3.)

Forming research questions ———

A common approach to moving from a research focus to planning a research study is by the development of one or more research questions. These research questions should be informed by the conceptual framework developed from reading previous research, and will inevitably be informed by our understandings of the nature of the phenomena being studied and the type of knowledge educational research can develop about those phenomena (see Chapter 3). It is worth pointing out here that there are two basic types of questions that can be asked, reflecting two main types of approach to educational research (as discussed in Chapter 3).

Question for reflection

In Chapter 3 two main types of educational research study were introduced, denoted ERP1 and ERP2. How might you expect research questions in ERP2 studies to differ from those in ERP1 studies?

A good research question guides your research plan and gives you a basis for later evaluating whether your research has been useful – and so it needs to have some level of specificity. However, in some ('provisional', 'exploratory') studies, research questions are quite open-ended.

In Healy's study to inform her introduction of Speaking and Listening and Drama activities with her Year 9 class, she set out her research questions in terms of her research objectives to:

- gain a better understanding of whether students felt Speaking and Listening activities and Drama could be helpful when preparing for an empathetic response to a novel;
- ascertain how they felt about their skills;
- know their preferences in terms of enjoyment (Healy, 2010, pp. 321–322).

Hypotheses and research questions

ERP1 research which is 'positivistic', informed by the experimental model derived from the physical sciences (see Chapter 3), will often be set up with the kind of question that looks for a definitive 'yes'/'no' response. For example, consider one of the issues given above:

- the teacher feels that boys in the class volunteer answers to questions much more than the girls

It may be that there are at least as many girls in the class as boys, and that it is so rare for the girls to put their 'hands up' to volunteer to answer a question that the teacher has little doubt there is a real issue here. However, we might ask: what if the situation was less clear-cut and the teacher *had a strong feeling* that girls were under-represented in volunteering answers to questions, but could not be sure if this was a real issue? One possible approach in this case might be to consider the teacher's belief as a testable hypothesis:

- girls in the class volunteer answers to my questions significantly less often than the boys

Alternatively, the same point may be phrased in terms of what is called the 'null' hypothesis:

- there is no significant difference in the extent to which the two genders volunteer answers to my questions in class

When specified in one of these forms, the hypothesis can be tested, although this may not be straightforward.

Question for reflection

Before reading on, it may be useful for you to consider how this question might be tested, and what the difficulties associated with this might be.

Exploratory research questions

If the teacher was sufficiently convinced that there was indeed an issue of girls not volunteering answers in class (either because the difference is so obvious or because the hypothesis has now been tested), then this raises further questions:

- why do the girls volunteer answers significantly less than the boys?

and

- what can I do to ensure that the girls are contributing in lessons as much as the boys?

These are much more open-ended questions that do not invite 'yes'/'no' type answers, and cannot be set up as testable hypotheses. Of course, a study that explored '*why do the girls volunteer answers significantly less than the boys?*' might well identify a range of candidate factors (in discovery mode as an ERP2 study), which might *then* lead to further research questions that could be set up as hypotheses (an ERP1 study). Notice that the first question here is about understanding the teaching–learning context, and the second is about improving it. For a study to be considered as action research it would usually be expected to be intended to change the research context for the better, but often it may only be possible to answer the 'what can I do?' question after the 'why?' question has been explored.

> ## Question for reflection
>
> Imagine you were undertaking a small-scale study and had chosen this issue as your focus. Your project advisor has strongly warned against taking on too much, and advises that in the time available you should limit your study to the 'why' question and not also investigate what might improve the girls' participation. Does this negate the value of the study? Does it become a completely 'academic' exercise without any useful outcomes?

We might even see this sequence of questions as a mini-research programme (see Chapters 1 and 4): moving from confirming there is a problem, to exploring the nature of the problem, and then to testing possible solutions.

The middle stage of this 'programme' is about exploring why girls in this particular class do not volunteer answers in class. There may be a range of answers to this question, and we should bear in mind that:

- just because girls are offering to answer questions less in this class, that does not mean this is a gender issue *per se* – it may relate to some other characteristic that just happens to correlate with gender in *this particular* class (see the discussion of generalisation in Chapter 7). It could just happen that these particular girls do not contribute as much as the particular boys in the group;
- just because girls are participating less in terms of offering to answer questions in class, that does not mean that the girls are participating less overall – there may be different patterns of participation for the boys and girls, with the reluctance to publicly give answers compensated in other ways (Taber, 1992).

As always, classroom teaching and learning are complex phenomena. Finding out why the girls are volunteering to answer questions less than the boys would help us re-examine whether this really is a problem of *girls'* lack of participation, and will suggest ideas about how to respond to improve participation if that is still deemed appropriate. At that point it could be that the teacher and class part company, after the focal issue has been explored but before there is a chance to try out any kind of intervention. In this situation, the research programme comes to an unfortunate stop. If the teacher-researcher is undertaking the study as an *academic* course requirement, then the data collected will still support the assignment or thesis. However, it could be asked whether the research has any value if there is no opportunity to apply what has been found out in the classroom.

This is a genuine concern. Research has costs. The teacher's time and effort may be considerable, and often (if not always) a study makes some additional demands on students. If learners have given up time to act as participants, there is an ethical dimension that needs to be considered: i.e., how does a teacher justify asking students to provide information for research purposes if that research is unlikely to have ben-efits for those informants? A key consideration here would be the extent to which the new knowledge developed through the study was likely to be of value in another context:

- If what has been found out about the class is only likely to inform that teacher when teaching that class, then the value of the research is limited.
- If the insights gained can be of value to another teacher taking over the class, or to the teacher-researcher in working with 'similar' classes in the future, then the research can have more value.
- If the research uncovers insights that are likely to be relevant to a wide range of teachers and classes, then it has *the potential* to be useful well beyond its initial context.

Ethical concerns are important in education, and for teacher-researchers are com-plicated by their dual role. Ethical issues are discussed in more detail in the next chapter.

Questions for reflection

If a teacher's classroom research leads to findings that seem to have genuine potential to inform the work of other teachers (whether in the school or more widely), should there be an obligation to disseminate/publish the findings to inform others? Should an obligation to disseminate research findings be part of a teacher's professional or ethical code?

Where a study has wider relevance, its value remains 'potential' unless and until it is disseminated. For research to be transferred to new contexts, other teachers have to know about it and appreciate its usefulness. So, no matter how *potentially* transferable a study may be, it can only have an impact if it is communicated. The issue of reporting research is the theme of Chapter 12.

From questions to research designs ——

The research design sets out what data will be collected (where, when, from whom, how?) and how it will be analysed to answer research questions. A good research question – whether a formal hypothesis to test or a more open-ended question – provides a focus that should inform the research plan. However, even an apparently clear question may need some additional clarification. For example, considering how to test the null hypothesis used as an example above ('There is no significant difference in the extent to which the two genders volunteer answers to my questions in class') leads to a number of complications.

In everyday life, language is used flexibly and in a fluid way – with word meanings taking on nuances depending on context. Each individual person has a unique variant of their language – none of us has exactly the same vocabulary, or the same precise understanding of what 'shared' words means. In conversation this can lead to misunderstandings, but the very inter-subjective nature of conversation – what Bruner (1987) calls constant transactional calibration – *usually* allows us to communicate meaning *well enough*. In a legal context, when drawing up contracts, that would *not* be considered sufficient, and it is important to ensure different parties appreciate exactly the same meanings. This is done by using a technical formalism with well-established terms, and by defining anything that might be ambiguous.

Similar considerations apply in research. (Remember, one of our metaphors for writing up research is the legal advocate.) Even in a simple statement there are likely to be potential areas of ambiguity. These need to be clarified by using accepted formalisms or defining terms. For example, Petri and Niedderer (1998) used the term 'learning pathway' in their research, and needed to explain to their readers exactly what they meant by this term (see Chapter 3). We all know what we mean by saying something is 'significant' in everyday usage, but when reporting research findings (at least, ERP1 studies) this is usually expected to imply *statistical* significance (see Chapter 4).

Some problems with testing hypotheses ——

The term 'significant difference' has a technical meaning when used in research. In effect, it means that some accepted statistical technique has been used, and has suggested that any differences between two sets of data are unlikely to be due to chance alone. Usually the meaning is actually more specific than that – that the difference is only likely to occur less than once on twenty occasions by chance (often represented as '$p < 0.05$'). Much educational research (i.e., from ERP1) uses statistical approaches to test hypotheses in this way, but there are a number of pitfalls that the teacher-researcher should be aware of:

- there is a range of common statistical tests, and all have to be applied following strict procedures for any results to be valid;
- for some tests these procedures include randomisation (e.g., of students to different 'treatments') that may be difficult to follow (see Chapter 4);

- different tests are appropriate for different kinds of data, and some tests only apply if data has a certain type of 'distribution' so that the test is only strictly valid if the data has been shown to fit the pattern (by using other tests);
- a statistically significant result can still be due to chance: if a study involved a great many comparisons and identified many significant results, it is quite likely that some are just due to chance (and there is no way of knowing which);
- a result which does not reach statistical significance may still be important, even though it is *not unlikely enough* to be judged 'significant';
- a *statistically* significant result may be a very small effect which has minimal importance;
- large data sets are often needed to identify statistically significant outcomes.

Inferential statistics: powerful, but specialised

This is not to say that there are no situations where the classroom teacher can use inferential statistics, but such an approach does require an understanding of the available tests and their ranges of application, and is only likely to be of value where large enough data sets are available to make identifying any significant factors possible. If the research involves counting and classifying many instances of some kind, the sample size may be sufficient. However, if in doubt, it is best to avoid inferential statistics.

Although statistical tests may be carried out with pencil and paper (supported by a calculator with basic statistical functions), it is more common these days to use a computer-based package such as 'SPSS' (Muijs, 2004). When using such a tool it is useful to bear in mind the adage 'garbage in, garbage out': the machine will perform calculations but cannot do the thinking for you, and the computer should only be used to analyse data according to your research design. In particular, student studies that test for relationships between every possible combination of variables almost invariably lead to the machine producing 'false positives' (see Chapter 4), and suggest research that is not informed by a strong conceptual framework.

Descriptive statistics: straightforward, but less informative

Descriptive statistics (such as reporting means, ranges, percentages) are much easier to use, but do not allow inferences to be drawn. For example, if a teacher kept records of when students volunteered answers in class over a two-week period and found that 41% of the time it was girls offering answers and 59% of the time it was boys, despite similar numbers of each gender being present, this would allow the teacher to report that in absolute terms the boys volunteered answers more often. This descriptive statistic is of interest, but cannot *in itself* tell us anything about whether this might have just been a chance effect that is likely to be reversed if the study was repeated. This could still be indicative enough to encourage the teacher to investigate why pupils in the class did or did not tend to volunteer answers, perhaps looking to see if any gender-related effect could be found. If follow-up work found that a number of the girls reported being intimidated by the boys in the group, then the descriptive statistics would have been useful as part of the 'programme' of research.

—— Defining terms ——

Even if the meaning of the term *statistically significant* is defined for us, we still have to ensure we are clear about what we mean by other terms in our research question. For example, it may seem obvious what we mean by 'the teacher's questions' and 'volunteering answers', but if we are to collect data that relies on these terms we should spend time clarifying them. In a study where several researchers collect data, it is important that they all know what such terms mean in the context of the research, but even in a single-researcher study we need to be precisely clear about what 'counts' as 'a question' (for example) before we set out to collect data.

You may feel we all know how to recognise a question, but time spent observing classroom interactions is likely to demonstrate that this is not so clear-cut. Are obviously rhetorical questions to count as questions?

- 'Do you want me to come over there and take that phone away from you?'
- 'Do you want to have to finish this during your break?'
- 'Would you like to get a good grade in this subject?'
- 'Are obviously rhetorical questions to count as questions?'

What about *statements* that seem intended to be understood as questions? 'I wonder if anyone can suggest why this play is considered a tragedy' is not technically phrased as a question, but as a report of an internal mental state. However, in normal social interaction, a person who treated such a statement as an observation rather than a question is likely to be suspected of autism or rudeness.

This is not simply a pedantic matter. If, when classifying classroom interaction, we limit 'volunteering an answer' to cases where students put their 'hands up', we may come to different conclusions than if we include calling out. (This is avoided when we have persuaded all the students to always put their hands up: otherwise it is quite conceivable, for example, that girls and boys could put hands up to a similar extent, but classroom interactions could be dominated by boys if they call out answers more.) We would also need to decide if we wish to define a boundary around the context of the 'questions' we are counting: are we interested in all questions ('can anyone see the remote control?' 'was that the bell?' 'didn't I tell you to stop chatting?' 'are you chewing?') or are we actually only interested in questions relating to the subject matter of the class? In different research studies, we might take different views of this.

Such decisions are important because they make a difference to what we find. A significant proportion of teacher–student interaction in some classrooms can concern administrative, procedural and social agendas rather than the 'academic' content of the lesson (Taber, 1992). This is not a criticism, as such interactions may have important functions, supporting teaching and learning, but it is quite possible that participation in these different aspects of lessons may vary according to gender. A class where girls answered fewer questions purely because they were less often the focus of disciplinary enquiries ('are you paying attention?') raises different issues from one where the girls are less involved in discussing the subject matter. Similarly, if the girls 'participate' in teacher–student interactions to the same extent as boys, but a much higher proportion of these interactions concern 'housekeeping' matters (distributing books and materials, tidying up – yes, I have observed this pattern), there may still be reason for concern.

If possible, pilot

These are issues that arose in my own classroom observations on teacher–student interactions for my Master's project undertaken when I was teaching in a comprehensive secondary school. I found it was helpful to do some pilot work to refine my thinking before starting the main data collection. This is generally a very useful thing to do. If we find that we do not need to change our approach, then the pilot data may be suitable for analysis as part of the main project.

When setting out on the classroom observation for my Master's research, I began with an observation schedule that had been used in a study on the same topic published in the literature. On piloting the schedule, I found I needed to develop it to make additional distinctions (relating to the kinds of issues I raise above). I also found that the schedule only made sense for the parts of the lesson where the teacher was working with the whole class (when the content of the conversation was public), and so I developed a different approach to recording data during parts of the lesson where the teacher was working with individuals and groups (when I could see how much each person talked, and to whom, but could often not hear what was said).

—— Exploratory research

Readers may ask how they will know how to define the key terms in their research question(s). Often this comes from reading the literature reporting studies of similar phenomena. However, it may often be the case, as I found, that it is not possible to be sure what *exactly* one is looking for until one has started looking. Research on a topic that has not been well studied (or at least not in comparable contexts) may be *exploratory* – looking to see how best to refine and define research questions.

In their 2004 study into self-regulated learning (SRL), introduced in Chapter 2, Corrigan and Taylor describe their work as an "exploratory research inquiry" (2004, p. 51), and suggest that such an approach would be the most appropriate because (a) a quantitative approach would be "of limited use" in view of their small sample size (six trainee primary teachers), and (b) they "wished to gain an in-depth understanding of the effectiveness of SRL as a pedagogy..." (2004, p. 51).

This type of research can be very useful (for example, at the start of a research programme), although may not always be an advisable approach when classroom enquiry is undertaken as a course requirement. The danger of exploratory research that is very open-ended is that it is difficult to know in advance what, if anything, will result. An enquiry with a more specific focus and a predefined research question is more likely to lead to a suitable assignment report (if not always being the most productive way of learning something useful about the classroom).

Whatever approach is taken, it is usually a good idea, as suggested above, to undertake some *pilot* work to try out both data collection *and* analysis techniques, and make sure that the research plan will provide the type of data needed. This allows the opportunity to revise the research design before too much time and effort have been committed to an approach that does not lead to the type of data needed. These issues are less acute in genuine action research, where the iterative process of cycles of action and evaluation in effect encompass pilot work as an integral part of the overall approach.

The research design ━━━

The identification of a focus, and the framing of a research question, inform the development of a research plan or design. Research designs vary considerably in their level of detail.

Question for reflection

How would you expect research plans for ERP1 and ERP2 studies (see Chapter 3) to compare?

Well-specified research designs

At one extreme, hypothesis-testing should follow a well-specified procedure. The research plan should show exactly what data is to be collected (the type of data, how much, how collected, the schedule) and how it is to be analysed (the specific statistical test(s) to be applied). There is limited flexibility in such a plan, as any attempt to change procedures once the process is underway may be considered to undermine the validity of the research. The type of test to be used will depend on the nature of the data, and the amount of data needed will depend on the tests to be used. When used properly these techniques are powerful, but – as pointed out above – results are only of any value when the researcher has the technical competence needed. Widely available software can be used to do the calculations, but the output only has any worth if an appropriate test is being correctly applied to suitable data – and the computer has no view about that!

Common tests include chi-squared, which tests for association (e.g., whether being placed in detention is associated with gender), and correlation coefficients that look at how well two ranks are aligned (e.g., whether the students' scores on the module 2 test correlate with their scores on the module 1 test). However, there are many statistical tests that can be applied in research to do different kinds of analysis.

Emergent research designs

The other extreme is an emergent design. As the phrase suggests, this is an approach to research where one has a starting point and sees where that leads. This is an important feature of grounded theory (GT) approaches (see Chapter 4). GT is a powerful research approach when exploring an issue where there is little available background to guide research. However, when done properly, a GT approach is an open-ended commitment, as the researcher has to follow leads indicated by the data collected ('theoretical sampling') and can only consider the study complete when the data analysis suggests that the model being developed (the 'grounded theory') has reached saturation, that is, when further data collection will not offer any further insights to refine the model. Although GT is a very valuable research approach, *it is unsuitable* for anyone needing to know they can complete a study within a limited time period. So GT is not a sensible choice for the teacher-researcher with limited time to draw conclusions and produce a report of their findings (see Chapter 5). However, it may be a very sensible way of exploring an issue of burning interest over many years with a succession of classes!

Allowing for the things that will go wrong

Generally, a sensible approach to most classroom research is to have a fairly complete but robust plan. Such 'robustness' should include the inclusion of some contingency:

- Allow time to pilot data collection whilst there is still time to amend the plan
- Allow enough time for data analysis and (where appropriate) for writing up within the schedule. It is best to assume that these stages will require a lot more time than you initially expect!
- Plan the type of data to be collected and how this will be done (Chapter 10 talks about data collection techniques)
- Have a schedule of when data will be collected, but
- Always assume that some of the expected opportunities for data collection will be lost (due to illness, unforeseen timetable changes, students going on unexpected school trips, school closures due to heavy snow, general elections, or various other factors beyond your control or ability to anticipate).

Inexperienced researchers will often find that the process takes longer than they expect, even when they think they have considered all likely contingencies. So a useful maxim is:

Assume everything will take longer than you expect ... even when you allow for that!

As a general rule, any schedule that does not allow for things going wrong is most unlikely to be met, so 'play safe'. It is also sensible to heed the warning offered by Robson (2002, p. 456): "naïve researchers may be injured by unforeseen problems with qualitative data. This can occur at the collection stage, where overload is a constant danger." Our planning should ensure that researchers, as well as other participants, emerge from our research unharmed by the process.

Perhaps the researcher undertaking an ERP2 study needs to heed the proverb:

Immerse yourself in your data, but avoid drowning in it.

———— Designing a case study ————

It was suggested earlier in the book (in Chapters 4 and 5) that some research methodologies require specific technical expertise (e.g., using inferential statistical tests) or require extended periods of time (such as grounded theory – GT). Teachers planning research to improve their own practice and solve problems in their own professional context may well undertake action research (AR). However, AR is a cyclic process that requires interventions to be implemented, evaluated, modified, and then implemented in their new form … and so on. As with GT, setting out on AR is an open-ended commitment to enquiry. AR also implies making decisions about when to move to the next stage of an intervention, determined by the needs of classroom practice (based on judgements of the balance of evidence), which will often be before there is sufficient evidence to 'make a case' that would satisfy the demands of academic rigour.

The teacher needs to act on what seems appropriate on the balance of available evidence: the academic researcher is looking to build an evidence-based argument that is supported strongly enough to persuade journal reviewers and editors. Different levels of evidence are fit for purpose in these different situations. It would often be as inappropriate for a teacher to delay a classroom decision until the evidence available was overwhelmingly clear as it would for a researcher to submit for publication a theory based on a hunch informed by a few casual observations. As suggested in Chapter 5, teachers who wish to undertake AR for their project for a higher degree should check with their university whether an account of AR would be an acceptable basis for a thesis. Where the focus of the degree is on reflecting on and developing professional practice (as is the case on some MEd–EdD routes), this may be possible. However, the usual expectations of an MPhil/PhD thesis would not be met by an account of a typical AR study. Tripp (2005, p. 457) suggests that "a dissertation cannot be achieved through performing action research, but through completing a case study of the action research performed". However, this may mean a good deal of extra work and/or compromising on AR principles to ensure the rich data needed for a case study.

For students required to undertake an empirical study in a restricted period of time, it is important to select a focus and methodology that allow such a study to be completed, and to be based on sufficient evidence to convince an examiner that findings are sound. This may mean investigating something because it is interesting rather than trying to solve a major problem in practice. In this situation the aim is *to demonstrate an understanding of and competence in small-scale classroom enquiry* rather than to make a major contribution to knowledge. Nonetheless, such projects can still lead to useful insights about teaching and learning to the person completing them. Often a suitable approach to meeting this type of course requirement is to set out on a case study (see Chapter 5). This means having a specific focus in theoretical terms and limiting the empirical phase of the research to a particular context. There are many possibilities, but a key feature will be to collect enough detailed information from a variety of sources (see Chapter 10) to provide the basis for writing an authentic account of the case.

Questions for reflection

What data would you collect to undertake a case study of:
Language use during a single lesson?
Student understanding of the concept of 'revolution' before teaching?
Student learning about climate over a two-week topic in Year 10 geography?
Students' affective responses to a range of learning activities in a topic?
The nature of teacher questioning during a week's lessons with a class?
The effectiveness of new teaching materials?
Student dialogue during group work over a two-week period?
Exploring whether analogies help students learn about electrical circuits?
The influence of students' religious beliefs on their learning about cosmological theories?

Identifying the case

It is important to be clear about what the case being studied actually is. Case study has long been recognised as an important approach in education, and is understood as "an umbrella term for a family of research methods having in common the decision to focus on enquiry around an instance" (Adelman, Jenkins, & Kemmis, 1980, p. 48). Although the case is embedded in a wider context, it is necessary for the researcher to be able to clearly draw a mental boundary around the case to support a clear description. For example, Mutton reports his case study, undertaken as part of his PGCE course, in *JoTTER*, as follows:

> The subject for this case study was a four-day Geography field trip at the beginning of March to Derbyshire for Year 12 students at the Vista Community College in Cambridgeshire. The school is an 11–18 mixed comprehensive school with about 300 pupils in the sixth form, approximately a quarter of whom study Geography. The trip aims to cover a wide sweep of the curriculum with opportunities for conducting fieldwork in a number of areas, including river studies, scree slopes, land use and glacial features. This year, 37 students went on the trip from a class of 40.
>
> (Mutton, 2010, p. 93)

It is clear from this that the case concerns a particular field trip undertaken by 37 Year 12 students as part of the wider context of studying geography in the particular placement school where Mutton was teaching.

The case needs to be manageable, so sometimes a subgroup of a teaching group may be identified as a case (if there is a clear logic to considering those individuals as being a group) or there may need to be sampling within the case – perhaps giving a whole class a questionnaire, but selecting a smaller number of students of varying characteristics for follow-up interviews. So in the report in *JoTTER* of her study of pupil perceptions of collective worship, undertaken for her PGCE, Rutherford refers to how "in this case, twelve Year 6 pupils formed the bounded group for study, partly due to pragmatism ... a small case study of twelve was chosen in order to produce rich data to analyse" (Rutherford, 2012, p. 69).

In the *JoTTER* report of Forbes' (2010) study for a PGCE assignment, she reports how she decided "to conduct a small-scale case study to determine the impact of a one-week Spanish exchange trip on four Year 8 pupils" (p. 115). Forbes

> decided to focus this case study specifically on the four Year 8 pupils, who will be referred to throughout this study as Ellie, David, Owen and Chris. These pupils particularly interested me as they had only been learning Spanish for 6 months prior to departure and even though they are all high ability, motivated pupils, they had only been working in class at National Curriculum level 3 across all skill areas. None of the four had ever been either to Spain, or on an exchange trip before; however, all have been abroad on family holidays.
>
> (Forbes, 2010, p. 116)

So although these were four students from among the larger group on the exchange trip, Forbes justifies considering them as a bounded case because they share particular characteristics of interest. She explains this decision is motivated by her review of previous research where she found a suggestion that "students with initially lower language proficiency make greater gains on an exchange trip" (p. 116). As she was not comparing Ellie, David, Owen and Chris with other students in the class, Forbes was not looking to test this suggestion; rather, she drew upon it to select, as participants in her study, students who were particularly likely to benefit from the experience. As has been suggested earlier, research studies should always build upon existing relevant research where possible.

The issue of what can reasonably be seen as a case is often mysterious to new researchers, probably because it may seem a dilemma that a case study reports on one bounded instance that is embedded in a wider context. However, this is not enigmatic if we consider a few examples (see Table 8.1).

Table 8.1 Some hypothetical cases embedded in their contexts

Potential case – can be clearly identified	Context – impinges upon the case
Year 11 (15–16 year old) students in a school – this group makes up a recognised subset of people in the school.	The characteristics of the Year 11 students of a particular school not only depends upon them as individuals, and how they interact with each other, but will also be influenced by the ethos and infrastructure (layout, amount of green space, comfort of teaching rooms, etc.) of the school, its locality (and perhaps how it is thought of by local people) and, most importantly, the other people working in the school – both staff and all the students in other year groups.
Behaviour of a group of disengaged students in a bottom maths set.	The behaviour is associated with one group of students, but will be influenced by many other factors, such as how other learners in the class respond to their behaviour, the attitude and skills of the teacher, and her/his teaching approach. The location of the classroom might feasibly be important: e.g., if a deputy head teacher is teaching another class in an adjoining room for one of the lessons each week, then this may influence the students' behaviour on that day. Understanding the significance of the behaviour may also involve knowing how the same students behave in other lessons.
Learning of a student with English as an additional language (EAL) in history.	Whilst the focus is on the learning of one student, this will clearly be influenced by the teacher's style and approach; the requirements of any syllabus or scheme of work; the presence of any learning support staff assigned to help; the relationship the student has with others in the class; the norms relating to whether it is acceptable for the student to work with and seek support from other students, etc. More broadly, school policies (and normal practices) relating to supporting EAL will be relevant, as well as issues such as class size and the level of learning technology available in the classroom.
A lesson to teach Year 7 (11–12 year old) students about the principle of inertia.	The case concerns a lesson by one teacher, to a particular class, in a particular classroom, with particular resources. However, as well as aspects of the intuitional context (the nature and norms of the school) there is also a temporal context to the lesson. The case-study lesson will be part of a sequence, and what happens in the lesson in terms of teaching and learning will in part be determined by what has been taught before and in what sequence. It will also be influenced by the relationship that the teacher has set up with the students and the expectations developed about such matters as whether it is OK to ask 'stupid' questions or admit when someone does not understand, and how others in the class respond in those situations.

The case-study researcher needs to be able to make justifiable decisions about what counts as a case – as an instance of some type of phenomenon or episode of educational interest – and which aspects of context need to be considered as potentially relevant to the case. Sometimes the boundaries between instances are drawn for us in obvious ways (by classroom walls or school bells indicating an end of a lesson; by the way the learners are arranged around several different tables in the classroom; by the way each member of teaching staff is assigned to one department or faculty). Sometimes we rely on less clear-cut classifications, perhaps provided by others (the EAL student, the gifted student, the autistic student). Sometimes the researcher needs to apply professional judgement to determine what might count as a case – for example, in considering critical incidents in a classroom, decisions have to be made about which incidents are critical, and when they begin and finish.

One of the main champions of case-study research suggests that "a teacher may be a case. But her teaching lacks the specificity, the boundedness, to be a case. ... The case is a specific, a complex, functioning thing" (Stake, 1995, p. 2). The teacher's teaching, in abstract, is not a case – but her teaching of a particular topic to a particular class could be, as we can 'draw' a boundary around those lessons (see Figure 8.1 below) and locate them as occurring in a particular place, at a particular sequence of times. In reality, education deals with complex, often messy, phenomena, and sometimes we just have to make judgements that we feel we can justify with reasons that others will find persuasive. Figure 8.1 offers a visual analogy of the situation facing case-study researchers.

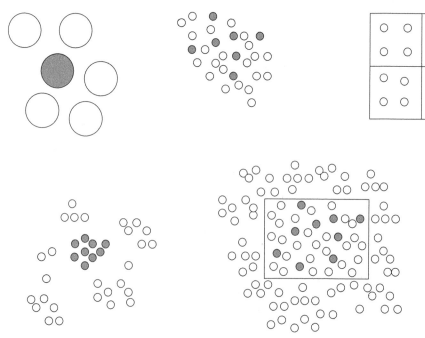

Figure 8.1 Representing instances

Question for reflection

Figure 8.1 offers a visual representation of five arrays of instances (the circles) – for example, each circle could represent a learner. Assume that in each of the arrays the closed (filled-in) circles represent instances that have been selected for investigation in a research study. Which of the images might be considered to include representation of a case study?

Note: this question is meant to allow you to explore your developing thinking about case study rather than have definite right and wrong answers (the images are open to interpretation!). If you have the opportunity, discuss this question with a colleague to see if you agree or, if not, can appreciate each other's take on this task.

If you found this task challenging, you may be reassured to know that one of the key thinkers about case study has suggested that case study "investigates a contemporary phenomenon within its real-life context, especially when the boundaries between phenomenon and context are not clearly evident" (Yin, 2003, p. 13).

The use of multiple data sources in case study

Chapter 10 discusses the collection and analysis of data. Case study is commonly based upon multiple data collection and analysis techniques. It is important when thinking about the choice of data sources needed in the case study to bear in mind that the use of different data sources supports two different features:

1   Because the case is a complex phenomenon, with many aspects, we need to collect data about different aspects of the case to fully understand it.
2   Because of the limitations of what we can infer from particular data, it is often useful to collect data of different types, or from multiple sources, to allow us to 'triangulate' – that is, to check we are drawing consistent inferences from the different data sources.

The best way to understand this is to set up a table showing how the different data sources link to particular things we need to find out in the case (perhaps the specific research questions). Indeed, this is a sensible way to think about and represent a research design whenever we are using multiple data sources and/or have several research questions, whatever methodology we are adopting. We should also be clear that we specify when different data will be collected, and from whom, and it may be useful to draw out a timeline for the study (cf. Figure 8.2 below).

As an example, consider Dry's (2010) study undertaken on teaching placement as part of his initial teacher training course (PGCE) and reported in *JoTTER*. Dry was responding to the requirement in the science curriculum to teach about the nature of science (or 'how science works', as it was described) as well as teaching about particular science topics. There are various arguments about how to teach about the nature of science in schools, and whether this should be achieved through discrete lessons or infused into the teaching of different topics (or a combination of these approaches).

Dry planned to teach a particular science topic about space by focusing on aspects of the nature of science, and he was interested in whether this would be effective in teaching the content of the topic and/or effective at teaching about the nature of science. He was also interested in whether teaching the topic in this innovative way would change the students' motivation to learn the science. So Dry had three particular research questions and he designed his study to collect data from a range of sources. He undertook tests before and after teaching the topic, and looked at data from two of the learning activities in the lessons. He also asked the students to complete a questionnaire at the start of the topic, after each lesson, and at the end of the topic. In addition, he selected three students to interview before and after they had studied the topic. In his published report, Dry (2010, p. 233) presents a table showing how he used these different data sources when considering his three research questions.

Dry's table includes a good deal of detail, and here (see Table 8.2) I have produced a summary of the key points (showing just the main types of data source). From this table it is clear that Dry had the potential to triangulate between data sources.

Table 8.2 Setting out how different data sources help address specific research questions (after Dry, 2010)

Research question	Student assessments	Student classroom work	Questionnaires	Interviews
Is focusing lessons on *How Science Works* an effective way of teaching *How Science Works*?	✓	✓	✓	✓
Is focusing lessons on *How Science Works* an effective way of teaching the *space* topic?	✓	✓	✓	
How does focusing lessons on *How Science Works* affect the motivation of students?			✓	✓

Question for reflection

Which feature of Table 8.2 shows that Dry could triangulate data sources when analysing his data and drawing conclusions from his study?

If you intend to use triangulation in your own study, you should plan carefully to ensure that you have *different* data sources relating to any particular research question. The data values need not always be of different kinds – it may sometimes be the same kind of data collected at a different time or from different participants. Whether that will support triangulation depends upon the particular question being considered. The imaginary examples in Table 8.3 may be helpful here.

Question for reflection

In which of the hypothetical examples in Table 8.3 will triangulation be possible?

Table 8.3 When can we claim we are able to triangulate between data sources?

Research question	Data sources
Do teachers and students agree about the characteristics of a 'good' lesson?	Interview with teacher; questionnaire given to students
Do students find discussion work in small groups challenging?	Observations of group work; interviews with students immediately after discussion lesson
Does student enjoyment of a subject change over time?	Questionnaire given to students at start of term; repeat administration of same questions at end of term.

In each case in Table 8.3 we have two different sources of data addressing a single research question, but in only one of these cases could we triangulate between the data sources. This is because two of the research questions are 'compound' in the sense that they look at relationships between two different things (the views of *two* groups of people; whether something is the same at *two* different points in time). So to answer those questions at all we must at least have distinct sources of data relating to the two different things that need to be related to answer the question. Only in one of the examples in Table 8.3 is there *redundancy* in the data. That is, only in one of the examples do the two data sources independently offer information about the same thing, allowing us to see *if the two different sources of data suggest the same answer to the research question*.

An example from a school placement

Usually we associate sign language with the deaf community, but there can be advantages to using sign language in classrooms for students with normal hearing. That was certainly what Mottley suspected when she introduced signing to the Year 2 (6–7 year old) students she was teaching on school placement, and investigated the innovation. Mottley (2012, p. 245) reported that she had two research questions (RQs) for her study:

1 Do children respond better to vocal or signed instruction?
2 Does the use of signing aid in the management of behaviour and actually reduce disruption?

Mottley introduced five specific signs – *toilet, quieten down, line up, sit down* and *wash your hands* (p. 249) – one per day over a week. The timeline for Mottley's study is represented in Figure 8.2, showing that she collected data before implementing signing, then repeated data collection after the new approach had been in place for long enough for the children to be familiar with using signing.

In the report, published in *JoTTER*, Mottley explains that she used "different data collection techniques, namely observations (use of timings and tallying – quantitative data) involving the whole class and interviews (qualitative data) involving eight children chosen … to include a spread of academic abilities" (p. 249).

Questions for reflection

How would you describe the methodology used in Mottley's study? Is there potential for triangulation in the design Mottley has adopted?

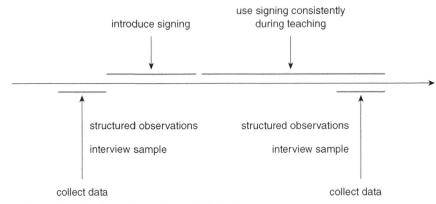

Figure 8.2 The timeline of Mottley's 2012 study

Mottley described her study as "a mixed-method approach" (p. 249). As we have seen earlier in the book, there is not always consistency in how different types of studies are described. However, as we saw in the case of Dry's work discussed in Chapter 5, this need not be important as long as the researcher offers a detailed report so the reader can make judgements about the appropriateness of research decisions, and thus the robustness of any conclusions drawn.

We might consider whether Mottley's study should be considered action research (AR), as it seems to be motivated by a desire to produce a more orderly, calm classroom to support teaching and learning – a definite case of seeking to improve the professional context. However, as noted in Chapter 5, not all teacher research to innovate and improve teaching is best understood as AR. Some would agree with Mottley that her research is a 'mixed-methods study', as she collects numerical data to test an implicit hypothesis (that certain indicators will improve after the implementation of signing) as well as interviewing some of the children to explore their perceptions of the classroom before and after the change. My own view is that this work is best seen as a case study evaluating the effects of introducing a change, as the report is focused on one classroom, and in particular a specified period of teaching; and the context is reported in some detail – with different 'slices of data' offering complementary insights into the case.

How can we understand 'triangulation'?

Mottley claims that she uses triangulation in her study: "Triangulation of data collection afforded me more than just the one perspective, providing me with convergence between my sources of data and thus a much deeper understanding of my study" (p. 249). As suggested above, triangulation involves having redundancy in our data, providing several viewpoints from which to consider the same question.

Mottley's second RQ is about reducing disruption of the teaching and learning in the classroom, and Mottley measures a range of indicators. Some of these relate to the number of times certain behaviours were observed during a sampling frame, and some concern the amount of time it takes for certain non-teaching activities to be completed. Mottley reports both that there are less potentially disruptive events and that the time spent on non-teaching activity is reduced. We might consider that as an example of triangulation, as two different indicators both suggest a decrease in classroom disruption.

Mottley's first RQ concerns how the students respond to the use of signed rather than verbal communication in the class. At one level, responses could refer to behaviour, which has been explored by the collection of the quantitative data. However, Mottley is aware of the importance of the children' own perceptions, and uses interviews to find out how they experience the classroom. She asked the children *before and after* the innovation is introduced, but that cannot be seen as triangulating as she is really interested in looking for shifts in their perceptions (cf. Table 8.3). What can be seen as triangulation here is the testing of whether the 'objective' measures of indicators (number of observed events; time spent away from learning activities) is consistent with the way the children themselves experience the change in the lessons.

In her study, Mottley found that the pupils interviewed were very positive about the change in their classroom, so her study suggests that the innovation was successful from the perspectives of both the researcher's objective measurements and pupils' reported experiences. Although only a sample of the class could be interviewed because of the constraints of small-scale teacher-research (see Chapter 5), the inclusion of a variety of interviewees nominated by the usual class teacher to represent different attainment levels in the class could also be considered by some as the basis of a type of triangulation between different classes of informants.

Triangulation, then, is something of a fuzzy concept. Sometimes (but not always) collecting data at different points in time can be considered triangulation – but not if we are looking for changes. Sometimes (but not always), collecting information from different informants counts as triangulation – but not if the original question was about the relationship between different people's views. Triangulation often (but not necessarily) involves comparing different kinds of data – but only when these different data types relate to the same research question. In effect, the key idea is *redundancy*: if we have different data that can separately offer answers to the same question, then we can triangulate between them to see if they suggest consistent answers to our questions. Ultimately, what is important (as always) is that the reader of a research report is provided with sufficient information about the research actions, and the thinking justifying those actions, to draw their own conclusions about the extent to which triangulation claimed by an author can increase our confidence in the claims made in the report.

Further reading ———

The Robson book in the list below is a helpful slim volume for anyone new to statistics. As I pointed out earlier in the book, I feel there are serious problems with

Creswell's notion of 'mixed methods' (which I specify in the review article from *Teacher Development*). Despite that, Creswell offers a very insightful account of many aspects of research design. I would recommend reading his book, but bear in mind the criticisms I raise in the review article.

Creswell, J. W. (2009). *Research Design: Qualitative, Quantitative, and Mixed Methods Approaches* (3rd edn). Thousand Oaks, California: Sage.

Robson, C. (1994). *Experiment, Design and Statistics in Psychology* (3rd Revised edn). London: Penguin Books.

Taber, K. S. (2012). Prioritising paradigms, mixing methods, and characterising the 'qualitative' in educational research. *Teacher Development, 16*(1), 125–138. doi: 10.1080/13664530.2012.674294

Yin, R. K. (2003). *Case Study Research: Design and Methods* (3rd edn). Thousand Oaks, California: Sage.

9

Teachers prioritising the ethical imperative in classroom research

This chapter:

- highlights the centrality of values to all educational work, including educational research
- discusses an example of a set of ethical guidelines
- considers the need to balance methodological and ethical priorities
- explores key ethical issues illustrated by examples from published studies
- considers the particular ethical issues arising when the researcher is also the teacher
- introduces some different approaches to thinking about ethical decision-making.

In general, we want to do the 'right' thing, and our values inform moral behaviour. Values are rightly often considered to be at the heart of education, and teachers, as a profession, are expected to demonstrate appropriate standards of professional behaviour. Codes of conduct, or professional ethics, have been developed over time to set out what the profession as a whole thinks is appropriate behaviour. Schwandt (2001, p. 73) suggests that "the subject matter of ethics is the justification of human actions, especially as those actions affect others". As researchers (as well as teachers) we wish to act morally, and to be seen as doing so. We generally think of research as a good thing, as it allows us to develop new knowledge; and as educators we tend to see knowledge as having higher value than ignorance. However, research has costs and consequences. As this chapter will demonstrate, selecting the 'right' course of action during a research project is not always clear-cut.

Guidelines that set out principles that need to be considered when planning ethical research have been developed by the research community. Ethical guidelines help us decide what is appropriate behaviour when planning and carrying out our research. By using the established ethical guidelines to inform our decisions, we protect our research participants from inappropriate requests and obligations. By explicitly justifying our actions in terms of such guidelines, we demonstrate that we are doing our best to carry out our research ethically, with due consideration for others.

———An experiment on learning ——————————————————————————

Consider, for example, a study that was carried out by psychologist Stanley Milgram (1973) in the 1960s. As you read this account, you should consider both the potential worth of research of this kind, and whether any aspect of the study might seem inappropriate in terms of your own system of personal values – what you feel is right and proper.

In the study two volunteers reported to a researcher, who asked them to draw lots to assign them to the role of 'teacher' or 'learner'. The experimenter explains that the study is concerned with the effects of punishment on learning. The learner was then taken to an adjacent room where he (the volunteers in the original study were men) was strapped into a chair and connected to electrodes. After seeing the 'learner' connected to the apparatus, the 'teacher' returned to the main room and was seated in front of an electric shock generator with a large sequence of switches. The teacher's job was to test the learner's ability to recall test items and to administer shocks each time the learner made an error (either giving a wrong response or failing to give a response in the allowed time). The teacher was to use the switches to ensure that each shock was somewhat more severe than the previous one: from a mild 15 volts to a more severe 450 volts – much more than mains voltage!

The teacher found that as the shocks became more severe, the learner showed increasing signs of discomfort, then increasing pain, and then became completely silent as if no longer conscious to respond. During this process the teacher was reminded (by the researcher), if and when needed, that it was important to continue and complete the experiment. Not surprisingly perhaps, many volunteers decided that they did not wish to complete the experiment, and refused to continue part way through the process, even though the researcher suggested the integrity of the study required them to complete the experiment. Perhaps more surprisingly, most of the 'teachers' obeyed the instructions to continue, and carried on giving electric shocks to the apparently unconscious (or worse) 'learner'. Over three-fifths of the 'teachers' continued with the procedure to the end, subjecting the 'learner' to the maximum voltage.

This might lead us to ask the question: Why did most of these volunteers think that research into the effects of punishment on learning was important enough to justify electrocuting another volunteer they had just met (and so presumably felt no malice towards), even when that other human being was begging them to stop and asking to be released from the experiment? The original study sought volunteers from US university students (leading to suggestions that the sample was not representative of normal people!), but it was later replicated with people from different walks of life, of both genders, in several parts of the world. The results were similar, and often even higher proportions of those who drew the 'teacher' role continued to the end of the process, administering potentially fatal shocks for the sake of completing the experiment. Was this because most volunteers assigned the teacher role thought that the potential benefits of the research justified the treatment of the experimental participant assigned the learner role? Perhaps you have your own view on this.

———— The ethics of educational research ————

Educational research is undertaken to increase knowledge and understanding of educational processes. This would seem to suggest such research is worthwhile, as it can inform educational activities – teaching and learning – that are generally considered to be important. The potential of educational research to improve education, and so be beneficial to the quality of human life, justifies the allocation of time and other resources.

The basic premise of this book would certainly support this general position: enquiry into teaching and learning can help teachers and learners and so is a worthwhile activity. However, as we have seen, individual research studies often only make a small contribution to knowledge; much research may seem to lead to only 'academic' outcomes, with no immediate and obvious transfer into the classroom; and research makes use of valuable, limited resources. This does not negate the *potential* contribution of educational research, but does suggest that it is sensible to weigh up the costs and benefits of studies. Research is worthwhile, but research studies are *not automatically* going to produce benefits that justify the time and effort involved.

Ethical guidelines

As well as this general consideration of the resource implications of any enquiry, there are other more substantial ethical concerns that need to be carefully considered by researchers setting out on a study. Most relevant professional associations have guidelines on ethical behaviour in research, and most academic institutions have policies and procedures to scrutinise research proposals. In the UK, the *British Educational Research Association* (BERA) sets out ethical guidelines (revised periodically) for educational research (British Educational Research Association, 2011).

This is now a well-accepted aspect of the research enterprise, although there was not always the expectation for researchers to make an explicit case that their research is ethical. The original version of the BERA guidelines were only published as relatively recently as 1992, following a seminar at Homerton College, Cambridge, four years earlier when the process of formalising a set of ethical guidelines for educational researchers was initiated. That is not to suggest that researchers did not generally act ethically before this, but sometimes studies published before ethical issues received such explicit attention may seem to us to use somewhat dubious approaches that might not be acceptable now.

The BERA guidelines suggest that all educational research should be carried out 'within an ethic of respect' for:

- the person
- knowledge
- democratic values
- the quality of educational research, and
- academic freedom (2011, p. 4).

The BERA guidelines are a useful starting point for anyone planning a research study. However, the same guidelines also point out that researchers often have responsibilities to a number of different groups of people. As well as participants in our research, we also have responsibilities to any sponsors (including schools or other institutions where we might be employed); to the wider community of educational researchers; and to the wider community (other teachers, policy-makers and the general public who pay for and send children to schools).

This means that there is an ethical imperative to make sure our research is rigorous, and is reported accurately and honestly, as it may have a role in informing the decisions of others far from the original site of the research. This also means that our responsibilities to our participants (to do them no harm; to ensure their participation is voluntary; to respect their anonymity and right to respond to what we write about them) needs to be balanced by our determination to be thorough so that our research can be as methodologically robust as possible. Sometimes these different considerations seem to pull us in different directions. A simple scheme for thinking about these considerations is shown in Figure 9.1, which represents the 'field' of concerns when ensuring our research is ethical.

At the centre of Figure 9.1 are the decisions that we make as researchers. These are influenced by principles (such as 'do no harm') and guidelines (such as BERA

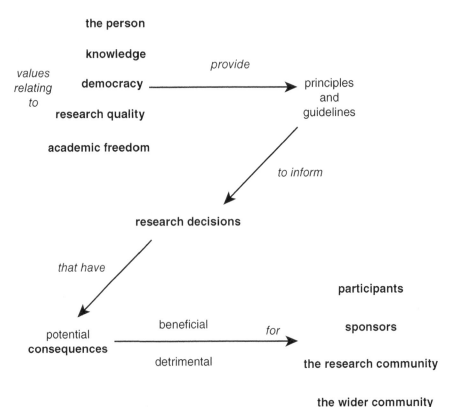

Figure 9.1 The ethical field: thinking about the ethical aspects of our research

guidelines and those issued by a university where we might be studying or teaching). However, those principles are themselves informed by values – such as valuing the rights of young people (to have a say in their education and any research they may be involved in), valuing honesty, valuing openness in our dealings with others, and so forth.

However, Figure 9.1 also reminds us that the decisions we make can have consequences which can be to the benefit or detriment of various groups of people – including, but not limited to, our research participants (and ourselves). Sponsors will wish to use our research to make policy decisions (e.g., should we move to a different way of organising pastoral support in the school?). The research community will use any published accounts of our research to inform decisions about what other research is needed, and how to frame it (just as we have been informed by the literature we have read in planning our research). Other teachers, other schools, and even governments may make decisions informed by their reading of research reports – potentially having consequences for everyone concerned with the education system. The ethical concern here is two-fold: just as reports of poorly carried-out (or worse, dishonestly reported) research can mislead, the lack of publication of potentially informative research can have consequences by failing to provide opportunities for informing others.

Question for reflection

Does the teacher-researcher, working in context-directed mode, avoid some of the potential ethical issues faced by professional academic researchers when his or her own enquiries are only intended to inform his or her own classroom actions and are not intended for dissemination or publication?

I strongly recommend that before setting out on any research, you should carefully read through the ethical guidelines that apply in your research context. Anyone doing educational research in Britain should certainly familiarise themselves with the BERA guidelines (available for free download from www.bera.ac.uk/publications/ethical-guidelines). This chapter will focus on some of the key issues likely to be of concern to teacher-researchers, but it is important to remember that ethical decision-making has to take all the relevant circumstances into account, and any set of *guidelines* are just that (a guide), as they cannot possibly specify all the myriad possibilities and combinations of considerations that might apply in any particular study.

Do no harm ——

In the medical profession, doctors are required to 'do no harm', and this is a general principle that should also apply in education. It is clearly not acceptable to plan any research where there are reasonable grounds for believing that some of the research participants may be harmed by the process. No educational researcher should want to deliberately – or even inadvertently – harm someone through research, and this principle has consequences for methodology and the development of knowledge.

What counts as harm?

In the 'experiment on learning' discussed above, people assigned as teachers were asked to administer increasingly dangerous electrical shocks to other people nominated as learners, when those learners failed to provide the correct answers to the teachers' questions. The teachers could hear that the shocks they were administering were causing discomfort, and then pain. The later shocks (that most of the 'teacher' participants proceeded to administer) were potentially capable of killing someone with a medical problem, such as a heart condition. It would seem there was considerable potential for harm here – but, as you may have guessed, all was not as it seemed.

> ## Question for reflection
>
> In Milgram's experiments the situation was manipulated so the participant who drew the 'learner' role was really a confederate of the researcher, and was reading from a script, pretending to be receiving electric shocks. Given that the 'learners' were not really shocked, do you think that the study might have done harm to anyone?

We can understand harm in a numbers of ways, not just as physical harm. A useful perspective is provided by Maslow's hierarchy of needs. Maslow (1948) suggested that, as human beings, we operate at a number of levels, each involving particular types of needs, which must be satisfied in a hierarchical fashion. In other words, at the most basic level we are physical organisms that require food and air and a suitable ambient temperature to survive. If those needs are not being satisfied, there is little point worrying about the subtleties of intellectual development: we will soon die.

Once immediate physical needs are satisfied, we need security – to be assured of our long-term survival and safety. The child who expects to be bullied at the next break, or to be beaten or sexually abused after school that day, or who is worried about a pending medical diagnosis, or the imminent break-up of their family, is in no state to concentrate effectively on school learning. Once basic security is stabilised, we all feel the need to be loved, cared for, and valued by others. So again, children who do not feel loved at home, believe they have no friends, and who do not think their teachers care about them are unlikely to engage effectively with school. Once we feel valued by others as a person, we can focus on feeling good about ourselves, by recognising our strengths, enjoying our achievements, and appreciating when others also recognise what we have achieved. Again, a child with limited self-esteem has little confidence in his or her abilities and is likely to struggle in school work.

Maslow thought that once these bases were in place, we can then focus on what he called self-actualisation, which involves developing our own value system, learning to be creative, etc. Beyond this, Maslow also thought there could be the possibility of what he called 'peak' experiences of an almost transcendental nature to which people could aspire. For our present purposes, the important point is that we can harm students and their educational progress at a number of levels. We must be aware not only of research that can put students or other participants in physical danger, but also of procedures that can perhaps lead them to lose self-confidence and start to doubt their abilities, or potentially even to start to question their own self-worth (such as, perhaps, the participants in Milgram's study who electrocuted strangers for the sake of a study on learning).

We would also consider any intervention that undermined effective teaching and learning as harmful. Consider, for example, the following two hypotheses:

- Students need to take in fluids during the day to function effectively as learners.
- Lower secondary students learn more when classrooms are organised to alternate boys and girls around the class.

We could imagine that it would be *possible* to test both ideas by some kind of quasi-experimental approach. In our first example, it would be possible (in theory) to randomly assign students to conditions where they are required to drink fluids regularly through the day, or where they are asked not to drink at all during school hours. As there are good reasons to believe that not taking in fluids for long periods of time is detrimental to learning, and indeed health, this would be an unethical study and totally inappropriate: ethical considerations would not allow the most 'scientific' approach to be used. (Having said that, there seems to be limited evidence for thinking that students usually need to drink water *during lessons* under normal classroom conditions as long as they are drinking during their breaks between lessons.) In this example, it is possible to imagine that students could be *physically* harmed by unethical research.

To test the second idea in a school with eight (mixed-ability) form entry, we might randomly assign four form groups to the treatment (sitting children boy–girl–boy–girl, etc. in class) and four forms to the existing practice (e.g., allowing pupils to sit with friends). There might be a case for saying that boys and girls generally have single-gender friendship groups in the lower secondary years, and requiring them to sit with pupils of the opposite sex either side is likely to decrease the proportion of student interactions which are off-task. (Some schools have implemented such arrangements for similar reasons.)

If a school were to carry out such a study, and intended to run the 'experiment' for a year, but found after a term that it seemed very clear that learning outcomes were significantly better in one arrangement than the other, then it might well be considered inappropriate to continue the study, requiring half the pupils to study in an arrangement that seemed to disadvantage their learning. In this example, provisional findings may well indicate that a study should end early. This assumes, of course, that there were no other considerations. A school might well take the view that children need to learn to regulate their own learning and behaviour, and their own social interactions, and so believe that any gains in learning of subject-matter following from forced seating arrangements need to be balanced against limiting the opportunities for learning in other important areas.

> ## Question for reflection
>
> Consider a researcher who has strong grounds for believing that students learn more
> effectively when organised in mixed-ability groups, and who wished to explore this issue
> and undertake research that could potentially inform teaching (i.e., producing findings that
> would encourage teachers to adopt more mixed-ability grouping in their classes). Would
> it be appropriate for this researcher to use similar-ability groups (to compare with mixed-
> ability groups) in his research if he strongly believed that learning is less effective with such
> groupings?

Ethical concerns may compromise research design

In his 1999 paper introduced in Chapter 2, Lyle reports research that argues for the value of mixed-ability grouping in teaching. The argument is supported by an empirical study of an intervention that provided literacy support for students in mixed-ability groups. Lyle's claims that the intervention was effective, and his suggestion that the mixed-ability aspect was an important feature, are undermined by the lack of any type of comparison group. This can be seen as methodologically problematic (see Chapter 6). However, Lyle informs his readers that "the decision to use mixed-ability groups was a principled one. The benefits of collaborative classroom learning have been well documented" (1999, p. 285). For a researcher who already believes there are strong grounds to think that students will benefit more from a mixed-ability context, requiring some students to work in similar-ability groups (purely for the sake of the research design) may be seen as ethically questionable. The potential dilemma here is represented in Figure 9.2.

Figure 9.2 suggests that values relating to producing quality research could be seen to be inconsistent with values relating to valuing the participants as people. Lyle made research decisions that compromised methodological robustness to avoid disadvantaging his participants. We might consider that he weighed potential benefits to his participants as more important than the potential detriment to the research community by publishing knowledge claims that were not supported by robust evidence. In situations such as this, judgements have to be made, balancing up the various considerations and their relative importance. In this case, some readers might feel that the quality of the research was so compromised as to undermine the value of the study to other researchers: but the ethical guidelines themselves cannot tell us what is the right thing to do in such cases, and professional judgement has to be used.

An important safeguard here can be institutional systems sometimes used to scrutinise research plans. A teacher undertaking research for a university qualification will probably have to seek ethical clearance from a supervisor or faculty ethics committee *before* undertaking the research. A teacher working in a school who is not undertaking a qualification should find out whether there is someone in the school management who takes on this scrutinising role as part of their responsibilities. If not, it may well make sense to seek informal clearance from a line manager or suitable senior colleague before proceeding with any research that seems to go beyond the normal evaluation of innovation that is part of the work of all fully professional teachers (see Chapter 1).

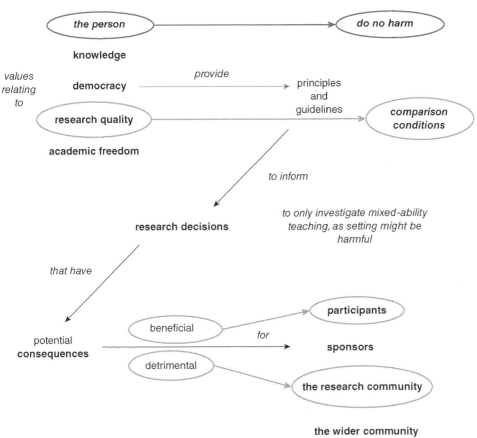

Figure 9.2 Features of the ethical field of Lyle's 1999 study

Voluntary informed consent ——

The area of consent is potentially a difficult one when undertaking research in schools, as most participants (the children) are, by definition, vulnerable. Teachers act *in loco parentis* (i.e., take on the parent's legal responsibility for the child during school hours), and a class teacher will act as a careful 'gatekeeper' who will not allow her charges to participate in what she judges as inappropriate research.

The 'gatekeeper' decides which researchers to admit

The gatekeeper admits, into the classroom, researchers who are undertaking studies seen as worthwhile and likely to benefit, or at least not be to the detriment of, students. However, the metaphorical gate is kept firmly shut in response to requests when, for example, the research seems pointless, ill-thought-out, or potentially stressful or disruptive for students (or teacher!). There is, however, clearly a potential for conflict of interest if the researcher is *also* the teacher – an issue considered later in the chapter.

Although it is suggested here that the gatekeeper is the class teacher, this is rather simplistic. For a trainee teacher on professional placement wishing to undertake some research in a teacher's class, that teacher should be approached for permission – usually after having planned the study in consultation with the university supervisor and school mentor (or their equivalents).

For a researcher who is not already known in the school, the initial request should be to the school head teacher or principal. (This applies in the UK, but see the note below.) If the researcher knows she wishes to work in a particular department or classroom, it makes sense to write to the head teacher, copying the letter to the head of department or teacher concerned. Most head teachers will only offer access on the basis that the individual classroom teachers concerned are also happy to cooperate in the research. When a researcher already has a relationship with the school, it may seem more appropriate to directly contact the teaching staff concerned for access to classes. However, unless the research is directly related to an existing role in the school, as in the case of the trainee teacher considered above, such approaches should be seen as complementary to a formal request to the school senior management.

Note: The approach to obtaining research access to schools varies in different places. In some countries requests to undertake educational research in schools need to be made at the level of district education offices, or even the national ministry. If the work is approved at that level, the schools may well be *expected* to cooperate with the researcher. If undertaking fieldwork abroad, it is important to check the procedures that would apply in the particular country.

Getting the green light for ECLIPSE

The author's own research within a personal research programme labelled ECLIPSE (*Exploring Conceptual Learning, Integration and Progression in Science Education*) has relied upon working with, and especially interviewing, secondary school and 'sixth-form' students about aspects of their thinking about science topics. One project undertaken for this research, labelled the *Understanding Science Project*, involved interviewing secondary school students about their understanding of the various science topics they were studying in class (some of the data collected is discussed at https://camtools.cam. ac.uk/wiki/eclipse/Eclipse.html).

A complication here is that although the direct focus of the study was the students' ideas, they would inevitably be talking to some extent about the teaching they were receiving, and therefore the study might be seen to have potential consequences for the teaching staff who were not direct participants (cf. Figure 9.1). Therefore, the research could be seen as potentially sensitive – why would teachers want a researcher taking the students' word for what was being taught in their classes?

The school where the research was carried out (over a period of five years) was selected carefully. The research was carried out in a state-funded comprehensive school that had a broad intake in terms of ability and a diverse student body in terms of social and ethnic background. It was also convenient to the researcher in terms of location and, as was suggested in Chapter 5, such pragmatic considerations can be important as travel costs and the time spent travelling to and from the research site can be minimised. The process of gaining access involved formally asking permission from the head teacher, informal enquiries with the head of department concerned, and attending a department meeting to explain to the teaching staff what I was hoping to do, and to answer their questions.

Obtaining informed consent

In some studies the approval of the gatekeeper may not be enough, and it may be necessary to explicitly seek parental consent for pupils to be involved in research projects. With the increasing trend for schools to see research into teaching and learning as a core activity, schools sometimes obtain blanket permissions from parents when children enter the school to cover basic types of research activity (such as recording lessons, collecting data by questionnaires, etc.). However, as schools vary in their policies on this, it is for the person doing the research to check on what permissions may already be in place.

It is also important that such policies and procedures do not remove the obligation on a particular researcher. It would be unethical to proceed with research on the basis of a blanket permission from parents if the researcher thought the nature of the research was such that particular permission should be requested, even if the person responsible in the school feels further permission is not necessary. I have known this situation to occur, when someone registered for a higher degree feels that they need to issue permission letters, and explain they have done this in their thesis, but the class teacher or head of department acting as the gatekeeper (trying to be helpful, I expect) feels this is not necessary. In this situation, the university supervisor can provide the researcher with support for their own judgement, allowing the researcher to take the line, "I know you think this is not needed, but my supervisor tells me that the university's ethical procedures require me to do this, and examiners will wants to see that I have done this when I write up."

Even when parents and/or teachers approve of the research, if it involves children individually (rather than something being done at a class level) it will usually be appropriate to seek the permission of the individual children. Research participants can only meaningfully give consent if they know what they are being asked to approve. Generally, the researcher needs to explain *why* he or she is doing the research, and *what* he or she will ask the participants to do. Participants should also know they are free *to withdraw* from a research study at any time, so it is often wise to enrol more participants than strictly needed if some level of drop-out seems likely. This is often the case with longitudinal research (looking at possible changes over time), where a whole range of factors can lead to original participants being unavailable for later stages of the study.

Questions for reflection

A researcher has a duty to obtain informed consent from participants in research. Consider a researcher who wishes to explore whether teachers interact differently with students according to gender – i.e., interacting more often with boys than girls (or vice versa), or interacting in a different way with boys and girls. The researcher needs to get permission – *informed* consent – from teachers to undertake observation in their classes. How much detail of the purpose of the observations should the researcher reveal in advance? Could it ever be ethically appropriate to deliberately mislead research participants about the nature and purposes of research when seeking their informed consent?

Is it ethical to revisit research data for a new purpose?

Harrop and Swinson's (2003) study of the nature of questions used by teachers was discussed in Chapter 3. Interestingly, the data analysed was not originally collected for the study reported in that paper, but consisted of recordings of lessons made as part of an earlier "investigation into teachers' uses of approval and disapproval in infant, junior and secondary schools" (p. 51).

Question for reflection

Is it appropriate to use data collected for one study for substantially different purposes in another study?

There is no *absolute* requirement that data used in a study should have been *specifically* collected for that study. However, there are two important caveats that should be considered. From a *methodological perspective*, any study is based around one or more research questions, or some similar focus, and ideally details of the methodology should be designed accordingly. This includes such matters as the type of data to be collected, the amount of data needed, and the approach to sampling. These steps are all short-circuited when data is re-used for a different purpose. It is important therefore to be confident that *a data set is appropriate* for use for the new purpose. Re-using a data set in this way probably means some compromise over research design features, but does provide considerable savings of time and effort!

Question for reflection

How much detail of the purpose of classroom observations should a researcher reveal in advance in order to obtain informed consent from teachers?

Balancing the methodological and the ethical imperatives

From an *ethical perspective*, data that is collected in schools is a gift to researchers from teachers and pupils. These individuals are the original 'owners' of their feelings, ideas, beliefs, utterances, etc. and, as suggested above, a researcher must get permission for the use of such material in research. (It is normally the parents who give consent for pupils under the age of 16.) For this to be *informed consent*, the informants must be told the purposes of the research. This in itself may be problematic, as people may well change their behaviour (if not always intentionally) when they know someone is scrutinising them, and so researchers will often be deliberately vague about their precise purposes.

If teachers gave Harrop and Swinson specific permission to record their teaching to explore their use of approval or disapproval, then the researchers should have sought renewed permission to then re-analyse the data for a new purpose. However, had the researchers' original request been this specific, the teachers' behaviour might have been modified, so it is more likely that the teachers gave consent to the recording being used for more general purposes, e.g., to 'investigate aspects of teacher's classroom talk' or to 'explore aspects of classroom interaction'. If this were the case, that would have covered Harrop and Swinson's (2003) study as well as their original research with the data.

What should we do with our data after the study is completed?

The re-analysis of data is only possible when it is available. Sometimes ethical guidelines issued by institutions suggest that data should be destroyed once analysis is completed. This is perhaps sensible if the data would allow participants to be identified, especially if it includes sensitive information and it would be difficult to ensure the data could be kept securely. A student doing a one-off project for an assignment, and with nowhere to safely archive data, may well feel that once the assignment is safely marked, the original data is best destroyed. However, given the investment of researcher time and effort, and the gift of data from participants, there is often a case for keeping data securely archived, when this is possible. This can allow:

- the original researchers or other researchers to go back and check the work;
- new analyses to be undertaken in the light of new research questions.

In Chapter 6 it was noted that when doubts were raised about the integrity of the research of one prominent researcher, it was not possible for other researchers to recheck his analyses because all his records had been destroyed. In that case it is now widely assumed that some of his work was fraudulent, based on non-existent data. Perhaps if his archives had been available, it might have transpired that this work was not dishonest, but simply contained errors. That would be important because the uncertainly casts doubt over the integrity of all of the research this person undertook in that topic. It may be that perfectly good research is being discounted.

Balancing costs and benefits

All of these ethical safeguards have the potential to compromise research design. The researcher also has a duty to any sponsors of research (such as a funding agency or a school that has safeguarded non-teaching time) to attempt to undertake a methodologically robust study, so that findings are more likely to be of value to inform future practice (and further research). There is clearly a balance here. For example, it may be considered an ethically *positive* thing to undertake secondary analyses on existing data sets (as Harrop and Swinson did) when existing research data has untapped potential to further inform practice. Certainly from a 'costs and benefits' consideration, such secondary analysis can lead to further potential benefits to knowledge creation and informing practice, with minimal additional costs (at least to the original participants). Funding agencies encourage the archiving of data sets in a form that protects the anonymity of original participants but allows possible further analysis.

Deception (misrepresenting the purposes of research) is generally considered unethical. However, it is often necessary to be deliberately vague about the *precise* purposes of research as research participants are likely to (deliberately or otherwise) change their behaviour when being observed. Any teacher being observed (whether by a researcher, senior colleague, or trainee teacher) is likely to be more careful than usual to demonstrate good practice, but knowledge of the precise focus of research may well lead to the observed teacher significantly changing his or her typical behaviour in relation to that focus.

In her report in *JoTTER* of her study on the challenge of being a left-handed learner in the primary classroom, Hayes wrote that:

> The first section of my research involved all thirty pupils in the class and is concerned with laterality. I required all pupils to participate in a laterality test which consisted of a series of nine exercises which pupils were asked to perform immediately. Their initial, instinctive responses were crucial for this test in order to ensure the most accurate results. Therefore, I presented the exercises to them as a game and did not tell them the reasoning behind the exercises until after they had completed them so as not to influence them.
>
> (Hayes, 2011, p. 94)

Hayes felt it was important to temporarily withhold information about what she was doing in order not to influence the student behaviour (but then to 'debrief' after the event). This seems sensible, as telling the children what she was doing might have provoked them to think about how they manipulate objects, rather than just acting spontaneously. Hayes's act of deception, if we consider it such, was undertaken for sound methodological reasons, and it would stretch credibility to see it as undermining the duty of respect to the children as people, or their expectation of access to information that would allow them to free determination of their own actions. We might also wish to bear in mind that as a (student-)teacher-researcher, it may be difficult to untangle her actions as a researcher from her actions as a trainee teacher, and question when research ethics (rather than the professional ethics of the teacher) become relevant. This issue is addressed later in the chapter.

The 'experiment on learning' discussed at the start of the chapter (Milgram, 1973) was not actually about learning, as the participants had been told. Stanley Milgram was actually interested in the extent to which ordinary people would be obedient to an authority figure. In his study, Milgram found that most of the people sampled would be prepared to administer unpleasant and potentially dangerous electric shocks to a stranger who was begging them to stop, based on the authority of a researcher with a white coat and clipboard, who argued that it was necessary for the integrity of the research. This area of research had been motivated by a desire to understand why apparently normal people are prepared to carry out atrocious acts when ordered to do so by an authority figure (for example, during the Nazi regime in Germany, but sadly there are many other examples).

Questions for reflection

The participants in Milgram's study were told they were involved in an experiment on learning. Do you think their behaviour would have been different if Milgram had been honest and told them that the experiment was designed to see how obedient they were to authority figures? Do you think your institution (e.g. university) would give ethical approval if Milgram were to submit a request for ethical clearance to carry out the same study today?

In Milgram's experiment, the participants were deliberately misled. This would seem to be unethical, but this raises the question of how we decide what is ethical. One approach is to have absolute rules. We might see lying as always wrong, and never acceptable. But perhaps even a scrupulously honest person might feel that such a rule can never be absolute. If a crazed gunman running riot in your school asks if you know where his potential victim went, and you know she's hiding in a cupboard, should you tell the gunman because it would be unethical to lie and pretend you do not know? That of course is an extreme example, but using extreme examples can be a helpful technique to test out whether we really think a rule should be absolute and have no exceptions.

Do you send a student home from school for a uniform violation if they have lost their tie in rescuing a child from drowning in a river on the way to school? I would hope you would decide to celebrate their actions rather than exclude them. So although one approach to ethics is to consider absolute rules, other approaches attempt to look at the wider context. Perhaps someone might tell the hypothetical gunman that his intended victim is hiding in the cupboard, despite not thinking honesty is an absolute rule, but because they are scared of what the gunman might do if they mislead him. Whilst that is more about fear than ethics, looking at potential consequences is one way of making ethical decisions. What are the consequences of bending our uniform rules for the student hero, and what are the consequences of sending the hero home because rules are rules and procedures must always be followed?

So one approach to ethics is to consider that a decision would be ethical if it leads to a greater good overall. Milgram's study was undertaken to help us understand better an important aspect of human behaviour – a potentially valuable outcome. To achieve this, Milgram had to deceive people, which is generally considered wrong, but was judged acceptable in these circumstances. At least, it was considered acceptable in the context of the particular time and place of the original study. It is very unlikely that Milgram would have got permission to run his study today. However, this is not because of the deception. It is generally considered that sometimes a level of deception is acceptable when a potentially useful study would be undermined by the participants knowing of its true purpose. This is sometimes the case in psychology experiments, and where deception is used it has to be explained in a full debrief at the end of the experiment.

The principle of informed consent means that although participants gave consent before taking part in the experiment, they can change their mind at the debrief because only then do they know the true purpose of the research, and so are actually in a position to give 'informed' consent. It is less likely that deception of this kind would be considered justified in classroom studies, especially where the researcher is a teacher who needs to develop trust with her/his students. Yet, as we have seen in Hayes' study above, some mild, temporary degree of deception may sometimes seem necessary.

Milgram's study would be unlikely to be approved today because of the potential to harm participants' self-esteem: imagine how you might feel had you participated in this study and been one of the majority prepared to give someone a potentially fatal shock just because someone in a white coat said an experiment into learning required it!

Confidentiality and anonymity

Usually it is also appropriate to promise (i) *confidentiality* in the research (which requires us to adopt procedures to keep data and documentation securely), to give assurances that research data will only be shared within the research team, and (ii) *anonymity* – to assure participants that a study will be written up in such a way that readers will not know the real identities of the people concerned. This may not be straightforward in studies that present 'thick description'. It is often also appropriate to offer to let participants see, comment on, or sometimes even veto, drafts of any writing about their contributions to the research (see below).

Question for reflection

Some researchers undertaking in-depth work with individuals seek to protect the identify of their informants by providing rich contextual accounts with some minor details changed (perhaps relocating the school from Manchester to Liverpool; perhaps reporting the teacher had undertaken voluntary work overseas for a while in Africa, when they actually served in South America). Is such deliberate inaccuracy acceptable in this situation?

As so often is the case in designing research, we need to balance different concerns. The need to protect a participant's identity needs to be balanced against providing a full report of our research (also an ethical requirement). It may not be easy to make judgements about how much to reveal.

Who's Nigel?

For example, an interview study published in 2001 by Coll and Treagust explored aspects of university students' understanding of a chemistry topic. The authors reported that "pseudonyms have been used to protect participants' identities" (Coll & Treagust, 2001, p. 361). This is quite appropriate, but in order to offer readers context to make sense of their study we are told something of the participants – which of course makes good sense in reporting research.

Clearly there is a tension between what is revealed and to what extent a participant's identity is protected. One of Coll and Treagust's interviewees was given the assumed name of Nigel. In the paper we are told (Coll & Treagust, 2001, p. 362) that:

- Nigel was a male PhD candidate;
- Nigel was studying in a West Australian university;
- Nigel was 26 years old at the time of the interview;
- Nigel appeared to be "reserved and hesitant and appeared to be rather under-confident despite being in the final year of his doctorate";
- Nigel had been "stimulated to study chemistry because of an inspiring high school teacher";
- Nigel was working on a thesis on "the use of activated carbon in the absorption of gold from solution".

This may not allow the typical reader to identify Nigel, but there cannot be many people who fit this profile (especially the thesis topic), and so arguably it might be possible to identify Nigel from this description.

Perhaps that does not matter, but the authors report that:

> The postgraduates used a number of concepts from other bonding or atomic models, typically describing the octet rule, but drawing on concepts from other models. Nigel also stated that covalent bonding results from the sharing of electrons. However, his drawing of the bonding in I_2 appeared to indicate that he has confused molecular orbitals and shells.

> (Coll & Treagust, 2001, p. 371)

To someone who knows about this topic (such as a potential employer), it might seem that here was a doctoral student who relied on rather simplistic metaphoric descriptions ('sharing' of electrons) more suitable for introductory study, and who was confused about basic models usually taught in college and undergraduate chemistry. Perhaps Nigel (possibly a professional chemist or chemistry teacher now) would prefer we did not know who he is.

Interestingly, Richard Coll (personal communication) recalls that, based on feedback from journal peer reviewers who raised this issue, the published account was modified compared with the original text in their submitted manuscript. Like a number of other examples in this chapter, it is likely that expectations in relation to ethical research and reporting have shifted in recent years to put a greater onus on researchers to protect research participants than was the case previously. Professor Coll reflects that "looking at [the description of Nigel in the published account] nowadays I would probably go further to obscure his identity but this was deemed by us, the reviewers and the editor of the time to be adequate" (personal communication, 2012).

Difficulties in ensuring anonymity

The study by Tobin and his colleagues (1990; discussed in Chapter 4) raises similar ethical issues. A key ethical concern is to do no harm (including psychological harm, such as damaging an individual's self-esteem), and a common safeguard is to make sure that the true identity of informants is not revealed in any reports. It is also common practice in research with a collaborative nature, as here, where two teachers volunteered to be subject to close scrutiny, to offer informants the chance to read, comment on, challenge and perhaps veto drafts of material that relates to them. In the Tobin et al. study, the two teachers, Peter and Sandra, were involved in reading and responding to the researchers' field notes and draft reports:

> When the field notes were written, we gave them to the teachers so that they would not feel anxious about what we were writing and so that they could give us feedback on their accuracy. ... Each teacher was provided with written reports of the study and the findings were discussed with them in depth. Feedback from the teachers about the written reports of the study was used as another data source.
>
> (Tobin et al., 1990, p. 16)

Although 'Peter' and 'Sandra' are assumed names, and the real names are not given, it is clear that colleagues (and students) who know these teachers will be aware of who they are: after all, not many teachers have been followed around school for an extended period in this way (and certainly not by this particular group of researchers). Sandra and Peter are not presented as representing 'good' and 'bad' teachers, but there is little doubt that Sandra comes out of the study rather well, at least compared with Peter. Beside his 'mind-set' being clearly considered by Tobin as less suitable for effective teaching, the study also suggests that Peter ("not a particularly popular member of the staff", p. 21), often behaved inappropriately for a teacher:

> Peter frequently was sarcastic and some of his remarks, which sometimes were belittling and sexist, could have discouraged some students. ... At times, Peter seemed to project himself in a manner that was slightly risqué and suggestive.
>
> (Tobin, 1990, p. 59)

It is not possible to know how such descriptions may have been greeted by 'Peter', or his colleagues and senior staff (or any parents of students in the school), but it is perhaps not surprising that Sandra (and not Peter) contributed the participating teacher's foreword to the book. Of course, researchers have a responsibility not only to protect their informants, but also to report their findings, and it may not always be easy to balance these expectations.

The process of carrying out and reporting research, and reflecting upon what we have done, provides an experience base that may lead to us changing our future approaches. Because I use the example above in my teaching, I wrote to Professor Tobin to ask him if he had any thoughts on this. He was kind enough to respond:

> The collaborative research models we use now and have used for the past decade typically preclude situations like this that arose with Peter. In fact, the strong feeling I had when we finished this study and asked Peter for his comments catalyzed

a strong value stance to include the voices of participants in research texts in ways that they would consider authentic.

(Kenneth Tobin, personal communication, 2009)

I do not necessarily feel that Tobin and colleagues 'got it wrong' in their 1990 work, but it is clear that reporting the project raised important ethical issues, and it is interesting to recognise that even professional academic researchers continue to struggle with the same kinds of issues that novice researchers must face.

Responsibilities to report research ———

Researchers also have an ethical responsibility to report research as fairly and as completely as possible. This has a number of features:

- providing enough details of methodology and also context (see Chapter 7) to ensure readers can make judgements about the quality of the research, and of its relevance to other contexts;
- not selectively reporting some studies over others because outcomes better fitted expectations;
- not selectively reporting data within papers because some data seems to better support preferred findings;
- highlighting recognised limitations in the study.

Each of these points is potentially problematic. For example, it is important to highlight the limitations in research studies – both because this contributes to a developing programme of research (by indicating how further research should look to improve or supplement existing studies) and because it avoids findings being over-interpreted. However, researchers will clearly also wish to make the strongest case for the significance of what they have found. These demands are not inherently incompatible. However, it is clearly a challenge for any researcher to 'stand back' from their research to write a balanced account which both argues for the study making a genuine contribution to knowledge *and* explains the inevitable compromises and limitations of the research.

A major problem for academic research is that many research journals limit authors to a modest word length (e.g., 4500–6000 words), which is a severe restriction on reporting a complex study. The British Educational Research Association (BERA) suggests that researchers should prepare detailed research reports that can be made available for anyone who wishes to find out further details after reading an account published in a research journal. The Association also recommends that researchers should consider writing up for different audiences – short, teacher-friendly accounts highlighting evidence and recommendations for practitioner journals, as well as more technical accounts for the research literature (BERA, 2000).

Avoiding bias in reporting research

The requirement that one should not merely select data that fits one's preferred outcomes may seem an obvious principle. However, in practice this is not so straightforward.

In much interpretivist (ERP2) enquiry, the researcher has to sift through and organise a good deal of material, and even make decisions about which data is relevant to the purposes of the study, to develop a model suitable for reporting. In writing-up, the most cogent segments of data are often chosen to clearly communicate the categories and ideas that have been developed through the analysis. It is normal practice, and quite *appropriate*, to selectively use data in this way – assuming all material collected is carefully considered whilst the model is being developed. The key question is the extent to which data is selected in terms of the emerging models rather than in terms of the researcher's pre-existing expectations and prejudices.

This is a difficult area as in many published studies the rigour and open-mindedness of the researcher has to be taken as given by the reader. Whilst it is reasonable to assume that academic researchers are not generally deliberately distorting research findings, it is much more difficult to know the extent to which analytical processes are inadvertently channelled by the researcher's existing ideas and beliefs. Grounded theory (GT, see Chapter 4) methodology is designed to offer techniques which safeguard against this problem, by setting out procedures that ensure that all data is fully considered, and reconsidered, and never prematurely dismissed. The rigorous application of a full GT methodology requires a good deal of time and an open-ended commitment to looking for what is called 'theoretical saturation'. However, many studies using qualitative data report the data analysis to have been undertaken with 'iterative procedures' or using an approach drawing up grounded theory techniques (i.e., 'constant comparison' of data during analysis), and this may offer reassurance about the robustness of findings.

Question for reflection

It is suggested that educational researchers are under an ethical obligation to report their findings – as selective reporting allows bias in which results reach the public domain.
To what extent should this obligation apply to teacher-researchers? Should those doing practitioner research be under an ethical obligation to publish their findings?

Even in the 'hard' sciences there are questions about scientists' decisions to omit from reports (what are judged as) spurious results considered to be due to some unexplained artefact, and so best ignored. Of course scientific apparatus can malfunction, technicians may make errors, electrical power supplies may go down for a period over night, chemicals may not be the claimed purity, measuring instruments may need recalibration, etc., and in many of these cases the reasons for an odd result may never be discovered. If the researcher cannot explain the odd result, and is unable to replicate it, then it may be sensible to discard it. However, science also presents many examples of potential discoveries being delayed years or decades because an anomaly that later was recognised as significant was initially dismissed as not worthy of attention. If these judgements can be so difficult in the so-called 'exact' sciences, then it can be even more challenging when enquiring into something as complex as classroom teaching and learning, where replication (repeating the precise conditions of the original study) is seldom a feasible option for checking an unexpected result.

⎯⎯⎯⎯⎯ The particular ethical issues facing the teacher-researcher ⎯⎯

All educational researchers, and especially those working closely with children as study participants, have to be aware of their ethical responsibilities. The situation is even more sensitive for the practitioner-researcher. Teachers who wish to research their own classroom need to be aware of the complications that can raise additional ethical dilemmas.

Question for reflection

How are the ethical responsibilities that *any* researcher must accept complicated when the researcher is *also* the teacher of the class being studied?

Universities, and their Education Faculties, will have their own procedures for ensuring that their research students plan their research in the light of ethical considerations. This may simply be based on including ethical advice in the research training, or may involve more formal recording and approval of research designs. In any case, research will be discussed with supervisors who have experience as researchers. A teacher who is planning research as part of their professional practice (and not taking a formal qualification) will probably not have their research plans subject to this external scrutiny.

The teacher-researcher is subject to the same expectations of high ethical standards as all researchers in education. However, having the dual role of class teacher and researcher, and so having a more complicated relationship with the learners, raises the potential for the teacher-researcher to abuse the privileged position of a teacher with responsibilities to students.

Does it matter if it is research or teaching?

Despite this complication, it is important to remember that classroom-based research and evidence-based practice should be the norm for all fully professional teachers (see Chapter 1), and that much of the research undertaken by teachers is primarily context-directed (see Chapter 5), seeking to improve the educational context and outcomes for the learners as well as the teacher. Earlier in the chapter an episode was discussed where Hayes temporarily misled her class about the purpose behind an exercise she set, to identify the dominant handedness of the pupils in the class she was working with on school placement. Given that the children were not aware of why Hayes wished them to undertake the 'game', they clearly had not given informed consent to this research activity. This raises the question of when a teacher should seek explicit consent for research carried out as part of the professional work of teaching.

As Hayes was a student-teacher-researcher, we might find it difficult to untangle her decisions and actions as a researcher from her decisions and actions as a teacher. There are many things that teachers try out in their professional work which would seem perfectly reasonable to most people as part of the job of trying to get the best out of students, but once we consider any of these innovations as 'research' it seems to raise new ethical concerns such as whether explicit informed consent should have been sought.

I would suggest that *the ethical status of an act carried out by a teacher as part of their professional work should be judged no differently depending upon whether we see it as teaching or research*. For example, the expectations of confidentiality should apply when the teacher has privileged information about a student, or their family, and this confidentiality relates equally to research reports, staffroom gossip, or talking to other members of the community outside school in social contexts.

In sending their children to school, parents are entrusting the school and teacher to seek to behave in the best interests of those children. If the teaching profession recognises that effective teaching is likely to depend upon regular, carefully evaluated innovation in classrooms, then the innovations, and the necessary collection of information for their systematic evaluation, should be accepted as part of teaching.

Of course a teacher's research actions should respect the learners and not expose them to harm: but this applies to all their teaching actions regardless of whether we think of them as research or not. We cannot expect the teacher to seek explicit consent from students or their parents before introducing a new poem to be analysed in class, or showing a new computer simulation of a laboratory experiment, or reorganising the order of topics in a scheme of work, or introducing a new rasp or drill into the technology room. Indeed, most parents would think that teachers had little idea of what they were doing if they constantly sought permission just to do their job.

The teacher-researcher has to decide when a particular activity goes *beyond* the norms of teaching (and the trainee should seek advice of the supervisor and/or mentor), as that is when it begins to make sense to think in terms of seeking explicit permission. Asking a student to give up part of their lunch-break to be interviewed would certainly be an example, but asking students to rate their enjoyment of a lesson at the back of their books at the end of lesson should not require specific permission. Common sense is a good guide here, supplemented by advice from more experienced colleagues when we are unsure of what should be reasonably considered part of normal, good teaching.

———The teacher-researcher's dilemma ————————————————————

All researchers have ethical responsibilities towards those they research. For a teacher-researcher wishing to enquire into teaching and learning in their own school, there are complications in the way ethical responsibilities are resolved. The complications arise from the potential abuse of power of the privileged position the teacher holds. Consider three examples:

- if the teacher-researcher is a head of department or senior member of staff, and asks to observe a less senior colleague's teaching, or to interview students in a range of classes within the department;
- if the teacher-researcher wishes to carry out an intervention study by using some form of innovative approach, or novel teaching materials, in her own class;
- if the teacher wishes to enrol volunteers from among her students to take part in interviews about their learning.

Gatekeepers and teacher research: *quis custodiet ipsos custodes*?

In each case the research may well be appropriate and potentially worthwhile. There is nothing in principle wrong with any of these scenarios. However, in each case, if an *external* researcher wished to do this work there would be the safeguards of additional gatekeepers (as discussed earlier in the chapter). An external researcher would normally first need to get permission from the head teacher to work in the school (unless the researcher was already known to the school through an existing partnership arrangement), and then arrange informed consent within the department for the work that was to be undertaken. Any teacher who had doubts about the nature or value of the research, or considered it potentially disruptive or uncomfortable for the students, would refuse permission. The head of department and/or teacher acts as a gatekeeper with the power to refuse permission to the researcher.

However, if the researcher is the person who would normally act as gatekeeper, then that safeguard is missing. The teacher-researcher who wishes to undertake the research must be able to also consider the research from an independent perspective to see how it might disrupt the normal teaching-learning in the class. Any research has the potential to complicate classrooms as well as the potential to improve them, but it may be difficult for one person (especially if under pressure to undertake research, for a university course, for example) to judge the balance between the potential value and costs of the research. For example, if an external researcher wishes to interview volunteer students about their learning, and the class teacher believed this was a worthwhile activity, she might well encourage students to help the researcher. However, if the teacher was also the researcher, and keen to collect the data, the students might feel under pressure to give up their free time and take part in an activity that may potentially make then uncomfortable.

This is not a good reason to discourage teachers from undertaking research into their own classrooms (which is often likely to be a valuable activity), but it does mean that the teacher-researcher needs to think very carefully about the way his or her students (or junior colleagues) are invited to participate in any research activity, to ensure there is no abuse of power. Whenever researching one's own students, it is important to prioritise the 'ethical imperative' and try to contextualise the enquiry within an ethical framework that ensures students know their involvement:

- is voluntary;
- is safeguarded by confidentiality;
- is not linked to any kind of formal class assessment; and
- may be cancelled at any moment by their choice, and without detrimental consequences.

Ultimately, we have to ask why others give us the gift of acting as informants in our research, and offer them the chance to decline or withdraw at any point where they feel participation is not in *their* interests (Taber, 2002b).

Moving the gate-posts

If a teacher-researcher suspects that others (other teachers, parents, etc.) could feel that any research they are carrying out with their own students goes beyond the normal innovation and evaluation that is part of being a fully professional teacher, they can avoid any risk of being suspected of behaving inappropriately by identifying a suitable colleague in the school to take on the gatekeeper role. This needs to be someone who is suitably senior so that they would be happy to take on the responsibility of saying 'no' if they thought anything being planned was inappropriate or misguided.

The teacher-researcher should seek permission for the research activities from parents/students, including a clear statement in the permission letter that in case of any concerns about the project, the student or teacher should contact the named colleague. It is important, in this situation, that the parents and student are clear who they can talk to, and know that that person has the authority to intervene in the case of worries or problems. The teacher-researcher, the senior colleague, the children and the parents should all be clear that it is the senior colleague who is acting as the 'gatekeeper' (although the term does not need to be used).

Ethical decision-making continues through a study

In my own doctoral research, when I taught in a further education college, I explored students' developing understandings of a key concept in chemistry (chemical bonding), and ideally wished to interview the same individuals at several points during their college course. However, I was also committed to emphasising the 'ethical imperative' to make sure my research was undertaken ethically, especially in view of my dual role as the teacher and researcher. I decided to explicitly set out the principles that would inform my study:

> To keep teaching colleagues informed; to ensure confidentiality of data; to ensure that all students involved in the case study work volunteered their time, and felt their involvement was worthwhile [by] (a) not assuming that colearners would wish to continue their involvement, but rather inviting them to each subsequent research session; (b) making it clear that colearners were free to leave the study at any time, and that they could decline to be involved on specific occasions; (c) making a point of asking colearners how they felt about each research session at its end.

(Taber, 2002b, pp. 441–442)

The term 'colearner' was deliberately used to remind me that my students came to class to learn about chemistry, whereas my research was designed to explore student thinking (albeit to inform my teaching and so support future student learning). Both teacher-researcher and student sought learning – but not about the same things. I considered that it was ethical to invite my students to give up their time to participate in the research as long as they could be considered to benefit from involvement in the research process. So I needed to consider (p. 436):

- What will the informant be asked to give to the study?
- What benefit will the informant gain from the study?

Moreover, as I was working with young people who were entitled to make their own judgements, it was important that *they* perceived being involved in the research process as a positive experience.

This of course had potential consequences for my ability to put my research design into practice, as students who found the research interviews boring, or stressful, or simply not the best use of the valuable time, might well decide to withdraw. It had been made clear that involvement was voluntary, and not linked in any direct way to their assessment on the course. Of course, it is not as simple as that: these were my students and may well have felt it was discourteous to decline a request from a teacher, or suspected they would get more positive treatment in some way if they cooperated, and so forth. Indeed, we might ask, for example, whether making a student feel good about themselves because they are helping with a teacher's research is itself a benefit worth their investment of time and energy.

As my purpose was to explore student understanding and how it changed over time, I also had to make clear to students that I would accept their answers, even if confused or wrong, and not try to correct them – somewhat unusual behaviour for a teacher (and indeed something that some teacher-researchers find very difficult when interviewing students). This would limit the potential value of the interviews at one level (they were not additional teaching), but my own views about the nature of the learning process suggested that giving students extra opportunities to talk through their ideas in response to iterative and challenging questions could be a valuable learning experience.

However, as the teacher, having professional responsibilities for facilitating student learning, I sometimes felt it necessary to break the 'no teaching' rule and provide feedback on particular points at the end of interviews. This could redirect student thinking – but if research interviews are learning opportunities for participants, then interview studies are already interventions that may modify the course of development of student thinking.

In the event, I found sufficient volunteers prepared to participate in the research, most of whom found the process interesting and useful enough to agree to follow-up interviews at different points in the course. I did have to negotiate convenient times to see students, fitting around their study and social priorities, somewhat compromising a neat pattern of interviews. But I also found some students who saw particular benefit in the process and volunteered to be interviewed more often, in one case allowing a very detailed case study to be built up. This particular student was not so keen on a card sorting activity included in some of the interviews, and negotiated a modified procedure that he found more useful, and which still allowed me to collect useful data. This student also got bored with being asked to complete my simple end-of-interview feedback sheet (designed to check that students were comfortable, not stressed, found the session useful, etc.) that I administered at the interview. So again I negotiated an alternative. This student agreed to complete a short diary of his experiences of being involved in the research rather than the feedback sheet. Whilst, again, this was a compromise on the original research design, it actually provided some very interesting insights on the experience of being a participant in intense research interviews (Taber & Student, 2003).

Ultimately, we have responsibilities to undertake research that is methodologically robust, whilst also being ethically sound. There are always going to be areas of uncertainty, where judgements have to be carefully made. Compromises to ideal research design will often be necessary, and sometimes plans will have to be changed once research is underway in response to how others experience the research process. As this brief account of my own teacher-research suggests, we may be required to make nuanced and difficult decisions. The important thing is that we are able to justify the basis for our decisions in such a way that others would recognise as reasonable in the circumstances.

To sum up some key points…

Clearly, ethical issues are often complex and nuanced, and so careful judgement is needed. However, most readers of this book will find that *several* of the following recommendations fit their situation:

---

i All education researchers need to follow the latest relevant ethical guidance on educational research (e.g., BERA, 2011)

ii Any researcher registered for a course at a university or similar institution should find out about, and follow, any ethics guidelines and/or procedures in place in that institution

iii Any external researcher wishing to undertake research in schools should seek access through the school senior management and class teacher(s) who will act as 'gatekeepers' for the research

iv A trainee teacher on professional placement should seek guidance on their planned research from their university supervisor and school mentor, as well as negotiating access with any specific classroom teachers

v A qualified teacher researching their own classroom through context-directed enquiry:

- o which they are confident falls within the usual range of innovation and evaluation activities that are a normal part of being a fully professional teacher
- o and does not make demands on the students outside normal classroom activity
- o and will not involve dissemination/publication beyond the institution

should rely on their professional judgement. However…

vi A qualified teacher

- o undertaking theory-directed enquiry, and/or
- o undertaking research on matters beyond the teaching and learning in their own classroom, and/or
- o undertaking activities that go beyond the usual range of innovation and evaluation activities that are part of being a fully professional teacher, and/or
- o requesting students to contribute to the research outside normal contact time (lessons, tutor periods), and/or
- o intending to disseminate/report findings beyond the institution

should seek guidance and approval from a suitable senior colleague in a position to act as the gatekeeper for the research

vii And for any potential researcher: if in doubt, seek guidance before acting.

—— Going deeper into ethics ————————————————

Many teachers undertaking classroom research appreciate the need for ethical behaviour in their professional work, including research. They know it is very important to behave

Figure 9.3 A simple model of approaches to thinking about ethics

ethically, and they are happy to be informed by ethical guidelines and the advice of more experienced researchers. However, as the examples above suggest, difficult decisions often have to be made where the best way to proceed is not always immediately clear. For those who find this topic particularly interesting, there is a great deal written about ethics, which is an important topic within philosophy.

An introduction to ethical perspectives

In keeping with the introductory nature of this text, and my treatment of other complex issues, I here offer a very simple model of four perspectives on ethics that can be drawn upon in decision-making (see Figure 9.3). As will be appreciated, this is a complex and nuanced topic, and this model should be seen as a taster of this area of scholarship. If you find issues of this type interesting, it is worth reading more widely. Of course, these approaches to ethics are not just relevant to decision-making in research: they apply just as much to how we make decisions about how to behave as teachers, as scholars and, indeed, as people.

Perhaps the most basic approach to ethical thinking is the deontological approach that concerns sets of rules for ethical behaviour. So, for example, if we believe it is wrong to lie, then a decision to deceive someone contradicts that ethical rule. We have already seen above that absolute rules can have limitations in complex or extreme situations. This leads us to consider a utilitarian position. This suggests that the ethical decision is the one that we expect to lead to the greatest good. In its pure form this suggests that we can ethically do 'evil' things if there are also good consequences that outweigh the evil. The author is old enough to remember when corporal punishment was regularly used in state schools (it is now illegal to use physical punishment in schools, at least in the UK and in many other countries). Rumours spread around my secondary school of particularly naughty students who had been sent to a deputy head to get hit with a cane. This seems like a story from the 'dark ages', but it is within living memory, showing how society has progressed in a few decades.

Presumably the deputy head teacher did not think it was inherently good to assault selected students with a piece of wood. However, the act was considered justified as a deterrent to bad behaviour both for those punished and others tempted to transgress. This view suggests that it is sometimes acceptable to cause a certain amount of discomfort or inconvenience in order to achieve something worthwhile. Many of us make such a decisions for ourselves (e.g., to give up most evenings and weekends to prepare for classes when we first start teaching as we want to be well prepared for lessons; to manage on a limited income whilst studying for a qualification that should lead to a rewarding and reasonably paid position): but the utilitarian researcher sets out a mental balance sheet on behalf of others involved.

Taken to the extreme, we might argue that it is worthwhile to put a class through a very unpleasant learning experience for research that can lead to a modest benefit for future students – as we multiply the costs and benefits by the numbers suffering them. A great deal of anguish for a class of 30 students is readily outweighed by a very small improvement in the lot of thousands of students who will be taught by teachers informed by the study concerned. Put in those terms, this might not seem a very ethical approach, but it is one very well-established and respected starting point for ethical thinking.

Given the obvious limitations of both of these approaches, it is perhaps not surprising that alternatives have been developed. One of these is informed by the idea that an educational professional, such as a teacher or educational researcher, should go beyond simply behaving ethically, and seek to actually work as a moral agent, effecting change with and for others that makes the world a better place. Such a perspective is likely to look beyond simple balancing of the potential benefits and costs of research, seeking to be seen to be acting as an example of correct behaviour.

Finally, there is a pragmatic approach to research ethics which acknowledges that education concerns complex processes, and therefore we cannot always know the precise consequences of our research (or other educational) actions, let alone balance up all the possible positive and negative outcomes. The pragmatist is dubious of establishing specific rules for ethical behaviour, and acknowledges the need to consider the complexity of each specific research context, and to customise decision-making for a particular study. The pragmatic researcher also acknowledges that this (as any) approach will sometimes lead to what seem in hindsight poor decisions, but will pay careful attention to the effect of decisions and be prepared to change plans in the light of experience (and to use such experience to inform future decision-making in subsequent research).

Question for reflection

Can you see evidence of research decision-making that seems to be based on any of the approaches introduced here (deontology, utilitarianism, virtue, pragmatism) in any of the studies discussed in this chapter, or indeed in the rest of the book?

Important to be ethical: important to be seen to be ethical

If research is being formally reported, for example in an academic assignment or thesis, then ethical considerations should be acknowledged in the report. As part of the methodology section of a report (see Chapter 12) it is important to acknowledge what precautions were taken to ensure the research is ethical. This is likely to include a reference to any ethical guidelines followed (e.g., British Educational Research Association, 2011) and an acknowledgement of any ethical clearance procedures followed that are required by the school or college where the researcher is teaching, and/or a university in the case of an academic assignment. In addition, specific decisions taken should be reported, as in this example from Hick's report in *JoTTER* of his work undertaken on school placement as part of his graduate teacher preparation course:

> To uphold the ethical standards of educational research this project has withheld the names of the school and pupils to ensure anonymity. Further, all those that took part in the research gave their consent to do so and were free to not take part at any point. A 'gate keeper' was used in the form of the students' normal classroom teacher to monitor the research and provide a point of contact for the students. In addition the classroom teacher ensured that the learning taking place as part of the study was still appropriate for the exam specification.

(Hicks, 2010, pp. 173–174)

As well as including pertinent points in our accounts of methodology, we should also report any ethical issues that arose during the research, and how we responded to them. It is sensible to revisit the ethical issues we faced when writing any discussion section of a report, to consider if there are things we would in hindsight do differently, or issues arising that can inform our future actions. Examiners (and journal editors) expect us to behave ethically, and also expect us to think that ethics are important enough for us to explain the decisions we made to ensure our work was informed by ethical considerations.

Further reading ———

Anyone undertaking research in British schools should read the BERA guidelines – and they would be invaluable for researchers elsewhere as well. The American equivalent may be found online as part of the 'Codes of ethics collection' of the *Center for the Study of Ethics in the Professions* (http://ethics.iit.edu/ecodes/introduction). A number of approaches to thinking about ethical issues have been proposed, and Stutchbury and Fox (2009) have drawn upon these to develop a tool to aid students and researchers in analysing the ethical issues involved in planning research. This would be a useful place to start reading more about the different approaches that can be taken to ethical decision-making. Kimmel's book is a more extensive treatment of the ethics of doing research with human participants.

American Educational Research Association (2000). *Ethical Standards of the American Educational Research Association.* (Available from: http://ethics.iit.edu/ecodes/ node/3178)

British Educational Research Association (2011). *Ethical Guidelines for Educational Research.* London: British Educational Research Association. (Available from: www. bera.ac.uk/publications/ethical-guidelines)

Kimmel, A. J. (2007). *Ethical Issues in Behavioral Research: Basic and Applied Perspectives* (2nd edn). Malden, Massachusetts: Blackwell Publishing.

Stutchbury, K., & Fox, A. (2009). Ethics in educational research: Introducing a methodological tool for effective ethical analysis. *Cambridge Journal of Education, 39*(4), 489–504. doi: 10.1080/03057640903354396

10

Teachers collecting evidence through research

This chapter:

- explains the importance of clarifying your 'unit of analysis' before beginning the analytical process
- introduces a range of the most common data collection techniques
- examines common sources of data used in educational work
- discusses features of instrument design, and administration of data collection, that can help to ensure the quality of the data collected
- includes discussion of data collection techniques that can be incorporated within normal classroom teaching.

This chapter offers some introductory advice to the teacher-researcher on data collection. The types of data collected in any enquiry should be determined by considering the information needed to answer the research questions. Two general considerations are:

- the 'subject' of the enquiry
- the unit of analysis

What is the 'subject' of the research?

Studies that are concerned with finding out what people *do* in classrooms will look for different data from those exploring what is going on in their minds. These latter studies will collect different data if the focus is what people (think they) know, rather than on what they believe is right, or what interests them. The following questions have different types of subject:

- What proportion of the students' time is spent on task?
- Do the students understand Newton's laws of motion?
- Do the students believe copying homework is a valuable activity?
- Why don't the students in this class seem to enjoy poetry?

What is the unit of analysis?

Studies also differ in whether they are focused on isolated individuals or interactions and groups. So, for example, research based on a conceptual framework (see Chapter 3) which includes a model of 'knowing' as a solitary activity is more likely to favour collecting data from individual learners, but research based on a conceptual framework which views knowing as a social activity might chose to explore student understanding by working with pairs or groups of students. Similarly, research from a view of teaching which sees the central relationship as being between teacher and student may focus on the interactions *between* teacher and individual learners, where a different view of classroom learning might lead to a focus on the interactions *within* groups when working on tasks set up by the teacher.

The unit of analysis refers to the types of 'things' that will be characterised and perhaps compared in a study. In educational research the unit of analysis could be a student, a lesson, a class, a teacher, a school, a group within a class, a question asked, an explanation given, a conversational exchange, a test script, a scheme of work, a lesson plan, etc. That is, we might characterise and compare different students; we might characterise and compare different lessons; we might characterise and compare different classes, etc.

So in a study looking at teacher beliefs about pedagogy, the unit of analysis is likely to be the teacher. In a study of the relationship between school ethos and exclusion rates, the unit of analysis is likely to be the school. In a study of student understanding of creation myths in different cultures, the unit of analysis is likely to be the student. In a study on the effect of gender on school science group work, the unit of analysis is likely to be the group (although a group does not have a gender, and so the *gender composition* of the group will need to be seen as the 'independent' (or input) variable).

———— Sampling in classroom research ————————————

The topic of sampling in classroom research was discussed in Chapter 4, where it was discussed as an important aspect of some common methodologies – such as surveys. It may seem that sampling is less important in small-scale classroom research, especially if we are undertaking context-directed research (see Chapter 5), as we are not looking to find out about some vast population (*all* secondary students studying geography, *all* students with hearing impairments, *all* gifted students in design lessons), but rather about our class, our lessons.

However, even in this situation we may need to sample. We might give a questionnaire to everyone in the class – but may well not have the time needed to interview them all. We may have to select particular lessons to focus on, within a teaching scheme. We may decide to look at a limited number of examples of student work or test scripts in some detail. We may wish to video group work, and need to choose one group to direct a camera at.

As suggested in Chapter 4, there are various ways to obtain a sample. One approach is to randomly choose from the 'population' of students, lessons, pieces of work, etc. the number of examples we wish to include in the sample. This allows us to claim some attempt at looking for typicality.

Questions for reflection

How do you select randomly? Why might selecting a random sample not always be the best approach in classroom research?

Random assignment: 'I randomly selected every third student…'

Although the term 'randomly' is much used, we know that most people are not good at appreciating what 'random' really means, and expect random events to appear much more evenly spread than is often the case. (I have to say 'often' here, because if we deal with random events, then no pattern is ruled out, as each possibility has some chance of occurring.) This leads to a question of how a researcher selects participants for a study in a truly random way. When we read accounts that report 'the teacher selected a student to interview at random', we might wonder how they went about that. (This is the kind of question that occurs to us when we read the research literature critically, but would probably not be considered by a casual reader.)

If we select students at random, then all students have an equal chance of being in the sample, and it becomes very unlikely we would get the same sample if we repeated the process. (Whereas if we decide instead to select every fifth student from a class list, we would get exactly the same sample if we started over.) The only way to be able to claim a random selection is to draw lots – so that it is a real lottery who gets selected. There are tables of random numbers, and computer simulations that give near-enough (quasi-) random assignations, and, of course, dice or tossing coins can be used. However, when a research report claims that a selection is random but does not indicate how the selection was made, I always become suspicious of the claim. If the 'random' selection is then reported to include both genders and an equal representation from different ability bands (or some other such variables) it starts to seem even less likely it really was random.

Of course, it is possible to set out a sampling frame in terms of, for example, gender, ability, etc., and *then* select randomly in each category from potential participants who match the particular characteristics. So you could write the names of all those in a class on pieces of paper that can be folded to be selected blindly from a hat or box, but then only select from one sub-pool at a time: e.g., two selected at random from girls of high attainment; then two selected at random from girls of middle attainment, etc. (see Figure 10.2). But if you want an even representation of different subgroups within a sample, do not expect this to occur if you use random selection *from the whole population* (e.g., class), as it is unlikely to be the outcome (see Figure 10.1).

Purposive sampling

Attempts to build a typical sample by random selection can be undermined by ethical considerations anyway – when some students may decline to be interviewed, for example. Also, it might actually be sensible not to interview those who have little to say, or speak very quietly, or are very easily embarrassed – as long as such pragmatic

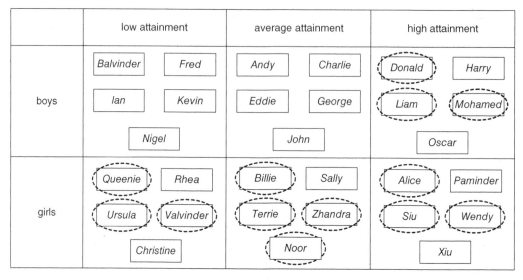

Figure 10.1 If a sample is selected at random (as above), it may provide an uneven representation of different identifiable subgroups

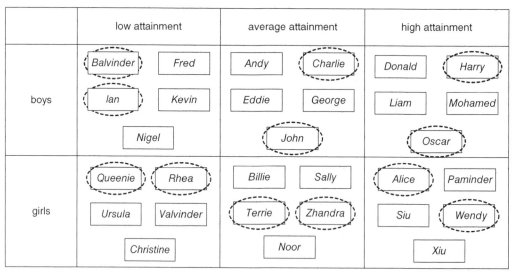

Figure 10.2 To ensure a sample contains representation of different subgroups in the class, you need to undertake any random selection from *within* each subgroup (as above)

concerns do not undermine our purpose. (It would be unfortunate to exclude students who say little if the study was about different levels of participation in discussion work!) We often also recognise that particular students (or lessons or whatever) could be especially informative in relation to our focus, and so deliberately wish to include them in our sample. As always we should make our decisions carefully, with good reasons, and keep records of both the decision and the rationale behind them.

——— Data collection ———

There is a range of data collection techniques that are open to classroom teachers exploring teaching and learning. Some of these are more problematic if a teacher is trying to research her own classroom. Available techniques include:

- interviewing
- observation
- questionnaires
- tests
- learner products
- documentary evidence.

Each of these can have a range of 'flavours', and so can be fine-tuned for particular types of study. In Chapter 3, it was suggested that research techniques are like a range of tactics that can be applied in a study. We can select more than one technique, as long as the techniques we do use are consistent with our overall strategy (methodology).

As suggested in Chapter 5, a useful methodological choice for many teachers exploring aspects of their own classrooms is case study, which focuses on an instance (a particular classroom, a particular sequence of lessons, etc.) but usually involves a range of data sources that allow the construction of a nuanced account reflecting the complexity of teaching and learning. It is also often an appropriate approach when academic researchers choose to investigate one particular context in some depth as the best way of better understanding an issue. When Taylor (2011) investigated how learners' perceptions of Japan in one English class changed due to learning about the country in geography lessons, she collected data in a range of complementary ways:

> In this project, materials resulting from a wide range of data-generation methods, including in-depth interviews, visual methods, classroom observation and audio diaries, were used to provide a detailed picture of students' representations of Japan and the ways in which these changed over a four-month period.
>
> (Taylor, 2011, p. 1037)

Often then, the types of data discussed here will be seen as complementary, rather than as alternatives from which we select.

——— Documentary evidence ———

Classrooms and teaching are often well documented. A range of documents may be useful in answering research questions. These include attendance records, mark-books, schemes of work, students' work and teacher feedback on that work. Other documents that are less centrally focused on a particular classroom but which may well be significant for what goes on there include departmental minutes, school policy documents (on marking, inclusion, literacy across the curriculum, etc.), inspection reports, papers presented to the governing body, school strategic plans, school brochures, etc. Such documents may in themselves only be sufficient to answer limited questions (e.g., 'Do cross-curricular school policies make reference to the needs of those students identified as gifted and talented?'), but documentary analysis can play an important part in enquiries comparing actual classroom experience with the intentions represented in school policies.

A particular area of documentary evidence that has traditionally been called upon for assignments on teacher training courses is that of lesson plans and evaluations. Although all teachers are expected to plan and evaluate their teaching, there is usually no requirement for qualified teachers to keep detailed paperwork (Department for Education and Skills, 2003). However, trainee teachers are usually expected to make detailed lesson plans, and to evaluate their lessons in writing.

Question for reflection

To what extent are lesson plans and evaluations likely to be reliable as evidence in classroom research?

Lesson plans represent the pedagogic intentions of the teacher (or trainee teacher). Their lesson evaluations attempt to identify what went according to plan, and why, and what did not go as expected – requiring the plan to be changed *in situ* and/or for teaching that lesson to a future similar class. To be useful, lesson evaluations have to be honest and analytical ('it went okay, I think it was a good lesson' is of little value to informing future practice), so that impressions are supported by evidence and are consistent with the models and theories of teaching and learning that the teacher uses to make sense of the classroom.

However, the teacher can make a very poor objective observer of the classroom – being intimately involved in the action, and often having a great deal invested in the outcomes. This can lead to lesson evaluations that miss key events, and are either much too self-critical or self-forgiving. This provides a major challenge to action research (AR, see Chapters 4 and 5) – an approach to classroom enquiry that has been described in terms of the teacher looking to account for their professional practice (McNiff & Whitehead, 2009). Indeed, it could be argued that one way of understanding AR is that it is a systematic approach to teacher planning and evaluation that provides support with overcoming the (inevitable) subjective nature of self-evaluation by using evidence and validation through the views of others.

As has been suggested earlier in the book, subjectivity is not always a bad thing (and is seen as important in certain types of 'qualitative' interpretivist writing). The distinction between bias and prejudice may be helpful here. It is quite right (and indeed unavoidable) for a teacher to bring some biases into their professional work, as our values inform such biases. (It is a 'bias' to view fairness as a better thing than unfairness; it is a bias to think that your teaching subject is especially interesting and important.) However, most readers would agree that prejudice – making judgements before considering all the relevant evidence and perspectives – is less desirable. (Then again, the belief that prejudice is a bad thing is of course itself a value judgement, and reflects my own bias. I hope it also resonates with the reader's biases.)

The validity of sources depends upon the research focus

Given this, it may seem that such teacher documentation is of very little value as research evidence. However, this again depends upon the research questions being investigated. By themselves, a teacher's lesson evaluations must be treated as having limited reliability in reporting the effectiveness of teaching. However, if the research questions concern teacher thinking (e.g., *'Does the teacher think about the needs of the full ability range when planning lessons?' 'Does the teacher consider she is meeting the learning needs of the full ability range?'*), then these documents may be a very useful source of information. Once again, we see that the issue of ontology (i.e., thinking about the nature of what it is we are enquiring into – see Chapter 3) is so important in research.

Many student projects are flawed when they do not clearly think about the ontological status of their research foci, and they present data about something quite different. It may well be that the students in a class do know when they have learnt 'Ohm's law' or the causes of the industrial revolution. Yet we cannot assume this will be the case. (I have undertaken many interviews with students who have told me that they have learnt things in science lessons that it is *very* unlikely the teacher was intending to teach!) If our research question concerns whether appropriate learning took place, rather than student perceptions of their learning, but our data only reports on whether students think they learnt what was intended, then we are not answering our research question. Similarly, there is plenty of research to suggest that teachers' beliefs about how they teach are not always reflected in what observers see them actually do in lessons.

Teaching diaries ———

A common approach to collecting data about teacher thinking about lessons planning and evaluation is to keep a research diary. This could take the form of a reflective notebook or diary, focusing on the issue of particular concern. The teacher can use this notebook as a record of thoughts about the topic, including ideas that feed into planning, and any relevant notes made when evaluating lessons. Such a reflective diary provides a record of the teacher's developing thinking as she explores the issue, and its significance and manifestations in her classes. Sometimes in research looking at classrooms, an external researcher may ask the teachers to keep such a diary, intending to use it as a source of data about the teachers' thinking – often alongside other sources of data. In teacher-research, the teacher-researcher may see such a document as the major source for developing and recording the research process.

A diary or set of notes in this form remains largely subjective – the thoughts, impressions and interpretations of one individual. This is a particular form of research data that has its value and limitations. This type of record can be useful in later explaining why certain ideas were used to plan actions – for example, why certain types of classroom interventions were undertaken rather than others. It may also record critical incidents that can provide useful clues for following up in other research. A student comment about why a particular activity was too difficult or too simple or too uninteresting may provoke a new research question.

Attitudes to the use of this type of information as research evidence vary. Where research is carried out for the professional development of the individual teacher, this can be a valuable record of critical reflection, and can help systemise and organise thoughts. If teacher-research is viewed as being primarily about the development of the teacher-researcher, then such documentation may play a major role in producing an account of the research (Whitehead, 2000). In action research, this kind of record can be very important in accounting for actions, and for claims that these actions have improved practice (McNiff & Whitehead, 2009). If, however, research is expected to produce new knowledge for the profession as a whole, then the personal reflections of one individual may not be considered to provide rigorous evidence. However, even here such accounts may provide useful starting points for the collection of other, more 'objective' types of data.

—— Tests

Teachers associate testing with assessment, but if classroom testing was a new invention it might well be considered a form of teacher-research. After all, tests are ways of collecting evidence about student knowledge and understanding. Indeed, formal examinations (such as SATs, GCSEs, etc.) provide an immense amount of data that has been used as the source of a great deal of educational research. Such research can provide substantial data sets for examination boards and others to use (for example, McClune's (2001) study discussed Chapter 4).

In the 1980s an organisation called the *Assessment of Performance Unit* (APU) was set up in the British government's education department, and tested large representative samples of the school population against some of the things they were expected to learn in school. For example, in science, the APU tested large numbers of students at ages 11, 13 and 15. The data from these surveys was made available to researchers, and was the starting point for major research programmes exploring student understanding of key science concepts. As the surveys were undertaken as research, and results could not be linked to individual schools or students, this survey process had potential to provide data on trends in student attainment over time. Unfortunately, as with so many national initiatives, it was abandoned before such trends could be established, and it was replaced with a system of national testing that required every student to be assessed and assigned 'levels' of attainment. The results from this system reported quite major improvements in student learning year-on-year, suggesting that teachers got much better at teaching core subjects in just a matter of a few years.

Question for reflection

Can you suggest an alternative interpretation for why the system of national testing and reporting seemed to show teachers getting so much better at their job year-on-year?

The confidential nature of the APU surveys, with anonymity assured for the schools and learners in the sample, gave teachers no reason to worry about the process if their class was selected for the sample. By contrast, the system of national testing not only labelled individual learners with information that would be passed to parents and other teachers, but allowed schools to be judged on the pupil results, and allowed school management to compare the results in classes taught by different teachers. Perhaps this motivated teachers to do a better job of teaching students – but it seems more likely that what most teachers got better at was preparing students for the specific nature of the tests. Government colluded in this, in some cases by providing specific materials to be used with students to 'boost' their attainment.

None of this would matter perhaps if tests were valid at assessing all the things we value students learning, but a common view of the high-stakes assessment systems in places like the UK is that they encourage teaching and learning that is targeted on answering test items rather than developing a broader understanding. Tests can only ever sample from the things we would like to assess, and assessing some things is much easier than others. So when standard test formats with similar items are used in high-stakes testing, the teachers tend to get very good at helping students learn how to pass the tests, rather than acquire the broader range of learning that the test items were meant to be sampling. In effect, the predictability of the assessment items can lead to a systematic sampling error. The tests may be useful in establishing league tables for schools, and claiming educational standards are improving, but become a rather poor measure of the actual quality of teaching and learning. Teaching to the test will only improve outcomes so far, and this was found with the system of national tests – the celebrated year-on-year improvements began to 'plateau' out, at which point the government abandoned much of the system.

Classroom teachers also use assessment at the end of modules to evaluate student learning and their own teaching; during learning sequences to inform teaching and learning; and at the start of a topic to check identified prerequisite learning is in place and to look for the presence of known common 'misconceptions'. Just because these processes are part of the normal work of the teacher does not exclude them as being part of a research plan. If undertaken in a systematic manner, to address a specified research question, summative, formative or diagnostic testing could all be used in classroom enquiry. However, as with national testing, the quality of the information obtained depends upon the nature of the measuring instrument and the way learning is sampled in testing.

Validity of test items

As with all assessment work, the validity of outcomes will in part depend upon the test items actually testing the knowledge or understanding they claim to test. Indeed, the validity of assessment items could be a suitable focus for classroom research (for example, comparing written answers given on tests with the knowledge and understanding students are able to demonstrate in interviews). Examination boards are responsible for setting papers which lead to assessments that will have public confidence (and are used for course progression, in evaluating job applicants, etc.) and so invest considerable resources developing and pre-testing examination papers. But they still occasionally find themselves severely criticised when something goes wrong.

Teachers (and researchers) should be aware of the difficulty of producing tests that are both valid (testing what they claim) and reliable (capable of giving reproducible results).

Examination boards have their own research units where they explore various aspects of setting and grading formal assessments. This is a complex area with many pitfalls. For example, the introduction of contextualised questions (where the question is framed in a familiar context) was meant to be helpful to learners by making questions seem less abstract and unfamiliar. However, this also introduces new complications (Taber, 2003): students have to 'process' more information, dis-embedding the principles behind the question from the context; the context may trigger everyday 'life-world' ways of thinking that do not match academic learning (although that learning may have occurred); and any context will be more familiar to some students than others (and so may introduce a cultural or gender bias).

Assessments may be a useful source of information for the teacher and the researcher, but it is important to appreciate that a poorly designed test will produce information of limited value. One should be especially wary of using any assessment for research purposes if it has not at least been carefully piloted with similar groups of students to those being tested in the enquiry. For that matter, using 'the test that the department always sets at the end of this topic' is not a fool-proof assurance that the assessment with be valid and reliable!

In many schools in England, tests are used which are meant to help teachers assign level of attainment to students. For this to be done properly, the different test items need to link to descriptors relating to the hierarchical nature of student learning in the subject, and the levels awarded should link to achievement on items which match those descriptors. Tests that are claimed to assign levels on the basis of simple mark bands (e.g., students getting 55–70% are awarded level X) should be treated with caution. As formal tests often lead to numerical scores, or the assignment of grades or levels, they appear to be very objective. However, such objectivity depends upon the quality of design of the assessment, the administration (no one cheating; all students having the full time in suitable conditions, etc.), and the care in marking. Many tests used in teaching are useful for getting a general impression of student knowledge and understanding of a topic, but little more.

Learner productions

A useful source of information about classroom teaching and learning is the wide range of outputs produced by learners as a normal part of the work of the classroom. Students' class work (and homework) can be analysed to provide information about learners' knowledge and understanding, work rate, ability to follow instructions, skills, etc. So, for example, Lang (2012) reports in *JoTTER* how he used students' drawings to collect data from primary phase children, including children in Year 1 (5–6 year olds), for his PGCE assignment undertaken on professional placement:

> I asked each child to imagine their ideal school, and in that school to imagine their ideal teacher. I asked them to draw their ideal teacher and write a little about them. Note the choice of language in this task; I have made sure not to use any he/she language to avoid leading the children, which would result in a bias in the results. I also made it clear that they are not to draw any of their current or past teachers,

that this is not a real teacher. The purpose of this activity is to see whether they will draw a male or a female teacher, without any leading language in the question and being utterly unaware of the task's overriding purpose.

(Lang, 2012, p. 8)

In principle, any work that a student produces individually or collectively that could be assessed in the normal course of teaching could be used as data. This should not be surprising, as teachers regularly assess work to obtain evidence of learning, and to guide teaching. The difficulties inherent in assessing work as part of normal teaching apply when we use this material as research data.

Question for reflection

What might be the difficulties of using 'work' produced by students as evidence of learning?

Complications of interpreting learners' productions

The things that students write (or draw, or perform, etc.) only provide *indirect* evidence of what they think, know and understand (and need not be reliable guides to what they believe). So:

- whatever has been written or said (or acted out) has to be interpreted by the teacher or researcher to find what the learner(s) 'meant';
- unless work is closely supervised, the teacher (or researcher) cannot be sure about the extent to which a product is any particular learner's 'own' work (although this may not be a problem if the study is informed by socio-cultural views of learning);
- if learning *is* seen as a socially mediated process, we might wish to reframe that previous point: unless work is closely supervised, the teacher (or researcher) cannot be sure about the extent to which learners interacted in producing a 'group' product;
- 'correct' answers can be guesses – for example, on 'objective' items such as those used in multiple-choice tests;
- 'incorrect' answers can be due to an inability to effectively represent thoughts into writing, or misinterpreting what the question required, or lack of concentration (or motivation), or due to pressures of time, etc., and may not always indicate lack of knowledge/understanding;
- 'correct' answers may demonstrate new learning, or simply pre-existing understanding that was already in place before teaching (so cannot be seen as evidence of new learning);
- responses reflect one way of thinking available to the learner, which may just be one facet of a repertoire of available ways of thinking ('manifold conceptions', or 'multiple frameworks');
- answers may reflect what the learners think they are meant to write, rather than what they actually think or believe.

Given all these potential problems, it may seem that students' work (or records of it, such as a video recording of a performance or role-play) has a limited part to play *in research*.

Question for reflection

Given the potentially flawed chain of associations between students' knowledge and understanding, and the teachers' assessment of their work, how can teachers justify using such 'data' to make judgements about learning?

Indeed, it seems reasonable to suggest that students' work (or records of it) should only have a limited role to play in *informing teaching* – whether as part of everyday practice or in the context of a research project!

'Fuzzy' data and iterative analysis

In everyday classroom practice, teachers *are* informed by their assessment of learners' work, but seldom put too much emphasis (or 'weight') on any one particular 'product'. Teachers usually consider student work (the products) collectively, and alongside their observations of the students working (the process), and their responses to oral questions (which are also technically productions, but not so easily collected in at the end of the lesson). We might say that teachers acknowledge that they are working with 'fuzzy' data where an individual datum offers a limited basis for drawing inferences. However, over an extended period of time, *teachers* naturally use an informal iterative process to learn from such data: for example, noting an especially poor response, or an unexpectedly insightful one, forming tentative hypotheses about what might be indicated, and looking for opportunities to test out these ideas. (We might refer to this as a kind of 'grounded practice'; see grounded theory, see Chapter 4). *Researchers* should see this type of data in a similar way. Student work outputs can be useful when seen as one 'slice of data' to be triangulated against other informative data sources.

Setting up teaching/learning activities to generate data

As well as the normal sorts of tasks that students regularly undertake in class, it is possible to set up particular activities that provide useful information. There is clearly an ethical issue here (see the previous chapter), as students should not be asked to put a lot of time and effort into creating material that is only intended as data for the benefit of the teacher's research! However, when planning teaching, it is often possible to incorporate activities that can be useful for *both* student learning and teacher-research.

Learner diaries

Given the importance of reinforcement in learning, and the value of learners developing metacognitive skills to work towards becoming self-regulated learners, it may be appropriate to ask learners to keep diaries of:

- what they have done in class
- what they have learnt

- whether they enjoyed activities
- what they need to put more effort into, etc.

The precise questions would clearly depend on the focus of the enquiry.

Concept maps

Concept maps (e.g., see Figure 10.3) have been widely used to collect data about learners' developing understanding of topics. They are also promoted as useful tools for planning teaching, and for helping students both as a learning tool and as way of monitoring their own developing learning about a topic (Novak & Gowin, 1984). Some (not all) students enjoy producing concept maps. Concept mapping can be scaffolded (as the task can be set from a blank sheet of paper, or with various degrees of structure and information already provided) and may be organised for individual study or a group activity.

Concept maps, then, offer great flexibility, and it is certainly easy to justify asking students to complete them. Interpretation of how concept maps reflect learners' ideas and understanding can be problematic (with a number of the problems listed above coming into play), but can potentially be very informative when used alongside other

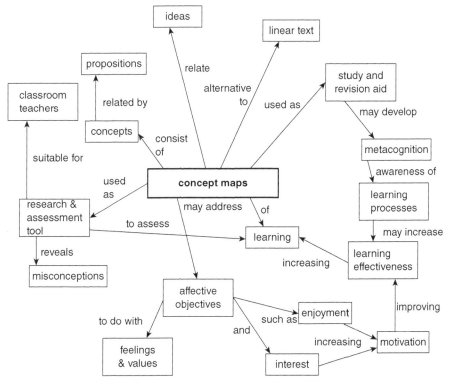

Figure 10.3 An example of a concept map (redrawn from Taber, 1994) (Reproduced with permission of Institute of Physics Publishing)

techniques, such as interviews ('Right, Pritpal, I want you to talk me through this concept map you drew for me').

———— Questionnaires ————

Questionnaires comprise sets of questions that are answered by an identified group of people (new first-year students; girls in the Year 9 class; my form group; pupils on the gifted register; anyone in school sports teams). Sometimes they are administered to a sample from such an identified group (see Chapter 4). Questionnaires are usually paper instruments that respondents complete in writing, although increasingly online questionnaires are being used. Questions may be of various types (e.g., see Box 10.1). However, questionnaires do not test learning, but provide questions that all respondents should be able to respond to. That is, we tend to use the term 'questionnaire' when we are exploring beliefs, values, opinions – where there are no right and wrong answers – rather than when we are testing knowledge and understanding. An examination paper asks questions, but would not be considered a questionnaire.

Box 10.1

Some types of questions that may appear in questionnaires

Questions may be:

closed	e.g., *how many nights a week do you normally do school work?* ☐ *less than 3 / ☐ 3–4 / ☐ more than 4)*
or open	e.g., *what do you most enjoy about your French lessons?*
about factual matters	e.g., *how many older brothers and sisters do you have?*
or opinions	e.g., *what are the good things about having to do homework? what are the bad things about having to do homework?*

Various types of response scales may be used in questions (e.g., how much do you enjoy your maths lessons? ☐ *a lot*; ☐ *a little*; ☐ *not really bothered*; ☐ *I dislike them*), and attitudes may be explored by asking about agreement with given statements (e.g., school is the highlight of my life: ☐ *strongly agree*; ☐ *agree*; ☐ *disagree*; ☐ *strongly disagree*). Items using these types of response options are known as a Likert questionnaire items.

Question for reflection

How might the nature of questionnaire items differ in an ERP1 study compared with an ERP2 study?

There are advantages and disadvantages to different types of items and scales. Closed questions only find out which *of the offered options* respondents chose, but are simpler to analyse. Open questions provide the opportunity for respondents to give an answer that better matches their views, but need later *to be categorised* if they are to be reported in an economic way. (Analysis of data is considered in Chapter 11.) Selection of illustrative comments always raises questions as to *how representative* such examples are. Sometimes a mixture of open and closed questions is useful, allowing the researcher to report proportions of responses in different categories, supported by selected quotations (see the comments on Kinchin's study in the following chapter).

Designing questionnaire items

There are techniques for increasing the *validity* and *reliability* of questionnaire items. One suggestion is that scales should *not* have central (neutral) points so forcing the respondent to make a decision about how they feel – but this may be an artificial choice if they genuinely have no feelings or mixed feelings about a topic. The inclusion of several equivalent statements, or opposite statements, may help to check the consistency of responses. Similarly, reversing the sense of some statements (e.g., I like French: ☐ *strongly agree*; ☐ *agree*; ☐ *disagree*; ☐ *strongly disagree*; I dislike German: ☐ *strongly agree*; ☐ *agree*; ☐ *disagree*; ☐ *strongly disagree*) is considered to encourage respondents to think about each item, rather than quickly tick the same point on the scale throughout!

Questions for reflection

People find filling in questionnaires an interesting activity:

  ☐ *strongly agree*; ☐ *agree*; ☐ *disagree*; ☐ *strongly disagree*

People get bored easily when filling in long questionnaires:

  ☐ *strongly agree*; ☐ *agree*; ☐ *disagree*; ☐ *strongly disagree*

People find it interesting to fill in questionnaires:

  ☐ *strongly disagree*; ☐ *disagree*; ☐ *agree*; ☐ *strongly agree*

People do not usually get bored when completing long questionnaires:

  ☐ *strongly agree*; ☐ *agree*; ☐ *disagree*; ☐ *strongly disagree*

Few people find completing questionnaires interesting:

  ☐ *strongly agree*; ☐ *agree*; ☐ *disagree*; ☐ *strongly disagree*

Many people find completing questions boring:

  ☐ *strongly agree*; ☐ *agree*; ☐ *disagree*; ☐ *strongly disagree*

Such advice is commonly given because it is recognised that questionnaires comprising many scale-type items may sometimes be completed with little thought. For any questionnaire, it is important not to ask too many questions, as this will increase the chance of respondents losing interest, concentration and good-will towards the researcher. You may be very interested in what your participants think about some topic that you believe is very important: your participants may not be especially interested in that topic, and may resent being asked a great many questions that seem to them to be asking much the same thing.

Questionnaires as providing one slice of data

Although questionnaires are limited as a means of eliciting in-depth information of the type usually needed in ERP2 studies, they may be a useful adjunct to other techniques. For example, in their study of "the experiences and understandings of a group of full-time further education trainee teachers", Avis et al. (2003, p. 191), report that:

> Our findings are based upon a series of focus-group discussions with the students, followed by in-depth individual interviews. A questionnaire was also used to seek information on the background and experience of the trainees.

> (Avis et al., 2003, p. 191)

How valid are questionnaire responses?

One of the severe limitations of questionnaires is that they only (at best, assuming honest and careful responses) elicit information about people's thoughts, beliefs and recollections; not actual behaviour. That teachers claiming to have constructivist views also report more frequently using pedagogy consistent with constructivist beliefs (see Chapter 4) is not surprising, but does not necessarily demonstrate these teachers *actually do* use these teaching activities as often as they think they do (or should!). It is interesting that Ravitz and colleagues (2000) found that most teachers in their survey thought students were more comfortable with traditional approaches, although Kinchin found most secondary students had a strong preference for learning in constructivist classrooms (as discussed in Chapter 2). This could indicate that teachers are 'out of touch' with their students.

Another issue worth considering, though, is the way that particular questions, and forms of questioning, may channel respondents' thinking. Ravitz and colleagues found that although most of their sample selected response categories that were not 'constructivist' in response to simple requests to select statements reflecting their views, a somewhat different outcome was elicited by a different approach. Ravitz, Becker, and Wong found that:

> Given a brief argument made between support for a philosophical position consistent with constructivist instructional reform and one reflecting a more traditional viewpoint, many more teachers will select agreement with reform than with traditional teaching practice.

> (Ravitz et al., 2000, p. 12)

It is important for the researcher (and reader of research) to remember that sometimes it is not just the questions asked, but the ways they are posed, that in part determine the responses elicited.

Questionnaire reliability

An instrument is reliable if repeating the administration under equivalent conditions would lead to the same results. Of course, 'equivalent' conditions may be hard to find. People learn from experience – so if a questionnaire provokes a person to think about an issue, then it may well be that if we later ask them to respond to the same questions, they might change their answers having previously reflected on the initial administration of the instrument. When working with large populations, we can test reliability by selecting two different random samples, and checking that – within experimental error – the results are consistent.

> ## Question for reflection
>
> If we consider opinion polls to be research instruments (a kind of questionnaire), and assume that respectable professional polling organisations are competent at administering the polls, then we might note that these polls sometimes show significant (i.e., beyond measurement error) shifts in responses to questions about political matters over a timescale of weeks or even days. Would you consider this to suggest that the polls lack reliability, or would you interpret these shifts differently?

All research techniques have limitations, and this is why classroom studies often use an array of different techniques allowing us to compare between data sources. Sometimes it may be appropriate to test the reliability of a technique by a form of retest to check that the same informants offer consistent responses. Smith (2012) offers an example of such reliability testing in a report in *JoTTER* of her study of Year 5–6 (9–11 year old) pupils' perceptions of intelligence, carried out on teaching placement during her PGCE course:

> Initially I gave the 32 students present the shortened version of Dweck's questionnaire, requiring them to rate three fixed statements. I used the shortened version due to the young age of the children and concern that they might be confused by a mixture of fixed and incremental statements. ... I used a longer, six statement questionnaire (also designed by Dweck) for the second questionnaire as this incorporated three statements for each mindset. ... I used the longer questionnaire because I wanted to eliminate the possibility that the children who had given fixed responses in the first questionnaire ... did so because they were more fearful about disagreeing with the statements ... rather than because it reflected their genuine opinions.
>
> (R. Smith, 2012, pp. 293–294)

Here Smith shows that she was aware of various potential disadvantages in each form of the questionnaire, but sought to ensure the validity of her interpretations by ensuring that learner responses were consistent across the two formats. We should note, however, that sometimes an instrument is used before and after an intervention to see if there has been any learning or change in perceptions as a result of the intervention (just as opinion polls are repeated close to elections to test for shifts in public opinion). Here we are in effect testing a hypothesis that because of the intervention the conditions of the second administration *are different* from those of the initial administration. In these circumstances we assume that any significant shifts in response are likely to be due to the intervention, and this would be undermined if the questionnaire itself was not reliable. Indeed, in this situation lack of reliability is a greater threat to the validity of our results than a biased instrument that would systematically distort response patterns in the same direction before and after our intervention (but probably still allow us to detect any major shift in what we are looking to measure).

In recent years it has been more common to use online forms of questionnaires. There are many advantages, as costs of postage and printing are avoided, and analysis is easier. Responses to close items may be tallied for us, and even though software cannot do much analysis of extended answers, they are automatically transcribed for us (saving time typing them into a computer). There are also free versions of software that allow the use of short questionnaires to be administered to modest numbers of participants without charge. However, not all respondents who might fill in a form will readily go to a website and complete an online questionnaire (both because it may seem more effort and because of worries about internet security).

━━ Classroom observation ━━

Observation has been used in classrooms to collect information about teaching and learning for a long time (Wragg, 2012). Classroom observation can be varied in a number of ways, influenced by our basic (paradigmatic) assumptions about the research.

Question for reflection

Classroom observation is a technique that can be used as a component of methodologies that fall within both main educational research paradigms (see Chapter 3). How might classroom observation be different in character within these two paradigms?

In principle, observers can be as unobtrusive as possible and avoid interacting with the class at all. The ultimate observer aims to be 'invisible' so that their presence does not influence what happens in the class (but when discretion becomes covert observation this raises ethical issues in relation to 'informed consent', see Chapter 9). At the other extreme, an observer might choose to be part of the classroom interaction being observed. A participant-observer would certainly observe something different from the lesson that would have taken place in her absence, but that may not be a problem (depending on the purpose(s) of the research).

Question for reflection

Participant observers try to become part of the group or activity that is being researched. Would you consider a teacher, researching into teaching and learning in one of her own classes, to be a participant observer?

Participant observation

An observer wishing to take an ethnographic approach might want to avoid altering the researched situation by becoming a participant-as-observer, by going 'undercover' as one of the class and not being spotted as an observer. This raises similar ethical issues relating to informed consent as the pure observer who is hiding from the class. It is an approach that could feasibly be used in some contexts (a parent's meeting, a class in an adult education college) but few teacher-researchers are likely to be able to go undercover with a typical class of 11 year olds!

Whilst this may be a ridiculous image, a viable (if risky) compromise might be for the researcher to tell the class that she wishes to be treated as one of them in the lesson. The class teacher and students obviously know the researcher is just taking on this role, so the situation is artificial, but nonetheless it could be a useful approach with some classes. If kept up for some time, the researcher may indeed come to be accepted at some level as one of the class, and may even have to keep in mind the dangers of 'going native' by coming to identify too closely with the new role!

More commonly, researchers may be present as adult participants: something that students may readily accept if they are used to teachers working in teams, or regularly having trainee teachers and/or learning assistants in lessons. The type of observation undertaken by Tobin and his colleagues in their study of teacher mind-sets (see Chapter 4) involved going into classes as participant observers, as people known (at least to the teachers) to be undertaking research, but choosing to get involved in the lessons and talking to the participants openly, rather than sitting quietly at the back making notes without interacting.

Teachers researching into teaching and learning in their own classes are already participants in the educational activity, and although they have a different role from the students, can reasonably be considered participant observers. They are a 'natural' part of the classroom situation, so their presence does not distort the context being studied.

Types of classroom observation data

Another key dimension of classroom observation concerns the type of data collected. This can vary from free-form notes, where anything that might prove to be of interested is noted, to the use of a formal observation schedule with clearly defined categories (where the observer's job may be to keep a tally of events identified as being in these categories). Again, the type of data collected depends upon the purposes of the research. A research question of the form 'What is it about 8F that leads to all their teachers judging them a "pleasure" to teach?' needs a different approach to data collection than the question 'Do the boys in 8F shout out answers to the teachers' questions significantly more often than the girls?'

The latter question derives from a pre-formed hypothesis that is going to be investigated within ERP1 (see Chapter 3), by collecting quantitative data suitable for statistical testing. The observer enters the field with pre-formed observation categories, and hopes that her presence does not lead to the teacher or students behaving any differently than in lessons without observers. The former question requires a more exploratory approach from ERP2, and the observer tries to free her mind from prior assumptions, and is looking for any useful clues.

In her study of the implications of being a left-handed learner in a primary school classroom, undertaken whilst on a professional school placement, Hayes (2011, p. 94) recounts how she centred her "research around both structured and naturalistic observations". She set the children "a laterality test which consisted of a series of nine exercises ... carried out with pupils in groups of five so that I could give them clear instructions and observe their reactions" (p. 94). This was a structured observation as there were clear categories into which to classify the observations. However, Hayes also used free-form observation notes to collect data during "an observation of left-handed pupils as they tried out various techniques when using scissors in order to see the effectiveness of the equipment and of their strategies for using it" (p. 95).

Both types of approach have limitations. Structured observations will only find out about the categories that have been built into the schedule. Open-ended observations are likely to produce useful hunches, but these will probably need to be *triangulated* against other data sources (see Chapter 5), or developed through more structured observations, before we can be confident that we have identified features that are significant.

Piloting/developing or adopting/adapting an observation schedule

As with assessment papers, observation schedules need to be *piloted* before they can be used in research. This piloting has two purposes:

- to check the validity of the schedule in collecting the data needed
- to provide practice in using the schedule to make observations reliable

In small-scale research where structured observations are chosen to collect data, it may be sensible to use a pre-existing schedule that has already been shown to be useful in answering similar research questions (and adapting it where needed), rather than constructing a new instrument that may need several stages of development. Ideally, the *reliability* of the data collection should be tested through inter-observer agreement – several observers using the schedule to observe the same classroom episodes, and then calculating how well their data matched. This is seldom possible in research carried out by classroom practitioners, so practice in using the schedule before collecting the research data is important.

Degrees of structure in observation schedules

Simple schedules may require the observer to check off each instance of certain events (teacher questions, pupil call-outs), perhaps for different groups within the class (e.g., by gender); or they may ask the observer to classify what is going on (teacher talk, teacher questioning, group work, students working individually) at regular periods in the lesson (e.g., every two minutes).

There are intermediate formats between highly structured schedules and a blank sheet of paper. For example, an observer could have a form with several categories or themes and be looking to make notes on any instances that seem relevant under the different headings. So, for example, if the research focus was the way a teacher responded to the needs of different learners in a class, the observer could be looking to identify *and describe* instances of where:

- the teacher differentiates by task
- the teacher differentiates by degree of teacher support
- the teacher differentiates by organising groups for peer support
- the teacher differentiates in evaluating outcomes.

How can we observe without seeing?

In Harrop and Swinson's (2003) study of the nature of questions used by teachers, the research was carried out using data collected on the teaching of 30 teachers, ten each from infant, junior and secondary schools. Harrop and Swinson describe how the data was collected, with teachers being "recorded by a radio microphone for 30 minutes whilst teaching a lesson". The analysis was based on the recordings of the classrooms. Understandably, perhaps, given this mode of data collection, certain types of lesson and lesson activity were excluded from the study:

> The lessons recorded were all classroom based, with literacy hour and numeracy sessions excluded, as were practical/activity sessions (e.g. physical education, craft, art).

> (Harrop and Swinson, 2003, p. 51)

Recording classroom dialogue can be a very useful way of collecting data, but only where an audio recording is able to 'capture' the information needed. Recordings of teacher-led classroom dialogue often only clearly pick up the teacher's voice. Recordings of group work often have a good deal of background noise (from the other groups in the class) and even when talk is audible it may be difficult to identify the different speakers in the group. Again, this is a technique that may often be best used as part of a battery of data collection approaches, so that each slice of data can be complemented by evidence from other sources. Video recording may provide richer data than audio recording, but is more obtrusive and difficult to set up.

Feedback from mentors/colleagues ———

The discussion above has assumed the researcher is the observer. However, when enquiring into *our own* teaching practice it can be very useful to get feedback from *other* suitably informed observers. Teachers-in-training will be used to receiving regular written feedback about their teaching. The feedback will be tied to specific issues that have been identified as the focus for development in trainee–mentor sessions. Focused feedback of this type can certainly be seen as suitable evidence in classroom research, especially when used alongside other 'slices of data'.

Being observed by colleagues is now one of the normal procedures in place for quality assurance and staff development in most schools and colleges. This type of observation is, however, usually infrequent, and undertaken to a pre-existing agenda. Nonetheless, this contributes to a professional ethos in most schools and colleges where observing colleagues is seen as acceptable and healthy, and a teacher-researcher may well find that a colleague will be prepared to help by observing teaching (although time commitments are unlikely to allow this to be more than occasional). The same considerations apply when we ask someone to observe our classes, as when we observe others teaching. If we wish to collect specific data about particular aspects of teaching and learning, then the observer has to be well briefed, and provided with a schedule with both appropriate headings/categories and a suitable level of structure.

——— Interviewing ————————————————

Interviews are very common in educational research. Like many teachers investigating aspects of their own practice, Greaves (2010, p. 208) used "a variety of methods in which to obtain data" in her school-placement study of the use of multi-modal texts to stimulate Year 9 (13–14 year old) students' creative story-telling. She reported how she found the interview process "the most enjoyable, interesting and insightful area of my research" (p. 209). As someone who has carried out a fair amount of interviewing for my own research, this comment resonates with my own experiences. Research interviews can be very intense for both interviewer and interviewee (Taber, 2002b), but are often fascinating and informative.

Interviews are often an especially useful way to explore how people experience situations, how they understand concepts, and what they think about things. In Chapter 2 an example was offered of how interview research clarified survey results that could readily have been interpreted to give misleading conclusions about how students understood a key mathematical concept (Stylianides & Al-Murani, 2010). Interviews with a sample of learners in a class can often usefully complement (and so triangulate) questionnaire responses, providing the opportunity to test our interpretation of the thinking behind questionnaire responses.

Interviews are special kinds of conversations (Powney & Watts, 1987): conversations designed so that the interviewer can find out information from a privileged informant. The interviewee is privileged in the sense of having access to information. This may because the interviewee was present at some time and place when the researcher was not around. However, often in educational research, the informant is intrinsically privileged as the information being sought is about some aspect of the way that that person thinks, understands, values or believes. The best way to find out what someone thinks can be to ask. This is not a guaranteed approach: both questions and answers can be misunderstood; the interviewer may be interested in some aspect of thinking or belief that is tacit (and so not consciously available to the informant); and sometimes interviewees may not give careful, complete or even honest answers. Despite these limitations, interviewing is often the *most direct* and trustworthy way to find out what someone knows, believes or thinks.

One strength of interviewing is its flexibility: it allows the interviewer to rephrase questions, clarify answers, seek elaboration, and so forth. Although most research interviews have an agenda or schedule of questions, this is often used as a guide rather than a strict set sequence of questions. A skilled interviewer can often obtain valuable data from an informant who is in a position to provide information and is prepared to do so. As Bruner (1987) has pointed out, conversation allows 'constant transactional calibration', allowing us to check that we are understood by, and understand the intended meanings of, people we are talking to. Whilst not a perfect means of communication, a conversation allows us checks that are absent from questionnaires, for example.

> By using substantial interviews ... as the main research technique there is scope for considerable 'internal validation' of the interviewer's interpretations of the [participant's] comments during a single interview.
>
> Such validation takes several forms...
>
> - confirming responses by repeating or rephrasing questions...
>
> - clarifying ideas by asking follow-up questions...
>
> - paraphrasing what one believes to be the co-learner's argument, and seeking confirmation...
>
> - returning to the same point in the same context later in the interview, to see if a consistent response is given by the co-learner...
>
> - approaching the same point through a different context later in the interview, to see if the co-learner gives a consistent response in the different contexts...
>
> (Taber, 1993)

Question for reflection

Is it more important for an interviewer to be able to be responsive to the informant's comments, or for the interviewer to follow the same procedures and schedule with each informant?

This flexibility has costs. An interviewer who takes advantage of the flexibility of this ('semi-structured') interview format will not be interviewing all subjects in identical ways. This would be a problem in some enquiries. For example, if one was testing the hypothesis that 'girls are just as likely to experience bullying as boys', then one would wish to make sure that the same question was asked in the same way, so that the respondents' judgements were not influenced by different phrasing of the question, or differently cued by the question sequence. (Asking the question 'can bullying be verbal, or must it always be physical?' just before asking 'have you ever been the victim of bullying?' could well lead to a different response to the second question.)

Types of interviewing and interview data

In this situation (an enquiry that is likely to be identified as within ERP1; see Chapter 3), a fully structured interview schedule would be appropriate. However, a study with a similar focus but from a more interpretivist perspective would indicate a different type of interview. A study to enquire into 'how boys and girls construe bullying, and feel about bullying' would be situated within ERP2. Here it is more important to uncover in-depth data about how individuals make sense of their experiences than it is to ask a large number of people identical questions. Both types of research question may be important, and be answered through interviewing as a data collection technique, but with different types of interview to collect (or 'construct') different types of data.

The distinction between data collection and construction is significant here. The researcher in the ERP1 interview is acting as a technician (cf. Table 3.1), to collect responses to precise, predetermined questions as effectively as possible. Indeed, in professional research, the individuals employed to collect the data may be trained specifically for this purpose and have little knowledge of, or other involvement in, the research.

Co-construction of interview data

This is not an approach a researcher in ERP2 could take. Here, the text produced in an interview (an 'InterView', Kvale, 1996) – the dialogue, the recording of the interview, the transcript of the interview – is a creative production of two authors. The text is constructed through the interviewer and informant interacting. (Note: this is anathema to the 'positivistic' assumptions of ERP1.) The researcher needs to be highly skilled, and have a good understanding of research purposes to help shape the data produced. The researcher brings those professional skills, and the interviewee brings their own understandings or views.

In this type of interview, the researcher is an intimate part of the data construction process, and it is neither reasonable, nor perhaps even desirable, to believe that another interviewer would have elicited exactly the same information. It is also worth noting that although the interviewer may feel she owns the text constructed, the other author (the interviewee) might be considered to share ownership (Taber & Student, 2003). As has been pointed out by Limerick, Burgess-Limerick, and Grace (1996), this type of interview, and the text constructed through it, is a gift from the interviewee. The interviewee gives their time and opens up their ideas to examination (and potential criticism or even ridicule) for the benefit of the researcher who hopes to benefit professionally. There is clearly an ethical issue (and potential for abuse of trust) here – and researchers need to make sure they are comfortable with the way they obtain information from informants, and use that information afterwards (see the discussion of ethical issues in Chapter 9).

Group interviews

Group interviews, where several informants are interviewed together, have a number of advantages. Some students are much more comfortable talking to a researcher in pairs or groups, especially where they are interviewed with friends. Group interviews also allow the comments of one student to act as a stimulus for another, perhaps eliciting information that would not otherwise have been revealed. Sometimes the closer match in levels of knowledge and language (compared with that of the researcher) may help the flow of the interview. This arrangement also takes some pressure off the informants, who can take 'time out' for thinking as a peer contributes.

The obvious disadvantage to this type of interview is that the responses that individuals give cannot be assumed to be the same as they might have offered if interviewed alone. This is particularly true if any of the respondents feel intimidated, embarrassed or uncomfortable 'opening up' in front of their peers. There are clearly some sensitive issues where group interviews are likely to be unproductive. Generally, though, there is no clear preference for individual or group interviews. The former are clearly appropriate in some situations where the presence of other learners would 'contaminate' the data being collected. However, for a study of student learning from a perspective that viewed the learning process as primarily mediated through interactions within a class, a researcher might well feel that group interviews give more pertinent data.

Focus groups

Focus groups (which are set up more as observed discussions than interviews) have become common in market 'research', and often involve quite large groups of (half-a-dozen or more) people talking through ideas. In this situation, discussion is encouraged, and the researcher might be more interested in any consensus positions that derive from the debates rather than individual viewpoints fed in. Focus groups are clearly not helpful in looking at individual learners' ideas in any depth, but are a useful way of involving more people as informants without significantly increasing the time available for interviews.

In Lyle's (1999) study of mixed-ability grouping in the primary school, evidence of the effectiveness of the intervention was collected when "two groups of 12 children were interviewed on separate occasions. The interviews were video-recorded and later transcribed" (p. 288). Interviewing a group of 12 pupils might well help overcome reservations children may have at being interviewed and videotaped by someone who is presumably not well known to them. However, this raises questions about the extent to which all 24 children contributed to the interviews, and whether each felt able to freely give their own view. As always, research decisions involve weighing up the 'pros' and 'cons' of the available alternatives.

Probes ——

Probes may be used in interviews to focus a student's thinking and provide a starting point for the dialogue (White & Gunstone, 1992). For example, in Watts' research of student thinking about forces (see Chapter 3), he used line diagrams as a focus to elicit student ideas. This has been called 'interview-about-instances', as the starting point for each diagram would be 'Is there an example of a force (or whatever) in this diagram?'

In Sade and Coll's (2003) study of the views of some Solomon Island primary teachers and curriculum development officers on technology education, the main source of data was "semi-structured interviews – typically of about 40–45 minutes duration, in which both the teachers and the curriculum development officers were asked non-leading, open-ended questions" (p. 102). However:

> During the interviews, a picture quiz questionnaire was given to the participants and they were asked to identify which pictures they associated with technology.
>
> (Sade & Coll, 2003, p. 102)

A similar approach to interviews-about-instances is called interviews-about-events, where the interviewer uses a simple demonstration (e.g., a candle burning) and asks the interviewee to explain what they think is going on during the event. For example, García Franco (2005) reported an interview-based study "based on semi-structured interviews with secondary students in English and Mexican secondary schools (Y8–Y11) using for the analysis a grounded theory approach". The research was looking at the types of explanation students use and, in particular, whether they consistently adopt the curriculum models of 'particles' (molecules). During the interviews she demonstrated simple phenomena (dissolving, mixing, burning), and "Students are asked to describe the phenomena, to explain 'why does it happen that way', and if they do not use particle theory in the construction of their explanation, they are then specifically asked to think about particles". This 'hierarchical focusing' approach (Tomlinson, 1989) allowed García Franco to see first if the students *spontaneously* introduced particle ideas in their explanations, and then – if not – whether they *were able* to build explanations using particle models.

Concept cartoons as stimuli

Kinchin (2004) used 'concept cartoons' as stimuli for collecting his data relating to students' perceptions of a preferred classroom environment (see Chapter 2). A concept cartoon is a simple line diagram of a situation, usually including a number of people offering different views about a phenomenon (Keogh & Stuart, 1999). In teaching, the cartoon is used as a stimulus to group discussion, with students asked to consider the range of ideas and to offer reasons for agreeing and disagreeing with them. Kinchin, in the spirit of 'student voice', involved students ("a focus group of Year 10 (15-year-old) secondary students" (2004, p. 304)) in designing the cartoons. This might be seen to increase the validity of the instrument, by ensuring that the ideas and language would be suitable for secondary students. Kinchin then used the cartoon to collect his data:

> Secondary students in Year 7 (12-year-olds) and Year 9 (14-year-olds) from two schools in south-eastern England were asked to examine the dialogue in each of the cartoons (A and B). They were then asked in which of the two classrooms each of them would rather be a student and to offer reasons for their choice in the form of a written free response. Responses were collected during form time on one day.
>
> (Kinchin, 2004, p. 304)

Kinchin reports that "these cartoons were intended to trigger talk among students about their epistemological beliefs" (2004, p. 304). In his conclusion, Kinchin (2004, p. 310) reports that "it seems that secondary students are capable of commenting upon their learning. ... Concept cartoons may provide a convenient starting-point for such classroom discussions."

The data collection instrument also differed from more familiar context cartoon approaches (that some students are likely to be familiar with) as instead of alternative views being presented within one cartoon, the instrument comprised two line diagrams, each one offering an exchange between an adult (presumably the teacher) and child (looking somewhat younger than those responding to the instrument). However, as the images are different (a computer features in one, a chalkboard dominates the room in the other) there is a danger of student preferences being influenced by the difference in the apparent nature of the classrooms, as well as the dialogue. Kinchin was aware of this, and reports that the images were swapped on "some question sheets" without making any difference to the results.

Probing for known misconceptions

In some school subjects it is well known that students commonly develop particular 'alternative conceptions', or 'misconceptions', of curriculum topics. Teaching is interpreted by learners in terms of what they think they already know and understand, leading to 'bugs' in the teaching–learning process (e.g., see https://camtools.cam.ac.uk/wiki/eclipse/learningdoctors.html), where any learning that takes place is quite different from the learning intended by the teacher. In some curriculum subjects, research into common student ideas and misconceptions in topics has led to the development of diagnostic assessment tools designed to help teachers identify where students adopt particular ideas known to lead to learning difficulties in the subject (e.g., in the case of chemistry, Taber, 2002a).

In a paper published in *JoTTER*, Armsby (2011) reports on her study (undertaken whilst on school placement as a trainee teacher) into using group work to support Year 7 (11–12 year-old) students' learning in earth science. In order to assess student understanding of topics before and after teaching, Armsby used concept maps (see above) and a set of multiple choice questions that could be answered quickly, informed by examples of common misconceptions identified from her reading of the existing research into student learning difficulties in the topic.

Using activities as probes: think aloud

In 'think aloud' techniques, students may be asked to talk through their thinking as they complete a task. This may allow us to identify thinking that is not directly observable, as when a sixth-form (post-16) student working through a physics learning activity on a computer reported that "so as I was reading through that [screen], I was thinking sort of what formulas do I know, erm, relating mass to, erm, energy, and distance to energy" (Taber, 2010a, p. 52). Think aloud can be very useful, but has some drawbacks. It can only access thinking the participant is aware of (and much of our thinking is pre-conscious, i.e., occurs without our conscious awareness), and it is only suitable for tasks where the person has capacity to talk about what they are doing as they do it. Moreover, it is suggested that in most studies about a tenth of potential participants prove incapable of talking about what they are doing, and still do it, whatever the task!

Where think aloud is not feasible, it may be possible to use stimulated recall, where students are video-recorded completing a task and then interviewed to ask them about what they might have been thinking or feeling at different points in the recording. The technique is designed to help the participants recreate their thinking during the original activity, but it clearly cannot guarantee that this will happen.

Research probes can be a bit like…

Teachers can be imaginative in setting up tasks that might elicit useful information from students. Fisher (2012) reports how she used 'metaphor elicitation tasks' to elicit students' perceptions of learning German. As well as asking students to think of something learning German was like, they were also asked to select which food and animal the German language was like, and to give their reasons if they could. By using the technique before and after a teaching intervention, it was possible to look for shifts in the way the student perceived German language learning.

Fisher's approach could tap implicit thinking, as a student may often be able to suggest a metaphor before being able to reflect on why that choice arose. Research into learning suggests that much of our thinking and learning occurs pre-consciously, with the conscious mind only catching up later, if at all. (Crossword puzzles often offer that strange phenomenon of knowing one has solved a clue … a moment or two before the solution is consciously available! For a few moments we are confident that we know the answer, without seeming to know what the answer actually is.)

A number of research approaches make use of elicitation techniques that seek to make explicit the thinking that is normally pre-conscious. An approach aimed at eliciting aspects of the way people perceive the world, which they may not be able to readily express, draws upon the work of therapist George Kelly, who developed a theory of 'personal constructs' (Kelly, 1963). Kelly believed that each person develops their own unique way of understanding the world in terms of a system of bipolar constructs (good–bad, up–down, positivist–interpretivist, scientific–non-scientific, valid–invalid, interesting–boring, etc.). Although he was not working in education, Kelly's work has informed much 'constructivist' (Taber, 2011a) thinking and research about learning.

One of Kelly's techniques, the 'method of triads', involves presenting study participants with cards showing words or images, three ('elements') at a time, and asking them to select an 'odd one out' that does not fit with the other two. Often people can make such discriminations even if they do not immediately know why, and this can help build up a model of how they understand the topic or issue being explored. There are no right or wrong answers, and participants will vary in the extent to which they can explain their choices.

Questions for reflection

Which 'element' is the 'odd one out' in Figure 10.4? Can you explain why? Is there more than one reason for selecting this option? Could another 'element' be considered the odd one out? (If possible compare your answers with another teacher or student learning to do classroom research.) Do you think this technique has potential to supplement direct interview questions in accessing students' thinking?

Figure 10.4 A 'Kelly's triad' of 'elements' to consider

The method of triads can be used, for example as part of an interview, in an exploratory and open-ended way – with the researcher selecting triads to test out hunches deriving from the participant's responses to earlier triads. This is often a useful enough technique in its own right. However, it can also be used as the first phase of a more systematic process where all of the elements in a deck are subsequently rated by the participant in terms of the 'constructs' (e.g., large–small, good–bad, complex–simple, etc.) participants used to discriminate between elements in triads. This 'repertory grid' method (Bannister & Fransella, 1986) is more formalised, and takes longer, but does allow forms of quantitative analysis to be applied to the response patterns. Whilst this is certainly a potentially useful method, it is quite technical and is probably not suitable for novice researchers unless they have sufficient time to learn and pilot the techniques.

The method of triads, however, is quite straightforward and suitable for incorporating into small-scale classroom research. Indeed, as with a number of other techniques described in this chapter (concept maps, concept cartoons), the method of triads can also be incorporated into normal teaching, offering an interesting basis for group discussion work when we want students to explore their thinking about a topic.

Collection and analysis of data

This chapter has described some of the techniques that can be used to collect data in the classroom. These different techniques can provide a range of different types of data for our research. However, before we can draw any conclusions from the data, we need to carefully and systematically analyse them – and that will be the focus of the next chapter.

Further reading —

This chapter has quickly covered a range of data collection techniques and it is worth reading in more detail about the specific research methods you select to include in your own research design. Comprehensive research texts (like the books by Cohen et al.

(2011) and Robson (2002), recommended in Chapter 1), discuss techniques in more detail than is possible here, but there are also books, guides and articles specifically concerned with particular research techniques, such as the examples listed here.

Fransella, F., & Bannister, D. (1977). *A Manual for Repertory Grid Technique*. London: Academic Press.

Novak, J. D. (1990). Concept maps and Vee diagrams: Two metacognitive tools to facilitate meaningful learning. *Instructional Science, 19*(1), 29–52. doi: 10.1007/bf00377984

Office of Educational Assessment (2006). *Tips for Writing Questionnaire Items*. Washington, DC: University of Washington Office of Educational Assessment. (Available from: www.washington.edu/oea/resources/surveys.html)

Powney, J., & Watts, M. (1987). *Interviewing in Educational Research*. London: Routledge & Kegan Paul.

Tan, K.-C. D., Goh, N.-K., Chia, L.-S., & Taber, K. S. (2005). *Development of a Two-tier Multiple Choice Diagnostic Instrument to Determine A-Level Students' Understanding of Ionisation Energy* (pp. 105). (Available from: https://camtools.cam.ac.uk/wiki/eclipse/diagnostic_instrument.html)

van Someren, M. W., Barnard, Y. F., & Sandberg, J. A. C. (1984). *The Think Aloud Method: A Practical Guide to Modelling Cognitive Processes*. (Retrieved from: http://staff.science. uva.nl/~maarten/Think-aloud-method.pdf)

Winterbottom, M. (2009). Taking a quantitative approach. In E. O. Wilson (Ed.), *School-based Research: A Guide for Education Students* (pp. 137–153). London: Sage.

Wragg, E. C. (2012). *An Introduction to Classroom Observation* (Classic edn). Abingdon, Oxon.: Routledge.

11

Teachers interrogating the evidence from classroom studies

This chapter:

- introduces the principles behind using descriptive and inferential statistics
- considers how to present the results of quantitative analyses
- explains the main approaches to analysing qualitative data
- offers examples of how the outcomes of qualitative analyses may be presented

Collecting data is clearly an important part of the research process, but the analysis of data is just as important. This may seem obvious, but what many students and teachers new to empirical research do not realise is that the analysis of data *needs to be planned*, just as much as the collection of data. It can also consume a significant proportion of the time available for a project, and the research schedule needs to allow for this taking into account when any report needs to be completed.

Analysing data

There tend to be different approaches to working with quantitative data (numbers) and qualitative data (which is usually text, but can also be other material collected – such as photographs – that will then be described and characterised in words as part of the analytical process). However, sometimes data that is initially qualitative leads to secondary quantitative data during processing. Where a study collects both qualitative and quantitative data to address the same question, the outcomes of the separate analyses will need to be compared and related in reaching any conclusions. Often a distinction is made between results (which are the outcomes of the analysis of data) and conclusions (which link these findings back to the research questions).

There are two main types of analysis that can be carried out with quantitative data, known as inferential and descriptive statistics. Inferential statistics were introduced in Chapter 4 and allow us to draw inferences from the analysis, whereas descriptive statistics offer a kind of description in numbers. For example, a study might report the average number of times certain categories of event were counted, giving an indication of how common those events were in the research context.

Inferential statistics are less commonly found in small-scale classroom research of the type used by teachers, and there are several reasons for this:

1 They are most useful for testing formal hypotheses, requiring experiments or representative surveys, and most teacher research is not of that form.
2 Often the requirements of statistical tests only make them suitable for data sets of a minimum size, and (depending on what is being counted) teacher classroom research tends to involve low frequencies of counts.
3 Many of the most useful statistical tests depend upon assumptions about the population being sampled, which may not be met in data sets collected in single classrooms.

That said, there are useful tests that can be used in classroom research, and they are probably under-used in relation to their potential. This is likely to be because the selection of appropriate tests, the collection of suitable data for particular tests, and the analyses themselves do require some specific knowledge and skills, and many teachers have limited background in this area. Moreover, an effective way to invalidate a study is to use an inappropriate statistical test, or to misinterpret the results of the statistics – issues sometimes identified by examiners of student projects. Inferential statistics are very powerful when they are relevant to the research questions and suitable data is available, but should only be used by someone who is confident they understand the tests they are using. However, all educational professionals should understand the *basic principles of statistical testing*, so that they can evaluate the research that they read to inform their own professional work.

Descriptive statistics are generally a useful way to summarise key features of quantitative data, and do not require a high level of statistical knowledge or mathematical skill. They cannot tell us how significant our results are in terms of how unlikely they are to have been obtained by chance (in the way inferential statistics do), but can summarise a great deal of data in a way that can often allow us to draw our own conclusions very quickly. Findings are often presented in the form of frequencies (often as percentages) of data falling into different categories. Results are tabulated, with means, standard deviations, etc. presented. Results may be presented graphically, using pie charts or bar charts to communicate findings visually.

——— Inferential statistics ————————————————————————

In much ERP1 research (see Chapter 3), data is collected that is basically quantitative, and designed to provide data sets suitable for inferential statistical tests (e.g., hypothesis testing). For example, in Button's study of pupil perceptions of music (see Chapter 2), he reports that the difference between the proportions of boys and girls in his sample who reported having access to a musical instrument at home was statistically significant.

According to Button (2006, p. 426), in his sample of students there were:

- 86 girls who said they had access to an instrument
- 29 girls who said they did not have access to an instrument
- 50 boys who said they had access to an instrument
- 51 boys who said they did not have access to an instrument

Button used a statistical test (known as χ^2, or chi-squared), which compares such 'observed' frequencies with what might be expected if there was no significant gender difference. So in this case, there were 216 students and 136 (i.e., 63%) had access to an instrument. All other things 'being equal', we might therefore have expected that about 72/115 girls and 64/101 boys would have had access to instruments. Clearly in this sample there was a *higher proportion* of girls reporting access to instruments than boys, but this could just be a reflection of the particular young people in the sample, rather than being true about 'boys' and 'girls' in general.

Button presents the statistic that he obtained from using the χ^2 test (p. 426), which tells him that the probability (p) of getting such a skewed sample by chance is less than one in a thousand ('p < 0.001'), so it seems very likely that this gender difference would be found in the wider population of Key Stage 3 students. Of course, this does assume that the sample can be considered typical of the wider population. Button selected his sample from six schools, a mixture of both urban and rural, to make it inclusive of gender, socio-economic class and student ability. Had he instead built a sample from boys at an inner-city school in an area of social deprivation and girls from a fee-paying school that offered free places to the children of members of the city orchestra, we might have less confidence that what was found in the sample reflects the wider situation. The statistics would still suggest Button's results were unlikely to occur by chance, but we could explain them in terms of the different backgrounds of the two sub-samples, and it would not make sense to infer that this was a gender issue *per se*.

Presenting the results of statistical tests

McClune's (2001) study of relative achievement in modular and terminal examinations (see Chapter 2) used quantitative methods of analysis (see Chapter 4), and his results were summarised in tables in his study. There were three compulsory questions common to the modular and terminal examination papers. When the three questions were considered together, it was found that the second-year students averaged 22.7 marks (out of 33 available) for these questions, whereas the first-year students scored 21.0 on average. This modest difference (1.7 marks) was statistically significant. In McClune's table 3 (p. 84), the probability value of this outcomes is given as p<0.001, meaning that such a difference would only be likely to be found by chance in a sample this size less than once in a thousand opportunities.

The scores of boys and girls are also considered separately. The average score for second-year boys was 23.0 compared with 21.3 for the first-year boys – a result likely to happen less than once in a hundred opportunities by chance (i.e., p<0.01). Among the girls, the second years also attained a higher average score on these questions, 22.8 compared to 21.8. However, this difference was considered non-significant (usually shown as 'n.s.'). This means that such a difference would happen more than once in twenty opportunities by chance, and *by convention* this is not considered a statistically significant finding. So among this group of girls, the average score was slightly higher for the second years, but we should not assume this would be repeated if we had compared the scores of all the girls who took the examination rather than just a sample.

McClune also presents the statistics for the three questions separately. Among the boys, the second-year students outscored the first years on all three questions, averaging 11.9 marks out of 17, compared to 11.1; 4.0 (/5) compared to 3.8; 7.0 (/11) compared to 6.2. Two of these differences (the first and third) were statistically significant (both reaching $p<0.01$). For the girls, the first years attained a higher average score on the first question (11.6 compared 11.3), but had lower average scores on the other two questions (3.8 compared to 4.0; 6.4 compared to 7.5). Only one of these three differences (the last) was statistically significant ($p<0.05$). Taking both genders together, this final question was the only one where the difference in scores reached statistical significance ($p<0.001$).

Question for reflection

McClune obtained findings that were *statistically* significant, but how much significance should we assign to such findings?

So, overall there was a statistically significant difference between the performance of first-year students (taking modular examinations) and second-year students (taking terminal examinations) – but this did not apply to the girls as a subgroup, and was only found on one of the three common questions. McClune summarises the findings:

> ...pupils in upper sixth (group 1) had a mean score which represented 69 per cent of the marks available, while those in lower sixth (group 2) gained 64 per cent of the available marks. Pupils in the lower sixth have not performed as well as those in the upper sixth when attempting these questions under the same examination conditions. This may seem to indicate that ... pupils opting for modular assessment midway through the course may be at a disadvantage compared to those who opt for assessment at the end of the course.

(McClune, 2001, pp. 83–84)

Statistics can only tell us about the specific data collected. Statistically significant differences become easier to identify in larger samples, and it may be that the smaller size of the girls' subgroup (205, less than half the 490 boys) is partially responsible for finding a significant overall attainment difference only among the boys.

False inferences

It is important to remember that statistical tests only tell us how likely/unlikely our results would be by chance. This assumes that there is no systematic bias in our sampling (as we have used randomisation techniques). So these tests only allow us to draw inferences. If we get a result, such as a difference between an experimental and control group, in the predicted direction, which statistical tests tell us is very unlikely to have occurred by chance, then it is reasonable to assume the result was probably due to the variable we are investigating. However, as this method is built around what is likely/ unlikely, it is inevitably going to lead to the wrong inferences sometimes. Unlikely events happen sometimes by their very nature – just not very often.

The author was once asked to examine a thesis where the student wrote excitedly about the positive results she had obtained, using the standard $p<0.05$ cut-off for inferring significance. However, she had undertaken several hundred different statistical tests in her thesis so it is almost inevitable that some unlikely results would occur by chance! As the vast majority of the students' statistical tests gave non-significant results, it is likely that most of her significant findings were just the unlikely chance effects that will sometimes occur if we play games of chance often enough. It is sensible to only use statistical tests to test hypotheses informed by existing theoretical considerations.

A result that reaches statistical significance by chance is sometimes referred to as a 'false positive' (see Chapter 4). We can reduce false positives by using a more stringent value of probability as our cut-off ($p<0.01$ perhaps, rather than $p<0.05$), but this would mean that more real effects will be missed (i.e., we will have 'false negatives') as they do not reach our more stringent test of significance. This is represented in Figure 11.1.

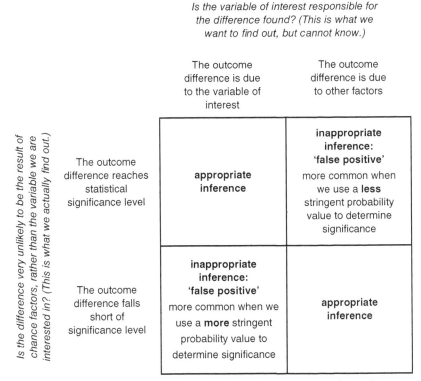

Figure 11.1   The probability value chosen as the cut-off for statistical significance determines whether we are more likely to discount real effects or misidentify 'fluke' chance results as due to the factor we are investigating

We can never completely eliminate false positives, as it is inherent in inferential testing that we are always comparing the probability of the result we got with what happens by chance. We should also be aware that even when our statistically significant results are due to a real effect, it does not always mean that the result is of great importance.

Significance and importance

The term 'significant' suggests something of importance, but when using statistical tests the term 'significance' has a rather specific meaning: it simply tells us the result was unlikely to be down to chance. Consider a hypothetical study where it was found that physics teachers were significantly more likely to smile at the girls in their classes than the boys. We might think there was something unfair going on here – a kind of gender discrimination. The government department might be concerned enough to wish to fund a follow-up study to understand why this was the case.

We can image various possibilities here. Perhaps most physics teachers are men, and men are generally more likely to smile at females than males, so it is a general gender issue and not actually about school physics? Perhaps teachers (regardless of their gender) generally smile more at girls: perhaps because secondary-age girls are more likely to smile at a teacher than secondary-age boys? Or perhaps teenage girls are at least more likely to smile at male teachers, as they have learnt to 'keep them sweet' for when they have to admit not having any homework to hand in – a technique they have discovered to be less effective with their female teachers? Or perhaps girls' behaviour in lessons, typically, is deemed more worthy of positive reinforcement than boys? Or perhaps physics teachers are very aware of the gender imbalance in progression from school science to more advanced physics courses, and they are especially trying to encourage girls in the hope they stick with the subject – positive discrimination through preferential smiling? … and so forth.

The reader can no doubt suggest a few more alternatives. We can soon come up with all kinds of possibilities here. Now what if we look at the results in more detail (remembering this is a hypothetical example) (see Table 11.1).

Now, according to the (imaginary) study, there was definitely a higher average number of smiles per lesson addressed to girls in physics classes than to boys. We might be told that this is significant at the 0.01 level (often indicated **, see Chapter 4). So, assuming a random sampling of lessons to observe, the chances of this being the effect of chance in the sampling process is less than one in a hundred. It looks like a 'real' general effect, not just down to the particular lessons/teachers/students that happen to be in the sample. Of course this assumes the sampling was representative of all physics teachers

Table 11.1 Results of an imaginary study finding a gender difference in teacher behaviour

Gender of student	Average number of smiles from physics teacher per lesson
Male	0.347
Female	0.351

who might smile at students in their class, and that data collection was sufficiently careful. Someone had to observe classes, note when the teacher smiled at someone, and ascertain and record whether the smile was directed at a boy or a girl. There must have been some missed smiles, or smiles where it was difficult to know who they were directed at. Perhaps in some classes the teacher just took some mental time out and imagined the lesson bell, the cup of coffee in the staff room, or the slippers waiting at home, and an observed smile was not actually meant for whoever the teacher's face seemed to be looking at.

However, given that the results are presented to three significant figures, it seems the sample of smiles observed must have been pretty large, so we might assume that missed or wrongly attributed smiles should average out over the large sample: as long as there were no systematic errors that would make it more likely that smiles directed at one gender were missed or miscounted. As always, once we get thinking about a piece of research (even an imaginary, and perhaps unlikely, study) we can start finding a great many possible complications.

Yet one of the most important things that Table 11.1 tells us is that although there was a significant difference, it was not a very large one. The teachers, on average, smiled at each student about once every three lessons. This was true for students of both genders. A difference that is proportionally very small can still reach statistical significance if the sample is large enough. In this (hypothetical) study, on average, girls received four smiles more for every thousand physics lessons they attended. (Or put another way, this would suggest that typically a girl will get smiled at by a physics teacher once more than a boy over their entire schooling.) Even if we accept the results, and recognise there is a real effect here, it may not be a large enough effect to be of any practical importance, and may not be worth further investigation (with the associated investment of resources).

So we must remember that 'statistical significance' means just that, and does not always imply an important result. For this reason, researchers are increasingly being encouraged to report 'effect sizes' for their statistical results as well as probability levels. The effect size is a measure of how big the effect is, given the overall pattern of the results, and suggests whether the results are likely to be important enough for us to need to act on the findings (see Table 11.2).

Table 11.2 Interpreting significance and effect size

Statistical significance	Effect size	Interpretation
n.s.	low	Any difference is not very great, and might have been a chance result.
$p<0.05$	low	There is a difference, which is probably not a chance result, but the difference may be too small to be of practical importance.
n.s.	high	Although the difference found is large, this could just be a chance result. If the sample was small, it is worth repeating with a larger sample to see if the difference is still found, and whether it reaches significance when the sample size is increased.
$p<0.05$	high	There is a difference, which is probably not a chance result, and it is large enough to be likely to be of practical importance.

The example used above, considering possible gender differences in how often physics teachers smile at students, is purely imaginary. However, consider the following claim made in a paper published in a journal called the *Electronic Journal of Research in Educational Psychology*:

> This study investigated the effects of a constructivist-based program on the attitudes of prospective teachers toward human rights education. The results show that the use of both constructivist teaching and learning activities, and traditional methods, increased the prospective teachers' degree of appreciation for human rights education. However, the use of constructivist methods and materials in the Human Rights course had a more positive impact on the student teachers' attitudes toward human rights. The results of the follow-up application show that using constructivist methods and materials leads to more permanent effects on these attitudes.

(Gündogdu, 2010, p. 344)

Questions for reflection

Do you think that Gündogdu's findings might be important for those teaching future teachers about human rights? How convinced are you about the effectiveness of the constructivist approach, given the following? 'The mean score of the experimental group was 72.67 for the pre-test; this mean score increased to 75.80 for the post-test, and was 74.64 in the follow-up. The mean scores of the control group were pre-test 73.68, post-test 74.43, and follow-up 71.83' (p. 342) – as shown in Table 11.3.

Table 11.3 Gündogdu's (2010) results, demonstrating the superiority of constructivist approaches in teaching about human rights

Teaching approach (size of group)	Average pre-test scores	Average post-test scores	Average delayed test scores
constructivist (experimental) (N=45 students)	72.67	75.80	76.64
traditional (control) (N=40 students)	73.68	74.43	71.83

We might be convinced that Gündogdu has identified a real effect, but we might take more convincing that the research should be seen as the basis for any major change in teaching, given what seem fairly modest changes in the overall scores in the experimental group.

——— Using descriptive statistics ———

The effect size is an example of a descriptive statistic that can be used to complement statistical tests. In many studies, especially small-scale studies, only descriptive statistics are used. Part of the logic of much statistical testing is to see whether the results we obtained from a sample are likely to indicate a difference in a wider population. Teacher researchers do sample (e.g., collecting data in one lesson with a particular class, rather than all the lessons they teach that class), but are not usually interested in extrapolating beyond their sample to other classrooms or schools. Especially when our research is context-directed (see Chapter 5), we are looking primarily to learn about teaching- and learning-related phenomena in a particular class (often our own class), rather than seeing the class as simply representing, say, all 14–15 years olds studying chemistry everywhere!

The kind of results commonly reported includes totals and averages (often the arithmetic mean, but mode or median may be useful sometimes). We may also use measures of the spread of results. So if students in the class scored between 12 and 78 marks on a test, we might report the range as 66. A distribution of scores with a mean of 59 and a spread of 66 is somewhat different from a distribution with the mean score of 59 but a range of only 22 points. A problem with reporting ranges like this is that atypical results have a large effect on the statistic. Perhaps everyone scored between 42 and 64 marks, *apart from* Minsha (72 marks) and Marty (12 marks). These two 'outliers' rather distort our impression of the spread of results, as most are quite tightly bunched around the mean score.

So, slightly more sophisticated approaches may be used. You may see reference to the inter-quartile range, which gives the range of scores of those who did not score in the top or bottom quarter of the class (i.e., the range of marks of the half of the sample 'in the middle'). That is a simple statistic to work out, which just helps avoid extreme results distorting our impression of the spread. If we have a scientific calculator, we can readily go one step further and measure the variance or standard deviation, which are ways of representing the spread by taking into account how far each result is from the average. This is a fairly simple process but, as always, we should avoid using any kinds of mathematical treatments unless we are confident that we know what we are doing.

Consider presenting results graphically

In any case, although quoting the mean result and the standard deviation gives a very succinct overview of a range of scores, most readers will actually find it easier to interpret results represented graphically. For many purposes, simple graphical forms, like scatter charts, bar charts and pie charts, are quite effective ways of presenting results. For example, Figure 11.2 reproduces one of the pie charts used in a paper reporting results from a project exploring student *Learning About Science And Religion* (LASAR) in secondary schools, directed by Dr Berry Billingsley at Reading University: 13–14 year-old students were asked to rate a number of statements reflecting ways of understanding the relationship between science and religion according to their level of agreement. In a published report of this stage of the project (Taber, Billingsley, Riga, & Newdick, 2011), pie charts were used to give a quick visual impression of the responses to some of the items.

In the example reproduced in Figure 11.2, it can readily be seen that a much higher proportion of the students in the sample agreed with the statement that *the scientific view is that God does not exist* than disagreed with the statement. This was seen of interest as these students studied in England where the relationship between science and religion was a recommended topic in the curriculum of 11–14 year olds. Whilst many individual scientists may think God does not exist (just as many others are devout believers), science itself has nothing to say about matters that are considered 'supernatural'

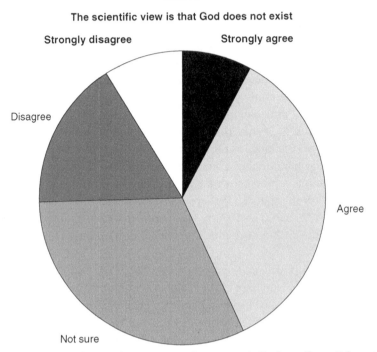

Item 19

The scientific view is that God does not exist

Figure 11.2 Example of a pie chart representing research findings (from Taber et al., 2011, p. 108) (Reproduced from *Science Education International*)

(i.e., beyond/outside nature), and so findings such as this suggest that despite the recommended curriculum, many young people have a distorted view of the nature of science. For many readers of the research report, the finding has more impact when represented graphically like this (Figure 11.2) than simply reported as numbers in a table.

In Dawe's (2012) study of Year 3 (7–8 year-old) students' perceptions of the nature of knowledge and intelligence, she collected data through a questionnaire and focus group discussions. Dawe presented her results thematically, using a series of bar charts to present questionnaire results, complemented by offering quotations from the focus groups. The use of bar charts allows the reader to quickly get an impression of the pattern of results. So, in her figure 1 (2012, p. 42), it is immediately clear that only a small minority of the pupils disagreed with the statement 'people are born clever or not clever', whilst only a small minority agreed that 'if I don't understand something straight away, I will never understand it'.

Using graphs in the process of analysis

It might seem that discussing the presentation of results would fit better in the next chapter, on reporting your work, than in a chapter on data analysis. However, the analyst, as well as the reader, often finds it easier to make sense of research results when they are presented graphically. Some teachers are very used to working with numbers and statistics, and can easily interpret results presented as numbers in tables, but for most of us graphs can be very useful tools in the analysis itself. Given how readily modern computers will quickly produce graphs for us with commonly available software, there is often a case for the analyst (i.e., the researcher) to convert suitable results into graphs whilst undertaking the analysis to help 'see' the patterns in data – even when it may only be appropriate to select a few key results to present in this way in a final report.

Approaches to working with qualitative data ———

There are different ways to approach the analysis of qualitative data, but the approach to analysis should be consistent with the research questions, and already set out in the research design. Robson (2002) refers to four approaches:

- Quasi-statistical – where initially qualitative data is analysed to produce counts, and so secondary data of a numerical kind. Sometimes this approach may be used to test hypotheses, even though the initial data collected was qualitative.
- Template – where a formal analytical framework was developed as part of the research design (informed by the conceptual framework for the study), so that the analyst knows just what they are looking for in the data from the start. There may even be a 'code book' already set up telling the analyst how to code specific items found in the data.
- Editing – where the participants' own words are used as text that can be edited into a form more suitable for reporting. This goes beyond selecting example quotes to illustrate findings (which might be used in reporting the *outcomes* of analysis undertaken, for example, using a template approach).
- Immersion – where the researcher spends considerable time reading and re-reading the data, 'immersing' herself or himself in the data to develop a deep understanding and allow insights to emerge.

Questions for reflection

Do you think these different approaches to analysis link with the terms 'quantitative research', 'qualitative research' and 'mixed-methods research' that are sometimes used to describe studies? Which of these approaches to working with qualitative data might fit with studies seen as ERP1 and ERP2 in the sense these terms are used in Chapter 3?

Of course, this suggestion of four approaches is, like many of the schemes we use to describe research, not meant to imply a strict typology of types of analysis, as variations and hybrid approaches are possible. As always, what *is* important is that decisions about analysis make sense in terms of the kind of data collected, and the research question being answered.

So, in general, there tend to be two basic approaches to coding data:

- drawn from the conceptual framework informing the research
- grounded in the data collected in the study itself.

In the former case, we already have a pretty good idea what kinds of information we are looking for in the data (i.e., confirmatory research), and sometimes we can be quite specific about this – depending on how strongly our reading of the existing literature has allowed us to make confident assumptions about the kinds of things we will find in our data. In the latter case, we have issues that we wish to explore, but feel that existing literature does not help us know exactly what we might be looking for, and so we use approaches that attempt to be open to what the data seems to be 'telling us' (i.e., discovery research). That is, we use an inductive approach which "builds theoretical categories, instead of sorting data pieces deductively into pre-established classes" and where "the units of analysis or data segments are not predetermined, but are carved out from the data according to their meaning" (Tesch, 1990, p. 90).

Robson (2002, p. 459) suggests that there is often a series of phases in undertaking this kind of work:

- coding the data, by marking up sections with suitable codes summarising the points that have attracted our interest;
- memoing, where we write ourselves reflective notes on the issues and themes we think we are seeing in the data, and the meaning we attach to the codes we are using;
- identifying themes, patterns, etc. (sometimes indicating what further data should be collected);
- developing generalisations from the overall patterns we find in the data set; and then
- constructing theory to show the relationships between the identified themes and variables, and to explain how they seem to link together.

The alert reader may note that this pattern seems familiar, as it seems to draw heavily on the general principles underlying grounded theory (GT) methodology (see Chapter 4), without being quite so demanding (and therefore so rigorous) as a full GT study.

As pointed out previously in the book, educational research is complex and multifaceted, and attempts to define and categorise different approaches should be seen as *useful models* rather than presenting absolute distinctions. In that spirit, I have presented a simple summary of (a model of) the main approaches to working with qualitative data in Figure 11.3.

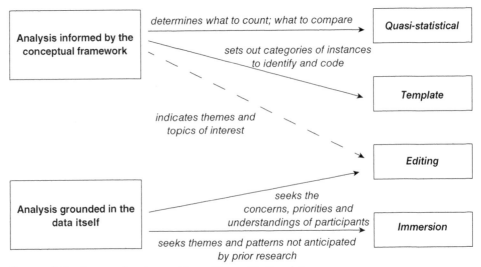

Figure 11.3 Approaches to working with qualitative data

Using scoring schemes ———

Sometimes quantitative data is obtained by direct counting of instances of different categories. However, sometimes scores are assigned to data according to where they appear on some perceived scale. In one of the studies discussed earlier in the book, McClune (2001) argues that students following modular courses (where some of the credit for final grade is awarded for examination papers taken early in the course) may be disadvantaged compared with students taking linear courses for the same award, and being examined on all aspects of the course in terminal examinations.

   McClune assumed the major factor that would indicate whether the two groups were comparable would be their previous examination success. He compared the students' GCSE (school leaving) grades and reported that there was no significant difference between the two groups. In order to make the comparison, examination grades have to be processed in some way. McClune chose to:

- only consider examination grades in three subjects
- weigh the three subjects as being equally important
- convert grades to a numerical scale: A*=6, A=5, B=4, C=3, etc., to give each student an overall numerical score.

Each of these decisions is reasonable, but clearly it is possible that making different decisions – such as including more subjects, giving most weight to science and maths (as he was looking at performance on physics questions), giving greater differentials between the highest grades – e.g., A*=10, A=7, B=5, C=3, D=2, E=1 – could all have led to a different outcome. In principle, when we are adopting somewhat arbitrary processes such as those in McClune's study, it may be possible to repeat the analysis having modified some of the parameters. If a different choice and weighing of subjects, and a different scoring system, still led to the same overall conclusions, then it would demonstrate that the findings were robust in relation to variations in the precise model used to represent prior attainment in the analysis.

Classification schemes ———

Frequency data is obtained when it is possible to assign data to a limited set of categories. For example, Harrop and Swinson (2003) used a classification scheme to characterise teacher questions. The type of scheme (or typology) used offers mutually exclusive categories to cover the full range of teachers' questions. That is, any question a teacher asks must fit into one, and only one, of the categories on the scheme.

Question for reflection

What are the limitations and potential problems of using a classification scheme to analyse classroom data such as teacher questions?

As we have seen in other studies, researchers have a responsibility to produce a simplified account of their data which is readable and readily appreciated by readers, although this can never reflect the full complexity of the educational phenomena studied. As suggested above (Figure 11.3), this is achieved either by selecting analytical categories from existing knowledge during the conceptualisation stage *before* collecting data, or by a process of 'induction' – of identifying 'emergent' categories that seem to represent the main patterns in data once it is collected.

In Harrop and Swinson's case, their initial conceptualisation of the field in terms of previously published research meant that they brought predetermined categories to the data – the types of questions identified in previous work. In this situation, the researcher would normally have a recording sheet in the form of a table set up to record instances of the different types of questions observed whilst listening to the lessons. In real time observation, the observer would identify the appropriate category and place a mark in the appropriate place on the recording sheet. If working from transcripts of lessons, it may be more sensible to use a set of codes for the different question types, and to code the transcripts (e.g., marking codes in the margin). In either case, the result makes it easy to tally up the instances and enter the tallies into a summary table, showing the total number of examples of each category observed.

Developing categories

Working with predetermined categories is more likely in studies from within ERP1 (see Chapter 3). Research that has a more interpretivist nature is likely to delay establishing categories until after data collection. In ERP2 approaches, the researcher develops the categories by interrogating the data, and deciding which classifications will best 'fracture' the data set in ways that represent the patterns in the original data. For example, in their 2004 paper on self-regulated learning (introduced in Chapter 2), Corrigan and Taylor outline the way they collected data (a "semi-structured interview protocol was constructed to detect perceptions, experiences, dilemmas and problems faced by students … student reports … were [also] examined", pp. 52–53), and analysed it ("all interviews were audio-taped and transcribed. After reading the transcripts, a number of categories were developed…").

Such categories are said to 'emerge' from, and be grounded in, the data (cf. grounded theory (GT) – see Chapter 4). Of course, the categories really emerge from the researcher's mind, and will be (often subconsciously) influenced by the analyst's own prior beliefs and ideas about the topic. This is inevitable, and is a possible source of bias in interpreting data.

Post-inductive resonance

However, there are ways of minimising such bias. Although the creative process of coming up with categories ('induction') is outside conscious control, it is certainly possible to carefully *check the fit* of categories against the data, and only retain those that fit well ('post-inductive resonance'). Iterative processes have been developed in GT that involve constantly checking (and modifying) the analytical codes against the data being collected. In effect, codes and categories should be treated as hypotheses being tested against new data.

Given such safeguards through the *context of justification*, the rather mysterious and subjective nature of the *context of discovery* is not problematic (see Chapter 6). In other words, we rely on personal insights to spot potentially pertinent themes and patterns in our data, and these insights ('aha!' moments) are the outcome of cognitive *processes* that we do not have conscious access to and so cannot validate. However, we can test the validity of *the outcomes* of these processes, the insights themselves, by treating them as hypotheses that are rigorously tested for match (resonance) with the data. Any insights which cannot be supported should be dropped from the analysis.

Whilst the seemingly haphazard nature of getting the original insight may seem at odds with a systematic approach to research, it is an integral feature in *all* research carried out by human beings. Whilst the emergence of insight is more obvious in interpretivist studies, exactly the same issues are met in the most traditional scientific studies, where the original hypothesis is a creative invention of human imagination, and is then objectively tested through the research (Taber, 2011b). The difference between confirmatory and discovery research is the stage in the overall research process where the insights to be tested are identified.

Identifying themes

In a paper in the journal *Teachers College Record*, Aldridge (2006) offers an account of how US history textbooks misrepresent the life of Martin Luther King, Jr., offering "a sanitized, noncontroversial, oversimplified view of perhaps one of America's most radical and controversial leaders" (p. 680). In his study, Aldridge identifies three 'master narratives' about King:

- as a Messiah;
- as the embodiment of the civil rights movement; and
- as a moderate.

This claim is based on the analysis of six American history textbooks that Aldridge characterises as "popular and widely adopted" high school texts (p. 664). He identifies the texts and justifies their selection for the study.

Aldridge describes his main methodological approach as *literary analysis*. This is described as a simple process of reading materials to identify evidence *to support* a perspective or argument. The approach, followed in the paper, has four stages: reading; identifying themes; discussing the themes identified; and offering examples that support the case being made (p. 664). Aldridge outlines his perspective early in his paper:

> History textbooks often presented simplistic, one-dimensional interpretations of American history within a heroic and celebratory master narrative … a teleological progression from 'great men' to 'great events,' usually focusing on an idealistic evolution toward American democracy.

> (Aldridge, 2006, p. 662)

The starting point for the study was a belief that "the dominance of master narratives in textbooks denies students a complicated, complex, and nuanced portrait of American history" (p. 663). Later in the paper, Aldridge, "illustrate[s] the master narratives that history textbooks present of one of America's most heroic icons, Martin Luther King, Jr" (p. 664).

The rhetorical nature of Aldridge's study

This study is particularly interesting in terms of some of the points raised earlier in the book, about research writing as rhetoric (see Chapter 1 and Chapter 6), and about the importance of a researcher's conceptual *frame*work for *framing* research studies (Chapter 3).

Question for reflection

Aldridge clearly expected and intended to find 'master narratives' about King in the books analysed, and his expectation was realised. Does this undermine the findings as being influenced by the researcher's biases?

It is clear that Aldridge sets his study within a rhetorical context – an argument that history teachers in the USA have to teach in ways that compensate for the limitations of the commonly adopted textbooks. Yet (as with Lyle's writing, see Chapter 6) Aldridge is always totally explicit about this position, and his description of his methodology makes it clear that the case of King is being used as an example to support (more than test) his argument. Indeed, the methodology might be seen as inherently self-fulfilling, as 'identifying themes' is seen as unproblematic. However, this methodological approach did not preclude the possibility of finding nuance and complexity (e.g., that the same books could have presented 'King as moderate' *and* 'King as radical' in interwoven themes).

If Aldridge's study had been set up as a test of the hypothesis that US history books presented history through oversimplified meta-narratives, then the methodological approach would be significantly deficient. However, Aldridge's acknowledged conceptual framework for the research was that such narratives *were* present, and the study sought to identify them. Accordingly, his study is best judged in terms of how well the three proposed narratives reflect the texts he analysed.

Following the leads to a core category

One of the papers referred to in Chapter 2 was Calissendorff's (2006) study of 5 year olds learning to play the violin. This study used a grounded theory (GT) approach to data analysis, and the author clearly explains the stages of the process in her account. For Calissendorff, 'leads' (i.e., insights) emerged during her study, as she interviewed and observed the young musicians, their teacher and their accompanying parents. A 'lead' derived "from an interesting event, statement or observation. It is followed up, and eventually either forms a category of its own, is placed within an existing category or is rejected" (p. 85). As well as reporting the 'leads' which emerged through her study, Calissendorff describes how some of these were modified or combined over the period of data collection to give a set of categories that organised her data: motivation, perception, time, and so on. Calissendorff then describes how she adopted the core concept of 'learning style', drawing heavily on an existing learning-style model she had read about.

Question for reflection

Is it acceptable in a GT study to organise the data around a core concept that is taken from a literature review rather than one that emerges from the data?

Calissendorff (2006, p. 91) adopts a concept from her reading to structure her findings because she found a strong match between her own categories and key elements of the published model ("what has been presented earlier is now integrated within the core category ... it includes everything"). However, she points out that her core concept is an *adaptation* of the published model, modified to fit the details of her own findings. This is within the spirit of GT (see Chapter 4), where models and schemes are modified to fit data, rather than data selected or interpreted according to pre-existing frameworks (as in Aldridge's study).

Editing data

The notion of editing in working with research data needs to be treated with care. If we are to select, modify and juxtapose what our participants have told us, then there is a great deal of scope for misrepresenting their thinking and views. However, a good editor does not change the message in the material being edited, but rather helps to make the message clearer by reorganising the material to help bring out the main points.

Of course, even the most well-meaning editor may inadvertently distort the original intended meaning in a text. After all, this is a technique of *interpretive* research, where the researcher makes sense of the text in terms of the cognitive resources they have available – the ideas they are familiar with. For this reason, it is useful to be widely read about an area when working in this mode, as it makes it less likely you will distort one of your participant's meanings in editing the text they have gifted you. Where the focus of the research makes it appropriate (for example, someone's beliefs and views, or their recollections of some experience), it can be very useful to validate your own interpretations through 'member checks', that is, asking the participants to read your edited text and confirm, or otherwise, that it catches the essence of their views.

Why would we need to edit?

The role of analysis is in part to take a large data set, and find the general patterns and messages it suggests. In terms of the visual metaphor introduced in Chapter 3 (see Figure 3.1), analysis is part of the second focusing phase of a project, where we seek to produce concise conclusions from our research that can provide succinct messages for future practice, and that can be readily be communicated to others.

A very common technique for collecting data in educational research is to interview people. The interviews can be transcribed, which often produces long documents which, although fascinating, take up a good deal of space when printed, and which are seldom in a very concise form. It is in the nature of this kind of data that:

- it will contain irrelevancies ('oh, let me move the voice recorder so your arm does not knock it', 'that's a nice broach', 'you are my last interviewee today', 'I was interviewed for some research when I was in primary school', 'I'm dying for a cup of tea', etc.);
- spoken English is seldom as tidy as written text, where we have time to adjust the final form. In a conversation we rely on the instant 'online' creation of utterances as we are speaking them, whilst both thinking ahead about where we wish the conversation to go, and also adjusting our own speech production in response to our ongoing analysis of what the other person is telling us;
- often many important responses by our interviewees do not make sense away from the context of our questions ('yes, I think that is so important'; 'well, perhaps, but not so much since I transferred to this school');
- even experienced interviewers find themselves sometimes talking over and interrupting the interviewee – we think they have finished speaking or we think they cannot think of an answer, so we go to rephrase the question just as the interviewee starts answering, etc.

An example of the transformation of qualitative data

As an example, consider the following short extract from a research report describing a student's understanding of some scientific concepts:

> Alice applied ideas about unbalanced forces being a cause of motion, and specifically acceleration, in a number of situations—falling apples, parachutists, etc. She described how increasing air resistance on a parachutist would lead to balanced forces, and so a terminal velocity. Although Alice identified unbalanced forces with acceleration, she apparently considered orbital motion to be the result of balancing centripetal and centrifugal forces, which kept the orbiting body moving round. Alice described velocity as speed with a direction, and acceleration as a change in speed, and so did not seem to consider a change of direction alone as sufficient criterion for an acceleration.

(Taber, 2008, p. 1927)

The data that led to this report was an interview that was transcribed to provide a text of what had been said. The transcript had the following format:

   ...

Keith: Why do you think the planets orbit the sun?

Alice: Say gravity again? [Laughs]

Keith: Yeah.

Alice: Okay.

Keith: You can say gravity.

Alice: There's forces between large bodies as in – the sun and planets, erm, I sup-
         pose like centripetal force, and

Keith: So what's centripetal force?

Alice: It links in with, erm [pause, approx. 3 seconds] objects circling [laughs] or objects
         orbiting, er keeping something in an orbit. But also erm the forces opposing
         that, which I think is centrifugal. Yeah, erm, which would send it out of orbit.

...

Sometimes in research, pauses and hesitations can be very informative. Indeed, in some research, transcripts record not only the words spoken, but changes in tonality and other features of speech that may reveal information about the speaker's think-ing and intentions. We need to make decisions about what we need to include in an analysis based upon consideration of the research question we wish to answer. Often words are enough. Sometimes, tidying up the grammar, and removing the hesitations is useful: and sometimes it loses information relevant to our study. As always, we will be judged according to whether we can offer a sensible rationale for our decisions as researchers – decisions that can only ever be justified in the context of the specific study and its research questions.

In analysing the interview, the researcher (the present author in this case) identified themes discussed in the transcript (in this case forces, energy, etc.), and cut and pasted material to bring together parts of the interview that were relating to the same scien-tific ideas. Then this material was edited into a narrative account, which comprised all the relevant material from the transcript, but reorganised to be more succinct. Part of this narrative account read:

> ...Alice thought that the planets orbited the sun due to "gravity again", explaining that "there's forces between large bodies as in the sun and planets, I suppose like centripetal force ... keeping something in an orbit, but also the forces opposing that, which I think is centrifugal ... which would send it out of orbit." Alice thought that the opposing forces were needed "to keep it in balance so that it carries on just going round, rather than veering off in either direction, away or towards the sun." Alice thought that hav-ing balanced forces "allows an object to remain either stationary, or at its, doing what it's doing in the same direction at the same speed, rather than, changing, you know accelerating or decelerating, or veering off either way". Similarly the moon did not move off into space as "it's being held by the same kind of forces" which being bal-anced meant the moon was continuing to move with "the same motion"...

The narrative account acted as a more reader-friendly version of the information in the interview: that is, it was an edit of the transcript, more useful in drawing together key ideas in this study. The aim in producing the narrative account in this study was to retain all of the relevant information in the original transcript, but to present it in a more organised and compact form. The edited-together narrative account was then used as the basis of the more concise research report, part of which was quoted above. The overall analytical process is summarised in Figure 11.4.

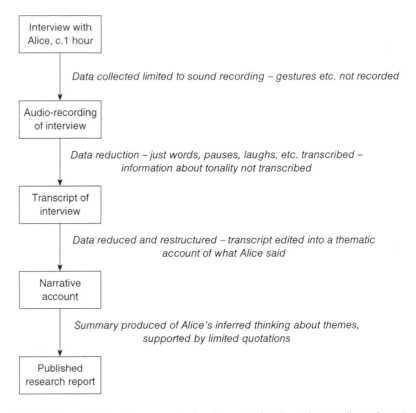

Figure 11.4 Data reduction in a case study of one student's understanding of curriculum topics

Producing a vignette

The editing process used to produce the narrative account stage in analysing Alice's interview was designed to reorganise the data in the transcript, whilst remaining faithful to Alice's actual utterances. Sometimes, however, researchers feel that an honest account can best be produced by taking more liberties with the 'facts' they have collected in their research. The following extract is from the penultimate chapter in my own Master's thesis from some years ago now. It describes the experiences and attitudes of Gill and Barry, two pupils in the school where I was teaching, and where I undertook a case study. This section of the thesis is described as being a 'vignette', and here just part of the vignette is reproduced (the full version may be found at https://camtools.cam.ac.uk/wiki/site/~kst24/vignette.html):

> Gill is likely to find she is taught science by teachers with a range of ideas about the desirability of distinct gender roles in society, and the role the school should have in effecting social change. Gill is unlikely to be subjected to any form of serious physical assault in the science classroom, although she will learn to expect – and probably accept – that occasionally some of the boys will insult her, physically manipulate and intimidate her, and subject her to the odd poke or slap. Gill will reciprocate much less often. Gill may interpret these incidents as boys showing

they are 'in charge' in the laboratory rather than any overtly aggressive intent. She is likely to find that her teachers consider such 'horse-play' to be a natural part of the interaction found in classrooms...

On entering the school at eleven Gill is most interested in studying [science] topics related to health, nature study and the human body, whereas Barry would rather study mechanical topics and 'spectacular science' such as space science and volcanoes. Although Gill is not especially interested in physical science topics as such, her interest is raised when biological aspects are considered – for example chemicals in food. Both Gill and Barry will have some ideas about which jobs involve science: for example, recognising that science is needed by doctors, electricians, and weather forecasters. They will both consider that some jobs, such as plumber, motor mechanic and pilot, are more suitable for men; whilst other jobs, such as nurse, hairdresser and junior school teacher, are more suitable for women.

(Taber, 1989, pp. 225–226)

Research writing should be non-fiction, but Gill and Barry did not exist. This is not an admission of research fraud, as all the data reported in my thesis were genuine – collected and analysed as reported. Moreover, there is no question of dishonest reporting in the thesis either, as it is explicitly reported that this particular chapter offered "a description of the perceptions and experiences which could be ascribed to a 'typical' female pupil passing through the school in comparison to her 'typical' male peers" but that "in reality all pupils are unique individuals, and probably no real girl in the school would recognise this composite report as being a precise account of her own case" (p. 224).

So Gill and Barry are not real people, but are narrative devices – inventions used to summarise a great deal of analysis in a simple, readable account that gets across the main messages of the study. This kind of approach is common in some types of research writing (Piantanida & Garman, 2009), but it is important to make sure that no reader could misinterpret such vignettes as actual reports of individuals, rather than composite summary accounts. (There are strong parallels here with the way Watts' accounts of student conceptual frameworks were stylised, composite accounts of data from a number of students, but treated by Kuiper as meant to report the discrete thinking of individuals – as discussed in some detail in Chapter 3.)

This takes much further the idea of the narrative account described above, where one data source (an interview transcript) was reworked to aid analysis – as the vignette from which this abstract is taken draws upon a wide range of data collected from a great many participants (through interviews, classroom observations, and questionnaires), and offers a preview or advanced organiser for the more detailed conclusions discussed in the subsequent rather 'dense' final chapter of the thesis.

Selecting a case for case study

In 1998 Petri and Niedderer published an account drawing on a case study (see Chapter 4) of one 18 year-old high school student's learning about the atom. Although they report the case of a single learner, Petri and Niedderer collected data from a class of nine students taught by two teachers. The researchers collected data over 12 weeks of the course. The authors then made a selection of Carl as the subject for a case study. They offer the reader two criteria that were used (p. 1078). They wanted a case study where the student made verbal contributions in class, and where the student was not at either extreme of the attainment range. The authors also give an overview of the main steps in the process of developing the case study (pp. 1078–1079):

- data was analysed using an iterative … interpretation procedure;
- data was transcribed selectively, using previous research results;
- hypotheses were formulated;
- further transcriptions were undertaken as indicated by hypotheses formed;
- transcripts were repeatedly read to (dis)confirm tentative hypotheses;
- the data on Carl's learning pathway was compared to selected data on other students.

Petri and Niedderer collected a good deal of data in their study, although in their analysis they 'transcribed selectively' and focused on the material relating to their selected 'case', Carl. It would not have been sensible to have identified a case to study at the outset as they could have made a poor choice of subject (perhaps a student who said little in class, and offered little in interviews, perhaps an atypically able learner) or even selected a student who dropped out or became ill and missed much of the course. By delaying their selection they safeguarded the study. They used an iterative process that involved developing hypotheses during data analysis, which then informed which other data should be interrogated in detail. The use of triangulation, from different 'slices of data', provides the richness of evidence to allow such an iterative process to be possible.

Multiple case studies

Multiple case studies use, as the name suggests, several case studies as part of the same overall research project. In a multiple case study it is important to analyse each case in its own terms (within-case analysis), and then only afterwards undertake a cross-case analysis (Stake, 2006). If the cases are not analysed in depth in their own terms, the work is not actually case study.

In his report in the *International Journal of Science Education*, of his MEd study, Dorion (2009, pp. 2255–2256) explained that he used a "two-tiered multiple case-study approach, which aimed first to analyse each case as an ideographic event, and only afterwards to employ cross-case comparisons [where] after the case studies had been analysed, a separate cross-case analysis focused again on the codings of the … themes". In reporting the results of a multiple case study, it may make sense to report the cases in separate sub-sections or chapters, before reporting the cross-case analysis.

————'Mixed methods'?

Earlier in the book (in Chapter 4) I discussed the common use of the descriptor 'mixed methods' for some research studies, and suggested the term is used in a variety of ways, some of which are not especially informative. In particular, it is common for research that collects both quantitative and qualitative data to be labelled as mixed methods (although it is of course quite possible for a mixture of methods, e.g., interviews, observations and document analysis, to produce purely qualitative data!)

A study presenting both quantitative and qualitative data

In his study of student preferences of learning environments (introduced in Chapter 2), Kinchin (2004) reports his results in two forms: he presents both quantitative and qualitative data. In Chapter 3, it was suggested that educational research tends to be associated with different traditions, based upon different assumptions about how useful knowledge about educational contexts may be generated. ERP1 (positivistic, nomothetic, confirmatory) is often considered to be largely a quantitative paradigm, where ERP2 (interpretivist, idiographic, discovery) tends to rely more on the use of qualitative data.

In Kinchin's study, students selected their preference for what Kinchin characterised as a constructivist (student-centred) or an objectivist ('traditional') classroom, and offered their reasons. The quantitative data consists of raw numbers that have been tabulated (p. 305): 310 of 349 respondents selected option B (the constructivist classroom) and the other 39 chose the option representing the 'objectivist' classroom. Kinchin reported that the response patterns were similar in the two age groups sampled.

Questions for reflection

Kinchin does not present any results from statistical tests to indicate if the difference between the proportions of students selecting the two types of classroom environment are statistically significant (89% selected the image representing a constructivist classroom; 11% selected the image representing an objectivist classroom):

i   Does the lack of statistical testing prevent you from drawing conclusions about whether the differences are likely to be simply artefacts of the study, due to chance factors?
ii Do you think the descriptor 'quantitative research' is appropriate for this study?

The qualitative data presented in the paper was a small selection of quotations from the justifications students offered. So, for example, in his analysis of responses from those favouring option A (the 'objectivist' classroom) Kinchin identifies two themes. His analysis of the data suggests that there were two main reasons for students making this preference:

- feeling this was an easier way of studying;
- it offered a more suitable basis for revising for examinations.

Kinchin's analysis of the responses from those preferring option B (the constructivist classroom) identified three main themes among student justifications:

- feeling that this type of classroom made learning more interesting;
- that it was more effective at supporting learning;
- that it gave them greater ownership of their own learning.

Again, these categories were supported with a small sample of quotes from the data collected.

Question for reflection

Would you consider Kinchin's study to be in the positivistic or interpretivist tradition, or is it an example of a distinct 'mixed-methods' approach?

The form of data analysis reflects the type of study being undertaken

In Chapter 3 it was suggested that the decisions made at the start of a research study may have implications throughout the enquiry (i.e., see Figure 3.4). The type of data analysis appropriate to a study depends upon the type of data collected, which should reflect the researcher's beliefs about the type of research (e.g., exploratory or confirmatory) being undertaken. There are some features of Kinchin's study that are positivistic. The main one is that he began the study with an assumption that the categories of constructivist and objectivist classroom, as he conceptualised them, were a suitable basis for exploring students' views. An alternative approach would have been to have undertaken research to explore student thinking about their preferred style of 'classroom' without preconceived categories. This might have produced a more authentic account of 'student beliefs about their preferred role as learners'. However, Kinchin's own conceptualisation of the project was in terms of official guidance supporting 'constructivist' teaching approaches, so setting up his research in terms of a dichotomous preference (with constructivism as one pole) better fitted his purposes.

Given that teaching and learning are complex phenomena, the educational researcher has a responsibility to produce findings that are a simplification: simple enough to be readily understood, and to provide the basis for teachers and others to act on them. Inevitably this means reporting results in terms of categories (or at least headings). In ERP1 it is usual to formulate categories at the outset, so that during data collection and/or analysis, 'forced choices' are made (by researcher, or respondents) in relation to the permitted categories. In ERP2 it is usual to collect data in a more open-ended way, but to identify categories during analysis which best reflect the main patterns in the data (inevitably filtered through the pre-existing conceptual structures of the analyst who interprets the data).

Kinchin's study shows that he felt that there was sufficient basis in existing research to support a simple model of classroom styles that could be used to force choices when collecting data about student preferences. However, he was more open-minded in terms of the reasons for those choices, and allowed categories for reporting student reasoning to emerge during analysis. The presentation of quantitative data is often associated with ERP1, but Kinchin does not offer an explicit hypothesis to be tested, and so does not present any inferential statistics (to show the *statistical significance* of findings). The discussion of the findings from student justifications is certainly presented as being closer to an interpretivist approach to educational research. Kinchin does not report bringing preconceived categories to his data analysis here (though the description, such as 'ownership' of learning, may not reflect the students' own language), but suggests the categories 'emerged' from his analysis of the data. Presumably, Kinchin's reading of the relevant literature provided him with a conceptualisation of the field, suggesting that the way students might justify their preference for an 'objectivist' or 'constructivist' classroom was still very much an open question.

Some readers might consider this a mixed-methods study, because of the way that different kinds of data values were collected to find out what student preferred and why. However, we could also describe this study as a kind of survey. As has been suggested at a number of points in the book, our choice of labels to describe studies is less important than thinking clearly about what we are doing and why, and carefully justifying our many research decisions. Often such justifications have to be made public in some form of report, and this is considered in the next chapter.

Further reading ————

There is a tendency for new researchers to plan data collection and assume data analysis will just follow. The following readings suggest data analysis is not always straightforward, and so sensibly needs to be considered before commencing data collection. The Miles and Huberman volume offers some quite advanced approaches to thinking about qualitative data analysis. The Evans and McLellan chapters provide useful introductory overviews. The Robson book offers a good introduction to some useful statistical tests.

Evans, M. (2009). Analysing qualitative data. In E. Wilson (Ed.), *School-based Research: A Guide for Education Students* (pp. 125–135). London: Sage.

McLellan, R. (2009). Analysing quantitative data. In E. Wilson (Ed.), *School-based Research: A Guide for Education Students* (pp. 154–170). London: Sage.

Miles, M. B., & Huberman, A. M. (1994). *Qualitative Data Analysis* (2nd edn). Thousand Oaks, California: Sage.

Robson, C. (1994). *Experiment, Design and Statistics in Psychology* (3rd Revised edn). London: Penguin Books.

12

Teachers making the case through reporting research

This chapter:

- considers when it is important for classroom research to be formally reported
- introduces different types of outlet for research reports
- offers a model structure for writing up research that suits most formal academic reports
- considers when the writing model may need to be modified for studies that do not readily fit the standard report structure

Should all research be reported?

There are two contrary opinions about reporting research, which need to be considered when deciding if, and how, to report classroom-based research:

- research is not of value until it has been put in the public domain so that it may be considered, replicated, criticised and become subject to professional dialogue
- practitioner research is intended to improve the professional context for both a teacher and her/his students: time and effort formally reporting the work is unnecessary and a distraction

Question for reflection

Consider your own research project. Which of these opinions more closely fits your own views about writing up your work? How would you argue against the other opinion?

The view taken here is that both of these (opposite) opinions are essentially correct! To appreciate how it is possible to agree with both of these contrary opinions, we should consider the purposes for which research may be undertaken, and so *the form of knowledge* that is being sought.

Academic researchers

In Chapter 5, I suggested that it is useful to consider two modes of research, with studies being either 'theory-directed' (primarily aimed at developing generalisable knowledge) or 'context-directed' (primarily aimed at understanding and/or changing a particular specific situation to inform professional practice). Academics employed to undertake research are expected to usually concern themselves with theory-directed research. Such researchers may undertake studies situated in particular settings, but they are always looking to learn something from the situation that is of general relevance.

Traditional academic research is about creating 'public knowledge' that is shared by the community. In the natural sciences, new 'discoveries' are only usually considered to be due to the person who *publishes* the ideas first, as only once published are findings open to scrutiny, and available to help develop the field. In these fields, ideas become part of a consensus and come to be considered reliable knowledge (Ziman, 1978/1991), once other competent investigators can confirm the findings. Although social science knowledge is often viewed differently from natural science knowledge, so that there is less expectation of consensus or potential for *direct replication* of studies, similar academic norms operate (see Chapter 6). The gatekeepers of public systems of knowledge are the journal editors, referees used by academic publishers, professional bodies, etc.; and publication in peer-reviewed research journals is considered the minimum requirement for claiming the production of new knowledge in a field. *Academic, professional researchers are judged by their ability to contribute to the development of knowledge in their field by publishing in appropriate forms.*

Publish or be damned?

For such researchers, the *intellectual* purpose of their enquiries may be primarily in terms of a desire to know more, to understand ('epistemic hunger'), but the *professional* purpose of research is to contribute through academic publications. For the professional researcher (in education or another field), publications are the sign of acceptable knowledge creation – and, to some extent, of professional worth. These researchers must report their research, and they must report it to a designated audience, and in a *format* that is considered acceptable to their peers. Their research must be written up in such a way that others in their field will judge they have reported their work in a form that contributes to the field. The criteria for acceptable writing are the norms established in the relevant journals.

Question for reflection

What are the criteria that are likely to be used to decide whether a research report submitted to an academic journal should be published?

In particular, a contribution to the academic literature has to offer some originality. This may be just a slight modification of existing ideas, or the finding that previously reported outcomes may (or may not) also apply in a slightly different context: from modern language teaching to geography teaching; from primary to lower secondary level, etc. The journal editor will wish to be convinced that by publishing the researcher's paper the readers will have access to something that was not previously available, whether a major new insight, or just increasing understanding of the properties of something that is already well known. (The status of the journal will largely determine where the line is drawn on *how* novel something has to be before it is likely to be accepted for publication.) The kinds of quality criteria that referees and editors apply are those that were considered in Chapter 6. As will be discussed below, the onus of *making the case* rests on the author.

Practitioner researchers

At the opposite end of the scale to the professional academic researcher is the practitioner, perhaps a newly qualified classroom teacher. The professional priority here is not to publish research, but to effectively teach students. The teacher will not be judged by publishing accounts of professional work. The research may be no more than trying out an idea that is already well reported in the literature to see 'will it help here?' The purpose is to support teaching, and so help students learn. The teacher wants to be able to evaluate these new approaches to find out if they improve professional practice. This would be context-directed research in terms of the distinction introduced in Chapter 5.

Questions for reflection

Research was described above in terms of knowledge-creation. Is this practitioner – who is using research as a systematic way to evaluate ideas used in teaching – actually creating new knowledge? It was suggested above that knowledge does not 'count' until it is published. Do you think anyone doing research in this way should feel obliged to publish their findings?

Let us assume that this teacher is competent in planning the research, in collecting the data, and in analysing it to draw conclusions that can inform practice. At the end of the process the teacher will have a better understanding of some aspect of the teaching and learning in the classroom. So, new knowledge has been produced that should inform future teaching.

Personal or public knowledge

However, this does not mean such a teacher should feel obliged to try to publish the findings. The teacher's personal research has led to new *personal* knowledge: knowledge of real value to professional work. This does not *in itself* make the findings a new potential contribution to *public* knowledge. It may well be that this new personal knowledge is strongly situated within the research context, and it would be difficult to disentangle any general lessons from the specifics of the particular classroom. This is particularly likely to be the case if the research has been set up in the context-directed mode, where the literature has been used to seek suggestions for action, but has not been formally reviewed to develop a strong conceptualisation of the issues underpinning the research.

This is often the case in action research (AR), where the focus is on effecting change and improving a professional context rather than developing formal theory.

Even if the personal knowledge could be made explicit (for personal professional knowledge is often at a tacit level, although the research process helps makes this explicit), and conceptualised in terms of a wide and relevant literature review, it is still likely that her study will be judged to have very limited significance in the public domain. (It is by no means *impossible* that a classroom teacher may discover something quite novel that should be brought to wide attention, but most practitioner research does *not* lead to such outcomes.)

As teachers, we should be very familiar with this distinction, because it is at the very heart of our professional work. After all, a great deal of school learning involves individuals developing new (personal) knowledge that is already widely known by others. In many school subjects, a significant part of the teacher's job is to help learners discover or appreciate or reconstruct well-established public knowledge. The lack of originality of this new knowledge certainly does not take away from its importance to the learners. We appreciate the value of one more person being able to solve quadratic equations, or having an understanding of key conditions that facilitated the industrial revolution. In a similar way, it is extremely valuable for a teacher to develop a better understanding of some aspect of their classroom work, even if it does not involve any major breakthrough in terms of developing new educational theory.

From this perspective, if the purpose of a teacher's research is purely professional development as a classroom practitioner, and much of the research involves evaluating existing ideas to find 'what works here?', or 'how can I solve this problem/address this issue in my professional practice?', then there may be little value in any kind of formal write-up. Indeed, the time needed to write up research could probably be used in more productive ways.

So the two key ideas here are:

- Purpose of research – just for my own professional development?
- Forms of knowledge – private or public knowledge?

However, the two scenarios discussed here represent the ends of a continuum. Teacher research is often intended only for use within the classroom where it is carried out. But this is not always the case.

Question for reflection

Can you think of any appropriate audiences for teacher-research beyond the teacher herself?

Audiences for teacher research ━━

There are a good many reasons why a teacher may wish to share research with others, some of which are considered here. As the purpose of research is a key consideration when deciding *if* and *how* to report research, these different reasons lead to different advice on sharing your research with others.

So, teachers may share research because:

- they are *required* to demonstrate research competence (e.g., if taking a formal academic qualification such as the PGCE or a higher degree);
- it is school policy (e.g., the school requires new staff to undertake a research project during
their first year in school; see McLaughlin et al., 2006);
- teaching is a collegiate activity (and so colleagues may share their findings, e.g., within the
department);
- research is supported (by the school, by an external sponsor);
- they wish to support the advocacy of a new policy (e.g., persuade the department to change
setting policy);
- they feel their experiences may be valuable to others in the profession or they wish to contribute at a professional level.

There are obviously many possible variations and graduations in these options. We shall here consider a number of possible audiences a teacher could have for his or her research, and the type of report likely to be indicated in each situation. A key issue will also be the basis upon which the research is undertaken. A busy classroom teacher inherently has little incentive to spend time and effort in *reporting* (as opposed to carrying out) research. The incentive normally comes from likely future 'rewards': a qualification, promotion, increased status in the subject association, seeing one's work in print. Often these are uncertain rewards even with considerable effort and perseverance!

The informal group

An informal research group, within a department, across a school, or among a group of local schools, is potentially a very powerful mechanism for supporting professional learning. Such groups lack formal structures, with members' strong interest in topics acting as impetus for attendance and contribution. The lack of formality also provides flexibility. It may be that simply discussing experience and sharing evidence over coffee is the extent of research dissemination. This allows members to find out what works in other classrooms in the same or similar institutional contexts, and also provides extra eyes and minds to make suggestions and offer criticisms in a supportive environ-ment. In the model of AR recommended by McNiff and Whitehead (2009), there is a strong expectation that the teacher-researcher accounts for her actions to others (e.g., departmental colleagues) and takes seriously their critiques and recommenda-tions. Such groups can also act as useful sounding boards for those who have to present more formal accounts of their work elsewhere.

The department or institution

Persuading the department to make changes or move in a particular direction may be difficult – even for the Head of Department. Arguing from evidence and showing that proposed ideas can work in the school can be very important. Depending upon the formality of procedures (and the level of cohesion and collegiality involved) a writ-ten paper may be an appropriate instrument *to make a case*. This is more likely to be appropriate at whole-school level, where talking to some sort of discussion paper may well be an accepted way of making the case for changes to policy or procedures.

In the context of the school or department, discussion papers are normally expected to be brief and 'to the point'; generally short papers with bullet points and clear summaries of the research evidence are likely to have more impact. A teacher involved in making a case in this way should look to produce a concise summary of the argument, but be prepared to answer questions to provide any additional background when presenting the case (at a departmental or staff meeting, for example). Colleagues are only likely to be convinced by an argument that seems to be well thought-out and based on a careful analysis of relevant evidence: they are, however, unlikely to have time to commit to reading a lengthy, detailed account. (This is where a small number of bar charts or pie charts or even a line graph may help to communicate key findings in a direct and reader-friendly manner – see Chapter 11).

The sponsor

Sponsors provide money for school research, and usually expect to see outcomes that suggest their money has been well used. A sponsor may well specify the form of report that needs to be undertaken as a condition of funding. So, for example, when government funding in the UK supported 'Best Practice Research Scholarships' (BPRS), there were minimum expectations in terms of an outline of the form the report must take. Reports had to be submitted to a central website so that other teachers could learn from the research. However, the limited level of detail required often led to reports that were insufficient to offer much guidance regarding the potential relevance of the research to other contexts. BPRS funding was available for a wide range of project areas that teachers might wish to research. Other sponsors may wish to find very specific research, or at least offer funding to explore a particular topic. The sponsor's requirements in terms of a report are likely to be tailored to their purposes in offering the money. The National Academy for Gifted and Talented Youth (NAGTY) was charged with researching and supporting teaching and learning for those classed as 'gifted and talented' in schools and colleges, so only funded teacher research that was targeted at that group of students.

Like many government-sponsored initiatives in Education in the UK, where having regular new initiatives seems to be a political imperative (see the Foreword), both BPRS and NAGTY were discontinued after a few years. When the government decided not to continue to offer BPRS, it was intended that funding would instead be available to schools directly to support research. Some schools already had established research policies and funds, and so had traditions of sponsoring their own staff to undertake research. Such sponsorship often takes the form of a small reduction of teaching load, with the expectation that the released time will be used to undertake the research. Schools may give an open agenda to teachers to suggest projects that would be useful, or they may have priority themes, or allocate money via a departmental structure. Sometimes schools may have specific research they wish to see undertaken, and so ask staff to work to a pre-existing brief. When teaching in Further Education, I was commissioned by my college to undertake a project exploring the use of value-added indicators. The project had set aims, and it was clear from the outset what form the outcomes had to take. This was in contrast to my other research projects as a school and college teacher which had followed my own research interests.

The professional journal

Professional journals are published by subject associations, and their editors are usually keen to publish material written by practising classroom teachers. These journals vary in the extent to which they are set up along the lines of an academic journal or a magazine (see Chapter 6). Editors of professional journals are often interested in publishing accounts of classroom work that might be of interest to other teachers. Practitioner research may often be ideal as a basis for such articles. A key advantage (for the busy teacher) of writing for a practitioner journal rather than an academic journal – apart from the likelihood that more teachers may actually read what you have written – is that the criteria for accepting articles tend to be less demanding. It is difficult to generalise, but many professional journals will publish articles which:

- are shorter (e.g., 2000 words perhaps, cf. typically 5000 words in an academic journal);
- are written in a more conversational style (as that makes them more readable);
- have limited conceptualisation (as they do not expect an extensive preamble setting out the issues around the topic: it is preferred that articles 'get to the point' to keep readers' interest);
- have limited use of literature (reference to a few key readings, not a literature review);
- are provocative or speculative (so that they encourage discussion and response from readers);
- and so are less rigorous (accepting illustrations from classroom practice without considering such issues as sampling bias, etc.);
- are interesting rather than needing to be novel.

The last point is particularly pertinent in view of the discussion earlier in the chapter about the nature of knowledge that derives from teacher research. Academic journals accept articles purely on quality grounds, and the specific topic is usually less important (as long as it is seen as being within the field covered by the journal). This means that the 'field' of researchers dictates (through what is submitted, and how articles are judged in peer review) which topics and themes are currently seen as important, and so which may seem to dominate or be under-represented in the journals.

A professional journal might be very interested in an account of teacher-research that exemplifies an important idea in teaching the subject:

- if it is written in a lively way (e.g., includes personal anecdote);
- if it offers some good illustrative material (photographs, snippets of student dialogue, etc.);
- if it makes clear recommendations to other teachers; and
- if the journal has not published an issue on that theme or topic for a while.

So where the academic editor asks 'does this tell us something new?', the professional editor may instead ask 'does this say something we have not had said for a while?' The academic journal will publish many articles on the same topic as long as each adds to the literature, and will happily reject papers that do not meet quality standards no matter which topic they are on. The professional journal editor wants to keep the content fresh, and to make sure that there is balance in the contents list. No tone of criticism is implied here, as these are exactly the types of criteria likely to produce journals that busy classroom teachers will subscribe to, and find time to read.

Academic and professional journals have different target audiences, and are read for different primary purposes (to inform research or to inform teaching). Articles in professional journals, aimed at supporting the professional development of other teachers, may often be very well written and be engaging and thought-provoking, but without offering any new contribution to public knowledge – just as teachers, aiming to support the learning of students, may offer interesting, well-thought-out, and engaging lessons, to offer learners access to public knowledge that is already well established.

Question for reflection

If a teacher undertakes research that seems to offer genuinely original insights that could contribute to public knowledge, and could be generalised to apply in other classrooms, should they look to report their work in a professional journal where other teachers are likely to read about it, or in an academic research journal, where it may be adopted and built upon by other researchers?

The academic journal

Academic journals rely for their status upon readers having confidence in the editorial procedures involved in handling manuscripts. In particular, editors send submissions to experts in the topic for comment, and are guided by these referee reports in making decisions about publication. International research journals with good reputations reject most submissions they receive. Those papers that are accepted are nearly always returned to authors with a list of requirements from the editor based upon referees' comments: 'We may be interested in publishing your paper if you can satisfy us that you have met the criticisms of the referees...'. In other words, even a 'positive' response from an academic journal is usually an invitation to undertake a lot more work before possible publication. On submitting a revised 'manuscript' the author will often be expected to offer a point-by-point response to referees' comments.

To get that far, the submission must be seen to meet basic quality criteria. The need for some level of originality has already been mentioned, but referees and editors also need to be convinced that the research has been thoroughly and expertly undertaken. Their concerns when evaluating submissions are likely to be very similar to the assessment criteria that university examiners (who are of course often the same people) will be applying when judging research at Master's and doctoral levels for students undertaking PGCE, MA, MEd, MPhil, etc. qualifications.

Generally, research journals have a strict rule that they only consider manuscripts for publication if they have not already been published, and are not under consideration for publication elsewhere. However, if a teacher's research seems to be suitable for reporting in the academic literature, he or she does not have to choose between publishing in a professional or an academic journal. As the purposes of the two types of publication are different, and different writing styles are needed, it is often possible to write a research paper (with full literature review section, full methodological details, details of findings, etc.) and also an article summarising the research for teachers and focusing on the implications for classroom teachers. This is not only acceptable, but is actually the approach recommended by the British Educational Research Association (2000).

The academic project report or thesis

Higher degrees normally involve the production of a long dissertation (perhaps 20 000 words, sometimes much longer) on a topic that has been studied in particular depth. Students undertaking research for a higher degree in education are expected to write up a report of their projects in the form of a thesis: in other words, a well-developed *argument*, making their case. Student teachers working towards a PGCE will usually be expected to undertake some kind of classroom-based research project which will be much smaller in scope than a Master's dissertation or doctoral project. However, this will still usually need to be written up as a research report, albeit a more modest one (e.g., 8000 words).

There are clearly differences between institutions and courses, and of what is expected at different levels. For example, a PhD project normally has to demonstrate the type of originality expected of a published research report, whereas a Master's project would also need to be rigorously carried out, but would not usually be expected to have such a high level of originality. There are also important differences in style: so that in some instructional contexts more discursive or personal modes of writing are acceptable. A PGCE project may be expected to be like a mini-Master's study, offering a taste of the full research experience, or it may be that some particular aspects of the research process are being emphasised at this level.

It is obviously important for any student to obtain and carefully read all information about the expected nature and format of the report, and the assessment criteria that will be used to judge it. It is also useful to know if a fairly formal 'traditional' research report is expected, or whether something that gives a more authentic feel for the actual personal response to the research experience is encouraged. Certainly at Master's level and above, reading good theses from previous years is very helpful. The open-access journal *JoTTER* (http://jotter.educ.cam.ac.uk/ – see Chapter 5) offers examples of PGCE project reports, but it should be remembered that these are all drawn from one particular teacher training context, and there will be differences in what is expected in different universities.

In view of the differences in requirements between different levels, and between institutions, it is not possible to offer comprehensive guidance for writing up a student research project. That caveat notwithstanding, in the next section I will offer an overview of a fairly 'safe' way of reporting an empirical research project that should satisfy the requirements of most academic courses. Indeed, this basic plan provides a suitable outline for writing for publication in academic journals as well. Indeed, although the requirements of writing for academic journals are rigorous, they parallel what university examiners are likely to be looking for in project reports. A good thesis at Master's level, for example, might well translate into a worthy submission for an academic journal. This same structure may also serve as a template for preparing an oral presentation, for example to a research conference such as the annual meeting of BERA (the British Educational Research Association).

Question for reflection

Consider that people who read your research reports will be critiquing them in the same way that you have approached your reading – asking the kinds of questions highlighted earlier in the book (see Chapters 6 and 7). Jot down a list of criteria that you consider to be useful for evaluating research reports you read. How will you ensure your own research writing will meet your own expectations as a reader?

Presenting at conferences ————

Conference presentations are more transient than written reports (the talk is over very quickly), but allow for more direct interaction with an audience – something many teachers are very comfortable with. As with journals, there are different types of conferences. Some, such as those organised by subject teaching associations, are often primarily aimed at teachers. Others, often organised by learned societies or research associations, are primarily for researchers. Some deliberately mix both practitioners and academics, and some are more successful at including policy-makers (such as government advisors and senior civil servants). Some conferences are specialised (e.g., only concerned with humanities teaching), where others are open to work on all educational themes. Some conferences are intended to have a national or regional flavour, and others are international where all presentations are expected to be sensible to an international audience. Presenters then need to contextualise their specific focus to make it widely relevant to those working in different national contexts, and avoid using parochial acronyms, like KS3, GCSE, SATs, OCR, etc., which will be meaningless to many delegates.

As with journals, conferences vary in how difficult it is to get to present your work. Some are very keen on teacher input, and very open to offers. Others have quite rigorous peer-review processes, much like academic journals, and are very picky. Sometimes detailed summaries of the presentations have to be submitted for vetting many months before the conference. Usually, details of all these aspects of a conference can be gleaned from a website, which allows potential delegates, and potential speakers, to see if a particular conference matches their needs and interests.

Types of conference presentation

There are various types of sessions arranged at most education conferences. Keynote sessions are usually substantive presentations (perhaps an hour) given by someone of note to the entire conference. Many other sessions may be arranged in parallel, so there are several sessions occurring at once and delegates choose which to attend.

Sometimes these are organised by theme, and the themes may run through the conference. Organisations like the British Educational Research Association or the European Association for Research into Learning and Instruction have 'special interest groups' which each organise one or more sessions during a conference.

Some conferences include workshops, where ideas can be demonstrated and perhaps tried out. Some conferences include 'round tables' or 'conversations' between different delegates, with varying levels of audience participation. However, the most useful types of contribution for the teacher-researcher looking to present are likely to be the paper and poster.

Giving a paper

Most conferences include parallel sessions of about 1–2 hours, where a number of people will talk, often on a similar theme. Most commonly, each speaker gets about 20 minutes or so to talk, and a few minutes for answering audience questions. As these are parallel sessions, the audiences tend to be quite small (maybe a dozen or so people), and relatively informal. There will usually be a chair to introduce speakers and keep them within time limits, and sometimes there is some kind of respondent or discussant who is charged with offering an overview at the end of the session.

One of the most important things to appreciate if presenting in this kind of context is that 20 minutes is not long enough to explain the full story of a research project: and it is very easy to use all the time setting the scene and describing the methodology … but then having to rush (or worse, omit) discussion of results and implications. If giving such a paper, it is useful to practise giving the talk to (real or imaginary) audiences. Having a script that can be quietly read through in 20 minutes on the train to the conference does not always translate to a presentation that takes 20 minutes when given to an audience – so at the least, time how long it takes to read the paper out loud to an empty room, with suitable pauses for effect and audience reaction. It is also important to recognise that actually reading a paper is very boring for the audience (I once travelled several hours to an after-school session at a university where an academic sat and quietly read out her paper), and there may be a danger that in actual presentation mode (with adrenalin flowing) one starts to offer all kinds of extra detail that was not planned.

When you give a verbal report of your research, the audience is entitled to ask about all the kinds of methodological details you would be expected to include in a written report, but there is likely to be insufficient time to offer that level of detail. So in preparing your talk it is sensible to prioritise the messages you want to get across, but also to have slides (as a kind of appendix) giving the technical information some people may wish to know about. Then in your precious 20 minutes, you can concentrate on your main messages, mentioning in passing that you have more details of the research design, questionnaire used, etc. available if anyone is interested. Then if someone wants to know about such matters, you can explain in response to questions at the end of the session, or even in a conversation over a break. You are happy to talk about these matters, but do not need to use up the limited time you have been allocated, which you have reserved to tell people about what you have found out in your research.

Presenting a poster

Often posters are seen as less prestigious than 'papers' (talks) and it may be easier to get a poster accepted into many conferences than a talk. Sometimes posters are used to present work in progress where final results are not ready, but they may also be a way of presenting for a teacher uncomfortable with talking to a research audience. Posters are just that, although the designated space may sometimes also allow the display of apparatus, teaching materials, etc. on a table by the poster. At some conferences posters are simply put up in a suitable room, and then left (perhaps for the whole conference, perhaps just for a morning or afternoon). They are often located near coffee points so that delegates can take a look at them at breaks.

Sometimes, however, specific times are assigned when the authors will be expected to be at their posters, so that those interested in the work can ask questions and hear more about the project. This may prove to be a context to talk about research which is more effective than actually giving a 'paper', as anyone who comes along to ask is likely to be genuinely interested in the work, and personal conversation may influence people (perhaps to try something in their own classroom, or to take up an idea in their own research) more than listening to a talk.

Poster presentation is often seen as less impressive on a CV than an oral presentation, just as conference presentation is generally less prestigious than publishing in a journal. That is something to be considered by anyone looking to build an academic career. However, for the teacher-researcher who is primarily interested in sharing ideas, each of these modes of dissemination affords opportunities to share what we have found out, and so to influence others.

The teacher as research writer ━━

Writing up research formally, as a report to a sponsor, a course assignment, or for publication, requires the author to adopt a style and structure that may not be familiar from other writing. One of the best ways to appreciate good writing is critical reading: reading other researchers' accounts and evaluating the strengths to aspire to, and the weaknesses to avoid. In Part II it was suggested that three useful analogies can help us understand the role of the author of research reports. These are author *as story-teller*, *as advocate*, and *as teacher*. That is, effective educational research writing can be seen in terms of:

- the literary analogy
- the legal analogy
- the pedagogic analogy.

The literary analogy

A good research report has a narrative that leads the reader through 'the story' of the research. It can be read from start to finish by an attentive reader, without constantly having to check back or read ahead. The reader knows what kind of story is being told, and where the story is going, at all points during reading.

The legal analogy

The author of a research report makes knowledge claims, and must be able to substantiate them. The author needs to make the case by a careful, logical argument, drawing upon convincing evidence.

The pedagogic analogy

The author is a communicator, charged with informing readers about the research. This is a form of teaching. Just as classroom teaching is planned, with careful attention to the structure of the subject matter, and due weight given to students' existing levels of knowledge, so must research writing be planned. The author-as-teacher provides a structure, with suitable use of advanced organisers and reinforcement, and appropriate examples to illustrate key points, and makes sure that the account both makes explicit connection to relevant information the reader already knows, and provides any essential background needed to make sense of the report.

So, for example, in her report of a project to increase the use of the target language by Year 7 (11–12 year-old) students, undertaken whilst on school placement, Morgan (2010) tells her reader that she has organised her writing into four main sections, as follows:

> Literature Review – a discussion of existing theories and research regarding second language acquisition and communication in the MFL classroom and how these impact upon my research.
>
> Research Methodology – an outline of the background to my research, its context and the methods I adopted to obtain the data.
>
> Discussion and Data Analysis – presentation of data and a discussion of the extent to which the evidence allows me to answer my research questions.
>
> Conclusion – a summary of my main findings and the implications thereof for my own practice in the light of my professional and academic understanding of this area of research.
>
> (Morgan, 2010, pp. 273–274)

This tells the reader that Morgan has an explicit plan, and that it is a plan with a rationale, and this prepares the reader for what is to follow. It is also useful for the reader (perhaps the examiner responsible for evaluating her report for the university) to help them readily find elements of the report. So Morgan does not include an explicit section called 'results' or 'findings', but has told us that she will present her analysis of data in one section, and then summarise her findings from this analysis in the subsequent section. Effective classroom practitioners will already have all the requisite skills for taking on these roles from their day-to-day work, and should be confident of being able to write as story-teller, advocate and (of course) teacher.

Writing up research: making your case

Any reader who has worked through this book in a linear fashion should already have a good feel for what a satisfactory project write-up must do and must look like. Chapter 6 presented a series of questions that we might ask to evaluate research studies. The task of the student writing up research for an academic assignment is to prepare a report that would satisfy the same criteria that we apply when critically reading research. Certainly, when it comes to research writing, the dictum should be 'expect of others, as you must be prepared for them to expect of you'.

A key feature of a research report is that it makes its case through a logical chain of argument. As we saw in Part I (e.g., Figure 3.4), the research process has a logic, where decisions are made sequentially, and each stage of the process builds on what has gone before, and prepares for what will come later:

- identify focus;
- conceptualise existing literature;
- develop research questions;
- identify appropriate paradigm for developing knowledge sought;
- identify suitable methodology to answer research questions;
- identify sample, data collection instruments, etc.;
- collect data;
- analyse data;
- formulate findings to answer research questions;
- relate back to initial focus – draw out implications of research.

The research report should reflect this logic, and set out the argument so that the reader can appreciate why key decisions were made, and how the research makes up a coherent study. This sequence will be developed as the basis for a writing plan. However, it would be foolish to pretend that real research is quite as neat as this description may suggest (Medawar, 1963/1990). Among the common objections to following such an 'ideal' prescription, the researcher might well argue:

- 'I'm doing action research (AR), so my work is cyclic, not linear'
- 'I'm doing grounded theory (GT), so my design is emergent, not planned at the start'
- 'my research went wrong, so I don't have a case to make!'

These possibilities will be explored below, after considering our 'default' writing plan.

Setting up your writing plan

A useful way of thinking about writing a research report is to consider entering into a dialogue with your reader – the supervisor, examiner, journal referee or editor, for example.

This is the type of dialogue you are already familiar with from your own critical reading of research. Of course, this is a dialogue separated in time and space: *the authors must anticipate and answer the reader's questions before they are asked*. Many students new to writing up research find this more difficult than it sounds – like most new skills, it takes time to develop competence.

A common error (also often made by inexperienced teachers in the classroom) is to forget to include information that you are familiar with and take for granted, but which needs to be made explicit if your argument is to be sensible and convincing. Do not assume readers know such things as the setting policy in your school, the details of a particular examination specification, the length of teaching periods, etc. – if any of these things are relevant, they need to be reported. Good writing practice explains any abbreviations or acronyms used: so if reporting work with KS3 or Year 11 students, explain what this means (e.g., 11–14 year olds; 15–16 year olds). This is especially important if writing for publication because many journals have readerships that extend beyond one particular country.

Almost certainly, your research report will need drafting and redrafting. You will need to become critical at reading your own drafts, and spotting the omissions, contradictions, lack of clarity, etc. This means being able to read as your audience will – without the benefit of the vast personal context you bring to your reading. If you are writing a report as a university requirement, you will almost certainly have a research supervisor who will be prepared to read and comment on your draft. It is important to make use of this resource, but that means planning your writing to give plenty of time for your supervisor to 'turn around' the draft whilst there is still time for you to respond to any criticisms.

Signposting your work to guide the reader

You will know that *as a reader* it is helpful if the author seems to be answering your questions in the order they occur to you – thus the importance of setting out a logically sequenced argument. It is also useful to use signposts, such as subheadings, which help lead your reader through the logic of your case. Clear subheadings, such as 'findings', 'description of sample' and so forth, may not seem very imaginative but they do offer useful signposts for your reader. It is often also helpful to include useful linking statements to explain the logic of the writing as you proceed:

- …before explaining the types of interviews used in this study, it is useful to consider the main purposes and types of interview used in educational research…
- …so in this section I have explained why I have rejected Aufbau's notion of constructivism and adopted instead the holistic learning theory of Gestalten. This will be reflected in the framing of the research questions set out in the next section…
- ….having earlier explained why a perspective on learning as a social process of constructing joint understanding has been adopted in this study, I will now show how this influenced the selection and application of particular data collection techniques…

The aim here is two-fold: to ensure that the reader follows the logically structured argument and to demonstrate that this structure is due to a deliberate and carefully considered writing plan. Let us consider, then, the typical form of the dialogue between the researcher and the examiner or other audience for the research report. Clearly, there is some potential for overlap and flexibility in where some information could be placed in the report, but the following plan acts as a useful guide.

A model for writing up

The teacher-researcher did it!

Writing up research is not like mystery writing, where the longer you keep the audience guessing the better. Quite the converse. The aim is to persuade – to make a case – and so it is important to offer the reader an immediate 'hook' on which to 'hang' the story you have to tell. Indeed, it is usual in research to preface your study with an abstract that 'gives away the ending' before the story even begins. This is discussed further below. (Even though the abstract appears at the start, it may be sensible to *write it* last of all.)

What is this study about?

A short introductory statement sets up appropriate expectations about what is to come. We might think of this as activating a schema, providing the foundations for developing a conceptual framework for making sense of the paper. Remember, even if your reader is an expert in the field, he or she is still a learner when it comes to reading about *your* project. There is no universal rule about how long the introduction should be, or what exactly it should contain, but I would suggest that when reporting classroom-based research the introductory section would be fairly brief, covering three areas that the reader will find useful:

- topic
- approach
- context.

It helps the reader to have an early indication that the general conceptual area being explored is differentiation, learning about chemical reactions, the use of teacher questioning, peer assessment, pupils' explanations in history, or whatever.

It is probably also very sensible to outline at the start something about the type of study being presented, i.e., 'This paper will report ...':

- a reflective account of some action research into my own teaching;
- a case study of the forms of pupil interaction in a single lesson;
- a small-scale evaluation of the usefulness of a learning style questionnaire...

It is also useful to provide some basic context about the research: for example, 'This study was undertaken during my Year 10 (for 14–15 year olds) geography lessons, whilst I was on professional placement at an 11–16 school in a small town in the Midlands.' Although it is likely that all the information in this section is either explicit or implicit later in the report, this still provides the basics to make a reader feel psychologically comfortable that they have a 'feel' for where your account is set, and where it will be taking them.

So what do we already know about this?

Having introduced the study in very general terms, it is usual to then offer the reader a review of the literature. The literature review is intended to offer a conceptualisation (yours) of the field where you are undertaking your research (see Chapter 3), to show that your thinking is influenced by existing scholarship, and that your research question(s) are important and/or pertinent.

Doctoral level students are meant to demonstrate through the literature review that they are aware of all the most relevant research in the field, and that there is some sort of 'gap' (or contradiction) in current knowledge that the present study is meant to fill (or address). That element of originality is less significant at Master's level. It is unreasonable to expect a PGCE student (probably undertaking the project whilst on teaching placement) to provide a comprehensive and exhaustive literature review. At PGCE level, the student will usually be expected to demonstrate an awareness of some of the key literature and a critical engagement with the literature that is reviewed.

A literature review is more than an annotated bibliography, which simply presents a list of relevant references with discrete notes on key points of each study (although preparing such a bibliography may be a useful preliminary stage in the process of undertaking a review). A review presents a story about the literature, organising the studies discussed so that it is possible to use them to offer a view of the field. In other words, the literature review demonstrates the author's personal take on the field – it reflects the author's creativity as well as their analytical abilities. Critical reading (as exemplified earlier in the book) will allow the weighing of the importance of different sources, so that an overall assessment of the state of the field can emerge.

The review will justify the author's views by pointing out where a study is considered to have inappropriate methodology, too limited a sample, inadequate controls, poorly phrased research questions, citation of limited evidence, etc. However, it is not expected that a major flaw will be identified in every study cited – the aim of a critical review is show informed judgement, not to criticise for its own sake. (In this book I have been critical of a good many studies, to set an example to readers of the kind of things you should look out for, but I hope to have done this in a fair and balanced way.)

So what's the issue/problem here?

The literature review leads to the identification of the specific focus of the study. Commonly, this will mean *setting up* one or more research questions that are being investigated in the study. The wording of those questions will reflect key concepts in the field (as understood from the literature review), and the conceptualisation of the field will also provide the justification for why the research is worth undertaking in the particular context discussed in the present study.

Of course, a full-time research student will *select* their research site(s) to best enable them to answer their research question(s). By contrast, for a teacher-researcher, the context will be their own institution, and often teaching and learning in one (or more) of their classes (see Chapter 5). It is clearly important that the topic being researched is appropriate to the context. This will not be a problem for context-directed research, where the identification of the issue/problem provides the impetus for the enquiry. However, when research is undertaken as a course assignment, such as on the PGCE course, and is theory-directed (motivated by interest in a particular topic in teaching and learning, rather than the current professional context, see Chapter 5), it is important to make sure that the research focus is pertinent to the class(es) where the enquiry will be carried out. Following the guidelines offered earlier in this section on *planning* the research should ensure this is the case (see Chapters 8 and 9). However, the researcher still has to ensure that this link is made explicit for the reader of the research report.

What are you trying to find out?

This will lead to the specification of the particular research questions being explored in this enquiry. The reader should be clear exactly what the aim of the research is. If there are formal research questions, or a hypothesis to be tested, then these should be stated. If the purpose is the evaluation of an activity, an approach, teaching resources, etc., then this should be specified. The reader will only be able to judge the research decisions made, and the analysis and conclusions offered, if the purposes of the research are made clear early in the report.

How did you go about it (and why)?

Once the background and purpose of the study are clearly presented, the researcher then explains the methodological decisions made in terms of an overall strategy (methodology, see Chapter 4), and the specific techniques employed to collect and analyse data (see Chapters 10 and 11). For higher degree theses, this discussion will normally be expected to start with a consideration of the type of knowledge that is sought, and how epistemological assumptions lead to working in a particular paradigm. At PGCE level, it may be sufficient to pass over this stage and discuss the choice of an overall approach (such as case study methodology), but it is important for the student to check what is expected in their institution at their level of study.

Although the researcher is expected to justify methodological decisions, it is accepted that a range of constraints (and opportunities) may channel these – as was discussed in Chapter 5. Pragmatic concerns (such as degree of access to students and available timescale) are quite proper considerations, as are personal research strengths: there is little point selecting statistical analytical methods if one lacks confidence and competence in statistics. Being open and honest about such matters is sensible, and should be appreciated by an examiner as long as such concerns do not compromise a coherent approach. It clearly would be inappropriate to avoid statistics if the research question is set up as a hypothesis about the statistical significance of some effect. Rather, if one wishes to avoid statistics (or for that matter, particularly wishes to use statistics), it is important that the research issue and questions make this a sensible decision.

Ethical concerns are very important and should be discussed in your report (see Chapter 9). It may be sensible to set out the particular ethical principles that guide your work and to make it clear how you applied these. In his account of research in students' understanding of mathematical proof, undertaken on school placement during his PGCE course, Payne (2012) sets out the 'code of practice' he developed based on his reading around ethical issues, and included this as an appendix to show he had given serious consideration to how he would approach ethical issue in his study. Examiners often comment that they expect to see evidence of engagement with ethics that goes beyond a tick-box mentality. That is, a concern with acting ethically, according to our professional and personal values, should be prevalent in our thinking at all stages of the research process – not just when we complete an ethics form as part of a required procedure. It is sensible to discuss ethics as part of the methodology, but it may well be appropriate to revisit the theme in the discussion later, especially where issues were faced in the research that were not (and perhaps could not have been) foreseen.

What data did you collect?

Before proceeding to look at the evidence collected, it is useful to give the reader an overview of that data. So if questionnaires were used, the reader should know (for example) that 27 questionnaires were issued to the class, and 24 were completed, with three students being unable to complete the questionnaire before having to move to another lesson. If a sample of students were interviewed, the reader should know that five interviews were held with pairs of pupils in the class, each interview being 10–15 minutes in duration. Potentially relevant features of the data collection process should also be described: for example, that the interviews were held during the lunch hour in a familiar classroom with no other students present. If informants make up a sample of a larger group (as when interviewing some students in a class), then the sample should be described and the basis for selecting the sample should be explained.

What did you find out (and how do you know)?

The findings section is potentially very problematic for any researcher. In writing up this section there is a need to carefully balance two key responsibilities:

1. The researcher, not the reader, bears the burden of analysis: the researcher should analyse the data and present the findings from the analysis	2. The researcher should assure the reader that findings are based upon a competent analysis of suitable and sufficient evidence

Responsibility 1 tells us that we should not be presenting a catalogue of data, but the results that derive from the careful analysis of that data. The examiner will not have the time to read through the raw data, and the analysis is a key part of the research process. Responsibility 2 tells us that an account which reports the methods of data collection and analysis to be used, and then presents the findings, often leaves the reader feeling somewhat cheated, feeling that they are being asked to trust the researcher's honesty and competence too much.

The solution to this dilemma is slightly different in the case of academics writing academic papers for publication, and students writing academic assignments for university courses. In the former case, there is usually a default assumption both that the researcher is competent (they normally hold a doctorate in the field or a related area) and that the journal has a premium on space. In the latter case, a large part of the purpose of the assignment or thesis is to allow the unproven researcher to demonstrate competence. The student still has to work within word limits, but usually has some freedom to *append* supporting material to the assignment or thesis.

Question for reflection

Is it possible to use appendices to overcome word limits by simply moving sections of an assignment or thesis text to appendices (or footnotes) until the overall length of the main text falls within prescribed limits?

In both cases, it will be expected that the findings section of the report draws upon the evidence base collected during the research to illustrate the claimed findings. Quantitative data analysis is actually less problematic in this respect, as it is usually quite simple to present enough numerical information (in tables and charts) to allow any reader to check the reasonableness of findings. Tables and figures should be numbered, either consecutively through a report, or within each chapter (as in this book). Qualitative data presents more of a problem since such material as lengthy interview transcripts or class sets of student work does not readily lend itself to being presented economically. However, an authentic account would normally still *draw* upon the data to illustrate the findings. For example, if the author is claiming that student interviews demonstrated three main classes of pupil attitudes to having to complete regular class tests, then one or two interview extracts may be presented to exemplify each of the categories.

The format of findings presented depends very much on the types of data collected. Descriptive statistics (as deriving from a simple questionnaire, for example) may be displayed in tables and simple charts (cf. Figure 11.2). Inferential statistics are normally presented in tables that cite calculated statistical test results and associated levels of probability. (And more complex statistical analyses may be presented through a variety of graphical forms of representation.) Where the data is interview dialogue, classroom dialogue, student written work, etc., it is likely that the findings will be in the form of prose. The findings will likely take the form of a model (e.g., a typology) or theory that describes or explains patterns in the data. Where various slices of data have been collected, the researcher needs to decide whether to present the findings from the different forms of data separately, and then integrate them, or present the overall findings drawing upon the triangulated data.

So, as we saw when considering some of the studies discussed earlier, a good research report does not just offer the final outcome of analysis, but also offers enough of a taste of the data and its analysis to give us confidence in the analytical process. The authors' job is to *make the case*, not just report the verdict. The report should present *enough* evidence to make a *persuasive* case, without 'drowning' the reader in the full data set.

When submitting a university course assignment it is common to make some use of appendices to help bridge the gap between data collected and the findings of the analysis. So it may well be appropriate to append a range of different materials (see Box 12.1). It is usually acceptable to also submit other media, for example data on CD or tapes, etc.

Box 12.1

Examples of typical content of Appendices to research reports

Appendices to research reports could include:

- sample questionnaires;
- sample interview transcripts;
- transcripts of classroom dialogues;
- photocopies of students' work;
- photographs or stills from digital video-recordings of students at work (subject to permission being available – sometimes digital techniques are used to disguise faces);
- photographs of displays or models put together by the students.

Where the main text of an assignment draws upon small extracts from the collected data to provide evidence that illustrates the findings, the appendices may be used to present evidence of competence in analysing data. For example, appending a transcript of an interview shows an examiner the care and detail with which the original recording has been transcribed. If the findings of a study claim that most of the class used anthropomorphic language when describing how electrons moved around an electrical circuit, then the findings may note that evidence was found in work from 18 out of 26 students, and quote one or two examples. Appending the full set of relevant extracts from the class would allow the examiner to see that the examples quoted in the main text were representative of what was found among a larger number of students. (However, see my 'appendix' below, about appropriate limits on the use of appendices.)

So what?

The findings report what was actually found. The researcher's final job is to explain how these findings may be used. In particular, near the start of the report, an issue, problem or research question was defined. It is important to clearly show how the findings relate back to this initial concern. It is also important to discuss how the present findings fit into the wider field, in terms of the initial review of literature, so this section usually cites some of the studies identified as especially relevant in the earlier literature review to show how the current findings are related to what previous researchers have found, and to briefly consider whether further research is indicated in the light of the present findings. The consequences for teaching and learning in the research context should be discussed, as well as the extent to which the present findings may have wider significance (in the department, school, elsewhere?).

Depending on the nature of the report, then, this section is likely to consider the implications of the research in terms of:

- the field (i.e., how does this research fit with and possibly extend the understanding of this topic?);
- the context (i.e., what have we learnt that might help us improve practice here?);
- future practice (i.e., how will this inform my future professional work?);
- personal development (i.e., what personal skills or capacities have I developed and demonstrated?);
- research (i.e., what does this work tell us about the further work that might be useful – perhaps in terms of new research questions; perhaps relating to methodological choices – either in this context, or in this area of research more generally?).

It is worth considering whether there is something to discuss in all of these areas, but the emphasis will be different in reports of theory-directed and context-directed research (see Chapter 5).

Do I want to read this study?

Having finished your report, you should finalise your abstract. The abstract is placed at the start of the report and is a brief overview of the whole project, including the findings. Abstracts are normally very short, e.g., 150–200 words, and so only outline the main points. Abstracts have an important role in research, as decisions to obtain and read particular studies are often based upon reading the abstract, which is often more readily available than the full report.

Give your sources

A full bibliography is placed at the end of the research report (usually a complete alphabetical list of all the sources cited in the main text), followed by the appendices separately numbered (or lettered) to allow them to be readily referred to in the main text.

Appendix: will anyone read the appendices?

As suggested above, appendices are commonly used to provide supplementary information to support a research report. However, there are two important caveats here. First, it is important to check that appendices are allowed (they usually are) and, if so, whether there are any restrictions on how they may be used – some examiners can get irritated if they are asked to look at great volumes of appended material.

Secondly, it is important to understand the status of appended materials. As an examiner, I am very aware that some students who find it difficult to work within word limits will attempt to get their report or thesis down to size by shifting material to appendices, footnotes or other places where the material is not counted towards the word limit. I am also aware that other students will manage to work within the limits without needing such devices – perhaps by spending a lot of time refining their writing; perhaps by omitting things they wished to include. There is therefore an issue of fairness and equity if some students put a lot of effort into carefully editing their text down to the required length, and others simply shift some of it to appendices whilst still expecting it to 'count' as part of the thesis.

When examining I have a personal rule about how to deal with this issue (and I believe many other markers take a similar view):

Textual material in thesis	Examiner's attitude
The main text which has to be within a specified maximum word limit:	This text must be carefully read during the assessment process.
Additional text included in footnotes, appendices or other forms that are not part of the word limit:	This material is not considered part of the main argument, but supplementary material that may be considered *at the examiner's discretion* to provide additional background to the argument in the main text.

That is, I may well read material in footnotes and appendices, but I do not feel *obliged* to do so. In evaluating the thesis, I am primarily judging the argument that can be made within the prescribed word limits. Examiners sometimes appreciate the supplementary information provided in addition to the main text, but will not allow it to be used as a way of ignoring the word limits that other students are working within.

———— Difficulties with the model structure for a research report ————

Although university regulations and most journals do not require papers to fit a single, formal format when reporting research, the type of structure outlined above is familiar to those judging the research and helps present the 'story' of the research and 'make the case'. As summarised in Table 12.1, this structure offers the reader answers to the key questions they would pose if talking to you about your research.

There may be good reasons to modify this structure in particular cases. However, research reports are a genre of writing and, as with any genre, the reader comes to the text with expectations about what to find. Confounding those expectations may act as an impediment to communicating your research story, and so to convincing the reader of the strength of your case.

What about action research (AR)?

At first sight the type of structure being recommended may seem inappropriate for reporting action research (AR). After all, a key characteristic of AR is its cyclic nature, and so any linear reporting structure will not do justice to the research. As suggested in Chapter 5, an AR study may be unsuitable for fulfilling the academic requirements

Table 12.1 Overview of the structure of a research report

Do I want to read this study?	Abstract – gives an overview of the issue, context, methods and findings
What is this study about?	Introduction – sets scene, introduces focus, context, type of enquiry
So what do we already know about this?	Literature review – developing a personal conceptualisation of the research field/topic
So what's the issue/problem here?	Setting for study – explaining the link between the literature and the current context for the research
What are you trying to find out?	Establishing the specific research questions, hypothesis or aim of the enquiry
How did you go about it (and why)?	Methodology – rationale for the selection of methodology and particular data collection and analysis techniques
What data did you collect?	Specifying the sample or providing an inventory of evidence collected
What did you find out (and how do you know)?	Findings – the results of analysing the data collected in the study, supported with illustrations from the evidence base
So what?	Discussion: conclusions and implications – how do the findings relate back to the initial concern, and what are the implications of the research for the research context, other contexts, and further research?
Where did you get your background information?	References – alphabetical lists of literature cited, giving full bibliographic details
Supplementary material?	Appendices: supporting evidence – sample data and sample analyses presented to demonstrate authenticity of account and competence in analysis

of some university courses, because the *balance of* evidence needed to inform professional decision-making may not readily provide the *weight of* evidence required to justify findings in a thesis. Where an AR approach *is* considered a suitable basis for a course project, writing up will present a challenge. A Master's level student undertaking a project with several cycles of action and evaluation will find it difficult to readily report the project within the structure recommended here. The structure would certainly seem to fit with one cycle of the action research process, but the student would need to discuss with the supervisor how best to represent the research in the thesis.

One approach would be to separate consideration of the methodology (overall strategy, i.e., choice of AR) and the specific data collection and analysis related to specific cycles of the study. In effect, each cycle can be reported in one chapter which moves the study forward by reporting what action was undertaken, what data was collected, what was learnt, and how this led to a re-formulation of the research question for the next cycle (see Figure 5.3). At the end of the thesis the project as a whole can be reviewed, evaluating the progress made towards addressing the initial problem or issue, and reviewing the learning from different cycles and its potential significance for further AR and future professional action.

For PGCE students adopting 'action research-flavoured' projects, it is likely that time will only allow one cycle of the AR process, in which case the structure given above can be used subject to little or no modification. As has been suggested earlier in the book (see in particular Chapter 5), many 'AR' studies reported by students are examples of single cycles of context-directed practitioner-research that are better considered as case studies than AR (cf. Figure 5.4). For a student undertaking a genuine AR project (see Chapter 4), that he or she is required to write up, but which does not need to be reported using the traditional research report format suggested above, McNiff and Whitehead (2009) offer an alternative model which is closer to the spirit of AR. These authors discuss how to structure an AR report that acts as a means for the teacher to account for their professional actions and explain why they believe the action they have taken has enabled them to better match their professional practice to their values.

What about grounded theory (GT)?

A genuine GT study presents a real challenge to the structure suggested. In this case the research plan is emergent, and there is a constant interplay between data analysis and 'theoretical' sampling of new data (see Chapter 4). However, it would still be possible *in retrospect* to present the report in the form suggested, making it clear it does *not* represent the chronological story. That is, the report may focus on 'the context of justification' more than 'the context of discovery' (see Chapter 6). However, when done thoroughly, the very processes of GT lead to the writing-up of the research as 'a grounded theory'. A Master's level student who is genuinely following this approach will be led to a suitable form of research report by the analytical methods employed.

As GT is an open-ended commitment in terms of sampling and time needed for analysis, it is a dangerous choice of approach for a higher degree student and should only be attempted with strong support. It is almost inconceivable that a PGCE student could develop GT within the constraints of a course assignment, so this is unlikely to be an issue on such courses. Despite this, it is certainly possible to borrow some analytical techniques from GT to search for emergent patterns in data, but from within a more tightly bounded research plan that could be reported within the structure modelled above.

Research that 'goes wrong'

Finally, a few words about research that 'goes wrong'. There is a lot that can go wrong in research. A failure to collect data relevant to the stated research question could be a serious impediment to writing a thesis for a higher degree. However, such problems should be avoided when the supervisor's advice is sought and heeded. Failure to learn what one hoped to learn is unfortunate, but may be perfectly understandable – after all, research is by its nature an uncertain process. It may still be possible to write up an account of what was intended, what was undertaken, and what was learnt from the process, which offers something of value to the reader – if only at the level that one approach to a problem may be usefully discounted.

In reality, given the complexity of teaching and learning as phenomena, much classroom research is only partially successful, and an honest report highlighting limitations of the work can be just as informative through setting out what did not go well, and what complications arose, as reporting the successful elements. So when Hicks attempted to introduce more active learning approaches into a sixth-form class he was assigned on teaching placement, he found positive outcomes, but these were tempered, as he reports in *JoTTER*:

The new methods can be seen to have successes as well as shortcomings. The learners enjoyed being involved in their own learning. They felt responsibility helped drive them to work. However they still felt a place existed for passive learning as well as not wanting too much responsibility. On the other hand their work did not always show a full understanding of the lesson objectives. … Certain activities were seen to be more successful than others, while all could be developed further with time.

The difficulties behind active learning were found to be the time constraints with preparation and class time. Additionally the behaviour of some class members during activities hindered their progress in the shift in responsibility over learning. A pressure to achieve in examinations means students need to learn information very quickly. If we look to teach all lessons using active learning this may not occur.

(Hicks, 2010, p. 187)

By offering a balanced, honest account of the work, Hicks not only demonstrates a respect for knowledge (see Chapter 9), but makes his report much more useful. Writing such a report is helpful for his own personal learning, to inform his future adoption of similar approaches in other classes; and reading the report offers a realistic idea of what can be achieved for other teachers or trainees interested in making learning more 'active' in their own classrooms.

In terms of PGCE assignments, demonstrating the ability to plan an enquiry, and collect and analyse appropriate data, is more important than answering the initial research questions. If the outcome of the research was to find that the data collected did not offer a clear pattern that could guide future practice, then so be it. An honest explanation of how analysis of the available evidence leads to this conclusion would be credit-worthy and appreciated by an examiner, whereas an attempt to conjure up some form of definite answer that is *not* supported by evidence would be intellectually dishonest *and* suggest the author does not understand what they are doing. The former case is a failure of the research, but demonstrates key research skills; the latter is a failure of the researcher and is more likely to lead to a failure in the assignment. Indeed, as the examples of published studies discussed in this book have illustrated well, we seldom get clear answers from single enquiries, especially at first attempt. But our failures may teach us something about what to do next, and where and how. This is all part of the research process, and of learning what it means to truly adopt research-based practice.

Little by little…

The teacher-researcher should be reassured that most of the published studies discussed in this book can be considered to be flawed. It is inevitable that educational research studies fail to build a complete chain of evidenced argument based *purely* on valid, reliable interpretation of data collected. Many studies are necessarily undertaken with small, non-representative samples, in limited contexts, or use simplistic concepts, categories or typologies that derive from previous studies and can only partially reflect the complexity of educational phenomena. Often studies use evidence that is indirect (inferring behaviour from self-reports, assuming informants can offer accurate and honest accounts of their belief and ideas), or are heavily reliant on the interpretations of the researchers in making sense of interviews, observations and other data.

Educational processes are complex, and seldom fully described or explained by single studies. Research in education is therefore both iterative and incremental, with studies building upon, and trying to overcome the limitations of, previous research. The community of researchers slowly builds up knowledge that might be considered valid and reliable (ERP1) or authentic and trustworthy (ERP2). The practitioner-researcher may feel that his or her contribution is necessarily quite limited in the wider context: but this may often be so for professional researchers as well. In the narrower, but very relevant, context of their own classes, however, the teacher can often use research to make a very real difference to the teaching and learning that is so important to their own students.

——— Further reading

Examples of studies completed as part of initial teacher education on a PGCE course (see Chapter 5) may be accessed from the open-access *Journal of Trainee Teacher Educational Research* at http://jotter.educ.cam.ac.uk/. Guidance on reporting research can be found in the BERA guide to good practice. The editorial from *Chemistry Education Research and Practice* sets out general criteria for publishable research papers in education.

British Educational Research Association (2000). *Good Practice in Educational Research Writing*. Southwell, Notts.: British Educational Research Association.

Taber, K. S. (2012). Recognising quality in reports of chemistry education research and practice. *Chemistry Education Research and Practice, 13*(1), 4–7.

References

Adelman, C., Jenkins, D., & Kemmis, S. (1980). Rethinking case study: Notes from the second Cambridge Conference. In H. Simons (Ed.), *Towards a Science of the Singular: Essays about Case Study in Educational Research and Evaluation* (pp. 47–61). Norwich: Centre for Applied Research in Education, University of East Anglia.

Aldridge, D. P. (2006). The limits of master narratives in history textbooks: An analysis of representation of Martin Luther King, Jr. *Teachers College Record, 108*(4), 662–686.

Armsby, S. J. (2011). Peer-assisted learning in a Year 7 classroom: Do structured group-work strategies impact upon the learning and engagement of pupils studying Earth Science? *Journal of Trainee Teacher Educational Research, 2*, 113–144.

Avis, J., Bathmaker, A.-M., Kendal, A., & Parson, J. (2003). Conundrums of our own making: Critical pedagogy and trainee further education teachers. *Teacher Development, 7*(2), 191–209.

Bannister, D., & Fransella, F. (1986). *Inquiring Man: The Psychology of Personal Constructs* (3rd edn). London: Routledge.

Bassey, M. (1992). Creating education through research. *British Educational Research Journal, 18*(1), 3–16.

Baszanger, I., & Dodier, N. (2004). Ethnography: Relating the part to the whole. In D. Silverman (Ed.), *Qualitative Research: Theory, Method and Practice* (2nd edn, pp. 9–34). London: Sage.

Behar, R. (2001). Yellow marigolds for Ochun: An experiment in feminist ethnographic fiction. *International Journal of Qualitative Studies in Education, 14*(2), 107–116. doi: 10.1080/09518390010023630

Biddle, B. J., & Anderson, D. S. (1986). Theory, methods, knowledge and research on teaching. In M. C. Wittrock (Ed.), *Handbook of Research on Teaching* (3rd edn, pp. 230–252). New York: Macmillan.

Biddulph, M., & Adey, K. (2004). Pupil perceptions of effective teaching and subject relevance in history and geography at Key Stage 3. *Research in Education, 71*, 1–8.

Biesta, G. J. J., & Burbules, N. C. (2003). *Pragmatism and Educational Research*. Lanham, Maryland: Rowman & Littlefield.

Brahler, C. J., & Walker, D. (2008). Learning scientific and medical terminology with a mnemonic strategy using an illogical association technique. *Advances in Physiology Education, 32*, 219–224. doi: 10.1152/advan.00083.2007

British Educational Research Association (BERA) (2000). *Good Practice in Educational Research Writing*. Southwell, Notts.: British Educational Research Association.

British Educational Research Association (BERA) (2011). *Ethical Guidelines for Educational Research*. London: British Educational Research Association.

Brooks, R., & Everett, G. (2009). Post-graduation reflections on the value of a degree. *British Educational Research Journal, 35*(3), 333–349. doi: 10.1080/01411920802044370

Bruner, J. S. (1960). *The Process of Education*. New York: Vintage Books.

Bruner, J. S. (1987). The transactional self. In J. Bruner & H. Haste (Eds.), *Making Sense: The Child's Construction of the World* (pp. 81–96). London: Routledge.

Burnard, P., & Swann, M. (2010). Pupil perceptions of learning with artists: A new order of experience? *Thinking Skills and Creativity, 5*(2), 70–82. doi: 10.1016/j.tsc.2010.01.001

Button, S. (2006). Key Stage 3 pupils' perception of music. *Music Education Research, 8*(3), 417–431.

Calissendorff, M. (2006). Understanding the learning style of pre-school children learning the violin. *Music Education Research, 8* (1), 83–96.

Carr, W., & Kemmis, S. (1986). *Becoming Critical: Education, Knowledge and Action Research*. Lewes, East Sussex: The Falmer Press.

Chapman, G., Cleese, J., Idle, E., Gilliam, T., Jones, T., & Palin, M. (1974). *Monty Python and the Holy Grail (1975) movie script*.

Cisneros-Puebla, C. A. (2004). 'To Learn to Think Conceptually.' Juliet Corbin in Conversation with Cesar A. Cisneros-Puebla. *Forum Qualitative Sozialforschung / Forum: Qualitative Social Research [Online Journal], 5*(3), Art. 32.

Coffield, F., Moseley, D., Hall, E., & Ecclestone, K. (2004). *Should We Be Using Learning Styles? What Research Has to Say to Practice*. London: Learning and Skills Research Centre.

Cohen, L., Manion, L., & Morrison, K. (2000). *Research Methods in Education* (5th edn). London: Routledge-Falmer.

Çokadar, H., & Yılmaz, G. (2010). Teaching ecosystems and matter cycles with creative drama activities. *Journal of Science Education and Technology, 19*(1), 80–89. doi: 10.1007/s10956-009-9181-3

Coll, R. K., & Treagust, D. F. (2001). Learners' mental models of chemical bonding. *Research in Science Education, 31*(3), 357–382.

Corrigan, G., & Taylor, N. (2004). An exploratory study of the effect a self-regulated learning environment has on pre-service primary teachers' perceptions of teaching science and technology. *International Journal of Science and Mathematics Education, 2*, 45–62.

Counsell, C. (2011). Disciplinary knowledge for all: The secondary history curriculum and history teachers' achievement. *Curriculum Journal, 22*(2), 201–225. doi: 10.1080/09585176.2011.574951

Creswell, J. W. (2009). *Research Design: Qualitative, Quantitative, and Mixed Methods Approaches* (3rd edn). Thousand Oaks, California: Sage.

Creswell, J. W., & Plano Clark, V. L. (2007). *Designing and Conducting Mixed Methods Research*. Thousand Oaks, California: Sage.

Dawe, A. (2012). Children's awareness of learning and knowledge: A study of Year 3 pupils' perceptions of the knowledge they need and how it is acquired. *Journal of Trainee Teacher Educational Research, 3*, 31–62.

Day, C., Sammons, P., & Kington, A. (2008). Effective classroom practice: A mixed-method study of influences and outcomes. End of Award Report submitted to the Economic and Social Research Council.

de Winter, J., Winterbottom, M., & Wilson, E. (2010). Developing a user guide to integrating new technologies in science teaching and learning: Teachers' and pupils' perceptions of their affordances. *Technology, Pedagogy and Education, 19*(2), 261–267. doi: 10.1080/1475939x.2010.491237

Demetriou, H., & Wilson, E. (2010). Children should be seen and heard: The power of student voice in sustaining new teachers. *Improving Schools, 13*(1), 54–69. doi: 10.1177/1365480209352545

Department for Education (2012). *Teachers' Standards*. London: Department for Education.

Department for Education and Skills (2003). *Excellence and Enjoyment: A Strategy for Primary Schools* London: Department for Education and Skills.

Dorion, K. R. (2009). Science through Drama: A multiple case exploration of the characteristics of drama activities used in secondary science lessons. *International Journal of Science Education, 31*(16), 2247–2270.

Dowley, L. (2012). A critical investigation of whether seating students by gender affects participation in discussion-based learning: A case study with a Year 8 class studying death. *Journal of Trainee Teacher Educational Research, 3*, 221–242.

Driver, R. (1989). Students' conceptions and the learning of science. *International Journal of Science Education, 11*(special issue), 481–490.

Driver, R., Squires, A., Rushworth, P., & Wood-Robinson, V. (1994). *Making Sense of Secondary Science: Research into Children's Ideas*. London: Routledge.

Dry, S. K. (2010). A critical analysis of how focussing lessons on How Science Works affects learning and motivation in Year 10 lessons on space: An action research project. *Journal of Trainee Teacher Educational Research, 1*, 219–270.

Duit, R., Roth, W.-M., Komorek, M., & Wilbers, J. (1998). Conceptual change cum discourse analysis to understand cognition in a unit on chaotic systems: Towards an integrative perspective on learning in science. *International Journal of Science Education, 20*(9), 1059–1073.

Edwards, D., & Mercer, N. (1987). *Common Knowledge: The Development of Understanding in the Classroom*. London: Routledge.

Eisenhardt, K. M. (1989). Building theories from case study research. *The Academy of Management Review, 14*(4), 532–550.

Elliott, J. (1991). *Action Research for Educational Change*. Milton Keynes: Open University Press.

Fisher, L. (2012). Discerning change in young students' beliefs about their language learning through the use of metaphor elicitation in the classroom. *Research Papers in Education*, 1–20. doi: 10.1080/02671522.2011.648654

Florian, L., & Black-Hawkins, K. (2010). Exploring inclusive pedagogy. *British Educational Research Journal, 37*(5), 813–828. doi: 10.1080/01411926.2010.501096

Forbes, K. (2010). A case study on the impact of a one-week Spanish exchange trip on the attitudes and productive language skills of four Year 8 pupils. *Journal of Trainee Teacher Educational Research, 1*, 107–152.

Freebody, P. (2003). *Qualitative Research in Education: Interaction and Practice*. London: Sage.

Galbraith, J., & Winterbottom, M. (2010). Peer-tutoring: What's in it for the tutor? *Educational Studies, 37*(3), 321–332. doi: 10.1080/03055698.2010.506330

Galton, M., Simon, B., & Croll, P. (1980). *Inside the Primary Classroom*. London: Routledge and Kegan Paul.

García Franco, A. (2005). Multiple representations about the structure of matter. *Royal Society of Chemistry Chemical Education Research Group Seminar*. Retrieved from: www.leeds.ac.uk/educol/documents/142648.htm

Gardner, J., & Cowan, P. (2005). The fallibility of high stakes '11-plus' testing in Northern Ireland. *Assessment in Education: Principles, Policy & Practice, 12*(2), 145–165.

Garet, M. S., Porter, A. C., Desimone, L., Birman, B. F., & Yoon, K. S. (2001). What makes professional development effective? Results from a national sample of teachers. *American Educational Research Journal, 38*(4), 915–945.

Geertz, C. (1973). Thick description: Toward an interpretive theory of culture. In C. Geertz, *The Interpretation of Cultures: Selected Essays* (pp. 3–30). New York: Basic Books.

Gilbert, J. K., & Watts, D. M. (1983). Concepts, misconceptions and alternative conceptions: Changing perspectives in science education. *Studies in Science Education, 10*, 61–98.

Gilbert, J. K., Watts, D. M., & Osborne, R. J. (1985). Eliciting student views using an interview-about-instances technique. In L. H. T. West & A. L. Pines (Eds.), *Cognitive Structure and Conceptual Change* (pp. 11–27). London: Academic Press.

Glaser, B. G. (1978). *Theoretical Sensitivity: Advances in the Methodology of Grounded Theory*. Mill Valley, California: The Sociology Press.

Glaser, B. G., & Holton, J. (2004). Remodeling grounded theory. *Forum: Qualitative Social Research, 5*(2), Article 4. Retrieved from: www.qualitative-research.net/index.php/fqs/article/view/607/1316

Greaves, C. (2010). A critical investigation, using approaches drawn from action research, into how Year Nine English students' creative storytelling can be stimulated through the use of multi-modal texts. *Journal of Trainee Teacher Educational Research, 1*, 195–218.

Greenbank, P. (2003). The role of values in educational research: The case for reflexivity. *British Educational Research Journal, 29*(6), 791–801.

Guba, E. G., & Lincoln, Y. S. (2005). Paradigmatic controversies, contradictions, and emerging confluences. In N. K. Denzin & Y. S. Lincoln (Eds.), *The Sage Handbook of Qualitative Research* (3rd edn, pp. 191–215). Thousand Oaks, California: Sage.

Gündogdu, K. (2010). The effect of constructivist instruction on prospective teachers' attitudes towards human rights education. *Electronic Journal of Research in Educational Psychology, 8*(1), 333–352.

Hallam, S., & Ireson, J. (2005). Secondary school teachers' pedagogic practices when teaching mixed and structured ability classes. *Research Papers in Education, 20*(1), 3–24.

Hamilton, D. (1980). Some contrasting assumptions about case study research and survey analysis. In H. Simons (Ed.), *Towards a Science of the Singular: Essays about Case Study in Educational Research and Evaluation* (pp. 78–92). Norwich: Centre for Applied Research in Education, University of East Anglia.

Hammersley, M. (1993). Introduction. In M. Hammersley (Ed.), *Controversies in Classroom Research* (2nd edn, pp. x–xxii). Buckingham: Open University Press.

Hardman, F., Smith, F., & Wall, K. (2005). Teacher–pupil dialogue with pupils with special educational needs in the National Literacy Strategy. *Educational Review, 57*(3), 299–316.

Harrop, A., & Swinson, J. (2003). Teachers' questions in the Infant, Junior and Secondary School. *Educational Studies, 29*(1), 49–57.

Hayes, E. (2011). Placing the left-handed child: A study of the implications of being a left-handed child within the primary classroom. *Journal of Trainee Teacher Educational Research, 2*, 89–112.

Healy, J. (2010). A critical investigation, using approaches drawn from action research, into how Year 9 students' learning about the novel *Stone Cold* is developed through Speaking and Listening activities and Drama work. *Journal of Trainee Teacher Educational Research, 1*, 311–346.

Hennessy, S., Ruthven, K., & Brindley, S. (2005). Teacher perspectives on integrating ICT into subject teaching: Commitment, constraints, caution, and change. *Journal of Curriculum Studies, 37*(2), 155–192.

Hicks, K. A. J. (2010). Yawning sixth formers: An action research project examining how we can move beyond passive learning in sixth form teaching of case studies in urban management. *Journal of Trainee Teacher Educational Research, 1*, 153–194.

Jegede, O. J., & Aikenhead, G. S. (1999). Transcending cultural borders: Implications for science teaching. *Research in Science and Technological Education, 17*, 45–66.

John, P. (2005). The sacred and the profane: Subject sub-culture, pedagogical practice and teachers' perceptions of the classroom uses of ICT. *Educational Review, 57*(4), 471–490. doi: 10.1080/00131910500279577

Kelly, G. (1963). *A Theory of Personality: The Psychology of Personal Constructs*. New York: W. W. Norton & Co.

Keogh, B., & Stuart, N. (1999). Concept Cartoons, teaching and learning in science: An evaluation. *International Journal of Science Education, 21*(4), 431–446.

Key Stage 3 National Strategy (2002). Framework for teaching science: Years 7, 8 and 9. London: Department for Education and Skills.

Kinchin, I. M. (2004). Investigating students' beliefs about their preferred role as learners. *Educational Research, 46*(3), 301–312.

Kind, V., & Taber, K. S. (2005). *Science: Teaching School Subjects 11–19*. London: RoutledgeFalmer.

Kington, A., Sammons, P., Day, C., & Regan, E. (2011). Stories and statistics: Describing a mixed methods study of effective classroom practice. *Journal of Mixed Methods Research, 5*(2), 103–125. doi: 10.1177/1558689810396092

Kuhn, T. S. (1959/1977). The essential tension: Tradition and innovation in scientific research. In T. S. Kuhn (Ed.), *The Essential Tension: Selected Studies in Scientific Tradition and Change* (pp. 225–239). Chicago: University of Chicago Press.

Kuhn, T. S. (Ed.) (1977). *The Essential Tension: Selected Studies in Scientific Tradition and Change*. Chicago: University of Chicago Press.

Kuhn, T. S. (1996). *The Structure of Scientific Revolutions* (3rd edn). Chicago: University of Chicago Press.

Kuiper, J. (1994). Student ideas of science concepts: Alternative frameworks? *International Journal of Science Education, 16*(3), 279–292.

Kvale, S. (1996). *InterViews: An Introduction to Qualitative Research Interviewing*. Thousand Oaks, California: Sage.

Lakatos, I. (1970). Falsification and the methodology of scientific research programmes. In I. Lakatos & A. Musgrove (Eds.), *Criticism and the Growth of Knowledge* (pp. 91–196). Cambridge: Cambridge University Press.

Lakoff, G., & Johnson, M. (1980). *Metaphors We Live By*. Chicago: University of Chicago Press.

Lang, J. (2012). My ideal teacher is…: Teacher gender preferences in Year One and Year Six children. *Journal of Trainee Teacher Educational Research, 3*, 1–30.

Limerick, B., Burgess-Limerick, T., & Grace, M. (1996). The politics of interviewing: Power relations and accepting the gift. *International Journal of Qualitative Studies in Education, 9*(4), 449–460.

Lyle, S. (1999). An investigation of pupil perceptions of mixed-ability grouping to enhance literacy in children aged 9–10. *Educational Studies, 25*(3), 283–296.

Macaruso, P., Hook, P. E., & McCabe, R. (2006). The efficacy of computer-based supplementary phonics programs for advancing reading skills in at-risk elementary students. *Journal of Research in Reading, 29*(2), 162–172.

Mahon, J., Bryant, B., Brown, B., & Kim, M. (2010). Using Second Life to enhance classroom management practice in teacher education. *Educational Media International, 47*(2), 121–134. doi: 10.1080/09523987.2010.492677

Maslow, A. H. (1948). 'Higher' and 'lower' needs. *The Journal of Psychology, 25*, 433–436.

McClune, B. (2001). Modular A-levels – who are the winners and losers? A comparison of lower-sixth and upper-sixth students' performance in linear and modular A-level physics examinations. *Educational Research, 43*(1), 79–89.

McIntyre, D., Peddar, D., & Ruddock, J. (2005). Pupil voice: Comfortable and uncomfortable learnings for teachers. *Research Papers in Education, 20*(2), 149–168.

McLaughlin, C., Black-Hawkins, K., Brindley, S., McIntyre, D., & Taber, K. S. (2006). *Researching Schools: Stories from a Schools-University Partnership for Educational Research*. Abingdon, Oxon.: Routledge.

McLellan, R., & Nicholl, B. (2011). 'If I was going to design a chair, the last thing I would look at is a chair': Product analysis and the causes of fixation in students' design work 11–16 years. *International Journal of Technology and Design Education, 21*(1), 71–92. doi: 10.1007/s10798-009-9107-7

McNiff, J. (1992). *Action Research: Principles and Practice*. London: Routledge.

McNiff, J., & Whitehead, J. (2009). *Doing and Writing Action Research*. Los Angeles: Sage.

Medawar, P. B. (1963/1990). Is the scientific paper a fraud? In P. B. Medawar (Ed.), *The Threat and the Glory* (pp. 228–233). New York: Harper Collins, 1990. (Reprinted from: *The Listener*, Vol. 70, 12 September 1963.)

Michell, H. (2011). A critical analysis of the effects of a videoconferencing project on pupils' learning about culture and language. *Journal of Trainee Teacher Educational Research, 2*, 51–88.

Milgram, S. (1973). The perils of obedience. *Harper's Magazine* (December), 66–77.

Modgil, S. (1974). *Piagetian Research: A Handbook of Recent Studies*. Windsor, Berkshire: NFER Publishing.

Morgan, J. (2010). Increasing pupil use of the target language through creative and cross-curricular contexts: An action research project focusing on a mixed top set Year Seven French class. *Journal of Trainee Teacher Educational Research, 1*, 271–310.

Mortimer, E. F. (1995). Conceptual change or Conceptual Profile change? *Science & Education, 4*(3), 267–285. doi: 10.1007/BF00486624

Mottley, A. (2012). The use of signing with hearing children as a means to communicate and manage behaviour: A study into the perspectives of children in a Year 2 classroom. *Journal of Trainee Teacher Educational Research, 3*, 243–286.

Muijs, D. (2004). *Doing Quantitative Research in Education with SPSS*. London: Sage.

Mutton, J. (2010). The confluence of methods: A case study investigating the benefits of fieldwork to Year 12 students studying rivers. *Journal of Trainee Teacher Educational Research, 1*, 83–106.

National Research Council Committee on Scientific Principles for Educational Research (2002). *Scientific Research in Education*. Washington, DC: National Academies Press.

Newton, D. P. (2000). *Teaching for Understanding: What It is and How To Do It*. London: RoutledgeFalmer.

Novak, J. D., & Gowin, D. B. (1984). *Learning How to Learn*. Cambridge: Cambridge University Press.

Payne, C. (2012). High-attaining Year 10 pupils' conceptions and learning of proof: A critical analysis. *Journal of Trainee Teacher Educational Research, 3*, 93–158.

Petri, J., & Niedderer, H. (1998). A learning pathway in high-school level quantum atomic physics. *International Journal of Science Education, 20*(9), 1075–1088.

Phillips, D. C. (1987). *Philosophy, Science and Social Enquiry: Contemporary Methodological Controversies in Social Science and Related Applied Fields of Research*. Oxford: Pergamon Press.

Phillips, D. C., & Burbules, N. C. (2000). *Postpositivism and Educational Research*. Oxford: Rowman & Littlefield.

Piaget, J. (1959/2002). *The Language and Thought of the Child* (3rd edn). London: Routledge.

Piaget, J. (1970/1972). *The Principles of Genetic Epistemology* (W. Mays, Trans.). London: Routledge & Kegan Paul.

Piantanida, M., & Garman, N. B. (2009). *The Qualitative Dissertation: A Guide for Students and Faculty* (2nd edn). Thousand Oaks, California: Corwin Press.

Pollard, A., & Filer, A. (1999). *The Social World of Pupil Career: Strategic Biographies through Primary School*. London: Cassell.

Pope, M. L., & Denicolo, P. (1986). Intuitive theories – a researcher's dilemma: Some practical methodological implications. *British Educational Research Journal, 12*(2), 153–166.

Powney, J., & Watts, M. (1987). *Interviewing in Educational Research*. London: Routledge & Kegan Paul.

Pring, R. (2000). *Philosophy of Educational Research*. London: Continuum.

QAA (2001). *The Framework for Higher Education Qualifications in England, Wales and Northern Ireland*: London: Quality Assurance Agency for Higher Education.

Ratinen, I. J. (2011). Primary student-teachers' conceptual understanding of the Greenhouse Effect: A mixed method study. *International Journal of Science Education*, 1–27. doi: 10.1080/09500693.2011.587845

Ravitz, J. L., Becker, H. J., & Wong, Y. T. (2000). Constructivist-compatible beliefs and practices among U.S. teachers. Vol. Teaching, Learning, and Computing: 1998 National Survey Report 4. Retrieved from: www.eric.ed.gov/ERICWebPortal/contentdelivery/servlet/ERICServlet?accno=ED445657

Reynolds, D. (1991). Doing educational research in Treliw. In G. Walford (Ed.), *Doing Educational Research* (pp. 193–209). London: Routledge.

Robson, C. (2002). *Real World Research: A Resource for Social Scientists and Practitioner Researchers* (2nd edn). Malden, Massachusetts: Blackwell.

Rogers, L., & Hallam, S. (2006). Gender differences in approaches to studying for the GCSE among high-achieving pupils. *Educational Studies, 32*(1), 59–71.

Rutherford, E. (2012). Pupils' perspectives of the purpose and value of collective worship: A case study of 10–11 year olds in a faith-school. *Journal of Trainee Teacher Educational Research, 3*, 63–92.

Sade, D., & Coll, R. K. (2003). Technology and technology education: Views of some Solomon Island primary teachers and curriculum development officers. *International Journal of Science and Mathematics Education, 1*, 87–114.

Sagarra, N., & Alba, M. (2006). The key is the keyword: L2 vocabulary learning methods with beginning learners of Spanish. *The Modern Language Journal, 90*(ii), 228–243.

Schraw, G., Wadkins, T., & Olafson, L. (2007). Doing the things we do: A grounded theory of academic procrastination. *Journal of Educational Psychology, 99*(1), 12–25. doi: 10.1037/0022-0663.99.1.12

Schwandt, T. A. (2001). *Dictionary of Qualitative Inquiry* (2nd edn). Thousand Oaks, California: Sage.

Shaw, M. (2012). Here endeth the three-part lesson. *Times Educational Supplement.* Retrieved from: www.tes.co.uk/article.aspx?storyCode=6219960

Smith, A. (2010). Testing Latin literature: A case study into the variety of ways to assess pupils in appreciation of Latin literature without focusing exclusively on language. *Journal of Trainee Teacher Educational Research, 1*, 35–82.

Smith, R. (2012). Barriers to learning: Exploring the relationship between Year 5/6 pupils' attitudes towards intelligence and how they cope with challenge. *Journal of Trainee Teacher Educational Research, 3*, 287–326.

Solomon, J. (1993). Four frames for a field. In P. J. Black & A. M. Lucas (Eds.), *Children's Informal Ideas in Science* (pp. 1–19). London: Routledge.

Spillane, J. P., & Hunt, B. R. (2010). Days of their lives: A mixed-methods, descriptive analysis of the men and women at work in the principal's office. *Journal of Curriculum Studies, 42*(3), 293–331. doi: 10.1080/00220270903527623

Staarman, J. K., & Mercer, N. (2010). The guided construction of knowledge: Talk between teachers and students. In K. Littleton, C. Wood, & J. K. Staarman (Eds.), *International Handbook of Research of Psychology in Education* (pp. 75–104). Bingley, West Yorks.: Emerald.

Stake, R. E. (1995). *The Art of Case Study Research*. Thousand Oaks, California: Sage.

Stake, R. E. (2006). *Multiple Case Study Analysis*. New York: The Guilford Press.

Strand, S., & Demie, F. (2005). English language acquisition and educational attainment at the end of primary school. *Educational Studies, 31*(3), 275–291.

Strauss, A., & Corbin, J. (1998). *Basics of Qualitative Research: Techniques and Procedures for Developing Grounded Theory* (2nd edn). Thousand Oaks, California: Sage.

Stutchbury, K., & Fox, A. (2009). Ethics in educational research: Introducing a methodological tool for effective ethical analysis. *Cambridge Journal of Education, 39*(4), 489–504. doi: 10.1080/03057640903354396

Stylianides, A. J., & Al-Murani, T. (2010). Can a proof and a counterexample coexist? Students' conceptions about the relationship between proof and refutation. *Research in Mathematics Education, 12*(1), 21–36. doi: 10.1080/14794800903569774

Sutherland, P. (1992). *Cognitive Development Today: Piaget and His Critics*. London: Paul Chapman Publishing.

Taber, K. S. (1989). Girls' under-representation in physics classes: A case study. MSc, University of Surrey, Guildford.

Taber, K. S. (1992). Girls' interactions with teachers in mixed physics classes: Results of classroom observation. *International Journal of Science Education, 14*(2), 163–180. doi: 10.1080/0950069920140205

Taber, K. S. (1993). Stability and lability in student conceptions: Some evidence from a case study. Paper presented at the British Educational Research Association Annual Conference, University of Liverpool. Available at: www.leeds.ac.uk/educol/documents/154054.htm

Taber, K. S. (1994). Student reaction on being introduced to concept mapping. *Physics Education, 29*(5), 276–281.

Taber, K. S. (1998). An alternative conceptual framework from chemistry education. *International Journal of Science Education, 20*(5), 597–608.

Taber, K. S. (2000a). Case studies and generalisability – grounded theory and research in science education. *International Journal of Science Education, 22*(5), 469–487.

Taber, K. S. (2000b). Finding the optimum level of simplification: The case of teaching about heat and temperature. *Physics Education, 35*(5), 320–325.

Taber, K. S. (2000c). Multiple frameworks? Evidence of manifold conceptions in individual cognitive structure. *International Journal of Science Education, 22*(4), 399–417.

Taber, K. S. (2001). Shifting sands: A case study of conceptual development as competition between alternative conceptions. *International Journal of Science Education, 23*(7), 731–753.

Taber, K. S. (2002a). *Chemical Misconceptions: Prevention, Diagnosis and Cure: Classroom Resources* (Vol. 2). London: Royal Society of Chemistry.

Taber, K. S. (2002b). 'Intense, but it's all worth it in the end': The colearner's experience of the research process. *British Educational Research Journal, 28*(3), 435–457.

Taber, K. S. (2003). Examining structure and context: Questioning the nature and purpose of summative assessment. *School Science Review, 85*(311), 35–41.

Taber, K. S. (2006). Beyond constructivism: The Progressive Research Programme into Learning Science. *Studies in Science Education, 42*, 125–184.

Taber, K. S. (2008). Exploring conceptual integration in student thinking: Evidence from a case study. *International Journal of Science Education, 30*(14), 1915–1943. doi: 10.1080/09500690701589404

Taber, K. S. (2009a). Learning from experience and teaching by example: Reflecting upon personal learning experience to inform teaching practice. *Journal of Cambridge Studies, 4*(1), 82–91.

Taber, K. S. (2009b). *Progressing Science Education: Constructing the Scientific Research Programme into the Contingent Nature of Learning Science*. Dordrecht: Springer.

Taber, K. S. (2010a). Computer-assisted teaching and concept learning in science: The importance of designing resources from a pedagogic model. In B. A. Morris &

G. M. Ferguson (Eds.), *Computer-assisted Teaching: New Developments* (pp. 37–61). New York: Nova.

Taber, K. S. (2010b). Paying lip-service to research? The adoption of a constructivist perspective to inform science teaching in the English curriculum context. *The Curriculum Journal, 21*(1), 25–45.

Taber, K. S. (2010c). Preparing teachers for a research-based profession. In M. V. Zuljan & J. Vogrinc (Eds.), *Facilitating Effective Student Learning through Teacher Research and Innovation* (pp. 19–47). Ljubljana: Faculty of Education, University of Ljubljana.

Taber, K. S. (2011a). Constructivism as educational theory: Contingency in learning, and optimally guided instruction. In J. Hassaskhah (Ed.), *Educational Theory* (pp. 39–61). New York: Nova. Retrieved from: https://camtools.cam.ac.uk/wiki/eclipse/Constructivism.html

Taber, K. S. (2011b). The natures of scientific thinking: Creativity as the handmaiden to logic in the development of public and personal knowledge. In M. S. Khine (Ed.), *Advances in the Nature of Science Research: Concepts and Methodologies* (pp. 51–74). Dordrecht: Springer.

Taber, K. S. (2012a). Recognising quality in reports of chemistry education research and practice. *Chemistry Education Research and Practice, 13*(1), 4–7.

Taber, K. S. (2012b). Vive la différence? Comparing 'like with like' in studies of learners' ideas in diverse educational contexts. *Educational Research International, 2012*(Article 168741), 1–12. Retrieved from: www.hindawi.com/journals/edu/2012/168741/ doi:10.1155/2012/168741

Taber, K. S., & Student, T. A. (2003). How was it for you? The dialogue between researcher and colearner. *Westminster Studies in Education, 26*(1), 33–44.

Taber, K. S., & Tan, K.-C. D. (2011). The insidious nature of 'hard core' alternative conceptions: Implications for the constructivist research programme of patterns in high school students' and pre-service teachers' thinking about ionisation energy. *International Journal of Science Education, 33*(2), 259–297. doi: 10.1080/09500691003709880

Taber, K. S., Billingsley, B., Riga, F., & Newdick, H. (2011). To what extent do pupils perceive science to be inconsistent with religious faith? An exploratory survey of 13–14 year-old English pupils. *Science Education International, 22*(2), 99–118.

Taber, K. S., Tsaparlis, G., & Nakiboğlu, C. (2012). Student conceptions of ionic bonding: Patterns of thinking across three European contexts. *International Journal of Science Education, 34*(18), 2843–2873. doi: 10.1080/09500693.2012.656150

Tan, K.-C. D., Goh, N.-K., Chia, L.-S., & Taber, K. S. (2005). *Development of a Two-tier Multiple Choice Diagnostic Instrument to Determine A-level Students' Understanding of Ionisation Energy* (pp. 105). Retrieved from: https://camtools.cam.ac.uk/wiki/eclipse/diagnostic_instrument.html

Taylor, A., Lazarus, E., & Cole, R. (2005). Putting languages on the (drop down) menu: Innovative writing frames in modern foreign language teaching. *Educational Review, 57*(4), 435–455.

Taylor, L. (2011). Investigating change in young people's understandings of Japan: A study of learning about a distant place. *British Educational Research Journal, 37*(6), 1033–1054. doi: 10.1080/01411926.2010.521235

Tesch, R. (1990). *Qualitative Research: Analysis Types and Software Tools*. Basingstoke, Hampshire: The Falmer Press.

Thayer-Bacon, B. J. (2000). *Transforming Critical Thinking: Thinking Constructively*. New York: Teachers College Press.

Tobin, K. (1990). Teacher mind frames and science learning. In K. Tobin, J. B. Kahle, & B. J. Fraser (Eds.), *Windows into Science Classrooms: Problems Associated with Higher-level Cognitive Learning* (pp. 33–91). Basingstoke, Hampshire: The Falmer Press.

Tobin, K., Kahle, J. B., & Fraser, B. J. (Eds.) (1990). *Windows into Science Classrooms: Problems Associated with Higher-level Cognitive Learning*. Basingstoke, Hampshire: The Falmer Press.

Tomlinson, P. (1989). Having it both ways: Hierarchical focusing as research interview method. *British Educational Research Journal, 15*(2), 155–176.

Treagust, D. (1995). Diagnostic assessment of students' science knowledge. In S. M. Glynn & R. Duit (Eds.), *Learning Science in the Schools: Research Reforming Practice* (pp. 327–346). Mahwah, New Jersey: Lawrence Erlbaum Associates.

Tripp, D. (2005). Action research: A methodological introduction. *Educação e Pesquisa, 31*(3), 443–466.

TTA (2003). *Qualifying to Teach: Professional Standards for Qualified Teacher Status and Requirements for Initial Teacher Training*. London: Teacher Training Agency.

Turner, J. (2010). The impact of pupil-set targets on achievement in speaking: An Action Research project involving a mixed-sex Year 9 German class. *Journal of Trainee Teacher Educational Research, 1*, 1–34.

Vygotsky, L. S. (1934/1994). The development of academic concepts in school-aged children. In R. van der Veer & J. Valsiner (Eds.), *The Vygotsky Reader* (pp. 355–370). Oxford: Blackwell.

Walford, G. (1991). Reflexive accounts of doing educational research. In G. Walford (Ed.), *Doing Educational Research* (pp. 1–18). London: Routledge.

Walsh, E. J. (2012). Bridging the gap: A study to enhance the learning of extra-curricular musicians within a mainstream Year 9 music classroom. *Journal of Trainee Teacher Educational Research, 3*, 159–220.

Warwick, J., Warwick, P., & Hopper, B. (2012). Primary teacher trainee perspectives on a male-only support group: Moving male trainee teachers beyond the 'freak show'. *Teacher Development, 16*(1), 55–76. doi: 10.1080/13664530.2012.669602

Watson, J. B. (1967). What is behaviourism? In J. A. Dyal (Ed.), *Readings in Psychology: Understanding Human Behavior* (2nd edn, pp. 7–9). New York: McGraw-Hill.

Watts, M. (1983). A study of schoolchildren's alternative frameworks of the concept of force. *European Journal of Science Education, 5*(2), 217–230.

White, R. T., & Gunstone, R. F. (1992). *Probing Understanding*. London: The Falmer Press.

Whitebread, D., & Coltman, P. (2010). Aspects of pedagogy supporting metacognition and self-regulation in mathematical learning of young children: Evidence from an observational study. *ZDM, 42*(2), 163–178. doi: 10.1007/s11858-009-0233-1

Whitehead, J. (2000). Living standards of reflection, research and renewal (Keynote address). Paper presented at the Ontario Educational Research Council Conference, Toronto.

Whitwood, L. (2012). 'Does age matter?' A study of Year 6 and Year 2 perspectives on learning Modern Foreign Languages as a new subject. *Journal of Trainee Teacher Educational Research, 3*, 327–360.

Wilkins, R. (2011). *Research Engagement for School Development*. London: Institute of Education.

Windelband, W. (1894/1980). History and Natural Science: Rectorial address, Strassbourg, 1894. *History and Theory, 19*(2), 169–185.

Wong, M. (2005). A cross-cultural comparison of teachers' expressed beliefs about music education and their observed practices in classroom music teaching. *Teachers and Teaching: Theory and Practice, 11*(4), 397–418.

Wragg, E. C. (2012). *An Introduction to Classroom Observation* (Classic edn). Abingdon, Oxon.: Routledge.

Yevsiyevich, Y. (2011). Religious Studies at Examination Level: A critical examination of the extent to which 'Evidence Sheets' can be used in AS Religious Studies lessons to help pupils access theological or philosophical thinking. *Journal of Trainee Teacher Educational Research, 2*, 1–50.

Yin, R. K. (2003). *Case Study Research: Design and Methods* (3rd edn). Thousand Oaks, California: Sage.

Ziman, J. (1968). *Public Knowledge: An Essay Concerning the Social Dimension of Science*. Cambridge: Cambridge University Press.

Ziman, J. (1978/1991). *Reliable Knowledge: An Exploration of the Grounds for Belief in Science*. Cambridge: Cambridge University Press.

Index

Tables and Figures are indicated by page numbers in bold print.